# The Complete GMAT® Sentence Correction Guide

Erica L. Meltzer

 THE CRITICAL READER

New York

ISBN-13: 978-0-9975178-0-4
ISBN-10: 0997517808

## ALSO BY ERICA L. MELTZER

· · · · · · · · · · · · · · · · · · · · · · · · · ·

# Table of Contents

# Introduction

I know you're probably eager to get down to business (literally), so I've done my best to keep this part short. Nevertheless, there are a few important points I feel obligated to make here; if you'll humor me, I've outlined them below.

First, you will be taking the GMAT® on a *screen*. This fact may seem so basic that it barely seems worth mentioning, but if you are doing the majority of your preparation on paper, it should not be discounted. Reading on a computer is not the same as reading in a book. Although you may have scratch paper to work out your answers on, you cannot physically draw lines through answer choices, nor can you cross out distracting information from sentences themselves. You are also more likely to overlook, insert, and misread letters and words—and unfortunately, the distinction between the correct answer and one or more of the incorrect answers can sometimes come down to a single word, even a single letter. Add in the fatigue factor and the second-guessing that often accompanies it, and you can end up losing points that you could have obtained easily given more favorable circumstances.

To guard against these pitfalls, you must make certain to pay extra close attention to which words the underlined portion of a sentence does and does not include.

For example, consider the following question:

> Among elephants living in families in the wild, <u>older females often have the greatest vulnerability because their large tusks, which make</u> the animals exceptionally attractive to poachers in search of ivory.
>
> (A) older females often have the greatest vulnerability because their large tusks, which make
> (B) older females are often the most vulnerable due to their large tusks, which make
> (C) older females often having the most vulnerability because of their large tusks making
> (D) older females are often the most vulnerable and due to their large tusks making
> (E) older females are often the most vulnerable because their large tusks make

If you happen to know that *because* rather than *due to* should be used (we'll get into why later), this is a relatively straightforward question; however, it does have the potential to be tricky for an entirely unrelated reason.

If you read carefully, you can see that the original version of the sentence is not a grammatically coherent statement. Because the verb *make* "belongs" to *which* rather than to *tusks*, its logical subject, the second half of the sentence is missing a main verb (*because their large tusks, which make the animals exceptionally attractive to poachers in search of ivory*). (A) is therefore incorrect.

What people can easily *think* they see in the original version, however, is this:

> ...older females often have the greatest vulnerability because **of** their large tusks, which make the animals exceptionally attractive to poachers in search of ivory.

That, of course, is perfectly acceptable as a sentence. The problem is that it's not what's written! But because it's what a lot of people are expecting to see, their eye automatically fills in the word *of*. As a result, they jump to pick (A) without reading the other answers carefully and get the question wrong, even though they understand perfectly well the concept being tested.

In contrast, (E), the correct answer, eliminates *which*, restoring the verb *make* to its proper subject, *tusks*. But if you mentally insert the word *of* into the original version, you might not even make it that far.

The difference between a pretty good score and a very good score is therefore not just a matter of what you know, but also of how carefully you work. On the GMAT, you have no choice but to sweat the details. As long as your proctor does not object, you may even want to physically put your finger on the screen as you read. Doing so might feel a bit ridiculous, but it can help ensure that you read what is actually written. If you find this technique distracting, you are of course free to disregard it; I mention it because I happen to find it useful.

Second, on the actual exam, Sentence Corrections are interspersed with Reading Comprehension and Critical Reasoning questions. Sometimes you may see a few Sentence Corrections in a row, while other times you may encounter a single Sentence Correction bookended by other question types. By necessity, you must be able to flip in and out of grammar mode very quickly. In addition, you cannot afford to let yourself get caught off guard by a first Sentence Correction that appears after four Reading Comprehension questions. Because the test is adaptive, a careless mistake early on can have serious repercussions for your score. Again, an obvious point, but one that cannot be overemphasized.

The good news is that among the various types of questions that appear on the Verbal portion of the GMAT, Sentence Corrections are typically the most straightforward. Unlike Reading Comprehension and Critical Reasoning questions, which ask you to juggle multiple ideas simultaneously, Sentence Corrections are always limited to one sentence. As a result, they can provide a welcome respite from the kind of mental contortions required by the rest of the section. If you're properly prepared, they can be a relatively easy source of points.

That said, if you don't have a solid understanding of what you're looking for, Sentence Corrections can also be a source of significant confusion. Like the other two Verbal question types, they present you with a mass of information, some of which is important and some of which is not. In order to conserve your energy for more involved, passage-based questions, you must be able to distinguish between information that is relevant and information that is present merely to distract you. In a sentence of 30 words, for example, the answer may depend on just 10 words or fewer. Conversely, you may not be able to determine the answer to a question in which only a single word is underlined without taking the entire sentence into account.

Throughout this book, I have sought to strike a balance between depth and clarity: I have attempted to discuss concepts in sufficient detail to allow you to understand their underlying logic as well as their application to a range of situations, but I have also tried to avoid detouring into potentially confusing nuances or exceptions not directly relevant to the GMAT. With the number of international test-takers growing, the GMAC has shifted the emphasis of the test toward reasoning skills and away from nitpicky idiomatic usage. So while correct answers may often sound less than elegant by non-GMAT standards, you can still determine many of them by thinking clearly about the most logical intended meaning.

One note about the exercises in this book: In my very considerable experience teaching grammar for a range of standardized tests, I have found that an excessive reliance on answer choices can be problematic. Rather, to master material to the point at which you are virtually unshakeable during the exam, you must be accustomed to correcting errors yourself. The more challenging the grammar, the better you will be served by the ability to predict corrections before you even look at the answers. Consequently, I have chosen not to place the exercises at the end of each chapter in multiple-choice format. Although you may find this setup somewhat tedious, it is designed to help you build a solid foundation rather than simply learn a few "tricks" and shortcuts.

To help you understand how the material in this book applies to actual released GMAT questions, I have also provided a list of relevant questions from the *Official Guide for GMAT Review 2020* and the *Official Guide for GMAT Verbal Review 2020* at the end of each chapter. In addition, I periodically discuss specific questions from those guides in order to illustrate the application of certain rules to the exam. You should, however, be aware that there are a handful of concepts covered in this book that are either not tested or deemphasized in the 2020 guides. When that is the case, the concepts have appeared either in earlier editions of the *Official Guides* or in official GMAT practice software. If a rule has been tested in recent years, it is reasonable to assume that it could be tested again. My goal is to help you anticipate the broadest possible range of Sentence Correction types you could encounter on the GMAT, and to give you the tools to master them.

~Erica Meltzer

# GMAT Sentence Correction Cheat Sheet

1.  Do NOT ignore the non-underlined portion of the sentence; it may include key information.

2.  Shorter = Better.

3.  –ING, especially BEING, usually = wrong. (Exceptions: idioms and participles used to join clauses). *Subjects + conjugated verbs* & nouns usually = right.

4.  Non-essential clauses are often used to distract from errors and "pad" sentences. Cross out to simplify.

5.  Semicolons separate two complete sentences.

6.  Singular/plural verb split = subject-verb agreement question. –S = singular verb; no –S = plural verb.

7.  *It* vs. *they* splits = pronoun agreement. *It(s)* = singular, paired with singular noun. *They/their* = plural, paired with plural noun.

8.  Collective nouns (*jury, agency, company*) = singular.

9.  *This* and *that* should be followed by nouns.

10. All items in a list must be parallel: noun, noun, and noun; verb, verb, and verb; -ING, -ING, and -ING. If items are long, focus on the beginning of each item. Also: remember that constructions on either side of a conjunction or word pair must be parallel.

11. *Which* often = wrong. This word must refer back to the noun that immediately precedes it.

12. *Which* = comma, *that* = no comma.

13. *Where* = places, not times, books, works of art, etc.

14. *Whose* = both people and things. *Who* = people only; *which* = things only.

15. *Due to* = caused by, usually wrong.

16. Keep comparisons equivalent: people = people; things = things. Correct comparisons are often introduced by *(un)like*.

17. *Such as* = introduce examples; *(un)like* = introduce comparison.

18. Participial phrase (e.g. *having gone, written by*) at the start of a sentence often = dangling modifier

19. Make sure modifiers (adjectives, adverbs, prepositional phrases) are placed next to the words they are intended to modify. A participle (–ING, –ED) at the start of a sentence often signals a dangling modifier.

20. Top word pairs: *not (only)...but (also); both/ between...and; so/such...that; from...to; (n)either...(n)or; just as...so.*

21. *Amount, much, less* = singular nouns; *number, many, fewer* = plural nouns.

## Parts of Speech

There are eight parts of speech in the English language, seven of which are tested on the GMAT.

### 1. Verb

Verbs indicate **actions** or **states of being**.

**Examples:**    To be
                    To have
                    To seem
                    To go
                    To increase
                    To believe

At the most basic level, a verb is a word that has an infinitive (TO) form. So, for example, *define* is a verb because it is correct to say *to define*, but *member* is not a verb because it is not correct to say *to member*.

All of the verbs listed above are infinitives. If you are uncertain whether a word can be used as a verb, a reasonably reliable shortcut for checking is to place TO in front of the word to check whether it can form an infinitive.

To indicate who is performing an action, it is necessary to **conjugate** a verb and provide its **subject**.

*To be* and *to have* are the most common verbs in the English language, and thus the most common verbs on the GMAT. Because they are **irregular**, their conjugated forms are different from their infinitives; you must therefore make sure that you are comfortable distinguishing between their singular and plural forms.

**To Be**

| Sing. (pres.) | Pl. (pres.) |
|---|---|
| I am | We are |
| You are | You (pl.) are |
| S/he, It is | They are |

| Sing. (past) | Pl. (past) |
|---|---|
| I was | We were |
| You were | You (pl.) were |
| S/he, It was | They were |

**To Have**

| Sing. (pres.) | Pl. (pres.) |
|---|---|
| I have | We have |
| You have | You (pl.) have |
| S/he, It has | They have |

*The past-tense form of *have* is always *had*.

The **tense** of a verb indicates when an action occurred.

| | |
|---|---|
| It is = Present | It would be = Conditional |
| It has been = Present perfect | It would have been = Past conditional |
| It was = Simple past | It will be = Future |
| It had been = Past perfect | It will have been = Future perfect |

## 2. Noun

Nouns indicate people, places, objects, and ideas, and can always be preceded by *a(n)* or *the*.

**Proper nouns** indicate specific people and places.

**Examples:** whale, company, notion, executive, Mark Twain, Chicago

- The **stock** has risen significantly over the last several **months**.

- A typical **drug** comes to **market** with about 12.5 years of patent **life** remaining.

**Gerunds** (verb + -ING) can also act as nouns:

- The **flourishing** of the Olmec Civilization began in Mexico around 1500 B.C.

## 3. Pronoun

Pronouns replace nouns.

**Examples**: she, you, one, we, him, it(s), their, this, that, which, both, some, few, many, (n)either

- The company was founded in the 1990s. **It** has tripled in size since that time.

- Stock prices are declining. **They** will soon be at their lowest point in nearly a year.

- Both of the stocks were expected to rebound, but **neither** has yet begun to rise.

Although pronouns can refer to both people and things, the GMAT is almost exclusively concerned with pronouns referring to **things**: *it, they, which, that,* and to a lesser extent, *this/these, that/those.*

## 4. Preposition

Prepositions are **"position" words**: they indicate where people/objects are located in relation to one another, or when an action occurred. The preposition *of* is also used to indicate possession.

Common prepositions include:

| | | | | |
|---|---|---|---|---|
| About | Among | Beside | In | Opposite |
| Above | Around | Between | Inside | Outside |
| Across | Before | By | Near | Toward |
| After | Behind | During | Next to | Under |
| Against | Below | For | Off | With |
| Along | Beneath | From | On | Without |

## 5. Adjective

Adjectives modify nouns and pronouns.

**Examples:** large, sharp, interesting, solid, wide, exceptional, smart, extreme

- Born in Spain in 1881, Pablo Picasso was one of the most **celebrated** and **revolutionary** artists of the twentieth century.

- The City Beautiful movement was embodied in the **stately** lines, **formal** balance, and **grand** scale of the buildings constructed according to its principles.

**Present participles** (-ING) and **past participles** (-ED, -OWN, -UNG, -UNK) can also act as adjectives.

- Dublin possesses a **thriving** theater scene whose productions regularly achieve international renown.

- Quebec City is home to the only **fortified** city walls in the Americas north of Mexico.

## 6. Adverb

Adverbs modify verbs, adjectives, and other adverbs. Many adverbs end in –LY.

**Examples:** rapidly, calmly, surprisingly, mildly, boldly, sharply, also, next

- Stock prices have risen **substantially** over the last several months.

- Many runners, even those who train **regularly**, do not have a clear sense of their potential.

## 7. Conjunction

Conjunctions indicate relationships between words, phrases, and clauses.

**Examples:** and, but, however, therefore, so, although, yet, when

- Some of the book's passages describe the physical realities of the Middle Ages, **whereas** others reflect the dazzling debates that would later lead to the Renaissance.

- Prairie dogs, once on the verge of extinction, were saved **because** naturalists lobbied for their perseveration.

*Chapter One*

# BUILDING A SENTENCE

The ability to determine when a statement is and is not a sentence is crucial to success on Sentence Corrections. No correct answer will ever contain a fragment; conversely, incorrect answers frequently do contain fragments.

Every sentence must contain two elements:

1) A **subject**

2) A **conjugated verb** that corresponds to the subject

A sentence can contain only one word (*Go!* is a sentence because the subject, *you*, is implied) or consist of numerous clauses, but provided that it contains a subject and a verb, it can be considered grammatically complete regardless of whether it makes sense outside of any context.

Before we look further at sentences, though, we're going to look at these two main components.

## What Can Be a Subject?

### I. Nouns

There are two types of nouns: **concrete**, which refer to physical objects (e.g., *book, chair, house*), and **abstract**, which refer to ideas and feelings (*belief, notion, theory*).

| | |
|---|---|
| Concrete: | **Bats** are able to hang upside down without discomfort because they possess specialized tendons in their feet. |
| Abstract: | **The theory** that bats are able to navigate in darkness by using their ears rather than their eyes was conclusively demonstrated by Donald Griffin, a biology student, in the 1930s. |

### II. Pronouns

Pronouns are words that replace nouns, e.g., *she, he, it, one, you, this, that, there, each, some,* and *many*.

Note that sentences that start with pronouns may not make sense out of context; however, **a sentence whose subject is a pronoun is grammatically identical to a sentence whose subject is a noun**. As long as it contains a main verb that corresponds to the subject, a clause that starts with a pronoun is still a sentence.

| | |
|---|---|
| Correct: | **They** are able to hang upside down without discomfort because they possess specialized tendons in their feet. |
| Correct: | **Some (of them)** are able to hang upside down without discomfort because they possess specialized tendons in their feet. |

Less commonly, the pronouns *how, that, what,* and *whether* can also be used as subjects, sometimes as part of a much longer complete subject (underlined below).

Correct:    **How** <u>bats hang upside down</u> was a mystery until it was discovered that they possess specialized tendons in their feet.

Correct:    **That** <u>Aldous Huxley exhibited many shortcomings in his ability to develop believable characters and create compelling storylines</u> was overshadowed by his capacity to navigate a staggering panorama of ideas in his fiction.

Correct:    Although the technologies necessary for space travel were developed only recently, <u>**what** drives humans' fascination with exploring the stars</u> has remained unchanged for hundreds of years

Correct:    **Whether** <u>markets will continue to rise or will begin to demonstrate signs of sluggishness over the next several months</u> remains to be seen.

While the use of these pronouns as subjects may sound odd to you, the construction is perfectly correct. In fact, answer choices that contain this usage are probably more likely to be correct precisely because so many people will work by ear and eliminate such answers automatically.

## III. Gerunds

Gerund = verb + -ING

Correct:    **Hanging** upside down for long periods is a skill that both bats and sloths possess, but bats race quickly away when startled whereas sloths make no attempt to move.

## IV. Infinitives

Infinitive = TO + verb

Infinitives are most commonly used to create the parallel construction "to do x is to do y."

Correct:    **To hang** upside down from a branch for a long period of time is <u>to experience</u> the world much as a bat or sloth does.

## What is a Verb?

To reiterate, there are two main types of verbs:

1)    **Action** verbs indicate specific activities, e.g., *talk, write, travel.*

2)    **Being** verbs, also known as **linking verbs**, indicate states of being, seeming, and feeling, e.g., *be, become, seem, appear.*

Either type of verb can be paired with any type of subject to create a full sentence. For example, *stocks plunge* is a complete sentence, but so is *they are.*

On the next page, we're going to look at a variety of sentence types as well as how they are constructed.

## A. Simple Sentence

Sentence:     The tomato grows.

This is known as a simple sentence because it contains only a subject (*the tomato*) and a verb (*grows*), which tells us what the subject does. Because it can stand on its own as a sentence, it can also be called an **independent clause**.

## B. Prepositional Phrases

If we want to make our sentence a little longer, we can add a **prepositional phrase**. A prepositional phrase is a phrase that begins with a preposition, a **time** or **location** word that comes **before a noun**. Common prepositions include *of, in, to, with, from, for, at, by,* and *on.* (For an extended list, see p. 11.)

Sentence:     The tomato grows **around the world**.

Sentences can contain many prepositional phrases, sometimes one after the other.

Sentence:     The tomato grows **in many shapes and varieties** **in greenhouses** **around the world**.

A prepositional phrase can also be placed between the subject and the verb. When that is the case, the prepositional phrase starts at the preposition and ends right before the verb.

Sentence:     The tomatoes **in the greenhouse** grow in many varieties and colors.

A prepositional phrase can also be placed at the **beginning** of a sentence:

Sentence:     **In the greenhouse,** the tomatoes grow in many varieties and colors.

A prepositional phrase **cannot**, however, stand alone as a complete sentence:

Fragment:     In the greenhouse

Fragment:     In many shapes and varieties in greenhouses around the world

## C. Pronoun as Subject

As discussed earlier, pronouns can replace nouns as subjects.

Noun:         **Tomatoes** grow in many shapes and varieties in greenhouses around the world.

Pronoun:      **They** grow in many shapes and varieties in greenhouses around the world.

Most sentences involving pronouns are fairly straightforward; however, one common point of confusion involves **pronouns of quantity**:

| One<br>Each<br>Either<br>Every | Both<br>Few<br>Some<br>Several | The majority<br>Many<br>More<br>Most | A number<br>Others<br>Any<br>All |
|---|---|---|---|

These pronouns can be used to begin clauses in two different ways, one of which creates an independent clause and the other of which creates a dependent clause.

Let's start with these two sentences:

Sentence:    Many tomatoes are grown in greenhouses around the world.

Sentence:    Most people believe that the tomato is a vegetable.

Most people don't have too much trouble recognizing that these are sentences. They have pretty clear subjects (*many tomatoes*, *most people*) and verbs (*are*, *believe*), and they make sense by themselves. The problem arises when we take away the nouns *tomatoes* and *people*, and start to deal with the pronouns on their own.

### Pronoun (of them) = sentence

In this usage, the pronoun simply acts as a subject and is used to replace a noun. It is often followed by the phrase *of them*, but it can be used by itself as well.

Sentence:    **Many (of them)** are grown in greenhouses around the world.

Sentence:    **Most (of them)** believe that the tomato is a vegetable.

Taken out of any context, the above examples don't make much sense, nor do they provide any real information. Regardless of how odd you find these examples, however, **they are still sentences** because each one contains a subject (*many*, *most*) and a verb (*are*, *believe*) that corresponds to it.

### Pronoun + "of which" or "of whom" = fragment

When an indefinite pronoun is followed by *of which* or *of whom*, it creates a **dependent clause**, which by definition cannot stand alone as a full sentence.

Fragment:    **Many of which** are grown in greenhouses around the world.

Fragment:    **Most of whom** believe that the tomato is a vegetable.

Which means:

Incorrect:    The tomato is used by cooks around the **world, most of them** believe that it is a vegetable rather than a fruit.

Correct:    The tomato is used by cooks around the **world; most of them** believe that it is a vegetable rather than a fruit.

Correct:    The tomato is used by cooks around the **world, most of whom** believe that it is a vegetable rather than a fruit.

## D. Adverbs

Adverbs **modify verbs** and **clauses**. Most adverbs are created by adding –LY onto adjectives.

Slow        →    Slowly
Current     →    Currently
Important   →    Importantly

A second type of adverb, however, does not end in –LY. Some of these adverbs are **adverbs of time**, which indicate **when** or **how often** something occurs. Others are **transitions** (also known as **conjunctive adverbs**) that indicate relationships between ideas.

| Again | Meanwhile | Next | Still |
|---|---|---|---|
| Consequently | Moreover | Now | Then |
| Furthermore | Never | Often | Today |
| However | Nevertheless | Sometimes | Yesterday |

**Important: Adverbs have no grammatical effect on a sentence. A sentence to which an adverb is added is still a sentence, regardless of where the adverb is placed.**

Sentence:    <u>Now</u>, the tomato grows in many shapes and varieties in greenhouses around the world.

Sentence:    The tomato **currently** grows in many shapes and varieties in greenhouses around the world.

Sentence:    The tomato grows in many shapes and varieties in greenhouses around the world **today**.

## E. Relative Clauses

Relative clauses are "embedded" in sentences and are used to describe nouns, often the subject of a sentence.

**Non-essential clauses** are set off by commas and often begin with "w-words" (**relative pronouns**) such as *who*, *whose*, and *which*.

When non-essential clauses are removed from a sentence, the sentence still makes both grammatical and logical sense.

Correct:    The tomato, **which is one of the most popular salad ingredients,** grows in many shapes and varieties in greenhouses around the world.

Crossed out:   The tomato…grows in many shapes and varieties in greenhouses around the world.

**Essential clauses** often begin with *that* and are not set off by commas. They differ from non-essential clauses in that they provide information that is central to the meaning of a sentence, but grammatically they are similar: they are normally followed by verbs, and when they are crossed out of a sentence, the sentence still makes grammatical sense.

Correct:    The small yellow fruit **that was grown by the Aztecs and that was known as the "tomatl"** was the ancestor of the modern tomato.

Crossed out:   The small yellow fruit…was the ancestor of the modern tomato.

While the second version no longer describes the small yellow fruit, the sentence is still grammatically acceptable.

## F. Participles and Gerunds

**Participles** are verbs that act as adjectives.

- They can modify **nouns**, e.g., *the ringing bell, the growing crisis, the required information*

- They can also modify **entire clauses**, e.g., *Tomatoes are an ancient crop, having first been cultivated during the first millennium B.C.*

Every verb has two **participles**:

### 1) Present participle

The present participle is formed by adding –ING to the verb.

| | | |
|---|---|---|
| Talk | → | talking |
| Throw | → | throwing |
| Ring | → | ringing |

### 2) Past participle

The past participle is usually formed by adding –ED. Irregular past participles often end in  –WN, –NG, or –NK. (For a list of common verbs with irregular past participles, see the chart on p. 59).

| | | |
|---|---|---|
| Talk | → | talked |
| Throw | → | thrown |
| Ring | → | rung |

A **participial phrase** begins with a participle and can be in either the present or the past. While participial phrases will sometimes involve past participles, they are generally more likely to involve present participles.

A participial phrase cannot stand alone as a sentence; it must be added to an independent clause, either before or after, to form a sentence.

Fragment:      **Originating** in South America during the first millennium B.C.

Sentence:      **Originating** in South America during the first millennium B.C., the tomato is an ancient crop.

Sentence:      The tomato is an ancient crop, **originating** in South America during the first millennium B.C.

A participial phrase can, however, be placed almost anywhere in a sentence.

Beginning:     <u>**Originating in South America**</u>, the tomato, one of the most popular salad ingredients, grows in many shapes and varieties in greenhouses around the world.

Middle:        The tomato, <u>**cultivated** initially in South America during the first millennium B.C.,</u> is now grown in many shapes and varieties in greenhouses around the world.

End:           The tomato is now grown in greenhouses around the world, **having first been cultivated in South America in the first millennium B.C.**

To form the past tense, we can use the present participle *having* + past participle of the main verb (*originated*).

Sentence: **Having originated** in South America, the tomato, one of the most popular salad ingredients, grows in many shapes and varieties in greenhouses around the world.

We could also use the past participle of the verb *grow*.

Sentence: **Grown originally** in South America, the tomato, one of the most popular salad ingredients, grows in many shapes and varieties in greenhouses around the world.

**Gerunds** are verbs that act as nouns.

They are identical in appearance to present participles: they are created by adding –ING to the verb.

Sentence: **Growing** heirloom tomatoes can be a profitable activity because tomato plants mature quickly, bearing fruit after only 60 days.

Because gerunds are not verbs, a phrase that contains only a gerund cannot be a sentence.

Fragment: Tomatoes **growing** in many shapes and varieties in greenhouses around the world.

In order to turn the fragment into a sentence, we must eliminate the gerund by conjugating the verb.

Sentence: Tomatoes **grow** in many shapes and varieties in greenhouses around the world.

## G. Conjunctions

There are two main types of conjunctions:

1) **Coordinating conjunctions** join two independent clauses.

There are seven coordinating conjunctions, known by the acronym **FANBOYS**: For, And, Nor, But, Or, Yet, and So.

These conjunctions should follow a comma, not a semicolon.

Incorrect: Originally, tomatoes were grown only in South **America; but** they are cultivated in greenhouses around the world today.

Correct: Originally, tomatoes were grown only in South **America, but they** are cultivated in greenhouses around the world today.

2) **Subordinating conjunctions** join an independent clause and a dependent clause.

Common subordinating conjunctions include the following:

| | | |
|---|---|---|
| After | Despite | When |
| (Al)though | Even though | Whereas |
| Because | Unless | Whether |
| Before | Until | While |

A clause that begins with a subordinating conjunction is known as a **subordinate clause**. Subordinate clauses are by definition dependent—they cannot stand on their own as sentences.

Fragment:     **Although** tomatoes have been cultivated since the first millennium B.C.

Fragment:     **Until** tomatoes were brought back to Europe in the early sixteenth century.

A clause that begins with subordinating conjunction can be used to start a sentence, however—provided that an independent clause appears afterward.

Sentence:     **Although** tomatoes have been cultivated since the first millennium B.C., they did not become popular in the United States until the mid-nineteenth century.

The order of the clauses can also be flipped so that the independent clause comes first.

Sentence:     Tomatoes have been cultivated since the first millennium B.C., **although** they did not become popular in the United States until the mid-nineteenth century.

When the dependent clause comes first, a comma is normally placed between the clauses. When the independent clause comes first, a comma is not usually necessary (except in the case of "strong" transitions such as *although* and *whereas*, a rule that you do not need to worry about for the GMAT).

Regardless of their order, the two clauses cannot be separated by a semicolon.

Incorrect:     **Although** tomatoes have been cultivated since the first millennium B.C.; they did not become popular in the United States until the mid-nineteenth century.

Incorrect:     Tomatoes have been cultivated since the first millennium B.C.; **although** they did not become popular in the United States until the mid-nineteenth century.

Note that a phrase begun by a subordinating conjunction should contain a subject and conjugated verb rather than an –ING word. Otherwise, a fragment is created. This principle is discussed more extensively in Chapter 14, but you should be aware that the GMAT tests it frequently.

Fragment:     Tomatoes have been cultivated since the first millennium B.C., **although** their popularity in the United States not <u>increasing</u> until the mid-nineteenth century.

Sentence:     Tomatoes have been cultivated since the first millennium B.C., **although** their popularity in the United States <u>did not increase</u> until the mid-nineteenth century.

In some cases, however, it may be idiomatically acceptable for an –ING word to follow a subordinating conjunction. This is primarily the case for conjunctions involving time, e.g., *before, after, while*.

Sentence:     **Before** <u>becoming</u> a staple of Italian cuisine, the tomato was rarely used in everyday cooking and was even suspected of being poisonous.

# *Chapter Two*
# NON-ESSENTIAL CLAUSES

Before we get started looking in-depth at the various types of errors, we're going to do some foundational work that will help you simplify questions and identify a variety of errors more quickly and efficiently. We looked at non-essential clauses briefly in the previous section, but now we're going to consider them in greater detail.

We're going to start with these clauses because they are an extremely common "distractor" item in GMAT Sentence Corrections. While they are directly tested in many questions, **they also appear in many questions in which they perform no function other than to make sentences longer and more difficult to follow**.

Remember that not all of the information that a given sentence contains will be relevant, and that you may only need to consider a small part of a very long sentence in order to determine the correct answer. Non-essential clauses are, as their name suggests, not essential to the meaning of a sentence. In many cases, eliminating a non-essential clause can provide a straightforward method of reducing a mass of confusing information down to something more manageable, thus preventing you from becoming sidetracked by irrelevant details.

For example, consider the following question:

> William Makepeace Thackeray and Charles Dickens were both renowned as authors during the nineteenth century, but today the novels of Dickens, once criticized for their sentimentalism and lack of psychological depth, <u>are more widely read than Thackeray</u>.

(A)  more widely read than Thackeray
(B)  more widely read than is Thackeray
(C)  more widely read than are those of Thackeray
(D)  more widely read than Thackeray has been
(E)  more widely read than Thackeray's novels would be

If we consider the sentence as a whole, we can see that it contains a non-essential clause that, when removed, brings the error more clearly into focus:

> William Makepeace Thackeray and Charles Dickens were both renowned as authors during the nineteenth century, but today the novels of Dickens...are more widely read than Thackeray.

With the non-essential clause removed, the error becomes easier to spot—namely, that the novels of Dickens (things) are being compared to Thackeray (person). In order to correct the sentence, novels must be compared to novels. That reduces the possibilities to (C) and (E). (E) contains an unnecessary tense switch, making (C) correct.

To be clear, you may not always find it necessary to spend time mentally eliminating non-essential clauses; however, being able to do so quickly, especially when you are stuck, can help you grasp the underlying structure of complex sentences and more easily identify any potential problems they contain. In order to apply this strategy effectively, however, you must be able to consistently recognize non-essential clauses.

Non-essential clauses have the following features:

1) They are usually set off by commas, but can also be set off by dashes.

2) If they are removed from a sentence, the sentence will still make grammatical and logical sense.

3) They can begin with "w-words" (e.g., *which* or *who*), nouns, or participles.

4) They are usually followed by verbs.

Let's look at some examples.

Correct:    Voltaire's satirical novel *Candide***, which was written sometime between 1757 and 1758,** has been referred to as the most clandestine work of the eighteenth century because of its obviously irreverent and illicit content.

Correct:    Voltaire's satirical novel *Candide* **— which was written sometime between 1757 and 1758 —** has been referred to as the most clandestine work of the eighteenth century because of its obviously irreverent and illicit content.

Although there is no grammatical difference between a comma and a dash here, the dash creates a stronger, more dramatic break between the parts of the sentence. **The GMAT, however, is not concerned with testing this type of stylistic nuance**; the only thing you need to know is that this use of a dash is acceptable.

**If you encounter a question that contains some answers with two commas and others with two dashes you can assume that the punctuation is a distraction tool and that the correct answer will depend on a separate factor.**

Note that some GMAT sentences may include multiple non-essential clauses. Although such sentences may strike you as unnecessarily complex and awkward, there is nothing inherently wrong with this type of construction.

Correct:    Cleopatra, the last of the pharaohs and presumably the only one fluent in the common speech, probably spoke Greek, the language of the ruling class, in private.

The sentence contains two non-essential clauses, which can be crossed out as follows:

Correct:    Cleopatra, ~~the last of the pharaohs and presumably the only one fluent in the common speech,~~ probably spoke Greek, ~~the language of the ruling class,~~ in private.

Because the sentence that remains when the non-essential clauses are removed makes perfect grammatical sense (*Cleopatra probably spoke Greek in private*), there is no error.

On the flip side, the presence of two commas does not always indicate a non-essential clause. (Dashes appear so infrequently that the presence of two is effectively guaranteed to signal a non-essential clause.)

Because GMAT sentences often contain multiple clauses and multiple commas, you must be able to distinguish between two commas that mark a non-essential clause and two commas used for other, unrelated reasons.

Let's start by considering the following pairs of sentences:

Sentence 1:    London**, which was one of the largest and most important cities in Europe during the Middle Ages,** remains an important financial and cultural center today.

When the non-essential clause is removed from the sentence, the sentence still makes sense.

Crossed out:    London…remains an important financial and cultural center today.

Now take a look at this sentence:

Sentence 2:    During the Middle Ages, **London was one of the largest and most important cities in Europe, and** today it remains an important financial and cultural center.

If we cross out the information between the commas, we get this:

Sentence 2:    During the Middle Ages…and today it remains an important financial and cultural center.

The remaining sentence does not make sense, indicating that the commas do not signal a non-essential clause.

**Important:** Sentences that contain commas setting off non-essential clauses may *also* contain commas that serve unrelated purposes. In such cases, you must consider the meaning of the sentence in order to determine whether and where non-essential clauses appear.

Correct:    The sport of sumo wrestling, whose competitors must attempt to force one another out of a circular ring, originated in Japan, which remains the only country in the world where it is practiced.

The above sentence contains only one non-essential clause that can be removed without creating a problem:

Correct:    The sport of sumo wrestling, ~~whose competitors must attempt to force one another out of a circular ring,~~ originated in Japan, which remains the only country in the world where it is practiced.

If the information between a different set of commas is removed, however, we are left with nonsense:

Incorrect:    The sport of Sumo wrestling, whose competitors must attempt to force one another out of a circular ring, ~~originated in Japan,~~ which remains the only country in the world where it is practiced.

Logically, a circular ring cannot be *the only country in the world where it is practiced* because a circular ring is not a country. The two commas thus do not create a non-essential clause.

If you cannot instinctively determine where a non-essential clause belongs, take your pencil (not a pen!), draw a line through the section you want to test out, and read the sentence without it. If that doesn't work, erase the line, cross out a different section, and try again.

To reiterate: While you obviously cannot cross anything out while you are working on the computer, this type of trial and error is an important aspect of paper-based prep. If you have difficulty identifying non-essential clauses on paper, you will almost certainly find that skill even more challenging when you work on a screen.

## Appositives and Participial Phrases

Although non-essential clauses frequently begin with "w-words," that is not always that case. A non-essential clause that begins with a noun is known as an **appositive**.

Correct: Voltaire's *Candide*, <u>**a satirical novel**</u> **written sometime between 1757 and 1758,** has been referred to as the most clandestine work of the eighteenth century because of its obviously irreverent and illicit content.

Some appositives begin by repeating a noun from earlier in the sentence, for stylistic effect.

Correct: Voltaire's satirical <u>novel</u> *Candide*, <u>**a novel**</u> **written sometime between 1757 and 1758,** has been referred to as the most clandestine work of the eighteenth century because of its obviously irreverent and illicit content.

Similar to appositives are participial phrases, either present (–ING) or past (–ED, –EN, –OWN, –UNK, –UNG).

Correct: Voltaire's satirical novel *Candide*, <u>**having**</u> **been written sometime between 1757 and 1758,** quickly developed a reputation as the most clandestine work of the eighteenth century because of its obviously irreverent and illicit content.

In the case of past participles, the "w-word" is implied but omitted from the sentence.

Correct: Voltaire's novel *Candide*, **(which was)** <u>**written**</u> **sometime between 1757 and 1758,** has been referred to as the most clandestine work of the eighteenth century because of its obviously irreverent and illicit content.

In addition, a modifier can also correctly be placed before the participle.

Correct: Voltaire's novel *Candide*, <u>**reputedly**</u> **written sometime between 1757 and 1758,** has been referred to as the most clandestine work of the eighteenth century because of its obviously irreverent and illicit content.

**Note that this type of modifying phrase can only begin with a past participle—it cannot begin with the simple past.** When a verb has different past participle and simple past forms, you must make sure that the correct form is used. (For a list of irregular verbs, see p. 59.)

Incorrect: Voltaire's satirical novel *Candide*, <u>**wrote sometime between 1757 and 1758,**</u> has been referred to as the most clandestine work of the eighteenth century because of its obviously irreverent and illicit content.

Correct: Voltaire's satirical novel *Candide*, <u>**written**</u> **sometime between 1757 and 1758,** has been referred to as the most clandestine work of the eighteenth century because of its obviously irreverent and illicit content.

Appositives and participial phrases can also appear at the beginning or end of a sentence. When an appositive appears at the end, either a comma or dash can be used.

Correct: **Written sometime between 1757 and 1758,** Voltaire's *Candide* has been referred to as the most clandestine work of the eighteenth century because of its obviously irreverent and illicit content.

Correct: Voltaire's satirical novel *Candide* has been referred to as the most clandestine work of theeighteenth **century, an epithet (or: century—an epithet) derived from its obviously irreverent and illicit content.**

You may also encounter sentences with short non-essential clauses or phrases that form brief interruptions. Do not be fooled by the unexpected syntax. This construction is perfectly acceptable.

> Correct: Voltaire's satirical novel *Candide*, **some critics believe,** is one of the most influential works of fiction ever written because it has inspired so many authors and artists in the centuries since it was composed.

A non-essential clause cannot, however, begin with a subject pronoun such as *it* or *they*:

> Incorrect: Voltaire's satirical novel *Candide*, **it was written sometime between 1757 and 1758,** has been referred to as the most clandestine work of the eighteenth century because of its obviously irreverent and illicit content.

The decision to construct a non-essential clause in a particular way is purely stylistic. As a result, if you encounter a GMAT question whose answer choices contain different types of correctly constructed non-essential clauses, you can assume that the answer will depend on a separate factor.

## When are Non-Essential Clauses <u>Not</u> Acceptable?

While correct answers may include multiple non-essential clauses and be somewhat convoluted structurally, incorrect answers may contain non-essential clauses that are awkward to the point of being unacceptable.

In addition, these answers may include an excessive number of non-essential clauses that break up sentences unnecessarily and illogically.

These clauses may also begin with prepositions (e.g., *in, from, to, with*) and/or contain unnecessary –ING words, constructions that are frequently awkward and unwieldy, and that create fragments.

Consider the following sentence:

> Incorrect: The country's human rights record, **in recent years, having come under close scrutiny,** is widely known to be poor, but leaders of the ruling party leaders have nevertheless managed to avoid international censure.

In the above example, the sentence still makes grammatical sense when the two non-essential clauses following the subject are crossed out, but the non-essential clauses themselves are problematic.

First, their placement after the subject creates an unnatural, jerky break in the sentence. Moreover, the use of a preposition (*in*) and a participle (*having*) respectively at the start of two consecutive clauses is extremely awkward.

So although the sentence does not directly violate a rule in quite the same way that, say, a subject-verb disagreement would, its overall construction is simply very poor. Were it an answer choice, you could pretty safely eliminate it.

For an authentic example, consider question #904 on p. 876 of the *Official Guide*. In the original version, the two non-essential clauses are appropriately set off by two commas, but the first is unnecessarily wordy (*an asteroid named Ida* as opposed to *the asteroid Ida*), and the second begins with a preposition (*in*).

# Exercise: Identifying Non-Essential Words and Phrases

In the following sentences, place commas around non-essential phrases as necessary. Note that some sentences may contain additional unrelated commas. (Answers p. 189)

| 1. | Over the next 50 million years, the cesium fountain atomic clock considered the most precise form of timekeeper ever created is expected to become inaccurate by less than a single second. |
|---|---|
| 2. | Each year, the field of fluid dynamics a field that is as mathematically demanding and challenging to the nonscientist as any field of physics produces compelling and beautiful videos by capturing motion and movement that cannot be seen with the naked eye. |
| 3. | More than any other recent innovation in entertainment, Internet streaming has the potential even the likelihood to create an entirely new narrative genre: one with elements of television, film and the novel. |
| 4. | Used in some martial arts, the Red Belt one of several colored belts intended to denote a practitioner's skill level and rank originated in Japan and Korea. |
| 5. | Patients who receive anesthesia during surgery are put into a semi-comatose state, not as many people assume a deep state of sleep. |
| 6. | Because dams supply relatively little water independent experts and most environmental groups argue aggressive modern methods of water storage and management are required. |
| 7. | Centered in Nantucket, Massachusetts, whaling a risky pursuit that led sailors halfway across the world and sometimes to the bottom of the sea was a lucrative business during the early nineteenth century. |
| 8. | Human "computers" once responsible for performing basic numerical analysis for laboratories were behind the calculations for everything from the first accurate prediction of the return of Halley's Comet to the success of the Manhattan Project. |
| 9. | Entertainment sources such as movies and books are not some critics claim responsible for shaping a culture, only for reflecting it. |
| 10. | The Environmental Protection Agency's Clean Power Plan a major component of governmental efforts to push electricity generators away from coal and toward natural gas provides businesses with incentives for renewable-power generation. |
| 11. | Illegal logging has declined in recent years, but the practice which was once nearly responsible for destroying the monarch butterfly's winter habitat persists in a number of regions. |
| 12. | Norman Rockwell's intricately conceived narrative paintings reproduced widely in magazines appealed to a vast audience of readers who recognized themselves in the stories the images told. |
| 13. | Unlike programs created for online distribution, network television shows which produce new episodes while the seasons air can alter their storylines midseason if ratings drop or a new character is rejected. |
| 14. | The right and left portions of the amygdala two almond-shaped groups of nuclei located deep and medially within the temporal lobes of the brain have independent memory systems but work together to store, encode, and interpret emotion. |
| 15. | Forensic biology the application of biology to law enforcement has been used for a wide range of purposes, including identifying illegal products from endangered species and preventing collisions between birds and wind turbines. |

# Official Guide Non-Essential Clause Questions

| Question # | Page |
|------------|------|
| **Official Guide** | |
| 823 | 860 |
| 847 | 865 |
| 899 | 874 |
| 904 | 876 |
| 929 | 880 |
| 939 | 882 |
| 961 | 887 |
| 975 | 890 |
| 981 | 891 |
| **Official Verbal Guide** | |
| 246 | 404 |
| 286 | 413 |
| 298 | 416 |
| 322 | 422 |
| 329 | 423 |

# Chapter Three

# SENTENCES AND FRAGMENTS

Because GMAT sentences and answer choices can be quite long and complex, and often contain multiple sub-clauses, the distinction between sentences and fragments is not always immediately obvious. Particularly when you are reading on a screen, it is easy to get lost and fail to notice that a particular statement is not actually a sentence. Becoming familiar with common types of GMAT fragments can thus help you avoid this type of confusion.

The GMAT tests two main types of fragments:

1) Relative clauses

2) Gerunds (-ING) replace verbs

To reiterate, gerunds and participles (*verb* + *–ING*) look like verbs but cannot substitute for them. As a result, a clause that contains only an –ING word lacks a main verb and is thus a fragment. To fix this type of error, it is necessary to provide a verb.

**Important: BEING and HAVING are the –ING words most likely to appear on the GMAT. While there are exceptions, you can generally start by assuming that answers containing these words (particularly BEING) are wrong**. Because the verb *to be* is irregular, you should make sure to be familiar with both its present and past forms.

|  | Present | Past |
|---|---|---|
| **Singular** | Is | Was |
| **Plural** | Are | Were |

Fragment:    Completed in the 1860s, Neuschwanstein castle in Germany **being** considered one of the seven wonders of the modern world because it represents such an incredible feat of architecture.

Fragment:    Completed in the 1860s, Neuschwanstein castle in Germany, **having long been** considered one of the seven wonders of the modern world because it represents such an incredible feat of architecture.

To turn a fragment containing a gerund into a sentence, simply replace the gerund with a conjugated verb:

Sentence:    Completed in the 1860s, Neuschwanstein castle in Germany **is** considered one of the seven wonders of the modern world because it represents such an incredible feat of architecture.

Sentence:    Completed in the 1860s, Neuschwanstein castle in Germany **has long been** considered one of the seven wonders of the modern world because it represents such an incredible feat of architecture.

Of course, verbs other than *to be* and *to have* are tested on the GMAT as well. In such cases, simply remove the –ING to create a verb and turn the fragment into a sentence. Then, check for answers containing that verb.

Fragment:     Believing that the creation of records represented an important form of social and economic power, activist and music publisher Harry Pace **launching** the African-American recording company Black Swan in 1921.

Sentence:     Believing that the creation of records represented an important form of social and economic power, activist and music publisher Harry Pace **launched** the African-American recording company Black Swan in 1921.

## Relative Clause Errors

In the previous section of this chapter, we looked at how to identify the two main types of relative clauses: essential (*that*) and non-essential (*which, who/whose*). Now, we're going to look at potential errors involving these types of clauses in greater depth.

A sentence that contains a relative clause must <u>also</u> contain a main verb that corresponds to the subject of the sentence. If the verb corresponds only to the subject of the relative clause—usually *that* or *which*—a fragment is created.

### Non-Essential Clauses

Let's start with the following base sentence (subject underlined, verb in bold):

Correct:      <u>George C. Williams</u> **was** an important biologist.

If we place the word *who* after the subject, we will create a fragment.

Fragment:     George C. Williams, <u>who</u> **was** an important biologist.

In the second version, the verb *was* becomes part of the clause begun by the *who*, not part of the main clause begun by the subject (*George C. Williams*). As a result, the sentence lacks a main verb that corresponds to the subject.

On the GMAT, however, you're much more likely to see something like this:

Fragment:     George C. Williams, <u>who</u> **is** considered one of the most important twentieth-century thinkers in the field of evolutionary biology because of his substantial contributions to a gene-centered view of evolution.

Although this sentence is much longer and more complex than the original version above, the problem is the same: the construction "comma + *who*" indicates that a non-essential clause is beginning, but the clause never ends. As a result, the verb *is* belongs to the pronoun *who* rather than to the subject of the sentence, George C. Williams.

The fastest and easiest way to turn this fragment into a sentence is to remove the comma and the relative pronoun, eliminating the relative clause and making the entire sentence into a single clause.

Sentence:     <u>George C. Williams</u> **is** considered one of the most important twentieth-century thinkers in the field of evolutionary biology because of his substantial contributions to a gene-centered view of evolution.

Another very common way of creating fragments involves placing a part of speech other than a verb after the non-essential clause, e.g., *and*, a pronoun such as *it* or *they*, or a gerund.

Fragment:    George C. Williams, who is considered one of the most important twentieth-century thinkers in the field of evolutionary biology, **and who made** substantial contributions to a gene-centered view of evolution.

In the above sentence, we can identify what appears to be a non-essential clause (*considered…biology*) because it begins with *who* and is surrounded by commas. If we cross it out, however, we are left with nonsense.

Fragment:    George C. Williams…**and who made** substantial contributions to a gene-centered view of evolution.

Clearly, this is not a sentence. Making it into a sentence, however, is simple. Since the first word after the end of a non-essential clause is typically a verb, we can cross out all the excess words before the verb. This leaves us with:

Sentence:    George C. Williams…~~**and who**~~ made a number of lasting contributions to a gene-centered view of evolution.

With the elimination of those two words, the fragment suddenly becomes a sentence. When we plug the non-essential clause back in, we get something much clearer:

Sentence:    George C. Williams, who was one of the most important twentieth-century thinkers in evolutionary biology, **made** a number of lasting contributions to a gene-centered view of evolution.

Another possible solution is to remove the non-essential clause entirely.

Sentence:    George C. Williams **was** one of the most important twentieth-century thinkers in the field of evolutionary biology and made a number of lasting contributions to his field.

## To sum up:

The easiest way to tackle sentences like this is to see whether there is a verb immediately following a non-essential clause. If there is not, the sentence will usually be incorrect. (The primary exception involves a modifier placed before the verb, e.g., *George C. Williams, who was one of the most important recent American thinkers in evolutionary biology, <u>also</u> made a number of lasting contributions to his field*, because the sentence still makes sense if the non-essential clause is eliminated.)

Eliminate everything after the second comma and before the verb, and usually, the sentence that remains will closely match the correct answer choice. **Note that you will most likely need to become accustomed to crossing out non-essential clauses on paper before you are able to easily eliminate them mentally on a screen.**

## Again:

Fragment:    Mobile robot technology, which was historically used by both the military and the police, and it **is** now becoming widespread at businesses and hotels.

Simplify:    Mobile robot technology~~, which was historically used by both the military and the police,~~ and it **is** now becoming widespread at businesses and hotels.

Cross Out:    Mobile robot technology…~~and it~~ **is** now becoming widespread at businesses and hotels.

Sentence:    Mobile robot technology, which was historically used by both the military and the police, **is** now becoming widespread at businesses and hotels.

You could also be asked to fix the beginning of a non-essential clause rather than the end.

Non-essential clause errors that appear in this format can be tricky to identify. Contrary to expectations, the beginning of the sentence may appear perfectly acceptable while the end seems problematic.

Fragment:     **Mobile robot technology** has historically been used by both the military and the police, is now becoming widespread at businesses and hotels.

Although the beginning of the sentence makes perfect grammatical sense, things fall apart later on. One possible correction involves recognizing that the comma after *police* can correctly signal the end of a non-essential clause and rewriting the beginning of the sentence to mark the start of the non-essential clause.

Sentence:     <u>**Mobile robot technology,**</u> historically used by both the military and the police, is now becoming widespread at businesses and hotels.

## Essential Clauses

Even though essential clauses beginning with *that* are not set off by commas, and by definition contain information essential to the meaning of a sentence, their <u>grammatical</u> function is the same as that of non-essential clauses: if an essential clause is crossed out of a sentence, the sentence will still make grammatical sense.

Fragment:     The mobile robot technology **that has historically been used by both the military and the police** and that is now becoming widespread at businesses and hotels.

Simplify:     The mobile robot technology…and that is now becoming widespread at businesses and hotels.

Cross out:    The mobile robot technology…~~and that~~ is now becoming widespread at businesses and hotels.

Sentence:     The mobile robot technology **that has historically been used by both the military and the police** is now becoming widespread at businesses and hotels.

Note, however, that a clause beginning with a "w-word" or *that* can acceptably end a sentence, provided that the sentence already contains a main verb:

Correct:      <u>Keyless entry systems</u> often **make** use of hidden cameras, which allow residents to screen visitors discreetly and determine whom to let in.

Correct:      <u>Keyless entry systems</u> often **make** use of hidden cameras that allow residents to screen visitors discreetly and determine whom to let in.

In this case, the clauses *which/that allow residents to screen visitors discreetly…* do not create fragments because the verb *make* already corresponds to the subject, *keyless entry systems*.

## Double Conjunctions

Every sentence, no matter how long, must contain at least one clause that can stand on its own as a complete sentence. If one clause in a sentence begins with a conjunction, the clause before or after it should not also begin with one.

While this type of error is easy to spot when sentences are short, it can be fairly easy to overlook in GMAT-length sentences, particularly if only a small portion of a sentence is underlined.

Incorrect: <u>Because</u> the opening and closing bells at the New York Stock Exchange receive extensive press **coverage, so** many companies schedule new product launches and other marketing events to coincide with the days on which company representatives participate in those ceremonies.

Correct: <u>Because</u> the opening and closing bells at the New York Stock Exchange receive extensive press **coverage, many** companies schedule new product launches and other marketing events to coincide with the days on which company representatives participate in those ceremonies.

Correct: The opening and closing bells at the New York Stock Exchange receive extensive press **coverage, so many** companies schedule new product launches and other marketing events to coincide with the days on which company representatives participate in those ceremonies.

In order to be able to identify this type of error, you must train yourself to always **back up and read from the beginning of a sentence**, no matter how far away from the beginning the underlined portion is located. Without the full context of the sentence, you may lack sufficient information to identify the error.

## Semicolons and Comma Splices

The GMAT tests semicolons and comma splices relatively infrequently, but incorrect answers involving these concepts can appear. Provided that you can distinguish between sentences and fragments, the rules are quite straightforward.

**Semicolons** should only be placed between two sentences (independent clauses); a semicolon placed between a sentence and a fragment/dependent clause is incorrect. Remember that a sentence need not make sense out of context to be grammatically complete, and that it must contain a subject and a verb that corresponds to the subject.

Incorrect: Following any learning event, new information is not deposited instantaneously in an individual's long-term **memory; rather, slowly assimilated** into the brain's long-term storage over time.

Correct: Following any learning event, new information is not deposited instantaneously in an individual's long-term **memory; rather, it is slowly assimilated** into the brain's long-term storage over time.

**Comma splice** errors are the flipside of semicolon errors. A comma splice consists of a comma incorrectly placed between two complete sentences.

Incorrect: Following any learning event, new information is not deposited instantaneously in an individual's long-term **memory, rather, it is slowly assimilated** into the brain's long-term storage over time.

Correct: Following any learning event, new information is not deposited instantaneously in an individual's long-term **memory; rather, it is slowly assimilated** into the brain's long-term storage over time.

## Passive Voice

In this construction, the subject and the object of a sentence are flipped in order to emphasize that someone or something is on the receiving end of an action. Whereas the active voice indicates that *x does y*, the passive voice indicates that *y is done by x*.

|  |  | Subject | Object |
|--|--|---------|--------|
|  |  |  |  |

Active:  As a result of poor sales and rising rents, <u>the company</u> laid off <u>several hundred workers</u> at the end of last quarter.

Subject

Passive:  As a result of poor sales and rising rents, <u>several hundred workers</u> were laid off by <u>the company</u> at the end of last quarter.

Object

Although the GMAT is generally not a big fan of the passive voice, there are some situations in which this construction is required to create a grammatically acceptable sentence.

Incorrect:  One of the least popular of all the Romance languages, **Romansch traditionally spoken** by people who reside in the southern regions of Switzerland.

Correct:  One of the least popular of all the Romance languages, **Romansch is traditionally spoken** by people who reside in the southern regions of Switzerland.

Even though the incorrect version of the sentence appears to contain a verb (*spoken*), it is unacceptable in this context to say *a language spoken*. The verb *is* must be used.

Note that if you are fatigued, your mind is more likely to fill in these types of missing verbs automatically. Because you know how the correct version should appear, you see what you expect to see.

## Jumbled Sentences

Finally, incorrect answers to GMAT Sentence Corrections sometimes consist of, or create, "jumbled" constructions—ones whose syntax is exceedingly wordy, awkward, twisted, and just plain wrong.

Although such constructions may contain multiple errors (e.g., gerunds, passive voice, misplaced modifiers), it is often unnecessary to spend time parsing the problems grammatically. If you have a reasonably good sense of standard English, you will likely be able to tell that there is something very off about them.

Problems may be restricted to one part of a sentence:

Incorrect:  Although the existence of Aesop remains uncertain, numerous tales **that it was credited to him** have been gathered in many languages and in many countries across the centuries.

Or they may be spread out across an entire sentence, creating a nonsensical mess:

Incorrect:  Although some animals can synthesize their own vitamin C, which humans and other animals like guinea pigs, bats, and some species of fish lack the enzyme L-gulonolactone oxidase necessary for such synthesis, and must obtain vitamin C through their diet.

If the former type of construction appears in the original version, you may be able to correct the error on your own, without looking at the answers. In case of the latter, however, you may need to work from the answer choices in order to determine the most logical correction.

# Exercise: Sentences and Fragments

Label each of the following phrases as either a sentence or a fragment. Rewrite all fragments as sentences. (Answers p. 189)

| | |
|---|---|
| 1. | The pyramids of ancient Egypt, constructed as monuments to the Pharaohs' greatness, and they were built with the help of immense armies of slaves. |
| 2. | Although the painter has earned praise for his ironic depictions of everyday life, neither humor nor self-awareness is apparent in his work; rather appearing to rely predominantly on cliché. |
| 3. | Puzzle-solving is an ancient and universal practice, depending on the kind of creative insight that led human beings to ignite the first campfires thousands of years ago. |
| 4. | Quasars, the most energetic and distant members of a class of objects called active galactic nuclei, often caused by collisions of galaxies, with the galaxies' central black holes merging to form either a supermassive black hole or a binary black hole system. |
| 5. | A recent trend of advertisers treating major awards ceremonies as platforms for new ads that will elicit an audience response seeming to be intensifying, with a variety of well-known companies planning to introduce new campaigns. |
| 6. | Throughout history there have been many senatorial bodies, two of which were the Spartan Gerousia and the Roman Senate, but all of them were founded on similar principles. |
| 7. | Recent findings from research on moose, suggesting that the development of arthritis in human beings may be linked to nutritional deficits as well as to the natural consequences of aging. |
| 8. | Although photovoltaic (PV) cells, first discovered in the 1950s, have long been the dominant source for solar power, but concentrated solar power (CSP) technology has been rising in popularity in recent years as well. |
| 9. | A popular novelist and playwright, George Barr McCutcheon, best known for the series of novels set in Graustark, a fictional country in Eastern Europe. |
| 10. | Nicollet Island is an island in the Mississippi River that is located just north of Minneapolis, Minnesota, and that was named after Joseph Nicollet, the French cartographer and astronomer who first mapped the upper Mississippi in the 1830s. |
| 11. | Brunei is the only sovereign state located entirely on the island of Borneo, the remainder of the island's territory is divided between the nations of Malaysia and Indonesia. |
| 12. | Although Rodin purposely omitted crucial elements such as arms from his sculptures, his consistent use of the human figure attesting to his respect for artistic tradition. |
| 13. | In recent studies, the Enlightenment has been viewed as the product of the Republic of Letters, the intellectual core of a nascent public sphere that emerged in opposition to a closed monarchy, which censored both books and speech. |
| 14. | When companies move from a traditional office model to an open office model, so discrete offices placed along a central corridor are removed in order to make way for large communal rooms. |
| 15. | In 1763, the signing of the Treaty of Paris marked the end of the Seven Years' War, also known as the French and Indian War; ushering in a period of British dominance outside of Europe. |

## Official Guide Sentence vs. Fragment Questions

| Question # | Page | |
|---|---|---|
| **Official Guide** | | |
| 828 | 861 | Jumbled Sentence (C), (E) |
| 830 | 861 | -ING Replaces Verb |
| 839 | 863 | Jumbled Sentence (C) |
| 842 | 864 | Comma Splice |
| 843 | 864 | Semicolon, Gerund Replaces Verb (D) |
| 852 | 866 | -ING Replaces Verb (A), Relative Clause (B), (E) |
| 875 | 870 | Semicolon |
| 896 | 874 | Semicolon, Gerund Replaces Verb |
| 905 | 876 | -ING Replaces Verb (E) |
| 932 | 881 | Passive, Missing Verb (D) |
| 933 | 881 | Relative Clause (B), (D) |
| 935 | 881 | Missing Verb (C) |
| 939 | 882 | -ING Replaces Verb (D), (E) |
| 956 | 886 | Relative Clause (C) |
| 961 | 887 | Passive, Missing Verb |
| 966 | 888 | Semicolon |
| 979 | 891 | Comma Splice |
| **Official Verbal Guide** | | |
| 238 | 403 | Jumbled Sentence |
| 264 | 408 | Comma Splice |
| 275 | 410 | Passive |
| 277 | 411 | Missing Verb |
| 286 | 413 | Jumbled Sentence |
| 299 | 416 | Missing Verb (A)-(C); Semicolon (D), (E) |
| 322 | 422 | Comma Splice (E) |
| 329 | 424 | Semicolon (C), (D) |
| 331 | 424 | Relative Clause (D) |
| 342 | 426 | Missing Subject |

# *Chapter Four*

# SUBJECT-VERB AGREEMENT

All verbs must agree with their subjects in number:

- Singular subjects take singular verbs.

- Plural subjects take plural verbs.

GMAT questions testing number ask about verbs in the 3rd person singular (*he/she/it*) and plural (*they*) forms.

**Important: 3rd person singular verbs always end in –S; 3rd person plural verbs do not. Note that this is the opposite of nouns, which take an –S in the plural.**

|  | Correct | Incorrect |
|---|---|---|
| Singular subject | The rate increases. | The rate increase. |
| Plural subject (simple) | The rates increase. | The rates increases. |
| Plural subject (compound) | The rate and the velocity increase. | The rate and the velocity increases. |

**Important:** *is/are, was/were,* and *has/have* are the most frequently tested verbs. When you see the conjugated form of one of these verbs underlined, you should immediately begin by identifying its subject.

Unfortunately, most subject-verb agreement questions that appear on the GMAT are considerably longer than the above examples, not to mention a good deal more complex. Furthermore, subjects and verbs are unlikely to appear next to one another, making disagreements difficult to spot.

That said, there are a limited number of ways in which subjects and verbs are likely to be separated from one another in GMAT sentences. The following pages detail these common constructions, as well as a number of additional formats in which subject-verb agreement errors could potentially appear.

## A. Subject – Non-Essential Clause – Verb

On the GMAT, non-essential clauses may be inserted between subjects and verbs in order to distract from the fact that the subject is singular and the verb is plural or vice-versa.

Incorrect:     Moroccan green tea, which is prepared with a healthy amount of sugar and mint leaves, **are** one of the most popular drinks across North Africa.

Correct:     Moroccan green tea, which is prepared with a healthy amount of sugar and mint leaves, **is** one of the most popular drinks across North Africa.

Whenever you encounter a non-essential clause, you should immediately cross it out. Most often it is used to distract you from spotting subject-verb agreement errors, but it can be used to distract from other types of errors as well (discussed later). Do not forget this step! Otherwise, you risk overlooking errors that can be easily spotted.

Subject-verb agreement errors can also appear *within* non-essential clauses, so if you've eliminated a non-essential clause and can't find another problem in the sentence, go back and check.

Incorrect:     Moroccan green tea, which **are** prepared with a healthy amount of sugar and mint leaves, is one of the most popular drinks across North Africa.

Correct:       Moroccan green tea, which **is** prepared with a healthy amount of sugar and mint leaves, is one of the most popular drinks across North Africa.

You may also encounter subject-verb agreement questions with essential clauses. Sometimes these clauses will be set off with *that*, but other times they may begin with another part of speech (typically a past participle).

Incorrect:     In large doses, many common chemicals (that are) found in household cleaners **has** devastating effects, but toxicologists insist that such substances are thoroughly innocuous in minuscule amounts.

Correct:       In large doses, many common chemicals (that are) found in household cleaners **have** devastating effects, but toxicologists insist that such substances are thoroughly innocuous in minuscule amounts.

## B. Subject – Prepositional Phrase – Verb

A prepositional phrase is a phrase that begins with a preposition, e.g., *in the box*, *under the table*, *over the hill*.

Prepositional phrases may be inserted between subjects and verbs to distract from disagreements. When this is the case, the verb will follow the last word of the prepositional phrase (or series of prepositional phrases).

Incorrect:     **Changes** in the balance of trade **seems** remote from everyday concerns, but they can drastically affect the ways in which consumers choose to spend their money.

Correct:       **Changes** in the balance of trade **seem** remote from everyday concerns, but they can drastically affect the ways in which consumers choose to spend their money.

The above sentence contains a classic trick: the subject (*changes*) is plural and thus requires a plural verb (*seem*). However, the prepositional phrase inserted between the subject and the verb ends with a singular noun (*trade*). If you are not paying close attention, *trade* can easily appear to be the subject of the verb that follows.

## C. (Prepositional Phrase) – Verb – Subject

**Note: this structure is not normally tested on the GMAT, but I am including it here for the sake of thoroughness.**

In this structure, the normal word syntax is reversed so that the prepositional phrase appears at the beginning of a sentence or clause (italicized), followed by the verb (bold) and then the subject (underlined).

Incorrect:     *Along the Loup Canal in Nebraska* **extends** parks, lakes, and trails owned and operated by the Loup power district, a public power utility serving residents of four separate counties.

Correct:       *Along the Loup Canal in Nebraska* **extend** parks, lakes, and trails owned and operated by the Loup power district, a public power utility serving residents of four separate counties.

The preposition can also appear as the second word in a clause. In such cases, it will most likely be preceded by a participle, either present (–ING) or past (–ED, –OWN, –UNG).

Incorrect:     Running *along the Loup Canal in Nebraska* **is** <u>parks, lakes, and trails</u> owned and operated by the Loup power district, a public power utility serving residents of four separate counties.

Correct:       Running *along the Loup Canal in Nebraska* **are** <u>parks, lakes, and trails</u> owned and operated by the Loup power district, a public power utility serving residents of four separate counties.

Although the reversed syntax makes the sentence sound odd, the syntax itself is not the problem. Rather, it is a distraction tool that makes the disagreement between the subject and the verb more difficult to hear.

In addition, errors may appear in which the verb comes before the subject but is not preceded by a prepositional phrase:

Incorrect:     Radioactivity is generally not considered harmful when people are exposed to it at low levels for brief periods, but less clear **is** <u>its long-term effects</u>.

Correct:       Radioactivity is generally not considered harmful when people are exposed to it at low levels for brief periods, but less clear **are** <u>its long-term effects</u>.

## D. Compound Subject

When two singular nouns are connected by *and*, the result is a **compound subject**. Compound subjects are always plural and require plural verbs.

If you only notice the second noun—the noun closer to the verb—you are likely to think that a singular verb is correct. As a result, you should always make sure to back up and determine the *complete* subject before deciding whether a given verb is correct.

Incorrect:     <u>Louise Erdrich's fiction and poetry</u> **draws** on their author's Chippewa heritage to examine complex familial relationships among Native Americans as they reflect on issues of identity and culture.

Correct:       <u>Louise Erdrich's fiction and poetry</u> **draw** on their author's Chippewa heritage to examine complex familial relationships among Native Americans as they reflect on issues of identity and culture.

Note that compound subjects can also appear in conjunction with other features, such as prepositional phrases or non-essential clauses. When this is the case, you must be very careful to identify the complete subject. If you only notice the noun closer to the verb and overlook the word *and*, you are likely to think that the subject is singular.

Compound subject with prepositional phrase:

Incorrect:     <u>The highly textured bark and distinctive silhouette</u> *of the Dutch Elm tree* **distinguishes** that species from the equally common English Elm tree.

Correct:       <u>The highly textured bark and distinctive silhouette</u> *of the Dutch Elm tree* **distinguish** that species from the equally common English Elm tree.

Compound subject with flipped subject and verb:

Incorrect:    In the galleries of the Louvre museum **hangs** Leonardo da Vinci's *Mona Lisa* and Eugene Delacroix's *Liberty Leading the People*, two of the best-known paintings in the world.

Correct:    In the galleries of the Louvre museum **hang** Leonardo da Vinci's *Mona Lisa* and Eugene Delacroix's *Liberty Leading the People*, two of the best-known paintings in the world.

## E. There is/There are, etc.

There is
There was          } take **singular** nouns
There has been

There are
There were         } take **plural** nouns
There have been

Incorrect:    In recent months, there **has been** <u>many questions</u> raised about the handling of the company's finances, increasing speculation that it may soon declare bankruptcy.

Correct:    In recent months, there **have been** <u>many questions</u> raised about the handling of the company's finances, increasing speculation that it may soon declare bankruptcy.

## F. Neither...Nor + Verb

When *(n)either...(n)or* is used, the verb must agree with the noun that comes right before the verb.

Incorrect:    Although both authors have written acclaimed novels, neither Maxine Hong Kingston nor <u>Amy Tan</u> **were** raised in a literary family.

Correct:    Although both authors have written acclaimed novels, neither Maxine Hong Kingston nor <u>Amy Tan</u> **was** raised in a literary family.

When *(n)either* is used without *(n)or*, a singular verb should be used. *(N)either* is short for *(n)either one*.

Incorrect:    Although Maxine Hong Kingston and Amy Tan have both written acclaimed novels, <u>neither</u> **were** raised in a literary family.

Correct:    Although Maxine Hong Kingston and Amy Tan have both written acclaimed novels, <u>neither</u> **was** raised in a literary family.

## In addition:

### Collective (group) nouns = singular

Collective nouns are nouns that refer to groups of people, e.g., *agency*, *company*, *board*, *institution*, *organization*, *team*, *family*, and *committee*. **Note that while British English considers these nouns plural, the GMAT follows American usage and only considers them singular.**

Incorrect: Founded in 1948, the World Health <u>Organization</u> **support** countries' attempts to improve the health of their citizens by coordinating the efforts of multiple sectors.

Correct: Founded in 1948, the World Health <u>Organization</u> **supports** countries' attempts to improve the health of their citizens by coordinating the efforts of multiple sectors.

### A number = plural

### The number = singular

Incorrect: Although company executives and labor leaders were able to reach a rapid agreement, <u>a number</u> of workers **has** unexpectedly begun to protest the new administration's economic policies.

Correct: Although company executives and labor leaders were able to reach a rapid agreement, <u>a number</u> of workers **have** unexpectedly begun to protest the new administration's economic policies.

Incorrect: Although company executives and labor leaders were able to reach a rapid agreement, <u>the number</u> of workers beginning to protest the new administration's economic policies **are** unexpectedly high.

Correct: Although company executives and labor leaders were able to reach a rapid agreement, <u>the number</u> of workers beginning to protest the new administration's economic policies **is** unexpectedly high.

### One = singular

Although this rule may seem obvious, it is easy to become confused if a prepositional phrase is inserted between the subject and the verb.

Incorrect: According to a view held by many economists, one of the fundamental causes of inflation **involve** changes in the demand for goods.

Correct: According to a view held by many economists, one of the fundamental causes of inflation **involves** changes in the demand for goods.

### Each (one) = singular

Incorrect: <u>Each</u> of the labor union's members **are** expected to attend the meeting at which next year's contract will be negotiated with company officials.

Correct: <u>Each</u> of the labor union's members **is** expected to attend the meeting at which next year's contract will be negotiated with company officials.

## Every (one) = singular

Incorrect:     Every one of the labor union's members **are** expected to attend the meeting, at which next year's contract will be negotiated with company officials.

Correct:       Every one of the labor union's members **is** expected to attend the meeting, at which next year's contract will be negotiated with company officials.

## Gerunds (-ING words) = singular

Incorrect:     Playing parlor games such as charades **were** a popular pastime in the early twentieth century, before the invention of radio and television.

Correct:       Playing parlor games such as charades **was** a popular pastime in the early twentieth century, before the invention of radio and television.

## Infinitives (TO + verb) = singular

Incorrect:     To train for competition in an athletic event at the Olympics **are** to be subjected to a grueling regime of discipline and training, one that must be followed strictly for months or even years.

Correct:       To train for competition in an athletic event at the Olympics **is** to be subjected to a grueling regime or discipline and training, one that must be followed strictly for months or even years.

## That, Whether, What = singular

Although the use of these words as subjects may sound odd to you, it is perfectly acceptable. If anything, answers containing these constructions are more likely to be correct, and should thus be considered very carefully, precisely because so many test-takers are likely to find them questionable.

Correct:       That Jane Goodall became the world's foremost expert on chimpanzees **was** hardly a surprise to those who had observed her childhood fascination with animals.

Correct:       What has been repeatedly criticized **is** the author's refusal to discuss her work publicly, not the content of her novels.

Correct:       Whether *The Tale of Genji* was actually written entirely by Murasaki Shikibu **is** unlikely to ever be determined unless a major archival discovery is made.

Note that some of these words are condensed versions of longer phrases, e.g., *that* = the fact that, *whether* = the question whether. In some cases, you may find it easier to understand what sentences are saying if you plug in the complete phrase.

## Subject-Verb Agreement on the GMAT

Being able to spot subject-verb agreement errors without the aid of the answer choices is of course ideal; however, you may not always be able to identify disagreements on your own. In such cases, you can work backwards from the answer choices. When the answer choices are split between singular and plural verbs, you can be confident that you are dealing with a subject-verb agreement question.

For example, consider the following set of answer choices:

(A)  remain puzzling to archaeologists, who in the
     mid-1980s began studying
(B)  remain puzzling to archaeologists, who in the
     mid-1980s began to study
(C)  remains puzzling to archaeologists, who in the
     mid-1980s began studying
(D)  remains puzzling to archaeologists, beginning in
     the mid-1980s to study
(E)  remain puzzling to archaeologists, who in the
     mid-1980s would begin to study

The first word of each answer choice provides a very important clue as to what the question is testing: choices (A), (B), and (E) all begin with the plural verb *remain*, while choices (C) and (D) begin with the singular plural verb *remains*.

Before you even start to consider the rest of the information in the answer choices, you must identify the subject of the verb in question and determine whether that subject is singular or plural. Doing so will allow you to eliminate at least two, even three, answers immediately, making it unnecessary for you to consider any additional errors in those choices.

Now take a look at the whole question:

> The presence of mysterious paintings in a cave
> located outside Columbia, Missouri, <u>remain puzzling
> to archaeologists, who in the mid-1980s began
> studying</u> the images created by ancient residents of the
> Mississippi Valley.

Be very careful when identifying the subject. While it is true that the mysterious paintings remain puzzling to archaeologists, the grammatical subject of the sentence is actually the singular noun *the presence*. The plural noun *mysterious paintings* is part of the prepositional phrase begun by the preposition *of*.

As a matter of fact, this sentence contains three prepositional phrases between the subject and the verb:

The presence **of mysterious paintings in a cave located outside Columbia, Missouri,** remain...
           1                         2                   3

When you are dealing with very long sentences, you must still remember to back up all the way to the beginning of the sentence. Subject-verb agreement questions can ask about verbs whose subjects are located anywhere in the sentence, and verbs can be separated from their subjects by large amounts of information. As a result, the subject of an underlined verb that appears close to the end of a sentence may be located all the way at the beginning.

If you cannot determine the subject of a verb logically, you should **cross out** any prepositional phrases and non-essential clauses that appear in order to reduce the sentence to its most basic elements.

The presence ~~of mysterious paintings in a cave located outside Columbia, Missouri,~~ remain...

Now the error is much more apparent.

With that information, we can return to our question.

> The presence of mysterious paintings in a cave
> located outside Columbia, Missouri, <u>remain puzzling</u>
> <u>to archaeologists, who in the mid-1980s began</u>
> <u>studying</u> the images created by ancient residents of the
> Mississippi Valley.

(A) remain puzzling to archaeologists, who in the
    mid-1980s began studying
(B) remain puzzling to archaeologists, who in the
    mid-1980s began to study
(C) remains puzzling to archaeologists, who in the
    mid-1980s began studying
(D) remains puzzling to archaeologists, beginning in
    the mid-1980s to study
(E) remain puzzling to archaeologists, who in the
    mid-1980s would begin to study

Because *The presence*, the subject of the verb, is singular, the verb must be singular as well: *remains*, not *remain*. (A), (B), and (E) can thus be eliminated.

Notice that the question of whether *began* should be followed by the gerund *studying* or the infinitive *to study* has become entirely irrelevant. (In fact, both versions are acceptable.)

Now let's consider just choices (C) and (D):

(C) remains puzzling to archaeologists, who in the
    mid-1980s began studying
(D) remains puzzling to archaeologists, beginning in
    the mid-1980s to study

Neither of these answers is flat-out grammatically wrong, although if you have a good ear, you can probably hear that (D) sounds somewhat awkward and be reasonably confident that (C) is correct.

Otherwise, you can think of it this way: the date *mid-1980s* indicates that the sentence is describing a completed action in the past, and that a verb in the simple past should therefore be used. (C) contains such a verb (*began*), along with a subject (*who*), whereas (D) contains only a participle (*beginning*). The construction in (C) is clearer and more precise, making that answer correct.

Note: For an excellent *Official Guide* example of how focusing on verb "splits" can help you narrow down answers quickly, see #959 on p. 887. Notice that (A), (B), and (D) all contain the plural verb *leave*, whereas (C) and (E) contain the singular *leaves*. If you can back up to the beginning of the sentence and identify the singular noun *absence* as the subject, you can immediately eliminate (A), (B), and (D).

# Exercise: Subject-Verb Agreement

In the following sentences, fix any subject-verb agreement error. Label subjects, verbs, and prepositional phrases, and cross out non-essential clauses. Some sentences may not contain an error. (Answers p. 190)

| | |
|---|---|
| 1. | First described by Aristotle in his *Poetics* (c. 335 B.C.E.), the process   of living vicariously through a fictional character in order to purge one's emotions are known as catharsis. |
| 2. | On the border between China and Tibet lies the Himalaya Mountains, which rise to more than 25,000 ft. above sea level and include some of the highest peaks in the world. |
| 3. | The buildings of Frank Gehry, including Gehry's private residence, attracts thousands of visitors annually because critics frequently praise his designs for embodying the most important principles of contemporary architecture. |
| 4. | Although Andrew Carnegie and Cornelius Vanderbilt eventually became two of the most powerful figures in business during the late nineteenth century, neither were born into a wealthy family. |
| 5. | The maps of historian and cartographer John Speed depict some of the first visual representations of many towns and cities throughout England, Ireland, and Scotland. |
| 6. | Playboating, a discipline of whitewater rafting or canoeing in which players stay in one spot while performing a series of complex maneuvers, involve specialized canoes designed specifically for the sport. |
| 7. | Often found in plastic drinking bottles is substantial amounts of a substance known as Bisphenol A, a potentially toxic chemical that may affect the brains and behaviors of infants and young children. |
| 8. | Louise Glück's seemingly straightforward language and unadorned style gives her poems an air of accessibility that masks the intensity of their content. |
| 9. | Among the finds from a recent archaeological dig in London was earthenware knobs originally used for "pay walls," boxes into which Elizabethan theater-goers deposited their admission fees. |
| 10. | One of the animal kingdom's best jumpers are the flea, whose ability to leap up to 200 times its own body length is virtually unsurpassed among either insects or other land-dwelling creatures. |
| 11. | According to entomologist Deborah Gordon, the popular depiction of ants as brave soldiers and dutiful factory workers is a human fiction, one entirely unrelated to true insect behavior. |
| 12. | The patent for the first mechanical pencils were granted to Sampson Morgan and John Hawkins in England in the early nineteenth century, a time when fountain pens were the most commonly used writing implement. |
| 13. | Each of the Taino's five chiefdoms, which inhabited the Bahamas before the arrival of Europeans during the late fifteenth century, were ruled by a leader known as a *cacique*. |
| 14. | Writing about scientific matters poses a problem because it requires the adoption of imprecise metaphors that allow new findings to be put in perspective for readers with minimal expertise. |
| 15. | Possible explanations for the suspicion surrounding Shakespeare's *Macbeth* includes the superstition that the witches' song is an actual incantation and the belief that theaters only mount the play when they are in need of money. |
| 16. | *Saint Maybe*, the twelfth novel by Pulitzer prize-nominated author Anne Tyler, revolves around a protagonist whose efforts to compensate for a single thoughtless act dictates the shape of his entire life. |

| 17. | The Hebrides islands have been continuously occupied since the Mesolithic period, and the culture of their inhabitants have been shaped by the successive influences of Celtic, Norse, and English-speaking peoples. |
|---|---|
| 18. | Found throughout England, stiles, structures that provides people with a passage through or over a fence, are often built in rural areas or along footpaths in order to prevent farm animals from moving between enclosures while allowing path users to travel freely. |
| 19. | In recent days, an increasing number of disturbing reports have filtered into the news agency — reports suggesting that the country's government, already reputed to be unstable, could be on the verge of collapse. |
| 20. | Opposition to rodeos from animal-rights workers center primarily on the poor treatment and living conditions of the horses that are ridden in competitions. |
| 21. | Because planes have been grounded and flights eliminated from schedules, the number of airplane tickets available to passengers have declined, causing prices to rise. |
| 22. | Preliminary studies of the new drug suggests that adverse effects are unlikely and, moreover, that any reactions that do occur will probably be minor. |
| 23. | The automotive company, whose products are at the center of a massive recall scandal, now faces an array of challenges, including servicing damaged products, handling lawsuits, and managing a general loss of business. |
| 24. | Dry stone structures, structures built from stones not bound together by mortar, achieves stability because of their unique construction method, which is characterized by load-bearing façades of carefully selected interlocking stones. |
| 25. | A landmark 2015 report that cast doubt on the results of dozens of published psychology studies has exposed deep divisions in the field, but neither the report itself nor the critique published in response have found evidence of data fraud or manipulation. |

## Official Guide Subject-Verb Agreement Questions

| Question # | Page | |
|---|---|---|
| **Official Guide** | | |
| 823 | 860 | Non-Essential Clause |
| 827 | 861 | Non-Essential Clause |
| 838 | 863 | Compound Subject |
| 843 | 864 | Compound Subject |
| 858 | 867 | Prepositional Phrase |
| 883 | 872 | Non-Essential Clause, Prepositional Phrase |
| 896 | 874 | Prepositional Phrase (A) |
| 900 | 875 | Prepositional Phrase |
| 905 | 876 | Non-Essential Clause |
| 910 | 877 | Non-Essential Clause |
| 940 | 883 | Essential Clause (C) |
| 941 | 884 | Essential Clause |
| 942 | 884 | Essential Clause (B), (D) |
| 947 | 890 | Non-Essential Clause, Prepositional Phrase |
| 977 | 891 | Prepositional Phrase |
| 989 | 893 | Infinitive as Subject (D) |
| 995 | 894 | Essential Clause |
| **Official Verbal Guide** | | |
| 236 | 402 | One, Prepositional Phrase (B) |
| 245 | 404 | Prepositional Phrase |
| 266 | 408 | Prepositional Phrase |
| 275 | 410 | Prepositional Phrase |
| 283 | 413 | Prepositional Phrase (D), (E) |
| 285 | 413 | Essential Clause |
| 312 | 419 | Prepositional Phrase (B) |
| 331 | 424 | Essential Clause, Non-Essential Clause |

# Cumulative Review 1: Chapters 1-4 (Answers p. 191)

1. Though established independently of the United Nations through its own international treaty, the IAEA Statute, which reports to both the United Nations General Assembly and Security Council.

    (A) treaty, the IAEA Statute, which reports
    (B) treaty, the IAEA Statute reports
    (C) treaty, the IAEA Statute and reports
    (D) treaty, the IAEA Statute that reports
    (E) treaty, the IAEA Statute, reporting

2. Hundreds of seismic sensors placed around the Pacific Northwest in order to detect "p" waves, the harmless, fast-moving signals that precede the "s" waves responsible for violent shaking during earthquakes.

    (A) sensors placed around the Pacific Northwest
    (B) sensors, which have been placed around the Pacific Northwest
    (C) sensors have been placed around the Pacific Northwest
    (D) sensors having been placed around the Pacific Northwest
    (E) sensors being placed around the Pacific Northwest

3. In the documentary *Behemoth*, the imagery and audio captured by filmmaker Zhao Liango over a year and a half of shooting convey the sheer physicality and scale of Inner Mongolia's coal mines.

    (A) convey
    (B) conveys
    (C) has conveyed
    (D) having conveyed
    (E) conveying

4. Tropical disturbances that reach the intensity of a tropical storm named from a predetermined list; however, storms that result in significant damage may have their names retired at the request of the affected nations in order to prevent future confusion.

    (A) that reach the intensity of a tropical storm named
    (B) that reach tropical storm intensity are named
    (C) that reach tropical storm intensity is named
    (D) reaching tropical storm intensity being named
    (E) reaching the intensity of a tropical storm is named

5. Because banks are hesitant to lend to potential home-owners with poor credit, seller-financed transactions beginning to draw interest from well-heeled investors, who sometimes purchase homes to sell at markups of several hundred percent.

    (A) transactions beginning to draw interest from well-heeled investors, who sometimes purchase
    (B) transactions, which have begun to draw interest from well-heeled investors, who sometimes purchase
    (C) transactions have begun to draw interest from well-heeled investors and purchase sometimes
    (D) transactions have begun to draw interest from well-heeled investors and sometimes purchasing
    (E) transactions have begun to draw interest from well-heeled investors, who sometimes purchase

6. Played professionally in jug bands comedy music and by amateurs everywhere, the kazoo, one of the first acoustic instruments developed in the United States, are also one of the easiest melodic instruments to play and requiring only the ability to vocalize in tune.

    (A) everywhere, the kazoo, one of the first acoustic instruments developed in the United States, are also one of the easiest melodic instruments to play and requiring
    (B) everywhere, the kazoo, one of the first acoustic instruments developed in the United States, is also one of the easiest melodic instruments to play and requiring
    (C) everywhere, the kazoo is one of the first acoustic instruments developed in the United States and also one of the easiest melodic instruments to play and requiring
    (D) everywhere, the kazoo, one of the first acoustic instruments developed in the United States, is also one of the easiest melodic instruments to play, requiring
    (E) everywhere, the kazoo, which is one of the first acoustic instruments developed in the United States, are also among the easiest melodic instruments to play and require

7. Conductor John Eliot Gardiner is considered one of the most eminent interpreters of <u>Bach; having studied the composer's work from both a musical and a scholarly standpoint</u>.

   (A) Bach; having studied the composer's work from both a musical and a scholarly standpoint
   (B) Bach; and he has studied the composer's work from both a musical and a scholarly standpoint
   (C) Bach, for he has studied the composer's work from both a musical and a scholarly standpoint
   (D) Bach and having studied the composer's work from a musical and as well as a scholarly standpoint
   (E) Bach and studying the composer's work from the standpoint of a both a musician and a scholar

8. Anchors, like many other types of maritime technology, <u>has evolved significantly since the nineteenth century, to make</u> it easier to identify their date of manufacture.

   (A) has evolved significantly since the nineteenth century, to make
   (B) has evolved significantly since the nineteenth century, making
   (C) and have significantly evolved since the nineteenth century, to make
   (D) have evolved significantly since the nineteenth century, making
   (E) which have significantly evolved since the nineteenth century, making

9. Most archaeologists agree that the <u>Anasazi, the forerunners of contemporary Pueblo peoples, emerged in the southwestern United States sometime around the twelfth century B.C.E.,</u> during the Early Basketmaker II Era.

   (A) Anasazi, the forerunners of contemporary Pueblo peoples, emerged in the southwestern United States sometime around the twelfth century B.C.E.,
   (B) Anasazi, the forerunners of contemporary Pueblo peoples who emerged in the southwestern United States sometime around the twelfth century B.C.E.,
   (C) Anasazi, the forerunners of contemporary Pueblo peoples emerging in the southwestern United States sometime around the twelfth century B.C.E.,
   (D) Anasazi, the forerunners of contemporary Pueblo peoples who emerged in the southwestern United States sometime around the twelfth century B.CE. and
   (E) Anasazi, the forerunners of contemporary Pueblo peoples and emerged in the southwestern United States sometime around the twelfth century B.C.E.,

10. Even though the broader phenomenon of shifting work from employees to part-time contractors <u>are difficult to quantify, data</u> on contingent workers suggest rapid growth in the part-time sector.

   (A) are difficult to quantify, data
   (B) are difficult to quantify, but data
   (C) is difficult to quantify, but data
   (D) that are difficult to quantify, data
   (E) is difficult to quantify, data

# Chapter Five

# VERB TENSE AND FORM

Unless there is a very clear reason for a shift to occur, verbs should generally remain consistent (or **parallel**) in tense or form throughout a sentence.

> Incorrect:    Florida <u>was</u> the site of some of the earliest European settlements in North America yet **increases/increasing/would increase** its population very slowly after it was established as a state.

> Correct:    Florida <u>was</u> the site of some of the earliest European settlements in North America yet **increased** its population very slowly after it was established as a state.

The sentence begins in the past tense, as indicated by the verb *was*, and must continue in the past tense because there is nothing to indicate that a tense switch would be logical.

## A. Present

The present tense is used to refer to actions that are currently taking place. Unlike other tenses, it has separate forms for singular (–S) and plural (no –S), e.g., *it contains, they contain*.

> Correct:    Over the past several years, the country's food prices have increased dramatically, and they **are** <u>now</u> at their highest rate in more than two decades.

Note that the present tense can be used to describe regulations, laws, treaties, etc. that were instituted in the past but that still apply in the present. The GMAT is fond of testing verb tense in this context.

> Correct:    Some companies have argued that the Unlawful Internet Gambling Enforcement Act, which **made** online gambling illegal <u>when it was passed in 2006</u>, **includes** an exception for fantasy sports.

## B. Present Perfect vs. Simple Past

Present perfect = *has/have* + past participle, e.g., *has been, has gone, have determined*

This tense is used for actions that **began in the past** and that are still **continuing in the present**.

The words *for, since, over*, and *during* usually act as tip-offs that the present perfect is required.

> Correct:    <u>Since</u> around 500 B.C., people **have cultivated** tomatoes in Mesoamerica.

> Correct:    People **have cultivated** tomatoes in Mesoamerica <u>for</u> around 2,500 years.

> Correct:    <u>Over the last 150 years</u>, the tomato **has gone** from being a relatively obscure fruit, one grown by only a handful of farmers, to being one of the most popular salad ingredients.

When a tip-off word is not present, the present perfect is also commonly used to describe recent events or discoveries. Although you are unlikely to be directly tested on this usage, you should be aware that it exists.

Correct:    Studies **have shown** that political preferences shape how individuals perceive reality, but offering people small sums can help correct those biases.

The **simple past** (also known as the **preterit**) is called "simple" because it consists of only one word. For most verbs, this tense is formed by adding –ED (e.g., *explained, declined, observed*), but some common verbs are irregular. Note that *to be*, the most common verb, is the only verb that has separate singular and plural forms.

| Infinitive | Simple Past |
|:---:|:---:|
| To be | Was |
| To have | Had |
| To go | Went |
| To do | Did |

Whereas the present perfect is used to refer to actions that are still occurring, the simple past is used to describe a **finished action in the past**. Often, it will be accompanied by a **date** or **time period** that clearly indicates that a particular event or action occurred a long time ago.

Correct:    Since serious drama unaccompanied by music **was** forbidden in all but two London theaters during the <u>eighteenth century</u>, the renowned Queen's Theatre **became** an opera house.

The time period *eighteenth century* indicates that the above sentence is describing an action that began and ended in the past: the Queen's Theatre's change from a theater into an opera house was a one-time occurrence.

## C. Past Perfect

Past perfect = *had* + *past participle*, e.g., *had been, had gone, had determined*

Sometimes, a sentence will describe two events or actions that occurred in the past. The **past perfect** can be used to refer to the **first (earlier) event** in order to emphasize that it occurred before a second, later event.

Incorrect:    Ragtime, a musical genre characterized by a syncopated, or "ragged," rhythm, fell out of favor as jazz claimed the public's imagination after 1917 but **had undergone** numerous revivals in the decades that followed.

Correct:    Ragtime, a musical genre characterized by a syncopated, or "ragged," rhythm, fell out of favor as jazz claimed the public's imagination after 1917 but **underwent** numerous revivals in the decades that followed.

In the above sentence, the phrase *decades that followed* indicates that ragtime *underwent numerous revivals* post-1917. Clearly, that action must have occurred <u>after</u> ragtime fell out of popularity. As a result, the verb *underwent* should not be placed in the past perfect.

**Important:** The word *by* and the phrase *by the time* are tip-offs that the past perfect is required.

Incorrect:    By the end of the seventeenth century, the tragedies of French playwright Jean Racine **became** more successful than those of his main rival, Pierre Corneille.

Correct:    By the end of the seventeenth century, the tragedies of French playwright Jean Racine **had become** more successful than those of his main rival, Pierre Corneille.

There are also instances in which either the past perfect or the simple past is acceptable.

| Correct: | Before a complete version of Louisa May Alcott's novel *Little Women* appeared in 1880, the book **had been published** in two separate volumes. |

| Correct: | Before a complete version of Louisa May Alcott's novel *Little Women* appeared in 1880, the book **was published** in two separate volumes. |

In the first sentence, the past perfect is used to emphasize the appearance of the book in two volumes before its appearance in one; however, the simple past in the second sentence is also correct because it describes two actions that took place in the past and keeps the tense of the sentence consistent.

On the GMAT, you may encounter sentences that contain only the simple past but that could also be written with the past perfect, or vice-versa. In cases in which both the simple past and past perfect are acceptable, you will never be asked to choose between them on that basis alone. A separate factor will always make one of the answers incorrect.

## D. Perfect Infinitive

Perfect infinitive = *to have* + *past participle*

The perfect infinitive is a construction that you are likely to encounter on the GMAT. The most important thing to know about it is that it is an **acceptable alternative to the simple past or past perfect**.

| Correct: | Legendary jockey and long-distance horseback rider Frank Hopkins claimed that he **had won** over 400 races, many of which were invented by Hopkins himself. |

| Correct: | Legendary jockey and long-distance horseback rider Frank Hopkins claimed **to have won** over 400 races, many of which were invented by Hopkins himself. |

Both of these sentences have the same basic meaning and, though not precisely the same, are more or less grammatically interchangeable. The use of the past infinitive in the second version simply emphasizes that Hopkins himself was responsible for making outrageous claims about his success.

# Verb Exercise 1: Present Perfect, Simple Past, Past Perfect, and Past Infinitive

**For each sentence, decide whether the tense of each underlined verb is correct or incorrect. If there is an error, write the correct tense. (Answers p. 191)**

1. The revival of economic development, beginning in the eleventh century, is acknowledged **to have allowed** Pamplona to recover its urban life after suffering repeated Viking invasions.

    **Correct**         **Incorrect**         Correction: _____

2. After traveling widely through Russia, where he discovered many previously unknown artistic masterpieces, Diaghilev **had mounted** a massive exhibition of Russian portraiture in St. Petersburg.

    **Correct**         **Incorrect**         Correction: _____

3. Although the ancient Egyptians abandoned Demotic more than 1,500 years ago, taking up Coptic and eventually Arabic, the language **has lived** on in words like "adobe," which entered Spanish before passing into English.

    **Correct**         **Incorrect**         Correction: _____

4. In 1915, the Dutch government approved the proposal for new ships to protect its holdings in the East Indies, not realizing that the request **has been** withdrawn because of the start of the First World War.

    **Correct**         **Incorrect**         Correction: _____

5. Abu Dhabi is full of archeological evidence indicating that civilizations, beginning with the Umm an-Nar Culture, **have been** located there since the third millennium B.C.

    **Correct**         **Incorrect**         Correction: _____

6. By the time Pearl Buck was awarded the Nobel Prize for Literature in 1938, she **was** a best-selling author in the United States for nearly a decade.

    **Correct**         **Incorrect**         Correction: _____

7. In 1847, Maria Mitchell became the first American astronomer to discover a comet, a feat she is reputed **to have accomplished** using only a two-inch telescope.

    **Correct**         **Incorrect**         Correction: _____

8. During the 1950s, the Detroit area emerged as a metropolitan region with the construction of an extensive freeway system that **has expanded** in the following decades.

    **Correct**         **Incorrect**         Correction: _____

9. The Arctic Council, a once-obscure body focused on issues such as monitoring Arctic animal populations, **has** in recent years **begun** to handle more important tasks.

    **Correct**         **Incorrect**         Correction: _____

10. In 1309, Pope Clement V moved the papacy from Rome to the French city of Avignon and **had left** Rome prey to the ambitions of local overlords.

    **Correct**         **Incorrect**         Correction: _____

# E. Will vs. Would

Future = *will + verb*

The future is used to refer to actions and events that have not yet occurred. On the GMAT, the need for the future is indicated primarily by context. Words such as *predict, propose,* and *project* often serve as tip-offs that the future is needed.

| | |
|---|---|
| Incorrect: | Critics of the <u>proposed</u> highway argue it **ruins** the city's character because of the increased traffic noise and confusing detours that will inevitably result. |
| Correct: | Critics of the <u>proposed</u> highway argue that it **will ruin** the city's character because of the increased traffic noise and confusing detours that will inevitably result. |

*Shall* can also be used instead of *will* to indicate future actions, but only in the first person (*I/we*). Because GMAT questions test the third person (*he/she/it/they*), this word is extremely unlikely to appear in correct answers. In addition, *shall* is generally considered overly formal in American English and is rarely used.

Conditional = *would + verb*

The conditional is used to refer to hypothetical actions—ones that could occur but that have not actually occurred.

| | |
|---|---|
| Correct: | Believing that real estate prices could not continue to increase indefinitely, the economist argued that the housing bubble **would burst**. |

When a sentence is referring to a situation in the past, the conditional can also be used to refer to events that have not yet occurred—even if, from today's perspective, those events occurred long ago.

| | |
|---|---|
| Correct: | In 60 B.C., Julius Caesar joined Crassus and Pompey in a political alliance that **would dominate** Roman politics for a number of years. |

**Important:** the construction *would + verb* can also refer to recurring actions in the past.

| | |
|---|---|
| Correct: | As a young child, Wolfgang Amadeus Mozart **would look on** in fascination while his older sister, Nannerl, received piano lessons from their father. |

If you are unsure when to use *would* vs. *will*, the general rule is that you should not mix past and future in the same sentence, unless there is an extremely clear reason for doing so.

- Sentences that contain verbs in the past tense should not contain the word *will*.

- Sentences that contain verbs in the present tense should not contain the word *would*.

| | |
|---|---|
| Incorrect: | William Shakespeare, who **will** become the greatest English dramatist, <u>was</u> born in Stratford-upon-Avon in 1564. |
| Correct: | William Shakespeare, who **would** become the greatest English dramatist, <u>was</u> born in Stratford-upon-Avon in 1564. |

Likewise, a sentence containing a verb in the present tense should not contain *would*.

| | |
|---|---|
| Incorrect: | If union members and company officials <u>reach</u> a compromise today, a labor crisis **would** most likely be averted. |
| Correct: | If union members and company officials <u>reach</u> a compromise today, a labor crisis **will** most likely be averted. |

## F. Past Conditional

Past conditional = *would have* + *past participle*, e.g., *would have been, would have gone, would have determined*

The past conditional refers to action that could have taken place in the past but that did not actually occur.

Correct:    When reporters asked the gubernatorial candidate to explain how he **would have** responded to the crisis, he seemed incapable of offering a coherent response.

## G. Future Perfect

Future perfect = *will have* + *past participle*, e.g., *will have been, will have gone, will have determined.*

The future perfect refers to an action that is expected to be completed at a certain time in the future. Like the past perfect, it often appears in conjunction with *by* or *by the time.*

Correct:    <u>By the time</u> the committee decides where the next Olympic games will be held, each city competing to host them **will have devoted** enormous resources to making its case.

## H. The Subjunctive

The subjunctive is used to express necessity, requests, and suggestions, and to refer to hypothetical situations.

In the **present subjunctive**, third person singular (*he/she/it/one*) verbs do not end in –S.

You can also think that the present subjunctive equals the infinitive minus the word *to*. Thus, the subjunctive form of *to be* = *be*; the subjunctive form of *to have* = *have*; and the subjunctive form of *to do* = *do*.

When the present subjunctive indicates a hypothetical situation, the word *should* can also be used to begin a clause.

| Indicative | Subjunctive |
| --- | --- |
| The building **is** constructed. | City planners <u>recommend</u> that the building **be** constructed. |
| The committee **adopts** the proposal. | Some board members <u>insist</u> that the committee **adopt** the proposal. |
| If the committee **adopts** the proposal | <u>Should</u> the committee **adopt** the proposal<br>If the committee should **adopt** the proposal |

The **past subjunctive** is used primarily for hypothetical situations.

In the past subjunctive, the verb *to be* is always conjugated as *were*. For other verbs, the subjunctive is formed identically to the past perfect: *had* + *past participle.*

| Indicative | Subjunctive |
| --- | --- |
| The building **was** constructed. | If the building **were** (to be) constructed<br>**Were** the building (to be) constructed |
| The committee **adopted** the proposal. | If the committee **had adopted** the proposal<br>**Had** the committee **adopted** the proposal |

# I. Sequence of Tenses

As we've seen, a number of tenses involve hypothetical situations, as indicated by the words *if* and *should*.

A clause that begins with one of these words is known as an **"if" clause** or **hypothetical clause**. Because this type of clause cannot be a grammatically complete sentence, it must always be accompanied by a **main clause** (also known as a **result clause**) that can stand on its own as a full sentence.

The tenses that can be used in each type of clause and then combined within a sentence follow a strict pattern. Some tenses can only be used in hypothetical clauses while other tenses can only be used in main clauses.

The chart below shows which tenses can be used in which clauses. (If you've studied a Romance language to an advanced level, it may look familiar.)

**Note:** Either the *if* clause or the main clause can appear first. Clause order does not affect the tense of the verbs.

| Hypothetical Clause | Main Clause |
|---|---|
| **Present**<br><br>If the pace of inflation increases,<br>(main clause = present or future)<br><br>Should the pace of inflation increase,<br>(main clause = future only) | **Present**<br><br>consumer spending declines.<br><br>**Future**<br><br>consumer spending will decline. |
| **Simple past**<br><br>If the pace of inflation increased,<br><br>If the pace of inflation were to increase,<br><br>Were the pace of inflation to increase, | **Conditional**<br><br><br><br>consumer spending would decline. |
| **Past perfect**<br><br>If the pace of inflation had increased,<br><br>Had the pace of inflation increased, | **Past conditional**<br><br>consumer spending would have declined. |

**Important:** although *would have* and *if* can both appear in the same **sentence**, the two should <u>not</u> appear together in the same **clause**. *Had* should be used in the *if* clause, and *would have* should be used in the main clause.

Incorrect:    <u>If</u> the pace of inflation **would have increased**, consumer spending **would have** declined.

Correct:    <u>If</u> the pace of inflation **had increased**, consumer spending **would have** declined.

## J. The Progressive

Every tense has a progressive equivalent, which emphasizes that a particular action or event is or was in the process of taking place.

The progressive form is created by adding the present participle (–ING) to the appropriate form of the verb *to be*.

For example, the following sentence can be correctly written the following ways.

Simple: Because most jurors **are** not compensated at rates sufficient to replace lost wages, many citizens **seek** to avoid jury duty by demonstrating financial hardship or claiming that they have urgent commitments.

Progressive: Because most jurors **are** not compensated at rates sufficient to replace lost wages, many citizens **are seeking** to avoid jury duty by demonstrating financial hardship or claiming that they have urgent commitments.

The two versions of the sentence have the same meaning; the second version simply emphasizes the fact that citizens are *currently* attempting to evade jury duty in the ways described in the sentence.

**As a general rule, the GMAT prefers that verbs be kept strictly parallel**—a simple tense (*go*) should be paired with a simple tense (*do*) rather than a progressive tense (*is doing*). If, however, the only grammatically or idiomatically acceptable answer pairs a simple tense with its progressive counterpart, as in the second example above, then the switch from one to the other is permitted.

The chart below provides a comparison of simple and progressive forms, using the verb *to go*.

| Tense | Simple | Progressive |
|---|---|---|
| Present | It goes | It is going |
| Present perfect | It has gone | It has been going |
| (Simple) past | It went | It was going |
| Future | It will go | It will be going |
| Conditional | It would go | It would be going |
| Past Conditional | It would have gone | It would have been going |

Note that *was* + *–ING* and *would* + *verb* can both be used to refer to ongoing actions in the past; however, the two constructions are typically used in different circumstances.

The past progressive is used to indicate that an action was performed repeatedly at a **particular moment in time**. In addition, it is often used to set up a contrast with a later action that stopped or interrupted the first action.

Correct: In the early eighteenth century, most British consumers **were still buying products** crafted by independent artisans, but by 1790, population growth and increasing foreign trade had created a greater demand for manufactured goods.

In contrast, *would* is used to indicate that an action was performed regularly over **an extended time period**.

Correct: As a student, paleontologist Roy Chapman rarely participated in excavations; instead he **would study** piles of fossils in an attempt to understood dinosaur physiology.

# Verb Exercise 2: All Tenses and Forms

**In the following exercises, underline the date or words that indicate a tense question, and fix any verb not in the correct tense or form. Some sentences may not contain an error. (Answers p. 192)**

| | |
|---|---|
| 1. | By the time suffragist Elizabeth Cady Stanton narrowed her political focus to women's rights, she was an active member of the abolitionist movement for several decades. |
| 2. | In 1498, the Dutch scholar Erasmus of Rotterdam moved from Paris to England, where he will eventually be appointed as a professor of ancient languages at Cambridge. |
| 3. | Were an earthquake to strike, the bridge's concrete piers will sway and absorb the majority of the shock, thus limiting the amount of damage sustained by areas that lack additional steel reinforcements. |
| 4. | First published in 1975 but frequently updated since, David Thomson's *Dictionary of Film* represents a singular attempt to appraise each significant director and star of movie history. |
| 5. | The hiring of musicians in Naples during the Baroque era rested largely on merit because the Spanish viceroys would remain in the city for fixed terms, making permanent patterns of patronage unsustainable. |
| 6. | Mahatma Gandhi, who was born in India, studied law in London and in 1893 moved to South Africa, where he had spent twenty years opposing discriminatory legislation. |
| 7. | Over the last century, several dozen boats are known to have sank off of the French Frigate Shoals, part of an enormous protected zone that covers nearly 150,000 square miles in the Pacific Ocean. |
| 8. | The country's economists speculate that thousands of additional jobs would have been lost if consumer demand for domestically manufactured products would have continued to decline. |
| 9. | Accidentally discovered by Procter and Gamble researchers in 1968, the fat substitute Olestra has been demonstrated to cause stomach upset in those who consume excessive amounts of the substance. |
| 10. | Since the 1950s, computer scientists struggle to create a machine capable of responding to human language, but despite their many attempts, they have achieved only limited success. |
| 11. | Many bird species have become endangered because rapidly modernizing societies are expanding roads, mines, and chemical plants into environmentally sensitive areas. |
| 12. | Should it be proven, the researchers' theory confirms that the first life evolved on Earth shortly after the Late Heavy Bombardment, a period during which thousands of asteroids slammed into the young planet. |
| 13. | After Great Britain achieved a decisive victory in the Seven Years' War, several successive ministries had implemented reforms in an attempt to achieve more effective administrative control and raise more revenue in the colonies. |
| 14. | Should an economic shock drive inflation down to extremely low levels, actual and expected deflation will likely persist, causing incomes to fall relative to debt. |
| 15. | Hot air balloons are made in every shape imaginable for over 40 years, although the traditional form remains most popular for both commercial and non-commercial uses. |
| 16. | Istanbul was virtually depopulated when it fell to the Ottoman Turks, but the city recovered rapidly and by the mid-1600s had become the world's largest city as well as the new capital of the Ottoman Empire. |

| 17. | Several members of the arts council have suggested that the sculpture, commissioned to mark the bicentennial of the city's founding, is placed in the city's main square. |
|---|---|
| 18. | Morgan Stanley Chairman Robert Baldwin predicted that hundreds of brokerage firms would go out of business if fixed commissions had been eliminated, a prophecy that was often quoted as its accuracy became increasingly apparent. |
| 19. | Even before the start of the twentieth century, when the electronic age was still in its infancy, the first attempts to generate sound from electricity were already beginning. |
| 20. | Since landing in a 96-mile-wide depression known as Gale Crater, Curiosity, the Mars rover, had made a number of discoveries, most notably that the crater once held lakes of fresh water. |
| 21. | Hardly a stranger to self-censorship, Mark Twain never hesitated to change his prose if he believed that the alterations would have improved the sales of his books. |
| 22. | A Federal Aviation Administration task force has recommended that drone operators are required to register their aircrafts, paving the way for regulations intended to help reverse a surge in rogue drone flights. |
| 23. | Harold Sheldon was a scientist ahead of his time: in 1929, he wrote the original introduction to *The Conquest of Space*, the first English-language book to suggest that human beings will one day visit other planets. |
| 24. | Passed in response to widespread calls for financial reform, the 2010 Dodd-Frank Wall Street Reform and Consumer Protection Act, commonly referred to as simply "Dodd-Frank," stipulates that markets are restrained by a set of comprehensive regulations. |
| 25. | When former space shuttle commander Pamela Melroy retired from NASA in 2009, more than a decade after being selected for its astronaut training program, she successfully logged close to 40 days in orbit. |
| 26. | Before playwright Lynn Nottage had been awarded a Pulitzer Prize for *Ruined* in 2009, seven of her plays were successfully produced in off-Broadway theaters. |
| 27. | More than 6,000 languages are now spoken around the world, but nearly half of them will be extinct by the end of the twenty-first century if current trends were to continue. |
| 28. | Although some oil industry experts warn of dire consequences if rules to prevent another catastrophic oil spill in the Gulf of Mexico go into effect, regulators project that such laws actually save money by preventing costly oil spills and saving lives. |
| 29. | Since Benjamin Franklin's invention of the lightning rod in 1752, the weather resisted numerous efforts at manipulation by meteorologists, physicists, and amateur scientists alike. |
| 30. | Ergonomic experts predict that workers face a greater risk of injury as they begin to communicate on more electronic devices in a wider range of professional situations. |

# Past Forms: Common Irregular Verbs

| Infinitive | Past Participle | Simple Past |
|---|---|---|
| To (a)rise | (A)risen | (A)rose |
| To (a)waken | (A)woken | (A)woke |
| To be | Been | Was |
| To become | Become | Became |
| To begin | Begun | Began |
| To blow | Blown | Blew |
| To break | Broken | Broke |
| To choose | Chosen | Chose |
| To do | Done | Did |
| To draw | Drawn | Drew |
| To drink | Drunk | Drank |
| To drive | Driven | Drove |
| To fly | Flown | Flew |
| To freeze | Frozen | Froze |
| To get | Gotten* | Got |
| To give | Given | Gave |
| To go | Gone | Went |
| To grow | Grown | Grew |
| To hide | Hidden | Hid |
| To know | Known | Knew |
| To ride | Ridden | Rode |
| To ring | Rung | Rang |
| To run | Run | Ran |
| To see | Seen | Saw |
| To sew | Sewn | Sewed |
| To shrink | Shrunk(en) | Shrank |
| To sing | Sung | Sang |
| To sink | Sunk(en) | Sank |
| To speak | Spoken | Spoke |
| To spring | Sprung | Sprang |
| To steal | Stolen | Stole |
| To stink | Stunk | Stank |
| To swim | Swum | Swam |
| To take | Taken | Took |
| To tear | Torn | Tore |
| To throw | Thrown | Threw |
| To wear | Worn | Wore |
| To write | Written | Wrote |

| Common Verbs that Take the Subjunctive | |
|---|---|
| Be necessary | Recommend |
| Demand | Request |
| Insist | Require |
| Propose | Suggest |

---

*Although *got* is used as the past participle of *get* in British English, *gotten* is considered standard in American English.

## Official Guide Verb Tense and Form Questions

| Question # | Page | |
|---|---|---|
| **Official Guide** | | |
| 824 | 860 | Present, Future, Conditional |
| 825 | 860 | Past Perfect (A) |
| 828 | 861 | Present Perfect, Simple Past, Past Perfect |
| 840 | 864 | Present, Conditional |
| 841 | 864 | Subjunctive (B), Note the incorrect usage |
| 853 | 866 | Progressive, Present Perfect (E) |
| 865 | 866 | Present, Future |
| 868 | 869 | Subjunctive (Misuse) |
| 869 | 869 | Future, Conditional, Infinitive |
| 879 | 871 | Past Perfect vs. Simple Past |
| 885 | 872 | Subjunctive/Sequence of Tenses |
| 911 | 877 | Present, Simple Past, Conditional |
| 915 | 878 | Present Perfect, Simple Past, Past Perfect |
| 925 | 880 | Present, Conditional |
| 944 | 884 | Perfect Infinitive |
| 961 | 887 | Present Perfect vs. Simple Past |
| 979 | 891 | Past Perfect |
| 989 | 893 | Subjunctive |
| 991 | 893 | Simple Past vs. Past Perfect |
| 992 | 893 | Present Perfect vs. Past Perfect |
| **Official Verbal Guide** | | |
| 306 | 418 | Present, Conditional/Sequence of Tenses |
| 308 | 419 | Present Perfect vs. Simple Past |
| 311 | 419 | Perfect Infinitive |
| 313 | 420 | Present vs. Future, Parallelism |
| 323 | 422 | Present Perfect vs. Simple Past |
| 336 | 425 | Simple Past vs. Past Perfect |

# *Chapter Six*
# NOUN AND PRONOUN AGREEMENT

Just as verbs must agree with their subjects, so must nouns and pronouns agree with their **referents**, or **antecedents**—the nouns to which they refer. Singular nouns and pronouns must be paired with singular referents, and plural nouns and pronouns must be paired with plural referents.

**Note:** A pronoun can refer to a noun that comes either before or after it. The prefix ANTE- means "before," a fact that can lead to confusion when the term *antecedent* is used to refer to a noun that appears after a pronoun. As a result, I have chosen to use *referent* here.

## Noun Agreement

When two nouns are paired by a linking verb such as *to be* or *to appear*, both nouns must be either singular or plural. Errors are typically created by incorrectly pairing a singular noun with its plural referent. To correct the error, the singular noun must be made plural.

| | |
|---|---|
| Incorrect: | When, in the 1830s, the Opium Wars introduced the power of European armies and technologies to China, <u>urban centers such as Shanghai and Ningpo</u> quickly ceased to be **an independent port city**. |
| Correct: | When, in the 1830s, the Opium Wars introduced the power of European armies and technologies to China, <u>urban centers such as Shanghai and Ningpo</u> quickly ceased to be **independent port cities**. |

Although it is unlikely, this error could also be tested the other way around.

| | |
|---|---|
| Incorrect: | Known for creating a unique sound and style through the use of non-traditional instruments such as the French horn, <u>Miles Davis</u> joined Louis Armstrong and Ella Fitzgerald as **the greatest jazz musicians** of the twentieth century. |
| Correct: | Known for creating a unique sound and style through the use of non-traditional instruments such as the French horn, <u>Miles Davis</u> joined Louis Armstrong and Ella Fitzgerald as **one of the greatest jazz musicians** of the twentieth century. |

Because the actual subject is Miles Davis alone, rather than Miles Davis, Louis Armstrong, and Ella Fitzgerald, the singular noun *greatest jazz musician* should be used.

## Pronoun Agreement

To review, a **pronoun** is a word such as *he*, *she*, *it*, *them*, or *their*, that is used to replace a noun.

For example, in the sentence *The Nobel Prize is awarded annually*, *Nobel Prize* can be replaced by *it*.

Likewise, in the sentence *Doris Lessing won the Nobel Prize for Literature*, *Doris Lessing* can be replaced by *she*.

When multiple nouns are present in a sentence, you must consider which noun a pronoun most logically refers to.

| | |
|---|---|
| Incorrect: | While the majority of editors are concerned with how accurate a biography is, some are more interested in how quickly **they** can be published. |
| Correct: | While the majority of editors are concerned with how accurate a biography is, some are more interested in how quickly **it** can be published. |

Logically, the pronoun *they* must refer to the singular noun *a biography* rather than to the plural noun *editors*—*editors* cannot be published. As a result the plural pronoun *they* must be changed to the singular pronoun *it*.

Remember that **collective nouns** such as *company*, *institute*, *agency*, *business*, *retailer*, and *board* are **singular.**

| | |
|---|---|
| Incorrect: | Because the country has been strongly criticized for producing a large amount of pollution, **their** environmental minister has recently issued manufacturing companies a series of strict warnings about uncontrolled development. |
| Correct: | Because the country has been strongly criticized for producing a large amount of pollution, **its** environmental minister has recently issued manufacturing companies a series of strict warnings about uncontrolled development. |

**Important:** Whenever you see a pronoun appear in an underlined section, you should start by determining its referent. Pay particular attention to *it(s)* and *they/them/their*. Note also that while you will typically be asked to change a pronoun from singular to plural or vice-versa, you may occasionally be asked to change a noun.

## A. People vs. Things

People (e.g., architects, executives, authors):

| | Singular | Plural |
|---|---|---|
| **Subject** | He, She | They |
| **Object** | Him, Her | Them |
| **Possessive** | His, Her | Their |

Things (e.g., cities, books, ideas):

| | Singular | Plural |
|---|---|---|
| **Subject** | It | They |
| **Object** | It | Them |
| **Possessive** | Its | Their |

People & Things:

| Singular | Plural |
|---|---|
| One | Few |
| Each | Both |
| Every | Some |
| Another | Several |
| The | Many |
| number | Most |
| | All |
| | Others |
| | A number |
| | Compound |
| | subjects |

**Note:** When the gender of a singular noun is not specified (e.g., an architect), the phrase *he or she* should be used; *they* is reserved for plural nouns. The GMAT is generally more concerned with pronouns referring to things, but occasionally this rule may be relevant.

When things and people are discussed in the same sentence, you must make sure not only that all the pronouns agree with their referents in number (singular vs. plural), but that the correct type of pronoun is used to refer to each noun.

Although errors involving this distinction may be obvious in short sentences (e.g., *Company leaders have published its quarterly profits*), they may be far less apparent in the lengthy, complex sentences that tend to appear on the GMAT.

Incorrect:    Strict adherence by <u>an athlete</u> to a program of training, particularly if it has led to successful performance on previous occasions, makes **it** inclined to overlook signs of injury when they arise.

This is complicated sentence, so let's take a moment and unpack it. Although there are multiple pronouns, we're going to focus on the bolded *it* in the second line. The first thing we want to do is simplify the sentence by removing the non-essential clause.

Incorrect:    Strict adherence by <u>an athlete</u> to a program of training…makes **it** inclined to overlook signs of injury when they arise.

Now the error is apparent. Logically, the pronoun *it* must refer to *an athlete*. (*Who is inclined to overlook sensations of discomfort? An athlete.*) But an athlete must be a person, and *it* can only refer to a thing.

One possible correction of that error could therefore look like this:

Correct:    Strict adherence by <u>an athlete</u> to a program of training, particularly if **it** has led to successful performance on previous occasions, makes **him or her** inclined to overlook signs of injury when they arise.

Another possible correction would involve replacing the singular noun *athlete* with the plural noun *athletes*.

Correct:    Strict adherence by <u>athletes</u> to a program of training, particularly if **it** has led to successful performance on previous occasions, makes **them** inclined to overlook signs of injury when they arise.

## B. Ambiguous and Missing Referents

Sometimes it is unclear which referent a pronoun refers to.

Incorrect:    Some game wardens have considered filing elephants' tusks in an attempt to deter ivory poachers; however, no action has been taken because of concerns that <u>visitors</u> will no longer travel to watch the <u>elephants</u> if **their** tusks are removed.

Logically, the intended meaning of this sentence is that tourists might not travel to watch elephants whose tusks have been removed.

The problem, however, is that there are two plural nouns, *visitors* and *elephants*, both of which could potentially serve as the referent of the pronoun *their*. Read literally, the sentence implies that the *visitors'* tusks might be removed—a meaning that is clearly absurd. In order to fix the sentence, we must make it clear that the tusks belong to the elephants.

Correct:    Some game wardens have considered filing elephants' tusks in an attempt to deter ivory poachers; however, no action has been taken because of concerns that <u>visitors</u> will no longer travel to watch the <u>elephants</u> if **the creatures'** tusks are removed.

Other times, GMAT sentences may omit a referent entirely. If a sentence includes a pronoun without a clear referent (noun, pronoun, or gerund), that sentence cannot be correct, no matter how obvious its intended meaning.

Incorrect:       In the report released by the treasury committee, **it** stated that significant budget cuts would be necessary for the following year, a pronouncement that has drawn complaints from executives and caused concern among shareholders.

In the above sentence, we do not know precisely what the word *it* refers to. The treasury committee? The report itself? To fix the ambiguity, we can either make the referent of *it* clear or eliminate the pronoun entirely.

Correct:       <u>The treasury committee stated</u> in **its** report that significant budget cuts would be necessary for the following year, a pronouncement that has drawn complaints from executives and caused concern among shareholders.

Correct:       <u>The report</u> released by **the treasury committee** stated that significant budget cuts would be necessary for the following year, a pronouncement that has drawn complaints from executives and caused concern among shareholders.

In other instances, a passive construction may be used to eliminate a missing or ambiguous referent.

Incorrect:       In international Morse Code, **they represent** the basic Latin alphabet and Arabic numerals as standardized sequences of short and long signals known as dots and dashes.

Correct:       In international Morse Code, the basic Latin alphabet and Arabic numerals **are represented** as standardized sequences of short and long signals known as dots and dashes.

In the incorrect version, the pronoun *they* logically refers to the people using Morse code. But because that information is not explicitly included in the sentence, the construction is ambiguous. The insertion of the passive construction eliminates the problem.

## Adjective as "Trick" Referent

One of the subtlest ways that referents can be presented in incorrect form is as follows:

Incorrect:       Constructed between the reign of Senusret I in the Middle Kingdom and the Ptolemaic period over a thousand years later, the Egyptian temple complex at Karnak, situated on the eastern bank of the Nile, was where **they** worshiped.

In the above version of this sentence, it can reasonably be assumed that *they* refers to the ancient Egyptians; however, no **noun** actually states who "they" are. When the word *Egyptian* appears earlier in the sentence, it functions as an adjective modifying *temple*—not as a noun, as is often the case.

As a result, the problem does not merely consist of a disagreement between the plural pronoun *they* and the singular referent *Egyptian*. Rather, the referent is missing altogether. The noun *Egyptians* must be added to make the sentence correct.

Correct:       Constructed between the reign of Senusret I in the Middle Kingdom and the Ptolemaic period over a thousand years later, the Egyptian temple complex at Karnak, situated on the eastern bank of the Nile, was where **the ancient Egyptians** worshiped.

What makes this error so tricky is that it plays with normal expectations about how words function grammatically. Even if people can sense that the sentence is "off" somehow, they probably can't pinpoint just why it doesn't seem quite right.

## Do So vs. Do It

To reiterate: only nouns, pronouns, and gerunds can act as referents. Any sentence that attempts to use another part of speech as a referent is incorrect.

Incorrect:   Activists who defend endangered species from poaching **do it/this** on the grounds that such animals, once gone, cannot be replaced.

What does *it* refer to in this sentence? *Defending* endangered species. But because the gerund *defending* doesn't appear, there is no real referent. The verb *defend* cannot fill that role. As a result, *do so* should be used.

Correct:   Activists who defend endangered species from poaching **do so** on the grounds that such animals, once gone, cannot be replaced.

## Referents ≠ Part of a Prepositional Phrase

Another one of the GMAT's subtlest pronoun errors involves prepositional phrases—in particular, prepositional phrases that create possessive constructions (*noun + of + noun*). This error is easier to illustrate than it is to describe, so let's look at an example.

Incorrect:   Houses of the inhabitants of Çatalhöyük, a Neolithic settlement that flourished around 7,000 B.C., contain murals and figurines, suggesting that **it** had a religion rich in symbols.

At first glance, this sentence might seem fine—and in fact, if you were to encounter it almost anywhere other than the GMAT, it would probably be considered acceptable.

For maximum clarity, however, **a pronoun should refer to the noun that is the subject of a sentence or clause**. It should not refer to a noun that appears *within* a clause as part of a prepositional phrase.

In the example above, the pronoun *it* can logically be assumed to refer to Çatalhöyük. The problem, however, is that the noun *Çatalhöyük* does not appear as the subject of the sentence. Rather, that word is part of the prepositional phrase/possessive construction *of the inhabitants of Çatalhöyük*.

In order to eliminate any ambiguity and make it absolutely clear who had a religion rich in symbols, it is necessary to replace the pronoun *it* with the noun *Çatalhöyük*.

Correct:   Houses of the inhabitants of Çatalhöyük, a Neolithic settlement that flourished around 7,000 B.C., contain murals and figurines, suggesting that **Çatalhöyük** had a religion rich in symbols.

Note that the same problem would be created even if the pronoun *they* were to appear instead.

Incorrect:   Houses of the inhabitants of Çatalhöyük, a Neolithic settlement that flourished around 7,000 B.C., contain murals and figurines, suggesting that **they** practiced a religion rich in symbols.

Even though *they* can logically be understood to refer to the inhabitants of Çatalhöyük, that noun again appears as part of the prepositional phrase *Houses of the inhabitants of Çatalhöyük* rather than as the subject of the sentence.

Correct:   Houses of the inhabitants of Çatalhöyük, a Neolithic settlement that flourished around 7,000 B.C., contain murals and figurines, suggesting that **Çatalhöyük's inhabitants** practiced a religion rich in symbols.

You can also use this **shortcut: given the choice between a noun and a pronoun, the noun option will usually be correct**. Pronouns have the potential to create ambiguity, whereas nouns are by definition specific.

Two additional points:

First, note that when *it* is used impersonally to express opinions or judgments, no referent is required (e.g., *it is preferable that, it is necessary that, it is clear that*).

> Correct: **It** does not appear that the city of Thebes was of great significance before Ancient Egypt's Eleventh Dynasty, and early temples there would have been relatively small.

Second, on rare occasions, incorrect answers may include pronouns that not only lack referents but that have no function beyond making sentences jumbled and awkward. To correct such constructions, the pronoun must be removed.

> Incorrect: Raising interest rates is one way of ensuring that currencies do not grow too strong or too weak, a strategy **that it leads** investors to earn more interest and attracts more investment.

> Correct: Raising interest rates is one way of ensuring that currencies do not grow too strong or too weak, a strategy **that leads** investors to earn more interest and attracts more investment.

## This, That, and Which

The same rule that applies to *it* applies to *this* and *that*: each of these pronouns must have a clear referent that appears within the sentence. Unlike the referents for *it* and *they*, however, referents for *this* and *that* (and their plural forms, *these* and *those*) must immediately follow those pronouns, e.g., *this increase, that belief*.

**Important:** you can generally assume that answers containing *this* or *that* without a noun immediately afterward are incorrect. The correct answer will either supply the noun or reconfigure the sentence to remove the pronoun.

> Incorrect: Cleota Davis, the mother of jazz legend Miles Davis, was an accomplished pianist in her own right, but she hid **this/that** from her son until he was an adult.

> Correct: Cleota Davis, the mother of jazz legend Miles Davis, was an accomplished pianist in her own right, but she hid **this/that fact** from her son until he was an adult.

> Correct: Cleota Davis, the mother of jazz legend Miles Davis, was an accomplished pianist in her own right, **a fact that she hid** from her son until he was an adult.

Although it is clear in the incorrect version that the pronoun *this* refers to the fact that Cleota Davis was an accomplished pianist, the sentence cannot be correct because the phrase *the fact that* does not actually appear.

*Which* works in a similar way. When used correctly, *which* should refer to the noun (or noun phrase) that immediately precedes it (aka the "which-touch" rule). If a part of speech other than a noun precedes *which*, the sentence is normally incorrect.

> Incorrect: Artists are not frequently associated with domestic serenity, **which** makes literary families rich sources of inspiration as well as psychological investigation for biographers and critics.

> Correct: Artists are not frequently associated with domestic serenity, **making** literary families rich sources of inspiration as well as psychological investigation for biographers and critics.

> Correct: Artists are not frequently associated with domestic serenity, **a phenomenon that makes** literary families rich sources of inspiration as well as psychological investigation for biographers and critics.

The noun immediately preceding *which* is *domestic serenity*, but logically that is not what the pronoun refers to. Domestic serenity would *not* make literary families rich sources of inspiration or psychological investigation. In fact, it would do just the opposite. People who *don't* have problems aren't usually all that interesting, artistically or psychologically.

In reality, the pronoun *which* refers to the <u>phenomenon</u> of artists' not being associated with domestic serenity. The missing referent can be fixed in a couple of ways. In the first version, the noun *phenomenon* replaces the pronoun; in the second version, the participle *making* is used. Both types of corrections appear on the GMAT.

**Important:** The misuse of *which* is tested frequently on the GMAT. I strongly recommend you pay particular attention to the relevant practice questions (labeled) in the *Official Guide* lists at the end of this chapter. For examples similar to the sentence above, see questions #954 on p. 886, choices (D) and (E); and #975 on p. 890 also choices (D) and (E).

You should, however, be aware that there is some flexibility to this rule. In certain cases, the referent of *which* may contain a prepositional phrase or begin a short clause.

For example, consider the following sentence:

> Correct: The term "Bollywood" is often incorrectly used to refer to the whole of Indian cinema; however, Bollywood is only a part of the larger **film industry** in India, **which** creates a wide array of films at a variety of production centers.

Logically, it is the film industry, not India itself, that *creates a wide array of films at a variety of production centers*. But although the words *film industry* do not appear immediately before *which*, the sentence is still acceptable because the phrase *film industry in India* can be considered the complete referent. The meaning is sufficiently clear that the placement of the words *film industry* is not problematic.

While cases such as this are rare, you will need to use your individual judgment if you do encounter them. To reiterate, the GMAT is less concerned with testing rigid adherence to a set of rules than it is to assessing whether you can determine whether constructions make sense. Sometimes there will be a slight element of subjectivity, and you will need to draw on your reasoning skills to make reasonable assumptions about when it is acceptable to bend rules for the sake of logic and clarity.

For an *Official Guide* example that puts a slightly different twist on this concept, see question #969 on p. 889. In (E), the correct answer, *which* is preceded not by the direct referent *high pressure* but by the clause *a broad area of high pressure builds*. Although constructions similar to this are included in wrong answers to many other questions, in this case (E) is the best option available—even if it is not 100% technically correct—and is therefore the answer.

## Exercise: Noun and Pronoun Agreement

**In the following sentences, label all pronouns and their referents. Some sentences may not contain an error. (Answers p. 193)**

| | |
|---|---|
| 1. | In the nineteenth century, Albany, the capital of New York State, became one of the first cities in the world to install public natural gas lines and electricity in the homes of their citizens. |
| 2. | Japan's status as an island country means that they must rely heavily on other countries for the supply of natural resources that are indispensable to national existence. |
| 3. | When the fossil of an enormous ancient penguin was unearthed in Peru, archaeologists discovered that their feathers were brown and gray rather than black and white. |
| 4. | The Free Basics service, a Facebook program that provides free access to certain online services, has drawn the ire of critics who insist that it runs contrary to principles of internet neutrality and who suggest that data providers avoid favoring some internet services over others. |
| 5. | The jewel beetle, along with the fire-chaser beetle, are insects that can thrive in trees scorched by wildfires or destroyed by other natural disasters. |
| 6. | Poor sleep habits among employees take a heavy economic toll because workers who fall asleep on the job or are tired to the point of incompetence can lose significant amounts of money for its employers as well as for the broader economy. |
| 7. | The chariot, together with the horse itself, was introduced to the Egyptians by the Hyksos in the sixteenth century B.C. and undoubtedly contributed to their military success. |
| 8. | Freemasonry consists of fraternal organizations that trace its origins to local guilds of stonemasons, which from the end of the fourteenth century regulated stonemasons' qualifications as well as their interactions with authorities and clients. |
| 9. | A new industry is emerging to shield fliers from large change fees, which generate billions of dollars for domestic airlines annually but create headaches for travelers. |
| 10. | Some demographers predict that the world's population could climb to 10.5 billion by 2050, which raises questions about how many people the Earth can support. |
| 11. | Apollo's sacred precinct in Delphi was a panhellenic sanctuary where every four years, beginning in the sixth century B.C., they gathered to compete in the Pythian Games, which served as precursors to the modern Olympics. |
| 12. | The grasslands of northeastern Montana have become a priority for the conservation movement because of its extraordinary biodiversity and high percentage of intact native prairie. |
| 13. | Although the two books include the same characters and recount the same series of events, they do it from different perspectives and are not intended to be read in any particular order. |
| 14. | The linear velocity of the Earth's surface is greatest towards the equator, and the southerly location of Cape Canaveral, a NASA launch site since the 1950s, allows rockets to exploit that phenomenon by launching east, the same direction as the Earth's rotation. |
| 15. | A *BusinessWeek* analysis has found that companies can cause their existing clientele significant anguish when they merge, leading it to experience a loss in profits and persistent declines in trust and satisfaction. |

| 16. | The ability of an executive to effect a change within a company depends on its capacity to engage successfully with key members of the franchise community. |
|-----|---|
| 17. | Consumer advocates caution that even seemingly low error rates in credit score calculations can affect numerous customers because each credit bureau has hundreds of millions of files in their possession. |
| 18. | The country's government is worried about alienating voters, and as a result, it is proceeding very cautiously in limiting benefits such as unemployment insurance. |
| 19. | Financial plans are valuable for a number of reasons, but perhaps the most significant one is that it can help people understand how to react to volatile markets. |
| 20. | Small population sizes and selective breeding have caused a number of changes in the DNA of domesticated dogs to increase, which has left the animals less able to reproduce. |
| 21. | Initially, the Ford Motor Company produced no more than a few cars a day, but within a decade they led the world in the expansion and refinement of the assembly line concept. |
| 22. | The secret behind the *Mona Lisa* lies in the matter of which retinal cells pick up the image of the iconic figure's enigmatic smile and how this channels the information to the brain. |
| 23. | According to social psychologists, there are two broad categories of human relationships: exchange relationships, which are based on trade for mutual benefit, and communal relationships, which are based on mutual caring and support. |
| 24. | Munich is situated at a high altitude and in close proximity to the northern edge of the Alps, which makes large amounts of precipitation common in both the city and its surrounding regions. |
| 25. | Though the federal income tax is progressive in principle, the dizzying provisions of the tax code make them less transparent, less efficient, and probably more regressive in practice. |

# Official Guide Noun and Pronoun Agreement Questions

| Question # | Page | |
|---|---|---|
| **Official Guide** | | |
| 823 | 860 | Noun |
| 837 | 863 | Missing Referent |
| 838 | 863 | Adjective as "Trick" Referent |
| 850 | 865 | This |
| 859 | 867 | Reflexive |
| 864 | 868 | Adjective as "Trick" Referent |
| 875 | 870 | Missing Referent, This |
| 883 | 872 | "Trick" Referent |
| 886 | 872 | Unnecessary Pronoun |
| 890 | 873 | Noun vs. Pronoun |
| 925 | 880 | Noun |
| 931 | 881 | Reflexive |
| 938 | 882 | Missing Referent |
| 947 | 884 | Noun vs. Pronoun, This |
| 949 | 885 | It vs. Them |
| 954 | 886 | Noun vs. Pronoun, Which |
| 962 | 959 | It vs. They, Missing Referent |
| 963 | 888 | Missing Referent |
| 967 | 888 | It, This, They, Which |
| 971 | 889 | It vs. They |
| 975 | 890 | Noun vs. Pronoun, Which |
| 986 | 892 | Which |
| **Official Verbal Guide** | | |
| 261 | 407 | Reflexive |
| 267 | 408 | It vs. Them |
| 279 | 412 | It vs. They (E) |
| 284 | 413 | Unnecessary Pronoun, (A) |
| 286 | 413 | Which |
| 291 | 414 | Noun vs. Pronoun |
| 292 | 414 | Which vs. Whom |
| 296 | 415 | Which |
| 297 | 416 | It vs. They |
| 310 | 419 | Ambiguous Referent, Noun vs. Pronoun |
| 313 | 420 | Which |
| 318 | 421 | It (Unnecessary Pronoun) |
| 323 | 422 | Which (E) |
| 328 | 423 | It vs. They |
| 332 | 424 | It vs. They |
| 335 | 425 | Noun vs. Pronoun, Which |
| 339 | 426 | "Trick" Referent, It vs. They |

# Chapter Seven

# RELATIVE PRONOUNS

We've just looked at the pronouns *which* and *that* through the lens of agreement, but now we're going to look at them—along with a few other pronouns—from a different angle.

## Which vs. That

Which = comma
That = no comma

Grammatically, relative pronouns join clauses. Stylistically, they allow writing to become more fluid and less repetitive. Let's start by considering the following pair of sentences:

Sentence #1:   Bats use a system of ultrasonic sounds in order to produce echoes.

Sentence #2:   These echoes allow them to identify their prey in complete darkness.

The two sentences can be joined with a relative pronoun, either *which* or *that*.

Correct:       Bats use a system of ultrasonic sounds in order to produce echoes **that** allow them to identify their prey in complete darkness.

Correct:       Bats use a system of ultrasonic sounds in order to produce echoes, **which** allow them to identify their prey in complete darkness.

These sentences have slightly different emphases. In the version with *that*, the focus is not simply on echoes, but on specific kinds of echoes: those that let bats identify their prey in complete darkness. In the version with *which*, the focus is on echoes in general; the fact that echoes let bats identify their prey in complete darkness is secondary.

In terms of the GMAT, this distinction is not directly tested, although it may in some cases help you understand subtle differences in meaning between answer choices. What you **need to know**, however, is that *which* follows a comma, while *that* never follows a comma. Note that although these words are often used interchangeably in everyday writing, particularly in British English, the GMAT adheres strictly to this rule.

Incorrect answers with these pronouns typically omit the comma before *which* rather than place an unnecessary comma before *that*. That said, both versions of the error are included below for the sake of thoroughness.

Incorrect:     The Mississippi and the Nile can be cited as examples of rivers **which** form large deltas as a result of the large quantities of sediment deposited at their mouths.

Incorrect:     The Mississippi and the Nile can be cited as examples of rivers, **that** form large deltas as a result of the large quantities of sediment deposited at their mouths.

Correct:       The Mississippi and the Nile can be cited as examples of rivers **that** form large deltas as a result of the large quantities of sediment deposited at their mouths.

## Who vs. Which

*Which* refers to things only. *Who(m)* should be used to refer to people.

> Incorrect: In classical Athenian democracy, <u>citizens</u> **which** failed to pay their debts were barred from attending assembly meetings or appearing in court in virtually any capacity.

> Correct: In classical Athenian democracy, <u>citizens</u> **who** failed to pay their debts were barred from attending assembly meetings or appearing in court in virtually any capacity.

## Who vs. That

Both *who* and *that* can refer to people; however, only *that* can refer to things.

> Incorrect: The field of handwriting analysis, otherwise known as graphology, is based on the belief that certain psychological states trigger <u>physical movements</u> in a writer **who, as a result, leads** to distinctive patterns of letter formation.

> Correct: The field of handwriting analysis, otherwise known as graphology, is based on the belief that certain psychological states <u>trigger physical movements</u> in a writer **that, as a result, lead** to distinctive patterns of letter formation.

What would lead to distinctive patterns of letter formation? The writers' *physical movements*, not the writers themselves.

The correct pronoun must therefore refer to the plural noun *physical movements* (things) rather than to the singular noun *a writer* (person). As a result, *who* is incorrect. *That* should be used instead.

Note that *whose* can be used to refer to both people and things.

> Correct: One marketing hypothesis suggests that <u>children</u> **whose** last names begin with letters that occur late in the alphabet are easier targets for limited-time offers because such children are often impatient from so frequently waiting to be acknowledged.

> Correct: Tarsiers, five-inch tall primates that inhabit the islands of Southeast Asia, are unusual in that they emit <u>sounds</u> **whose** frequencies are entirely above the range perceptible to the human ear.

## Where, When, and "Preposition + Which"

*Where* is for places (physical locations) only and can often be used interchangeably with *preposition + which*.

> Correct: Although Einstein predicted the presence of black holes, regions of space **where/ in which** gravity is so intense that not even light can escape, he had difficulty believing that they could actually exist.

Although it is common in everyday speech to use *where* when referring to works of art (e.g. books, movies) and situations, this usage is incorrect. *In which* should be used instead.

> Incorrect: The novel *Life of Pi*, written by Yann Martel, is a story **where** the protagonist survives on a raft in the ocean for nearly a year, accompanied only by a tiger.

> Correct: The novel *Life of Pi*, written by Yann Martel, is a story **in which** the protagonist survives on a raft in the ocean for nearly a year, accompanied only by a tiger.

Note that although *where* is often interchangeable with *in which*, a preposition other than *in* is sometimes required.

Correct:        One of the turning points in the modern dance revolution occurred at Bennington College, **where** Martha Graham and other influential choreographers gathered to refine their techniques during the 1930s.

Correct:        One of the turning points in the modern dance revolution occurred at Bennington College, **at which** Martha Graham and other influential choreographers gathered to refine their techniques during the 1930s.

Because <u>at a college</u> is standard usage, the preposition *at* should be used. Note that in all of the examples above, *where* and *preposition + which* are equally correct. When these two constructions appear in different answer choices, you can assume that a separate factor will also be present to make one answer correct and the others incorrect.

*When* is for times. Like *where*, it can often be used interchangeably with *in which* (or *during which*). It cannot, however, be used interchangeably with *where*, even though this construction is common in everyday speech.

Incorrect:     The musical *Gypsy* is set in Seattle during the Great Depression, a period **where** vaudeville was beginning to lose popularity as a form of mass entertainment in the United States.

Correct:        The musical *Gypsy* is set in Seattle during the Great Depression, a period **when** vaudeville was beginning to lose popularity as a form of mass entertainment in the United States.

Correct:        The musical *Gypsy* is set in Seattle during the Great Depression, a period **in which/ during which** vaudeville was beginning to lose popularity as a form of mass entertainment in the United States.

## Whereby

In some cases, *whereby* can also be used in place of *by which* or *according to which*. This construction typically appears in the context of systems or processes/procedures. Although this pronoun may strike you as odd or antiquated, it is perfectly acceptable.

Correct:        Scientific inquiry is process **whereby** researchers traverse the abyss between the known and the unknown, suspended by intuition, adventurousness, a healthy dose of stubbornness, and a measure of luck.

## Exercise: Relative Pronouns

**In the following sentences, identify and correct any relative pronoun error that appears. Some sentences may not contain an error. (Answers p. 194)**

| | |
|---|---|
| 1. | In classical Athenian democracy, citizens which failed to pay their debts were barred from attending assembly meetings and appearing in court in virtually any capacity. |
| 2. | In order to treat elderly patients whose bodies cannot handle the rigors of modern medicine, some doctors are now rejecting the assembly line of modern medical care for older, gentler options. |
| 3. | The poet's works are unusual for the period where they were written because they frequently include elements such as short lines and unconventional punctuation. |
| 4. | Supercells, the massive thunderstorms with rotating hearts which form the most intense tornadoes, contain winds that increase in strength and change direction with height, generating horizontal tubes of rotating air parallel to the earth's surface. |
| 5. | In his utopian novel *Walden Two*, B.F. Skinner invents a world in which emotions such as envy have become obsolete because people are conditioned as children to reject unpleasant feelings. |
| 6. | When readers who obtain their news from electronic rather than printed sources send articles to their friends, they tend to choose ones which contain intellectually challenging topics. |
| 7. | Speed bumps are used in many countries around the world, and they are found most frequently in regions where speed limits are legally imposed. |
| 8. | Alexander von Humboldt resurrected the word "cosmos" from the ancient Greek and assigned it to his multi-volume treatise *Kosmos*, where he sought to unify diverse branches of scientific knowledge and culture. |
| 9. | In an era where women painters were not easily accepted by the artistic community or patrons, Artemisia Gentileschi (1593-1656), who painted many pictures of strong and suffering women from myth and the Bible, became the first female member of the Accademia di Arte del Disegno in Florence. |
| 10. | Some scholars believe the economy of the Kingdom of Kush was based on a redistributive system whereby the state would collect taxes in the form of surplus produce and redistribute the excess crops. |
| 11. | There are more than 200 known Upanishads that the first dozen are considered particularly important; consequently, they are referred to as the principal or main Upanishads. |
| 12. | Few countries are tilting toward a cashless future as quickly as Sweden, whose residents have become accustomed to the convenience of paying with cellular telephones and credit cards. |
| 13. | William Etty's *The Wrestler* was painted at a time where sports were becoming increasingly popular, and the work is both a reflection of that trend and a part of the English tradition of copying poses from classical Hellenistic works. |
| 14. | Many unicorn startups—private companies with a valuation of more than $1 billion—have raised hundreds of millions of dollars, of which the majority must be repaid to investors and other preferred shareholders before employees receive any funds. |
| 15. | The Rorschach test, also known as the Rorschach inkblot test, the Rorschach technique, or simply the inkblot test, is a psychological test in which subjects' perceptions of inkblots are recorded and then analyzed using psychological interpretation, complex algorithms, or both. |

# Official Guide Relative Pronoun Questions

| Question # | Page | |
|---|---|---|
| **Official Guide** | | |
| 943 | 884 | In Which, Where |
| 964 | 888 | Where |
| 981 | 891 | Who, That |
| 991 | 893 | Where, That |
| **Official Verbal Guide** | | |
| 261 | 407 | Who, Whom |
| 292 | 414 | Which, Whom |
| 316 | 420 | That, Whose, Whom |
| 328 | 423 | Which vs. That |

# *Chapter Eight*
# ADJECTIVES VS. ADVERBS

**Adjectives** modify nouns or pronouns. They may either be placed before nouns, or paired with nouns/pronouns by linking verbs such as *to be*, *to become*, or *to seem*.

| | |
|---|---|
| Correct: | Despite the **poor** <u>economy</u>, bank loans to small businesses have begun to increase in recent months. |
| Correct: | <u>The gubernatorial candidate</u>, previously known for his open and candid manner, has become **evasive** about his positions on a number of key issues. |
| Correct: | Barcelona is the capital city of the autonomous community of Catalonia as well as Spain's second most populous city, and <u>it</u> is **famous** for its beauty and architectural masterpieces. |

**Adverbs** most often modify verbs, but they can also modify adjectives and other adverbs.

| | |
|---|---|
| Correct: | Many of the texts in the library of St. Catherine's monastery were written in common languages such as Arabic and Latin, but others were inscribed in ones that scholars **rarely** <u>encounter</u>. |
| Correct: | Over the course of the novel, the author's prose, already known for its sharpness and incisiveness, becomes **increasingly** <u>lucid</u> and <u>spare</u>. |
| Correct: | Gravity is the dominant force on earth: without it, many common chemical processes would behave **very** <u>differently</u>. |

Most adverbs are formed by adding –LY to the adjective, e.g., *clear*, *clearly*.

When an adjective already ends in –Y, the adverb is formed by adding –ILY, e.g., *noisy*, *noisily*.

(Note that you do not need to worry about irregularly formed adverbs, e.g., *good* and *well*.)

On the GMAT, adverbs may be incorrectly replaced with adjectives and vice versa.

| | |
|---|---|
| Incorrect: | The candidate, previously known for his open and candid manner, has in recent months begun to <u>speak</u> **evasive** about his positions on a number of key issues. |
| Correct: | The candidate, previously known for his open and candid manner, has in recent months begun to <u>speak</u> **evasively** about his positions on a number of key issues. |

The incorrect adverb is fairly easy to spot in the above example. When sentences involve adverbs placed before adjectives, however, errors can be far more difficult to notice. Try to spot the problem in the sentence below.

| | |
|---|---|
| Incorrect: | Located in what is now southern Iran, the ancient city of Persepolis, the capital of the Achaemenid Empire, was a relative cosmopolitan place during an era that was notable for its barbarity. |

Did you notice it? The adjective *relative*, which modifies the adjective *cosmopolitan*, must be changed to an adverb.

Correct:      Located in what is now southern Iran, the ancient city of Persepolis, the capital of the Achaemenid Empire, was a **relatively** <u>cosmopolitan</u> place during an era that was notable for its barbarity.

Interestingly, test-takers tend to experience difficulty with this question type not because they have trouble understanding when adverbs rather than adjectives should be used, but rather because their eyes automatically correct the error by adding –LY to the ends of adjectives.

If you didn't have a problem with this sentence, consider yourself lucky — but be aware that this trap is very easy to fall into. If you don't see an error initially, try putting your finger on the page/screen, making sure to place it under each word as you read. The physical connection to the page will focus your eye and make you less likely to overlook errors.

The comparative (-ER) form of an adjective may also be incorrectly used in place of *more + adverb*.

Incorrect:      Almost 30 kinds of paint were used on each Model T produced by the Ford Motor Company because different types of paint <u>dried</u> **quicker** on some parts of the automobile than it did on others.

In the above sentence, the adjective *quicker* is incorrectly used to modify the verb *dried*. Only adverbs can modify verbs, so the adjective must be replaced with *more + adverb*.

Correct:      Almost 30 kinds of paint were used on each Model T produced by the Ford Motor Company because different types of paint <u>dried</u> **more quickly** on some parts of the automobile than it did on others.

You could also potentially (although less probably) encounter a sentence that incorrectly uses an adverb in place of an adjective. This type of error would almost certainly involve a verb of being or feeling (e.g., *be, become, seem, appear, feel*).

Incorrect:      Researchers have found that just being exposed to words associated with money can <u>cause</u> people to <u>feel</u> more **independently** and be less inclined to help others.

Although the above version of this sentence makes grammatical sense, it does not make logical sense. It implies that being exposed to words causes people to feel independently — that is, to feel without the help of others. Obviously, feeling is not something that people normally need help doing.

A much more logical interpretation is that exposure to money causes people to have a greater sense of independence. The use of the adjective *independent* conveys that meaning.

Correct:      Researchers have found that just being exposed to words associated with money can <u>cause</u> people to <u>feel</u> more **independent** and be less inclined to help others.

# Exercise: Adjectives vs. Adverbs

**For the following exercises, fix any error in adjective or adverb usage. Some sentences may not contain an error. (Answers p. 195)**

| | |
|---|---|
| 1. | Both bizarre and familiar, fairy tales are intended to be spoken rather than read, and they possess a true inexhaustible power over children and adults alike. |
| 2. | According to economists' predictions, the country's rate of growth will drop to 0.4% from 0.5% because the key services sector, which accounts for well over 70% of economic activity, is growing more slowly than expected. |
| 3. | Examined under a microscope, a glass of apparently crystalline water can reveal a hodgepodge of microscopic drifters that appear quite differently from other aquatic creatures. |
| 4. | Though few people believe that human beings are entirely rational, a world governed by Voltaire and Locke would, in all probability, operate fairer than one governed by anti-Enlightenment principles. |
| 5. | Italian nobleman Cesare Borgia was ruthless and vain, but he was also a brilliant Renaissance figure who was exceeding well-educated in the Greek and Latin classics. |
| 6. | Surrounded by a well-known racing circuit that was created in the 1960s Lake Pergusa, the only natural occurring lake in Sicily, has in recent years hosted a number of international sporting events. |
| 7. | When Mt. Vesuvius first began to show signs of eruption, many of the people living at the base of the volcano hasty abandoned their villages in order to seek cover in nearby forests. |
| 8. | The sportswear company has announced that it expects its sales and net profits to rise faster next year than this year, aided by aggressive marketing and major events such as the European soccer championship and the Summer Olympics. |
| 9. | More is known about Augustine, Bishop of Hippo, than is known about any other figure from the ancient world, and his personality and perceptiveness shine brighter than those of his contemporaries. |
| 10. | Tests on the germination rates of *Salsola imbricata*, a shrub known for its salt tolerance, show that the plant sprouts quicker at 20°C than at higher temperatures and that it shows higher germination rates at low salinity levels than at high ones. |

# Official Guide Adjective vs. Adverb Questions

| Question # | Page |
|---|---|
| **Official Verbal Guide** | |
| 292 | 414 |
| 314 | 420 |
| 321 | 421 |

1. South Africa experienced a series of massive and devastating blackouts in 2008, and consequently their electricity has been rationed ever since that time.

   (A) their electricity has been rationed
   (B) their electricity had been rationed
   (C) its electricity had been rationed
   (D) the country has undergone electricity rationing
   (E) the country's electricity is being rationed

2. In order for the international climate accords to be effective, governments must reject ever-more-affordable fossil fuels in favor of policies requiring that renewable energy sources are found.

   (A) policies requiring that renewable energy sources are found
   (B) policies which require that renewable energy sources are found
   (C) policies requiring that renewable energy sources be found
   (D) policies to require that sources of renewable energy is found
   (E) policies that requires sources of renewable energy be found

3. A plan to place new restrictions on Maine's scalloping industry, some fishermen believe, is the most effective way to ensure they do not become depleted.

   (A) they do not become depleted
   (B) it does not become depleted
   (C) they will not become depleted
   (D) scallops have not become depleted
   (E) scallops do not become depleted

4. Military officials have recently stated that new technologies, and in particular that which involves artificial intelligence software, will help, rather than replace, human soldiers.

   (A) that which involves
   (B) those involving
   (C) those involve
   (D) that involving
   (E) that which has involved

5. When the Punic Wars, a series of conflicts between Rome and Carthage, were fought during the second and third centuries B.C., they probably formed the largest military clash that had ever taken place.

   (A) they probably formed the largest military clash that had ever taken place
   (B) it probably formed the largest military clash which had ever taken place
   (C) it probably formed the largest military clash that has ever taken place
   (D) this probably formed the largest military clash which had ever taken place
   (E) they probably formed the largest military clash having ever taken place

6. The usual assumption about domestic animals is that the process of taming and breeding them happened once; nevertheless, pigs were domesticated twice, and the same can be true for other species.

   (A) pigs were domesticated twice, and the same can be true for other species
   (B) pigs were domesticated twice; the same being true true for other species
   (C) pigs were domesticated twice, and the same could be true for other species
   (D) pigs were domesticated twice, and other species had been the same
   (E) the domestication of pigs occurring twice, and the same is true for other species

7. A joint venture between Boeing and Lockheed Martin is intended to create inflatable habitats that are delivered to low Earth orbit beginning sometime in the next several years.

   (A) habitats that are delivered
   (B) habitats that will be delivered
   (C) habitats that is delivered
   (D) habitats which are delivered
   (E) habitats and are delivered

8. Venture capitalists in India are discovering that they can easily build large and profitable businesses without significant long-term technological advantages because <u>many of them are operating</u> in areas with little or no competition.

(A) many of them are operating
(B) many of these are operating
(C) many businesses operate
(D) many would operate
(E) many of them have operated

9. Since the 1920s, most major motion picture studios, including Paramount <u>Pictures, accumulate</u> tangled lists of owners and corporate relations.

(A) Pictures, accumulate
(B) Pictures, which accumulate
(C) Pictures and have accumulated
(D) Pictures, accumulates
(E) Pictures, have accumulated

10. When it comes to remembering numbers or binary digits, <u>each competitor in the World Memory Championships has its</u> own systems for converting these items into images.

(A) each competitor in the World Memory Championships has its
(B) each competitor in the World Memory Championships has their
(C) each competitor in the World Memory Championships have their
(D) all of the competitors in the World Memory Championships have its
(E) all of the competitors in the World Memory Championships have their

11. Analysis of handwriting on pottery shards found in Israel <u>suggests that literacy, and perhaps also the written Bible,</u> might have spread in the Middle East much earlier than previously thought.

(A) suggests that literacy, and perhaps also the written Bible,
(B) suggest that literacy, and perhaps the written Bible as well,
(C) suggests that literacy, and maybe also the written Bible, which
(D) suggesting that literacy, and maybe the written Bible also,
(E) suggests that literacy, and perhaps also the written Bible, and

12. In 2002, deemed the International Year of Gaudi by the Barcelona city council, <u>several of his houses were still in private hands but were opened</u> to the public for the first time, triggering a massive surge in the architect's popularity.

(A) several of his houses were still in private hands but were opened
(B) several of his houses were still in private hands but opened
(C) several of Gaud's remained in private hands but had been opened
(D) several of Gaudi's houses remained in private hands but were opened
(E) several of his houses have remained in private hands but were opened

13. <u>In the Nasca region of Peru, an area famous for the Nasca lines,</u> enormous geometric images carved into the landscape to form a sophisticated hydraulic system that retrieved water from underground aquifers and made the arid land habitable.

(A) In the Nasca region of Peru, an area famous for the Nasca lines,
(B) In the Nasca region of Peru, an area famous for the Nasca lines, which are
(C) In the Nasca region of Peru, an area famous for the Nasca lines and
(D) The Nasca region of Peru, an area famous for the Nasca lines,
(E) The Nasca region of Peru is an area famous for the Nasca lines,

14. Planets with atmospheres that orbit <u>too close to their host stars are bombarded by a torrent of high-energy radiation, which</u> strips away the gaseous outer layers of these worlds.

   (A) too close to their host stars are bombarded by a torrent of high-energy radiation, which
   (B) too close to their host stars are bombarded by a torrent of high-energy radiation,
   (C) too closely to their host stars being bombarded by a torrent of high-energy radiation, which
   (D) too close to their host stars are bombarded by a torrent of high-energy radiation and
   (E) too closely to their host stars are bombarded by a torrent of high-energy radiation, and this


15. Although certain genetic mutations inevitably result in the development of disease, <u>patients which have identical mutations can nonetheless display widely varying symptoms</u>.

   (A) patients which have identical mutations can nonetheless display widely varying symptoms
   (B) patients who have identical mutations nonetheless displaying symptoms of a wide variation
   (C) patients with identical mutations can nonetheless display a wide variety of symptoms
   (D) patients having identical mutations can nonetheless display wide varying symptoms
   (E) but patients who have identical mutations can nonetheless display widely varying symptoms

# Chapter Nine
# MODIFICATION

In any given sentence, modifiers should be placed as close as possible to the nouns, pronouns, or phrases they modify. Sentences that separate modifiers from the elements they modify are often unclear and sometimes completely absurd.

Two main types of modification errors are tested on the GMAT:

1) Dangling modifiers

2) Misplaced modifiers

## Dangling Modifiers

Dangling modification is a type of misplaced modification, one that appears in a very specific form. A sentence containing a dangling modifier will include a phrase that describes a noun, usually the subject, but does not name that noun.

This phrase most often appears at the beginning of a sentence, but it can appear later on as well. Regardless of where it is placed, it is followed by a comma.

| | |
|---|---|
| Correct: | **Able to grow in only a limited habitat,** Texas wild rice may soon become extinct because the area where it is usually planted is being destroyed by pollution. |
| Correct: | King Louis IX of France was seized by the Egyptian army during the Battle of Al Mansurah in 1249 and, **following his release from captivity,** he used his influence to show crusaders how to rebuild their defenses and conduct diplomacy. |

Whenever a sentence contains this type of descriptive phrase, the noun or pronoun it modifies must be placed immediately after the comma. If that noun or pronoun does not appear, the modifier is dangling.

| | |
|---|---|
| Incorrect: | **An elementary school teacher from Arkansas,** increased funding and support for public libraries were advocated for by <u>Bessie Boehm Moore</u>, who in 1999 was named one of *American Libraries'* 100 most important twentieth century leaders. |

The above sentence contains a descriptive introductory phrase (*An elementary school teacher from Arkansas*) that describes but does not name the subject—it does not tell us who the elementary school teacher from Arkansas *is*.

We must therefore ask whom that phrase is describing. When we look at the rest of the sentence, it is clear that the description can only refer to Bessie Boehm Moore.

The words *Bessie Boehm Moore* do not appear immediately after the comma, so the modifier is dangling. In order to fix the sentence, we must place Bessie Boehm Moore's name after the comma.

Correct:   An elementary school teacher from Arkansas, **Bessie Boehm Moore** advocated for increased funding and support for public libraries and was in 1999 named one of *American Libraries'* 100 most important twentieth century leaders.

Be on the lookout for possessive versions of the subject immediately after the introductory phrase. In general, any possessive noun placed immediately after an introductory phrase will be incorrect.

Incorrect:   An elementary school teacher from Arkansas, **Bessie Boehm Moore's goal** was to achieve increased funding and support for public libraries, and in 1999, she was named one of *American Libraries'* 100 most important twentieth century leaders.

At first glance, this sentence looks and sounds correct. But who is the elementary school teacher from Arkansas? *Bessie Boehm Moore*, not her *goal*. And here, *goal* is the subject, not *Bessie Boehm Moore*. So the modifier is dangling.

Correct:   An elementary school teacher from Arkansas, **Bessie Boehm Moore** had the goal of achieving increased funding and support for public libraries, and in 1999, she was named one of *American Libraries'* 100 most important twentieth century leaders.

Note, however, that it is acceptable to begin the main clause with an adjective or phrase modifying the subject—such modifiers are considered part of the **complete subject**.

Correct:   **Born** in a small town in Missouri, <u>singer and actress Josephine Baker</u> spent the majority of her career performing throughout Europe.

Note also that the presence of a participle, particularly a present participle (-ING word), at the beginning of a sentence often signals a dangling modifier.

## Present Participle

Incorrect:   **Stretching** from one end of the city to the other, the efficiency of <u>the new tram system</u> often surprises both tourists and city residents.

Correct:   **Stretching** from one end of the city to the other, <u>the new tram system</u> often surprises both tourists and city residents with its efficiency.

## Past Participle

Incorrect:   **Born** in a small town in Missouri, the majority of <u>Josephine Baker</u>'s career was spent performing throughout Europe.

Correct:   **Born** in a small town in Missouri, <u>Josephine Baker</u> spent the majority of her career performing throughout Europe.

When fixing dangling modifiers, you should **focus on identifying the subject** because when you look at the answer choices, you are looking for an option that places the subject immediately after the introductory phrase. If the subject is placed elsewhere, you can immediately eliminate the option.

For example:

> One of the twenty-two official languages of India, <u>many Hindu ceremonies and Buddhist rituals make use of Sanskrit in the form of hymns and mantras</u>.
>
> (A) many Hindu ceremonies and Buddhist rituals make use of Sanskrit in the form of hymns and mantras
> (B) many Hindu ceremonies and Buddhist rituals would make use of Sanskrit in the form of hymns and mantras
> (C) playing a role in many Hindu ceremonies and Buddhist rituals is the use of Sanskrit, having the form of hymns and mantras
> (D) Sanskrit is used in many Hindu ceremonies and Buddhist rituals in the form of hymns and mantras
> (E) Sanskrit being used in many Hindu ceremonies and Buddhist rituals in the form of hymns and mantras

Logically, what is one of twenty-two official languages of India? Sanskrit. So *Sanskrit*, the subject, must be placed immediately after the comma. That eliminates everything except (D) and (E).

(E) is a fragment because it substitutes the gerund *being* for a conjugated verb, eliminating that option. Besides, *being* almost always signals a wrong answer.

That leaves (D), which is correct.

In some cases, however, you may have no choice but to rearrange the entire sentence. For example, the question above could also be asked like this:

> <u>One of the twenty-two official languages of India, many Hindu ceremonies and Buddhist rituals make use of Sanskrit in the form of hymns and mantras</u>.
>
> (A) One of the twenty-two official languages of India many Hindu ceremonies and Buddhist rituals make use of Sanskrit in the form of hymns and mantras.
> (B) One of the twenty-two official languages of India, many Hindu ceremonies and Buddhist rituals would make use of Sanskrit in the form of hymns and mantras
> (C) One of the twenty-two official languages of India, playing a role in many Hindu ceremonies and Buddhist rituals is the use of Sanskrit, having the form of hymns and mantras
> (D) Sanskrit, one of the twenty-two official languages of India, is used in many Hindu ceremonies and Buddhist rituals in the form of hymns and mantras.
> (E) One of the twenty-two official languages of India, Sanskrit being used in many Hindu ceremonies and Buddhist rituals in the form of hymns and mantras

In this case, (D) is still the correct option, but it reconfigures the sentence using a non-essential clause rather than preserving the introductory phrase and placing the subject after it.

## Exercise: Dangling Modifiers

In the following exercises, identify the subject of each sentence, and rewrite as necessary to eliminate any dangling modification. Some sentences may not contain an error. (Answers p. 195)

| | |
|---|---|
| 1. | Once known to live throughout much of Europe and North America, the destruction of the gray wolf's natural habitat has caused its population to decline. |
| 2. | Widely considered to be among the greatest pianists of her age, Clara Wieck's musical studies began when she was five years old; by the age of twelve she was renowned as both a performer and a composer. |
| 3. | Precise, unforgiving, and frequently unnatural, no artistic pursuit is more physically or mentally demanding than the form of classical ballet developed at the French court in the 1700s and perfected in Russia two centuries later. |
| 4. | Often thought of as a modern sport, one that has only gained popularity during the last half-century, surfing was an important activity in Polynesian culture long before Europeans first observed it. |
| 5. | A recipient of the Presidential Medal of Freedom, Barbara Jordan's election to Congress made her one of the most politically accomplished African-American women in the United States. |
| 6. | Subject to Moorish rule until the twelfth century, Arabic was still spoken by many Spaniards when their cities first came under the control of European monarchs. |
| 7. | Historically based on the carving of walrus ivory, which was once found in abundance, the inclusion of prints and figures made from soft stone has characterized Inuit art since the mid-twentieth century. |
| 8. | Projecting an image of pain and brutality that has few parallels among advanced paintings of the twentieth century, *Guernica* was painted by Pablo Picasso in the aftermath of a World War II bombing. |
| 9. | Predicting renewed interest in their country's natural resources, a plan has been established by political leaders to create mines in the most underdeveloped regions. |
| 10. | Raised in Hong Kong and Shanghai before he moved to the United States in 1935, the buildings designed by I.M. Pei are immediately recognizable because of their characteristic glass exteriors and use of geometrical forms. |
| 11. | A staple in grocery stores since the 1970s, environmentalists now estimate that close to a trillion plastic bags are distributed worldwide each year. |
| 12. | Recent studies have shown that by consuming a small amount of dark chocolate daily, overall health can be improved in most people. |
| 13. | Having left her native Dominican Republic for the United States in 1939, Rhina Espaillat wrote many works in both English and Spanish and became the most prominent translator of Robert Frost's poetry. |
| 14. | Often spending their time hidden under submerged ledges or in crevices within reefs, a preference for specific resting sites is exhibited by many nurse sharks, which return to them each day after the night's hunting. |
| 15. | Drawn in black and white, Marjane Satrapi wrote her graphic novel *Persepolis*, a combination of comic-strip form and astute political commentary, as a semi-autobiographical depiction of her childhood and adolescence in Tehran and Vienna. |

# Misplaced Modifiers

Misplaced modifiers generally do not involve introductory phrases and occur later in sentences. They do, however, also involve modifiers separated from the words or phrases they are intended to modify, and can sometimes result in statements whose meanings are unintentionally ridiculous.

## Adjectives and Adverbs

Misplaced modifiers can be very short. In fact, some of them consist of only one word.

Recall from the beginning of the chapter that modifiers should be placed as close as possible to the words or phrases they modify in order to make meanings as clear as possible. Some incorrect GMAT answer choices will put modifiers in places that are illogical or confusing.

Incorrect:    Hersheypark was opened in 1907 as **only** a leisure park for <u>employees of the Hershey Chocolate Company</u>, but Hershey executives later decided that members of the public should be given access as well.

The placement of the word *only* before *a leisure park* implies that later on, Hersheypark also became something other than a leisure park.

However, the statement that members of the public were later given access to the park suggests an alternate meaning: when Hersheypark opened, employees of the Hershey Chocolate Company were the only people given access to it. Logically, then, the word *only* should modify the phrase *employees of the Hershey Chocolate Company*.

Correct:    Hersheypark was opened in 1907 as a leisure park for <u>employees of the Hershey Chocolate Company</u> **only**, but Hershey executives later decided that members of the public should be given access as well.

This version of the sentence makes it clear that *only* refers to the employees rather than to the park itself.

## Phrases

Misplaced modifiers can also consist of various types of longer phrases, including prepositional phrases.

Incorrect:    When President James K. Polk officially confirmed <u>the discovery</u> by James Marshall **of gold flakes** at Sutter's Mill in Coloma, California, in 1848, hopeful prospectors immediately began planning to travel there.

Logically, the discovery was of gold flakes, so the modifier *of gold flakes* must be placed next to *the discovery*.

Correct:    When President James K. Polk officially confirmed <u>James Marshall's discovery</u> **of gold Flakes** at Sutter's Mill in Coloma, California, in 1848, hopeful prospectors immediately began planning to travel there.

You should also be careful with phrases beginning with *which* and *that*. These pronouns must refer to the noun that appears immediately before them. Otherwise, a misplaced modifier is created.

Incorrect:    Some of the world's fastest trains run between the Japanese cities of <u>Tokyo and Kyoto</u>, **which can reach speeds of up to 200 miles per hour.**

Clearly, the trains can reach speeds of up to 200 miles per hour—not, as the sentence indicates, Tokyo and Kyoto.

Correct:    <u>Some of the world's fastest trains,</u> **which can reach speeds of up to 200 miles per hour,** run between the Japanese cities of Tokyo and Kyoto.

Now let's look at an example with *that*.

> Incorrect:    Paul Conrad was a cartoonist known for his political satires that spent nearly three decades on staff at *The Los Angeles Times* and provided a critical perspective on numerous United States presidential administrations.

Even though it's pretty obvious what the sentence is *trying* to say (Paul Conrad spent three decades working at the *Los Angeles Times*), there is a problem with what the sentence is *actually* saying—namely, that the political satires spent three decades on staff at *The Los Angeles Times*. Clearly, it was Paul Conrad who did so.

To fix the sentence, must make it clear that Conrad, not the political satires, worked at the newspaper. There are a variety of ways to make the correction; some possibilities are listed below.

> Correct:    Paul Conrad, a cartoonist known for his political satires, spent nearly three decades on staff at *The Los Angeles Times* and provided a critical perspective on numerous United States presidential administrations.

> Correct:    Known for his political satires, cartoonist Paul Conrad spent nearly three decades on staff at *The Los Angeles Times*, providing a critical perspective on numerous United States presidential administrations.

> Correct:    A cartoonist known for his political satires, Paul Conrad spent nearly three decades on staff at *The Los Angeles Times*, providing a critical perspective on numerous United States presidential administrations.

### Gerunds

Yet another type of misplaced modification involves gerunds.

> Incorrect:    In ancient Rome, the first aquariums were created when **bringing sea barbels indoors** in order to be housed in tanks of marble and glass for houseguests to observe.

Read literally, the above sentence implies that the first aquariums themselves brought sea barbels indoors. Logically, however, an aquarium could not transport anything.

Note that a passive construction is typically required to correct this error—one of the few instances in which the passive voice is preferable.

> Correct:    In ancient Rome, the first aquariums were created when **sea barbels were brought indoors** in order to be housed in tanks of marble and glass for houseguests to observe.

# Exercise: Misplaced Modifiers

**In the following sentences, correct any misplaced modification error that occurs. Some sentences may not contain an error. (Answers p. 196)**

| | |
|---|---|
| 1. | Investors and executives typically receive preferred stock in startup companies, a class of shares that is often accompanied by a guaranteed payout when the companies go public. |
| 2. | The printing press was introduced in Europe by Johannes Gutenberg in the mid-fifteenth century, a goldsmith who devised a hand mold to create metal movable type and adapted screw presses and other existing technologies to create a printing system. |
| 3. | When economic activity weakens, monetary policymakers can push interest rate targets below the economy's natural rate, lowering the real cost temporarily of borrowing. |
| 4. | Some of the gold-diggers known as "forty-niners" traveled alone to California during the gold rush of 1849, but most formed companies that enabled them with other miners to share expenses and supplies during the long journey. |
| 5. | Born in Jamaica and first educated by his older brother, who possessed a considerable library of novels, poetry, and scientific texts, Claude McKay became one of the most important poets of the Harlem Renaissance that moved to New York after studying agronomy in Kansas. |
| 6. | Thousands of forged stamps, some very similar to their authentic counterparts, have been produced over the years, and a thorough knowledge of philately only offers any hope of detecting the fakes. |
| 7. | Throughout the Middle Ages, cities across Europe were protected from bands of invaders by fortresses that roamed in search of settlements to plunder. |
| 8. | The trees and rivers of the Ardenne provided the charcoal industry with assets that enabled the great industrial period of Wallonia during the late 1700s and early 1800s, arguably the second most important industrial region of the world. |
| 9. | The earliest type of armor to be invented was chainmail, a protective covering made from thousands of interlocking metallic rings that a master craftsman and his apprentices had linked together by hand. |
| 10. | A recent discovery by astronomers suggests that for the past 2.5 billion years, a B-flat has been continuously emitted by a black hole 250 million light years from Earth, the lowest note ever detected. |
| 11. | Prohibition movements in Europe and the United States coincided with the advent of women's suffrage; newly politically empowered women strongly often supported policies that curbed alcohol consumption. |
| 12. | Bioluminescence, a phenomenon occurring primarily among sea-dwelling creatures but also found among land-dwelling ones, involves light produced within a living organism that is created by a chemical reaction. |
| 13. | Only after joining Miles Davis's Second Great Quintet did Herbie Hancock, who professionally had performed as a musician since the age of seven, succeed in finding his voice as a pianist. |
| 14. | Based on studies in mice, one way of improving health involves sharply restricting the consumption of meals to a narrow window during the day and extending the time between dinner and breakfast. |
| 15. | Praised by consumer magazines for being both versatile and affordable, the food processor performs a wide range of functions, including chopping, dicing, and pureeing, when flipping a switch. |

## Official Guide Modification Questions

| Question # | Page | |
|---|---|---|
| **Official Guide** | | |
| 826 | 860 | Dangling (D), (E) |
| 855 | 866 | Dangling |
| 862 | 868 | Dangling |
| 870 | 869 | Dangling |
| 876 | 870 | Misplaced (Adverb), (B) |
| 882 | 880 | Dangling |
| 888 | 872 | Dangling |
| 894 | 874 | Dangling |
| 899 | 875 | Misplaced |
| 904 | 876 | Dangling |
| 909 | 877 | Dangling |
| 918 | 878 | Dangling |
| 932 | 881 | Misplaced |
| 934 | 881 | Dangling |
| 936 | 882 | Misplaced |
| 955 | 886 | Dangling |
| 959 | 887 | Misplaced |
| 966 | 888 | Misplaced |
| 976 | 890 | Dangling |
| 978 | 891 | Dangling |
| 985 | 892 | Dangling |
| 986 | 892 | Misplaced (Adverb) |
| 993 | 893 | Dangling |
| **Official Verbal Guide** | | |
| 235 | 402 | Dangling |
| 240 | 403 | Dangling |
| 246 | 404 | Dangling |
| 253 | 406 | Dangling |
| 255 | 406 | Dangling (E) |
| 270 | 409 | Dangling (B), (C), (E) |
| 295 | 415 | Dangling (C) |
| 296 | 415 | Dangling |
| 304 | 417 | Dangling |
| 305 | 418 | Dangling (C) |
| 306 | 418 | Misplaced (Adverb) |
| 312 | 419 | Misplaced |
| 315 | 420 | Dangling (E) |
| 324 | 422 | Dangling (C), (E) |
| 329 | 423 | Dangling |
| 330 | 424 | Dangling |
| 336 | 425 | Dangling (B), (C) |

# *Chapter Ten*

# WORD PAIRS

On the GMAT, a number of pairs of words and phrases (formally known as **correlative conjunctions**) must appear together; any deviation is considered incorrect. Knowing these pairs can allow you to simplify seemingly complex questions and immediately eliminate several answers, or even jump right to the correct answer. Not only does this type of shortcut save you time, but it also saves you considerable energy.

For example, consider the following:

> Goethe, an amateur scientist as well as a renowned poet and novelist, was **so** impressed with the work of British chemist Luke <u>Howard and publishing</u>, in German translation, an autobiographical letter that Howard had sent to him.

- (A) Howard and publishing
- (B) Howard to publish
- (C) Howard, and he published
- (D) Howard **that** he published
- (E) Howard; indeed, he published

At first glance, this might appear to be a fairly complicated sentence. There are perhaps several options that seem reasonably acceptable, and you might not be sure how to choose between them.

There is, however, a shortcut. If you read the sentence carefully from the beginning, you can see that the word *so* appears. *So* must be paired with *that*, and there is only one answer choice that includes the word *that*. (D) is thus correct. By zeroing in on the key words, you eliminate the possibility of becoming distracted by irrelevant information and turning the question into something much more complicated than it is.

## A. Not (only/just)...but (also)*

Correct:    Elizabeth Barrett Browning's "Cry of the Children," published in 1842, **not only** denounced the use of child labor **but (also)** helped bring about legislation to prevent it.

## B. (N)either...(n)or

Correct:    Because the Articles of Confederacy did not provide for **either** the creation of executive agencies **or** judiciary institutions, they were rejected in favor of the Constitution in 1787.

Correct:    Although Italian Renaissance painter Palma Vecchio's work demonstrates superior richness of color, Vecchio excelled in **neither** invention **nor** vigorous draftsmanship.

**C. So**
**Such** } **that***

Correct: The first lesula monkey seen by researchers bore a strong resemblance to the owl-faced monkey, but **so** unusual was the lesula monkey's coloring **that** experts suspected the animal was a new species.

Correct: The first lesula monkey seen by researchers bore a strong resemblance to the owl-faced monkey, but the lesula monkey had **such** unusual coloring **that** experts suspected the animal was a new species.

**D. Both**
**Between** } **And**
**At once**

Correct: The Egyptian queen Nefertiti ruled alongside her husband, Pharaoh Akhenaten, more than 3,300 years ago, during an era of **both** tremendous affluence **and** unprecedented social upheaval.

Correct: Asked to choose **between** the gorilla **and** the chimpanzee, experienced primate researchers generally do not hesitate to declare the chimpanzee the smarter animal.

Correct: Patrons find the experience of dining in the restaurant **at once** impressive because of the exceptional food **and** disappointing because of the poor quality of the service.

**E. From...to**

Correct: The shift **from** a monarchical form of government **to** a totalitarian one occurred in Russia over a remarkably short period of time at the beginning of the twentieth century.

**F. X is to...what y is to**

Correct: The plays of William Shakespeare **are to** the history of theater in England **what** the plays of Molière (Jean-Baptise Poquelin) are to the history of theater in France.

**G. As**
**Not so much** } **As**

Correct: In his poems and essays, Dan Chiasson proves **as** adept at rigorously interrogating his own psychology **as** he is at intellectually probing the outer world.

Correct: Although her plays have garnered praise from many critics, Toni Morrison is known **not so much** for her theatrical works **as** she is for her novels.

---

*Please note that there is an exception to this pattern in Question #863 on p. 868 of the *Official Guide*. Incorrect answers contain *so...that*, while the correct answer contains an alternate construction: *so...as to*. In this case, the overall logic and coherence of choice (A) outweigh strict adherence to the usual version of the word pair.

## H. Hardly/scarcely…any

When this word pair is presented incorrectly, *scarcely/hardly* will almost certainly be paired with *no* rather than *any*, creating a double negative.

Incorrect: Although many people have attempted to solve the mystery of Stonehenge, its purpose is **hardly/scarcely no** clearer than it was centuries ago.

Correct: Although many people have attempted to solve the mystery of Stonehenge, its purpose is **hardly/scarcely any** clearer than it was centuries ago.

## I. Comparative } than
## No sooner

Correct: Although Jane Austen's novels are **more** widely read **than** those of her contemporaries, Austen was hardly the only female author in nineteenth-century England.

Correct: **No sooner** had the senator announced her intention not to run for re-election **than** the media began to speculate about the next stage of her political career.

Any comparative form of an adjective (-ER or *more* + *adjective*) should be paired with *than*.

## J. Just as…so

Correct: **Just as** Thomas Edison is known for revolutionizing the electric industry by inventing the electric light bulb, **so** is Albert Einstein known for revolutionizing the field of theoretical physics by developing a theory of general relativity.

**Note:** The GMAT has included correct answers that include *just as* but not *so*. That said, if *just as* does appear in a question, you should always start by checking for answers that include *so*. If such answers do appear, one of them is most likely correct.

## K. Only when
## Only after } did
## Not until

Correct: **Only when** technology began to advance during the eighteenth century **did** the first real breakthroughs in the study of meteorology take place.

Correct: **Only after** technology began to advance during the eighteenth century **did** the first real breakthroughs in the study of meteorology take place.

Correct: **Not until** technology began to advance during the eighteenth century **did** the first real breakthroughs in the study of meteorology take place.

"Not" and "after" expressions can also be paired with a form of the verb *to be*.

Correct: **Not until** technology began to advance during the eighteenth century **was** it possible for the first real breakthroughs in the study of meteorology to take place.

Correct: **Not until** technology began to advance during the eighteenth century **were** the first real breakthroughs in the study of meteorology made (by scientists).

**Note:** the expression *not since* also exists and should be paired with a form of the verb *to have*.

Correct: The cellular telephone allows people to hold long-distance conversations while carrying out a range of activities; **not since** the car radio **has** a device so altered the experience of driving.

L.  **It was only when**
    **It was only after**  } **that**
    **It was not until**

Correct: **It was only when** technology began to advance during the eighteenth century **that** it became possible for the first real breakthroughs in the study of meteorology to take place.

Correct: **It was only after** technology began to advance during the eighteenth century **that** it became possible for the first real breakthroughs in the study of meteorology to take place

Correct: **It was not until** technology began to advance during the eighteenth century **that** it became possible for the first real breakthroughs in the study of meteorology to take place.

# Exercise: Word Pairs

**In the following sentences, identify and correct any word pair error that appears. Some sentences may not contain an error. (Answers p. 197)**

| | |
|---|---|
| 1. | When a white dwarf takes on enough mass from a neighboring star, the pressure becomes so great at its center, with the result that runaway fusion occurs and the star detonates in a thermonuclear supernova. |
| 2. | Among ancient languages, Latin and Greek are to the literary cultures of Europe what classical Sanskrit is to the literary culture of the Indian subcontinent. |
| 3. | It was not until the late seventeenth century when some English writers began to challenge the traditional view of commerce, which held that money-making was a source of moral corruption to be avoided at all cost. |
| 4. | Long Island was the setting for F. Scott Fitzgerald's novel *The Great Gatsby*, but finding traces of the characters there is as much a job for the imagination as it is for a map and a guidebook. |
| 5. | India's natural resources, which range from the frigid lakes of the Himalaya Mountains and the tropical forests that lie hundreds of miles to the south, are home to an astounding variety of birds and other animals. |
| 6. | The original British settlements in Australia, chosen exclusively for their strategic locations, had rocky soil and produced scarcely no food to support their inhabitants. |
| 7. | Just as the machine age transformed an economy of farm laborers and artisans into one of assembly lines, so the technology revolution is replacing factory workers with robots and clerks with computers. |
| 8. | So great was the surplus of food created by the ancient Mesopotamians and it led to the establishment of the first complex civilization in human history. |
| 9. | Obedience to authority is not only a way for rulers to keep order in totalitarian states, and it is the foundation on which such states exist. |
| 10. | Normally associated with airplane construction, wind-tunnel testing has also been applied to automobiles, not so much to determine aerodynamic forces than to determine ways to reduce the power required to move the vehicle on roadways at a given speed. |
| 11. | The time devoted to books by publishing companies, experts suggest, has been reduced by both financial constraints and as well as an increased emphasis on sales and marketing considerations. |
| 12. | A leading figure in the Pop Art movement, Andy Warhol was at once celebrated for his depictions of everyday objects, but he was denounced for his embrace of consumerist culture. |
| 13. | New Zealand has been so geographically isolated throughout its history to a level at which unique forms of fauna have arisen there, making the island nation one of the most ecologically distinctive places on Earth. |
| 14. | Between the early 1870s until the 1910s, when his health began to fail, Thomas Eakins painted exactingly from life, choosing as his subject the people of his hometown of Philadelphia. |
| 15. | One of the main effects of industrialization was the shift from a society in which women worked at home with one in which women worked in factories and brought home wages to their families. |

## Official Guide Word Pair Questions

| Question # | Page | |
|---|---|---|
| **Official Guide** | | |
| 826 | 861 | So…That |
| 845 | 864 | Just as…So |
| 854 | 866 | Not only…But |
| 857 | 867 | More…Than |
| 866 | 868 | More…Than |
| 867 | 868 | As…As |
| 873 | 870 | More…Than |
| 891 | 873 | (Neither…)Nor |
| 897 | 874 | So…That |
| 907 | 876 | More…Than |
| 934 | 881 | Are to…What |
| 952 | 885 | Both…And |
| 957 | 886 | Between…And |
| 960 | 887 | Comparative…Than |
| 976 | 890 | As…As |
| 977 | 890 | More…Than |
| **Official Verbal Guide** | | |
| 262 | 407 | Not only… But also |
| 265 | 408 | Between…And |
| 266 | 408 | Neither…Nor |
| 279 | 412 | So…That |
| 280 | 412 | Both…And |
| 303 | 417 | Both…And |
| 311 | 419 | From…To |
| 338 | 425 | As…As, Comparative…Than |

## *Chapter Eleven*

# PARALLEL STRUCTURE

The term "parallel structure" refers to the fact that equally important parts of a sentence should match—that is, they should be presented in the same format. Parallel structure is among the most frequently tested concepts, and it can appear in many guises. These questions are often signaled by the presence of lists, with each item set off by a comma, but they can also involve only two items joined by a conjunction such as *and* or *but*.

Most GMAT lists will contain three items, but occasionally a list may contain four. Regardless of the number of items, the word *and* (or, in some cases, the word *or*) should only be placed before the last item.

Incorrect:     The closing of the recreation center has been strongly protested because it <u>provides</u> a gathering place for community members, <u>offers</u> activities to senior citizens, **and sponsors** lectures on a variety of topics, **and hosts** a number of continuing education classes for adults.

Correct:     The closing of the recreation center has been strongly protested because it <u>provides</u> a gathering place for community members, <u>offers</u> activities to senior citizens, **sponsors** lectures on a variety of topics, **and hosts** a number of continuing education classes for adults.

**Important:** Because each item in a given list can consist of an entire phrase, the fastest and most efficient way to identify inconsistencies in a list is to **start by focusing on the beginning of each item**.

Although parallel structure questions are not necessarily difficult, they can be very tedious. They can also be visually overwhelming, causing you to overlook information that is present and insert information that is not actually there. Initially focusing on a limited amount of information helps you avoid these pitfalls.

Incorrect:     The closing of the recreation center has been strongly protested because it <u>provides</u> a gathering place for community members, <u>offers</u> activities to senior citizens, and **hosting/to host** a number of continuing education classes for adults there as well.

Incorrect:     The closing of the recreation center has been strongly protested because it <u>provides</u> a gathering place for community members, <u>offers</u> activities to senior citizens, and **a number of continuing education classes** for adults are hosted there as well.

Correct:     The closing of the recreation center has been strongly protested because it <u>provides</u> a gathering place for community members, <u>offers</u> activities to senior citizens, and **hosts** a number of continuing education classes for adults.

In the incorrect versions of the sentence above, the first two items in the list are both verbs (*provides, offers*), whereas the third item is either a gerund (*hosting*), an infinitive (*to host*) or a noun (*a number of continuing education classes*). In order for the sentence to be correct, the third item must also be made into a verb (*hosts*).

Sometimes, you may be able to determine the correct answer just by looking at the beginning of each item, as in the example above. In other instances, you may be able to eliminate two or three options but will then need to consider the remaining possibilities more closely in order to arrive at an answer.

For example, consider this question:

> One of the most accomplished women in seventeenth-
> century English as well as a remarkable self-publicist, Margaret
> Cavendish, duchess of Newcastle-Upon-Tyne, was <u>a composer
> of poetry, a writer of philosophy, and inventing romances.</u>

(A) a composer of poetry, a writer of philosophy, and
    inventing romances
(B) composed poetry, wrote philosophy, and to invent
    romances
(C) a composer of poetry, a writer of philosophy, and an
    inventor who wrote romances
(D) composed poetry, wrote philosophy, and inventing
    romances
(E) a composer of poetry, a writer of philosophy, and an
    inventor of romances

Looking only at the beginning of each item, we can eliminate (A), (B), and (D) because they contain a motley assortment of nouns, verbs, and gerunds.

In contrast, all three items in (C) and (E) begin with nouns. As a result, we need to look more carefully at the full construction of the third item in both answers. Because the construction "noun + *of* + noun" appears in the first two items, it must appear in the third as well. Only (E) contains that construction, so it is correct.

Although identifying and correcting errors in parallel construction is often a reasonably straightforward process of making all of the items match, as in the example above, some questions may include a twist. As an example, we're going to return to the sentence from the previous page.

> The closing of the recreation center has been strongly
> protested because the center <u>provides a gathering place for
> community members, offers activities to senior citizens,
> and a number of continuing education classes for adults
> are hosted there as well.</u>

(A) provides a gathering place for community members,
    offers activities to senior citizens, and a number of
    continuing education classes for adults are hosted there
    as well
(B) provides a gathering place for community members,
    offering activities to senior citizens, and to host a
    number of continuing education classes for adults
(C) provides a gathering place for community members,
    offering activities to senior citizens and hosting a
    number of continuing education classes for adults
(D) provides a gathering place for community members,
    to offer activities to senior citizens, and hosting a
    number of continuing education classes for adults
(E) has provided a gathering place for community members,
    offers activities to senior citizens, and hosting a
    number of continuing education classes for adults

The first thing to notice about a question like this is that it asks you to deal with a substantial amount of information. If you're not aware of the various ways in which the question can be solved from the start, it is exceedingly easy to become confused.

It is entirely reasonable to approach the question by focusing on the beginning of each item in the list, but if you work this way, you'll quickly encounter a problem: not one of the answers makes all three items parallel—or so it seems.

The key to answering this type of question correctly is to reframe it as a *two-part* parallel structure question, one that uses the second and third items to modify the first item.

Let's look at the correct answer, (C):

> The closing of the recreation center has been strongly protested because it provides a gathering place for community members, **offering** activities to senior citizens and **hosting** a number of continuing education classes for adults.

The participial phrase created by *offering* and *hosting* modifies the information before the comma, clearly and logically linking the two halves of the sentence. The solution is perfectly acceptable—it's just not the solution most people are expecting.

## Two-Part Parallel Structure

"List" parallel structure questions are not the only type of parallel structure question you'll encounter on the GMAT. Just as common are parallel structure questions containing only two parts, one on each side of a conjunction (e.g., *and, or, but*) or comparison (e.g., *more, less, as*). **As a rule, the construction on one side of the conjunction/comparison must match the construction on the other side of the conjunction or comparison as closely as possible.** If the constructions of the two sides do not match, the result is an error in parallel structure.

Incorrect:    The Mayflower, which weighed over 200 tons and measured 100 feet long, **was** chartered by a group of British merchants <u>and</u> **setting** sail from Plymouth, England in 1620.

The word *and* tells us that the constructions on either side of it must match. But the first side begins with a verb (*was*) whereas the second side begins with a gerund (*setting*). In order to make the sentence correct, a verb must be used in both instances.

Correct:    The Mayflower, which weighed over 200 tons and measured 100 feet long, **was** chartered by a group of British merchants <u>and</u> **set** sail from Plymouth, England in 1620.

The error could also appear this way:

Incorrect:    The Mayflower, which measured over **100 feet in length** <u>and</u> more than **30 feet high**, was chartered by a group of British merchants and set sail from Plymouth, England in 1620.

Correct:    The Mayflower, which measured over **100 feet long** <u>and</u> more than **30 feet high**, was chartered by a group of British merchants and set sail from Plymouth, England in 1620.

Correct:    The Mayflower, which measured over **100 feet in length** <u>and</u> more than **30 feet in height**, was chartered by a group of British merchants and set sail from Plymouth, England in 1620.

# Parallelism and Word Pairs

Sometimes, two-part parallel structure questions can also double as word pair questions. If you can spot the word pair upfront, you can often eliminate at least one answer, or even jump directly to the correct answer, very quickly. As a result, it is well worth your while to spend some time memorizing the word pairs listed in the previous chapter.

You should also keep in mind the importance of taking the entire sentence into account. The first half of a word pair can easily appear in the non-underlined portion of the sentence, and if you focus too hard on the underlined portion, you are likely to miss an important clue.

It has been said that the purpose of the Sherman Antitrust Act (1890) is not just to protect competitors from illegal monopolies <u>but also the promotion of a competitive economic landscape</u>.

(A) but also the promotion of a competitive economic landscape
(B) but also to promote a competitive economic landscape
(C) but promoting also a competitive economic landscape
(D) and promote a competitive economic landscape
(E) and the promoting of a competitive economic landscape

If you notice that the non-underlined portion of the sentence contains *not just*, and you know that the *not just* must be paired with *but (also)*, you can eliminate (D) and (E) immediately.

Now check the construction after the first half of the word pair. *Not just* is followed by the infinitive *to protect*. As a result, *but also* must be followed by an infinitive as well. Only (B) fits.

In other instances, the word pair itself may be presented correctly in all the answer choices, but each half may be used to modify a different part of speech.

Incorrect:     During the Middle Ages, knights wore armor to protect **not only** <u>themselves</u> in battle **but also** <u>to demonstrate</u> their elevated social status.

In the first half of the sentence, *not only* is followed by a pronoun (*themselves*) whereas in the second half, *but also* is followed by an infinitive (*to demonstrate*). In order for the sentence to be parallel, both halves of the word pair must modify the same part of speech.

Correct:     During the Middle Ages, knights wore armor **not only** <u>to protect</u> themselves in battle **but also** <u>to demonstrate</u> their elevated social status.

You can also think of the issue in terms of modification: placing *not only* before *themselves* implies that knights wore armor to protect other people as well as themselves. However, the emphasis here is really on the fact that knights wore armor for two purposes:

1) to protect themselves in battle

2) to demonstrate their elevated social status

Because the focus is on the action, each half of the word pair must be placed before a verb (infinitive).

For an authentic example, see question #913 on p. 877 of the *Official Guide*. Only (C) places a noun (*an explosion, an intense interest*) after both sides of the word pair while avoiding the wordy and redundant construction in (E).

Now we're going to try something a little harder.

Incorrect:    In the early 1920s, a time when new technologies revolutionized leisure activities, the music business became a major sector of the entertainment industry by **producing** millions of dollars worth of goods <u>and</u> **it began** to exert a strong influence on popular culture.

This sentence is quite long, but we can simplify it slightly by removing the non-essential clause:

Incorrect:    In the early 1920s…the music business became a major sector of the entertainment industry by **producing** millions of dollars worth of goods <u>and</u> **it began** to exert a strong influence on popular culture.

As in the previous example, the construction on either side of the conjunction *and* must be the same. So next we want to look at the construction of the items on either side of the conjunction. The sentence tells us that the music business became a major sector of the entertainment industry by doing two things:

1)  **producing** (gerund) millions of dollars worth of goods

2)  **it began** (pronoun + noun) to exert a strong influence on popular culture

Clearly, the two sides do not match.

In order to make the two sides parallel, and to make the second side work grammatically after *by*, we must make the second side begin with a gerund as well.

Correct:    In the early 1920s…the music business became a major sector of the entertainment industry by **producing** millions of dollars worth of goods and **beginning** to exert a strong influence on popular culture.

But wait! What if you were to see this sentence accompanied by the following set of answer choices?

In the early 1920s, a time when new technologies were revolutionizing leisure activities, the music business became a major sector of the entertainment industry by producing millions of dollars worth of goods and <u>it began to exert a strong influence on popular culture</u>.

(A)  it began to exert a strong influence on popular culture
(B)  began in exerting a strong influence on popular culture
(C)  beginning that a strong influence on popular culture was exerted
(D)  began to exert a strong influence on popular culture
(E)  beginning that popular culture should have a strong influence exerted on it

If you went through the steps outlined above, you would most likely narrow the answer choices down to (C) and (E) right away because you would assume that the correct answer contained a gerund.

Upon closer inspection, however, neither of those answers works particularly well. Both contain the construction *beginning that…*, which is awkward and ungrammatical. In standard English, the verb *begin* can be followed by either a gerund (*began exerting*) or an infinitive (*began to exert*), but not by the word *that*.

So now what do you do? You've understood the question, worked through it logically, determined the information the right answer must contain… But the answers with that information clearly don't work.

**At this point, you must resist the temptation to pick an answer with an ungrammatical construction simply because a different part of that answer is acceptable. Rather, you must be willing to go back and reconsider your initial assumption about the error.**

Take another look at the original sentence. We're going to use the simplified version for the sake of clarity.

> In the early 1920s…the music business **became** a major sector of the entertainment industry by producing millions of dollars worth of goods and **it began** to exert a strong influence on popular culture.

If you back up all the way to the beginning of the clause and read the sentence very carefully, you'll find that there is actually one other verb that the verb in the underlined portion can be made parallel to: *became*.

If the sentence is read this way, the phrase *by producing millions of dollars worth of goods* becomes part of the <u>first</u> item in the list: *…became a major sector of the entertainment industry by producing millions of dollars worth of goods.*

Because the first item begins with a verb in the simple past (*became*), the second item must also begin with verb in the simple past (*began*).

So instead of this:

> In the early 1920s…the music business **became** a major sector of the entertainment industry by
>
> 1) **producing** millions of dollars worth of goods
>
> 2) **beginning** to exert a strong influence on popular culture

We get this:

> In the early 1920s…the music business
>
> 1) **became** a major sector of the entertainment industry by **producing** millions of dollars worth of goods
>
> 2) **began** to exert a strong influence on popular culture

Now we're going to look back at the remaining choices:

> In the early 1920s…the music business **became** a major sector of the entertainment industry by producing millions of dollars worth of goods and <u>it **began** to exert a strong influence on popular culture</u>.
>
> (A)  it began to exert a strong influence on popular culture
> (B)  began in exerting a strong influence on popular culture
> (D)  began to exert a strong influence on popular culture

(A) is incorrect because the lack of a comma before *it* creates a run-on sentence, and because the inclusion of that pronoun before *began* is unnecessary and slightly awkward. In (B), *began in exerting* is not idiomatic. That leaves (D), which correctly creates a parallel construction.

## Parallel Structure with Verbs

Parallel structure questions involving verbs are generally straightforward: the verb on one side of the conjunction must match the verb on the other side of the conjunction.

Incorrect:     Researchers are struggling to explain why some groups of patients <u>have responded</u> well to the new course of treatment while, in contrast, other groups **are/do not**.

Correct:       Researchers are struggling to explain why some groups of patients <u>have responded</u> well to the new course of treatment while, in contrast, other groups **have not**.

Because the verb *have* is used earlier in the sentence, the same verb should be used at the end of the sentence as well. Pretty straightforward, right?

Now, consider this pair of sentences. It's almost the same, but there's a slight twist.

Incorrect:     Researchers have long struggled to explain why some groups of patients <u>do</u> respond well to a particular course of treatment while, in contrast, other groups **have not**.

Correct:       Researchers have long struggled to explain why some groups of patients <u>do</u> respond well to a particular course of treatment while, in contrast, other groups **do not**.

It is also correct to omit the first *do*.

Correct:       Researchers have long struggled to explain why some groups of patients <u>respond</u> well to a particular course of treatment while, in contrast, other groups **do not**.

In this case, the phrase *do not* serves as a shortened substitute for the complete phrase *...other groups do not respond well*. It is unnecessary to repeat the verb *respond* in order to maintain parallel structure.

Sometimes, parallel structure questions involving verbs may also have correct answers that contain two different forms of the same verb. Often, this shift occurs because a tense switch is necessary for the sentence to make sense.

Consider the following sentence:

Correct:       Energy costs are projected to be lower this winter than last because homeowners <u>are</u> installing solar panels about 10% more frequently than they **were** last winter.

Although the sentence starts out in the present tense (*are*), the phrase *last winter* clearly indicates that a past tense verb (*were*) is required.

Alternately, we could again use a form of the verb *do* to rewrite the sentence.

Correct:       Energy costs are projected to be lower this winter than last because homeowners <u>are</u> installing solar panels about 10% more frequently than they **did** last winter.

In this case, *did* serves as a shortened substitute for the phrase *...more frequently than they installed solar panels last winter*.

Note that in normal circumstances, *did* is the only verb that can be used to substitute for a <u>different</u> verb while maintaining parallel structure. On the GMAT, you are likely to see various other verbs appear in incorrect answer choices.

For example, consider the following question:

> While "super centenarians," people who live to be well
> over 100 years old, eventually succumb to a variety of
> age-related maladies, such individuals resist illness until far
> later in life than most people <u>have</u>.

(A) have
(B) would
(C) are
(D) do
(E) could

The word *than* indicates a comparison between people who resist illness until extremely late in life and people who **do not** resist illness until extremely late in life. If we were to "expand" the second side of the comparison, we could rewrite it as *...until far later in life than other people resist illness*. The only verb that can replace *resist* is *do*, making (D) correct.

## Parallel Structure with Prepositions

When parallel structure involves word pairs, the construction after the first half of the word pair must match the construction after the second half. Often, each half of the word pair will be followed by a preposition. When this is the case, the same preposition should be used both times.

| Incorrect: | As one of the greatest American dancers and choreographers of the twentieth century, Martha Graham was praised <u>both</u> **for** the brilliance of her technique <u>and</u> **in** the vividness and intensity of her movements. |
|---|---|
| Correct: | As one of the greatest American dancers and choreographers of the twentieth century, Martha Graham was praised <u>both</u> **for** the brilliance of her technique <u>and</u> **for** the vividness and intensity of her movements. |

It is also acceptable to omit the preposition in the second item. The preposition *for* "applies" to the nouns on both sides of the word pair (*the brilliance, the vividness and intensity*).

| Correct: | As one of the greatest American dancers and choreographers of the twentieth century, Martha Graham was praised <u>both</u> **for** the brilliance of her technique <u>and</u> the vividness and intensity of her movements. |
|---|---|

When a sentence involves two verbs that require different prepositions, however, the appropriate preposition must follow each verb. A preposition cannot "apply" to a verb that it does not idiomatically follow.

| Incorrect: | Car dealers are showing scant **interest or enthusiasm <u>for</u>** electric cars, despite widespread popular support and governmental pledges to fund development of new automotive technologies. |
|---|---|
| Correct: | Car dealers are showing scant **interest <u>in</u> or enthusiasm <u>for</u>** electric cars, despite widespread popular support and governmental pledges to fund development of new automotive technologies. |

Because it is incorrect to say *interest for*, the preposition *in* must be added after *interest*.

## Parallel Structure with Adjectives

As is true for parallel structure with prepositions, two adjectives can be paired with a single (linking) verb, making it **unnecessary** to repeat the verb for the second item. This construction falls into the category of "sounds wrong but is perfectly acceptable."

Correct:    After waiting more than an hour for the candidate to make his scheduled appearance, the voters **grew** impatient and the reporters irritated.

In the above sentence, the verb *grew* "applies" to the second adjective, *irritated*, as well as the first, *impatient*. Most people's inclination, however, would be to rewrite the sentence as follows:

Correct:    After waiting more than an hour for the candidate to make his scheduled appearance, the voters **grew** impatient and the reporters **grew** irritated.

While this version of the sentence is correct, it is not inherently *more* correct than the first version, and you should be aware that both constructions are acceptable.

The GMAT also tests a form of parallel structure involving the comparative form of adjectives: *the –ER, the –ER.*

Incorrect:    The major effect of inflation is that consumers must spend more currency to obtain necessities: **the higher** the rate of inflation, savers and investors have lower purchasing power.

Correct:    The major effect of inflation is that consumers must spend more currency to obtain necessities: **the higher** the rate of inflation, **the lower** the purchasing power of savers and investors.

## Parallel Structure with *That*

This is a construction that the GMAT is rather fond of testing; if it appears in an answer choice, there is a very good chance that that option is correct. As a result, you should make sure to be on the lookout for it. It's best illustrated with an example:

> The globe's southernmost continent hasn't always been ice-bound: the discovery of fossil ferns from the Cretaceous Era indicates **that** Antarctica was once a warm <u>place, and many plant and animal species living quite comfortably close</u> to the South Pole.
>
> (A) place, and many plant and animal species living quite comfortably close
> (B) place, and many plant and animal species would live quite comfortably close
> (C) place and **that** many plant and animal species lived quite comfortably close
> (D) place, and many plant and animal species had lived quite comfortably in close proximity
> (E) place, with many plant and animals species lived quite comfortably and in close proximity

The appearance of the word *that* in the non-underlined portion provides an important clue, namely that the correct answer will also include *that*. The only option to include this word is (C), the answer.

If we strip the relevant section down to its basic structure, we can see how the parallelism works: *the discovery of fossil ferns from the Cretaceous Era indicates **that** Antarctica was…and **that** many plant and animal species lived…*

# Exercise: Parallel Structure

In the following sentences, identify the conjunction or comparison indicating that parallel structure is required, and rewrite the sentence to include a parallel construction. Some sentences may not contain an error. (Answers p. 197)

| 1. | Seeing the Grand Canyon, standing in front of a beautiful piece of art, and to listen to a beautiful symphony are all experiences that may inspire awe. |
|---|---|
| 2. | The most important reforms introduced by France in the Rhineland during Napoleon's reign resulted from the abolition of all feudal privileges and historic taxes, introducing legal reforms through the Napoleonic Code, and the reorganization of the judicial and local administrative systems. |
| 3. | The Delphic Oracle exerted considerable influence throughout the Greek world as well as in its peripheral regions, and she was consulted before major undertakings such as battles and colonies being established. |
| 4. | Supporters of legislation to ban plastic beads from beauty products claim that the new regulations would require the Environmental Protection Agency to set clear priorities for assessing the risk of chemicals and substantially increase the number of chemicals reviewed by federal regulators. |
| 5. | In addition to providing badly needed space in cramped cities, skyscrapers fulfill an important social role because they connect people and creativity is fostered in them. |
| 6. | The Euphrates River receives most of its water in the form of rainfall and melting snow, resulting in peak volumes during the spring months and volumes that are lower during the summer and autumn ones. |
| 7. | Because human behavior is erratic and driven by emotion as well as using logic, it is exceedingly difficult to predict the short-term directions of major markets, even when events would seem to be entirely predictable. |
| 8. | Except in very rare cases, photographers and artists seem to instinctively arrange compositions in order to make the experience of looking at the images dramatic, impressive and, above all, to engage viewers. |
| 9. | It is almost as difficult to find consistent information about the Fort Pillow incident, which took place in Tennessee during the American Civil War, as determining the significance of its outcome. |
| 10. | Spiders use a wide range of strategies to capture their prey, including trapping it in sticky webs, lassoing it with sticky bolas, and mimicking other insects in order to avoid detection. |
| 11. | There is evidence of vast economic disparity in Viking society as early as the first century A.D., with some people living with animals in barns and others dwell nearby in large, prosperous homes. |
| 12. | The title role of Bellini's opera *Norma*, one of the most difficult roles in the soprano repertoire, calls for a wide vocal range, dynamic control, and being able to convey a wide range of emotions. |
| 13. | Taking actions without fully considering their risks is a form of wishful thinking known as exaggerated expectation—a phenomenon that is known as "reaching for yield" and it has been observed in many areas of life. |
| 14. | The term "single family house" describes how a house is built and who is intended to live in it, but it does not indicate the house's size, shape, or where it is located. |
| 15. | Among Marie Curie's most significant achievements were the development of the theory of radioactivity, inventing techniques for isolating radioactive isotopes, and the discovery of polonium and radium. |

| 16. | Although 68 of the female delegates at the Seneca Falls convention signed the Declaration of Sentiments, a document that included demands for many basic rights for women, only 32 of the male delegates have. |
|---|---|
| 17. | Listings by the Fish and Wildlife Service treat lions in different regions as genetically distinct subspecies, a division that echoes international classifications and supported by scientific data. |
| 18. | The biggest beneficiaries of the Grateful Dead archive may prove to be business scholars who are discovering that the Dead were visionaries in the way they created customer value, promoted networking, and implemented strategic business planning. |
| 19. | In contemporary education, there is a disturbing contrast between the enormous popularity of certain pedagogical approaches and credible evidence for their effectiveness is lacking. |
| 20. | Antiques are typically objects that show some degree of craftsmanship or attention to design, and they are considered desirable because of their beauty, rarity, or being useful. |
| 21. | The coelacanth was long considered a "living fossil" because it was believed to be the sole remaining member of a species otherwise known only from fossils and to have evolved into its current form approximately 400 million years ago. |
| 22. | Many procrastinators find themselves trapped in a vicious circle: the longer they put off working on an unpleasant task, the harder it becomes for them to get started. |
| 23. | At the peak of its power, the Roman army was virtually unconquerable because its soldiers were extraordinarily disciplined and its troops exceptionally well-organized. |
| 24. | Known for her musical compositions as well as for her poems and letters, Hildegard of Bingen was just as renowned in the twelfth century as the twentieth. |
| 25. | Drawing on a wide range of influences and ideas, including modernist and avant-garde developments, Stanislavsky's work was as important to the creation of socialist realism in the Soviet Union as it was to developing psychological realism in the United States. |
| 26. | Experiments on animals have in recent years challenged conventional thinking about heredity, suggesting that environmental factors play nearly as important a role in determining an individual's appearance and personality as genetic ones have. |
| 27. | The development of identity was one of psychologist Erik Erikson's greatest interests, dominating his own life as well as in his theoretical writings. |
| 28. | Science fiction is shaping the language that companies are using to market virtual reality technologies, influencing the types of experiences for which headsets are designed and even defining long-term goals for developers. |
| 29. | Though no longer a household name, nineteenth century English biologist Richard Owens published more than 600 articles and made discoveries that were nearly as important as Darwin's did. |
| 30. | Hans Holbein was one of the most exquisite draftsmen of all time, renowned for the precise rendering of his drawings, and his portraits were compellingly realistic. |

## Official Guide Parallel Structure Questions

| Question # | Page | |
|---|---|---|
| **Official Guide** | | |
| 821 | 859 | Two-Part |
| 822 | 860 | Word Pair (As...As) |
| 828 | 861 | Two-Part |
| 830 | 861 | Word Pair (Both...And) |
| 833 | 862 | The –ER, The –ER |
| 835 | 862 | List |
| 839 | 863 | Word Pair (Both...And) |
| 844 | 864 | Two-Part |
| 845 | 864 | Word Pair (Just as...So) |
| 859 | 867 | Parallel Clauses |
| 860 | 867 | Two-Part |
| 871 | 869 | Word Pair (Not...But) |
| 874 | 870 | List |
| 879 | 871 | Word Pair (As...As; Not only...But) |
| 880 | 871 | Word Pair (As...As) |
| 883 | 872 | Two-Part |
| 884 | 872 | List |
| 891 | 873 | Two-Part (Preposition: With/Without) |
| 892 | 873 | Two-Part |
| 895 | 874 | Word Pair (From...To) |
| 898 | 874 | That |
| 900 | 875 | List |
| 913 | 877 | List |
| 916 | 878 | That |
| 922 | 879 | Two-Part (Verb, Did) |
| 923 | 879 | List |
| 930 | 881 | Two-Part |
| 932 | 881 | Two-Part |
| 941 | 883 | Two-Part |
| 942 | 883 | Missing Preposition (C), (D) |
| 945 | 884 | Two-Part |
| 948 | 885 | List, Preposition |
| 951 | 885 | List |
| 954 | 886 | Preposition |
| 970 | 889 | Preposition (Unnecessary) |
| 972 | 890 | Preposition |
| 980 | 891 | That |
| 982 | 891 | That |
| 983 | 891 | Preposition |
| 986 | 892 | Two-Part |
| 987 | 892 | Two-Part |
| 988 | 892 | List |
| 990 | 893 | Preposition |
| 994 | 894 | Preposition |

| Question # | Page | |
|---|---|---|
| **Official Verbal Guide** | | |
| 237 | 402 | List |
| 239 | 403 | List |
| 241 | 403 | List |
| 248 | 405 | Two-Part |
| 251 | 405 | Two-Part |
| 252 | 405 | List |
| 254 | 406 | Two-Part |
| 258 | 407 | Two-Part |
| 259 | 407 | Two-Part |
| 260 | 407 | List |
| 262 | 407 | Word Pair (Not only… But also), Preposition |
| 285 | 413 | Two-Part |
| 288 | 414 | List |
| 295 | 415 | Two-Part |
| 300 | 416 | Two-Part |
| 301 | 416 | Two-Part |
| 303 | 417 | Two-Part |
| 307 | 418 | Two-Part |
| 317 | 421 | List |
| 319 | 421 | Word Pair (Either…Or) |
| 332 | 424 | Word Pair (Not only…But also) |
| 340 | 426 | List |
| 341 | 426 | List |

# Chapter Twelve
# FAULTY COMPARISONS

The rule for forming comparisons is as follows: **compare things to things and people to people.**

Whenever you see a word or phrase signaling a comparison (e.g., *as*, *more*, *less*, *like*), you should make sure to check that the items the sentence is comparing truly are equivalent.

In the examples below, the items being compared are underlined, and the comparison word or phrase is in bold.

## Singular Faulty Comparison

Incorrect:     In the United States during the mid-twentieth century, **Norman Rockwell's art** was <u>more familiar</u> to most people than **Russian painter Wassily Kandinsky**.

In the above sentence, art (thing) is being compared to Wassily Kandinsky (person). In order to make the sentence correct, art must be compared to art.

Many people will instinctively correct the sentence as follows:

Correct:     In the United States during the mid-twentieth century, **Norman Rockwell's art** was <u>more familiar</u> to most people than **Russian painter Wassily Kandinsky's art**.

The GMAT may very well allow you to correct a faulty comparison by supplying the necessary noun; however, it may also ask you to fix such errors with pronouns.

Let's start with an intermediate step. Because an apostrophe indicates possession, the sentence above can also be written correctly in the following way:

Correct:     In the United States during the mid-twentieth century, **Norman Rockwell's art was** <u>more familiar</u> to most people than **the art of Russian painter Wassily Kandinsky**.

The singular noun *art* can also be replaced by the singular pronoun *that*.

Correct:     In the United States during the mid-twentieth century, **Norman Rockwell's art was** <u>more familiar</u> to most people than **that of Russian painter Wassily Kandinsky**.

What cannot be done, however, is this:

Incorrect:     In the United States during the mid-twentieth century, **Norman Rockwell's art was** <u>more familiar</u> to most people than **that of Russian painter Wassily Kandinsky's**.

Because *that of* and *apostrophe + -S* mean the same thing, it is redundant to use both. The sentence is no longer referring to the art of Wassily Kandinsky, but rather to the art of Wassily Kandinsky's *art*. Clearly, that meaning does not make sense.

## Plural Faulty Comparison

Plural faulty comparisons are often corrected with *those of*. The plural pronoun *those* replaces a plural noun.

> Incorrect: Although **the buildings of architect Benjamin Marshall** are <u>just as innovative as</u> **Frank Lloyd Wright**, Marshall, while much admired by designers, has been largely forgotten by the general public.

> Correct: Although **the buildings of architect Benjamin Marshall** are <u>just as innovative as</u> **those of Frank Lloyd Wright**, Marshall, while much admired by designers, has been largely forgotten by the general public.

It is also incorrect to use both *those of* and an apostrophe because *those of* already indicates possession.

> Incorrect: Although **the buildings of architect Benjamin Marshall** are <u>just as innovative as</u> **those of Frank Lloyd Wright's**, Marshall, while much admired by designers, has been largely forgotten by the general public.

This version compares Marshall's buildings to the buildings of Wright's *buildings*—a wholly illogical meaning.

You should also make sure to be on the lookout for faulty comparison errors involving singular vs. plural nouns and pronouns. Unless there is a clear reason for a switch in number, singular nouns should be compared to singular (pro)nouns, and plural nouns should be compared to plural (pro)nouns.

> Incorrect: The maker of the 2011 documentary *Summer Pastures* suggests that for all the hardships they endure, Tibetan nomads lead **lives** <u>no more stressful than</u> **the life** of most city dwellers.

Logically, city dwellers lead *lives*, plural, rather than a single *life*.

> Correct: The maker of the 2011 documentary *Summer Pastures* suggests that for all the hardships they endure, Tibetan nomads lead **lives** <u>no more stressful than</u> **the lives** of most city dwellers.

We can also rewrite the second side using pronouns, according to the same rules. Plural noun = plural pronoun.

> Incorrect: The maker of the 2011 documentary *Summer Pastures* suggests that for all the hardships they endure, Tibetan nomads lead **lives** <u>no more stressful than</u> **that** of most city dwellers.

> Correct: The maker of the 2011 documentary *Summer Pastures* suggests that for all the hardships they endure, Tibetan nomads lead **lives** <u>no more stressful than</u> **those** of most city dwellers.

**Note:** The verb on the second side of a comparison is often placed immediately after the comparison itself, instead of in its expected position at the end of the clause/sentence. For example, the following sentence can be written two different ways:

> Correct: A dog's ears are far more sensitive than <u>those of a human</u> **are**: they pick up frequencies at more than twice the range that human ears can perceive.

> Correct: A dog's ears are far more sensitive than **are** <u>those of a human</u>: they pick up frequencies at more than twice the range that human ears can perceive.

## Comparing Equivalent Things

You could also encounter faulty comparisons that do not involve comparing things and people but rather two things. In such cases, you must make sure that the two things being compared are truly equivalent.

Incorrect:      **Unlike** <u>a train, the length of a tram</u> is usually limited to one or two cars, which may run either on train tracks or directly on the street.

This sentence compares a train the length of a tram. Even though both are things, they are not equivalent. A train can be compared to a train, or a length can be compared to a length, but a train cannot be compared to a length.

Correct:      **Unlike** <u>the length of a train, the length of a tram</u> is usually limited to one or two cars, which can run either on specially designed train tracks or directly on the street.

Correct:      **Unlike** <u>that of a train, the length of a tram</u> is usually limited to one or two cars, which can run either on specially designed train tracks or directly on the street.

## "Reverse" Faulty Comparison

On the GMAT, you may also encounter answers that construct faulty comparisons "in reverse" — that is, the side of the comparison you are asked to change will incorrectly contain a possessive construction (*that/those of*), and the other, non-underlined side of the comparison will not contain one.

For example:

> Because domesticated canines, <u>unlike wolf society,</u> do not naturally live in hierarchical pack structures, some scientists scoff at dog-training approaches that require humans to act as pack leaders.
>
> (A) unlike wolf society
> (B) unlike **that of wolves**
> (C) unlike wolves
> **(D) in contrast to those of wolves**
> (E) as opposed to wolf society

What does the non-underlined side of the comparison refer to? Animals (*domesticated canines*). There is no possessive construction involved in *domestic canines*, so the correct answer cannot contain a possessive construction either. The phrases *that of* in (B) and *those of* in (D) both indicate possession, so those answers can be eliminated immediately.

## Any vs. Any Other

When two things from the same category are compared, the phrase *any other* should be used to indicate that one of the things is better, faster, more difficult, etc. than the other items in that category.

Incorrect:      BASE jumping, which involves parachuting or wingsuit flying from a fixed structure or cliff, is often considered to be more dangerous than **any sport**.

Because BASE jumping is itself a sport, it is inaccurate and illogical to say that is more dangerous than *any sport*.

Correct:      BASE jumping, which involves parachuting or wingsuit flying from a fixed structure or cliff, is often considered to be more dangerous than **any other sport**.

Sometimes, faulty comparisons may require slightly more complex corrections.

Incorrect:    **The range of sounds perceptible to an owl** is <u>similar to</u> **a human being,** but an owl hears so acutely that it is capable of determining the location of a mouse covered by a foot of snow.

Here again, a thing (range of sounds) is compared to a person (a human being). In order to make the two sides of the comparison parallel, a thing must be compared to a thing.

Correct:    **The range of sounds perceptible to an owl** is <u>similar to</u> **the range (of sounds) perceptible to a human being,** but an owl hears so acutely that it is capable of determining the location of a mouse covered by a foot of snow.

The sentence can also be fixed using a pronoun. Again, the entire phrase from the first side must be repeated.

Correct:    **The range of sounds perceptible to an owl** is <u>similar to</u> **that (=the range) perceptible to a human being,** but an owl hears so acutely that it is capable of determining the location of a mouse covered by a foot of snow.

While identifying the items involved in comparisons is a fairly straightforward process most of the time, you may occasionally stumble across a question whose answer choices are designed to confuse you about just what is being compared to what.

For example, consider the following question:

In 2013, more than three times as many serious automobile accidents were caused by drivers under the age of 20 <u>than</u> over it.

(A)  than
(B)  than caused
(C)  than were caused
(D)  than there were caused
(E)  than had been caused

Although this sentence is fairly short and seemingly clear-cut, it also has the potential to be surprisingly tricky—especially if you encounter it on a screen, at the end of a section, after having already sat through several hours of testing.

When you first read the sentence, (A) might seem fine to you. *...under the age of 20 than over it.* That makes sense, right?

But then you look at (B) and (C), and suddenly you're not so sure anymore. You remember that corrections to faulty comparison often involve repeating portions of the first side on the side second, and (A) starts to look a little *short.*

(D) is extremely awkward, and (E) contains an unnecessary tense switch, so you can eliminate those answers pretty easily, but you're still stuck between (A), (B), and (C).

You reread the sentence, but now you can't seem to wrap your head around which items are actually involved in the comparison. Are automobile accidents being compared to drivers, or are drivers being compared to drivers, or are drivers being compared to the age of drivers?

In fact, the original version of the sentence correctly compares drivers under the age of 20 to drivers over the age of 20 (*it* = the age of 20). So the answer is (A).

To understand why (B) and (C) are so effective as distractors, it's useful to take a closer look at how the comparison in this sentence functions.

Let's start with the fact that the sentence can be correctly written two ways. In the first way—the way that appears in the question—the comparison involves only the drivers' ages. Remember that *it* = the age of 20.

> Correct:    In 2013, more than three times as many serious automobile accidents were caused by drivers under the age of 20 <u>than</u> over it.

Now consider this version:

> Correct:    In 2013, more than three times as many serious automobile accidents were caused by drivers under the age of 20 <u>than</u> were caused by drivers over it.

In the second version, the number of accidents that were caused by x drivers is compared to the number of accidents that were caused by y drivers. In order for the comparison to be presented in equivalent terms, the entire construction from the first side must be repeated on the second side.

This second version is just as correct as the first version; the focus of the comparison has simply shifted.

The distractor answers play on the fact that the sentence can acceptably be written both ways. When elements of the two versions are combined, however, a faulty comparison is created.

> Incorrect:    In 2013, more than three times as many serious automobile accidents were caused by drivers under the age of 20 <u>than</u> (were) caused over it.

Now, the number of serious automobile accidents is incorrectly compared to the age of 20. If we "expand" the sentence again, the error becomes easier to see.

> Incorrect:    In 2013, more than three times as many serious automobile accidents were caused by drivers under **the** age of 20 <u>than</u> (were) caused over the age of 20.

Without the phrase *by drivers*, the second side of the comparison makes no sense.

## Comparison Phrases

Sometimes, the phrase used to form comparisons will itself be incorrect. As a general rule, the GMAT prefers *like* and *unlike*, although other expressions can appear in correct answers. Although some of these errors could be classified as diction/preposition errors, I am including them here for the sake of logic.

| Correct | Incorrect |
|---|---|
| (Un)like | In similarity to |
| Similar to | In contrast with |
| In comparison to | Contrasting with |
| In contrast to | Opposing/in opposition to |

This idiom can be made incorrect in a variety of ways, e.g., *in contrast with, contrasting with, opposite to*. You should simply know that if answers with *in contrast to* appear, one of them is most likely correct.

> Incorrect:    **Contrasting with** household surveys, store surveys can be used to compare prices of similar items across many different locations and types of stores.

> Correct:    **In contrast to** household surveys, store surveys can be used to compare prices of similar items across many different locations and types of stores.

## Like vs. As

Both *like* and *as* can be used to indicate similarities between two items. Although these words have the same basic function and are often used interchangeably in everyday writing, they are **not interchangeable on the GMAT**.

The most important thing to know is that *like* is a preposition that is primarily used to compare **nouns** and **pronouns**: *noun x is like noun y*, NOT *noun x is as noun y*.

**Important:** on the GMAT, *(un)like* is generally associated with correct answers, while *as* tends to be associated with incorrect answers.

Incorrect:    **As (with/in)** other forms of insurance, health insurance allows people to pool their risk of incurring expenses for unforeseen illness or other medical emergencies.

Correct:    **Like** other forms of insurance, health insurance allows people to pool their risk of incurring expenses for unforeseen illness or other medical emergencies.

In contrast, *as* is a conjunction used to join **clauses**. Unlike prepositional phrases, clauses contain verbs.

Incorrect:    Health insurance allows people to pool their risk of incurring expenses for unforeseen illness or other medical emergencies, **like** other forms of insurance <u>do</u>.

Correct:    Health insurance allows people to pool their risk of incurring expenses for unforeseen illness or other medical emergencies, **(just) as** other forms of insurance <u>do</u>.

As an **exception**, note that *as* can be followed by a noun or pronoun when it is used idiomatically with certain verbs (e.g., *regarded, viewed, known*).

Incorrect:    Sold for significantly lower prices than their name-brand counterparts, medications that are manufactured and distributed without patent protection are known **like** <u>generic drugs</u>.

Correct:    Sold for significantly lower prices than their name-brand counterparts, medications that are manufactured and distributed without patent protection are known **as** <u>generic drugs</u>.

## Exercise: Faulty Comparisons

In the following sentences, identify and correct any faulty comparison that appears. Some sentences may not contain an error. (Answers p. 199)

| | |
|---|---|
| 1. | The writings of John Locke, unlike Thomas Hobbes, emphasize the idea that people are by nature both reasonable and tolerant. |
| 2. | In similarity to bears, coyotes are expanding into new habitats in recent decades because human settlements have encroached upon the wooded areas where they once lived. |
| 3. | Doctors in Norway prescribe fewer antibiotics than in any other country, so people do not have a chance to develop resistance to many kinds of drug-resistant infections. |
| 4. | Gustave Caillebotte was a both a member and a patron of the circle of painters known as the Impressionists, although his works were much more realistic than many other artists in the group. |
| 5. | As with modern joint-stock companies, the Roman publicani were independent of their members, whose ownership was divided into shares known as parties. |
| 6. | Very little is known about the ancient Druids: they left fewer artifacts of their existence than did other Iron Age peoples, and the only traces that remain are descriptions left by Greek and Roman writers. |
| 7. | Contrasting with merchants in coastal regions of central Asia, merchants in landlocked regions had fewer trade options because of their distance from maritime routes of commerce and because the aridness of the steppes made agriculture difficult. |
| 8. | Even though the university has been wracked by recent administrative scandals, its reputation remains significantly better than most other schools of comparable size and location. |
| 9. | During the period between 1870 and 1900, the United States saw an influx of millions of European immigrants because wages in the United States were at that time much higher than Europe. |
| 10. | Unlike motor vehicles, which run on a prepared flat surface but can move in any direction, drivers of rail vehicles are directionally guided by the tracks on which they run. |
| 11. | Archaeologists have long been far more puzzled by members of the Saqqaq culture, the oldest known inhabitants of Greenland, than by that of other prehistoric North American cultures. |
| 12. | A source of intense fascination for both art historians and museum patrons, the *Mona Lisa*, which has been exhibited continuously at the Louvre since 1797, is perhaps more famous than any work of art in Europe. |
| 13. | At an apparent magnitude of 8.4, a brightness comparable to Saturn's moon Titan, the Crab Nebula is not visible to the naked eye but can be perceived with binoculars under favorable conditions. |
| 14. | Company officials announced that there would be no major changes made to the eligibility requirements for the benefits package, an offering that makes the plan more generous than those of other major retailers. |
| 15. | The reproduction of ciliates, opposite to the reproduction that occurs in other organisms, takes place when a specimen splits in half and grows a completely new individual from each piece. |

# Official Guide Faulty Comparison Questions

| Question # | Page |
|---|---|
| **Official Guide** | |
| 829 | 861 |
| 836 | 863 |
| 849 | 865 |
| 866 | 868 |
| 878 | 870 |
| 912 | 877 |
| 917 | 878 |
| 922 | 879 |
| 946 | 884 |
| 949 | 885 |
| 955 | 886 |
| 963 | 888 |
| 968 | 889 |
| **Official Verbal Guide** | |
| 257 | 407 |
| 273 | 410 |
| 276 | 411 |
| 284 | 413 |
| 293 | 415 |
| 301 | 416 |
| 302 | 417 |
| 343 | 427 (Note the non-essential clause between the two sides of the comparison.) |
| 348 | 428 |

**Cumulative Review 3: Chapters 1-12 (Answers p. 199)**

1.  The signing of the Treaty of Paris in 1763 marked the end of the Seven Years' War, also known as the French and Indian War, <u>and signaling</u> the start of British dominance outside of Europe.

    (A)  and signaling
    (B)  signaled
    (C)  and signaled
    (D)  and has signaled
    (E)  and to signal

2.  Tiny houses, generally defined as dwellings that are smaller than 400 square feet <u>and often being built on wheels</u>, first appeared in the early 2000s and have become mainstream in the years since.

    (A)  and often being built on wheels
    (B)  and has often been built on wheels
    (C)  that have often been built on wheels
    (D)  and that are often built on wheels
    (E)  and that have often built on wheels

3.  Chatbots, text-based services <u>let users complete tasks such as checking news, organizing meetings, or booking reservations, are</u> usually powered by artificial intelligence but can also rely on humans.

    (A)  let users complete tasks such as checking news, organizing meetings, or booking reservations, are
    (B)  that let users complete tasks such as checking news, organizing meetings, or booking reservations, are
    (C)  which lets users complete tasks like checking news, organizing meetings, or booking reservations,
    (D)  that lets users complete tasks like checking news, organizing meetings, and booking reservations, is
    (E)  which let users complete tasks such as checking news, organizing meetings, or booking reservations by sending short messages, are

4.  So voracious is the hippo's appetite for tasty greens <u>and, when given the chance, they do not hesitate</u> to maraud farmers' cash crops.

    (A)  and, when given the chance, they do not hesitate
    (B)  and, when it is given the chance, it does not hesitate
    (C)  and, when it is given the chance, not hesitating
    (D)  that, when given the chance, hippos do not hesitate
    (E)  that, when given the chance, does not hesitate

5.  In the 1960s and '70s, leaders of the self-sufficiency movement urged their audience to return to a more traditional way of <u>life and to become less reliant on the outside world because they believed that doing this</u> would free people from their dependence on a damaging industrial society.

    (A)  life and to become less reliant on the outside world because they believed that doing this
    (B)  life and become less reliant on the outside world because they believed that doing so
    (C)  life and becoming less reliant on the outside world because of their belief that this
    (D)  life and becoming less reliant on the outside world because they believed that it
    (E)  life and they became less reliant on the outside world because they believed that doing so

6.  In nineteenth century China, the Qing Dynasty was weakened not by a single event but rather by a large number of factors, including <u>widespread social strife, an exploding population, and economic stagnation</u>.

    (A)  widespread social strife, an exploding population, and economic stagnation
    (B)  widespread social strife, a population that was exploding, and the stagnation of the economy
    (C)  widespread social strife, a population that was exploding, and a stagnating economy
    (D)  the wide spread of social strife, an exploding population, and the stagnation of the economy
    (E)  widespread social strife, an exploding population, and the stagnation of the economy

7.  Once primarily restricted to a single season, <u>some places now are experiencing forest fires as a constant threat,</u> burning earlier and later in the year.

    (A)  some places now are experiencing forest fires as a constant threat,
    (B)  some places experience forest fires now are a constant threat,
    (C)  forest fires are now a constant threat in some places,
    (D)  forest fires are now a constant threat in some places and
    (E)  some places experience forest fires as a constant threat now,

8. A report from the security firm Symantec suggests that <u>in comparison to 2014, the number of fake technical support scams reported rose by 200% in 2015</u>.

(A) in comparison to 2014, the number of fake technical support scams reported rose by 200% in 2015
(B) as compared to 2014, the number of fake technical support scams reported had risen by 200% in 2015
(C) there were 200% more reports of fake technical support scams in 2015 than in 2014
(D) there were 200% more reports of fake technical support scams in 2015 than 2014 was
(E) there have been 200% more reports of fake technical support scams in 2015 than 2014 had

9. In the early 1960s, shortly after lasers were invented, Robert Forward, a physicist and science fiction writer, <u>had suggested that it could be used</u> to push sails in space.

(A) had suggested that it could be used
(B) had suggested that they can be used
(C) has suggested that they could be used
(D) would suggest that it could be used
(E) suggested that they could be used

10. In order to protect their property, owners of historical homes are being encouraged to update electrical, plumbing, and heating systems in accordance with local code requirements <u>and insuring</u> their properties for their full assessed values.

(A) and insuring
(B) and to insure
(C) and will insure
(D) and insured
(E) and have insured

11. With a call that exceeds 188 decibels, the blue whale is often thought to vocalize <u>louder than any creature</u> in the animal kingdom.

(A) louder than any creature
(B) louder than any other creature
(C) more loudly than any creature
(D) more loudly than any other creature
(E) louder in comparison to any other creature

12. Many successful startup companies have raised hundreds of millions of dollars, <u>of which the majority must be repaid to investors and other preferred shareholders before employees receive any funds</u>.

(A) of which the majority must be repaid to investors and other preferred shareholders before employees receive any funds
(B) of which the majority must be repaid to investors and other preferred shareholders before employees had received any funds
(C) the majority of it must be repaid to investors and other preferred shareholders before employees receive any funds
(D) the majority of this must be repaid to investors and other preferred shareholders before the reception of any funds by employees
(E) the majority of which are repaid to investors and other preferred shareholders before employees receive any funds

13. By the time the Spanish arrived in Central America in 1517, the political and economic power that had erected the region's iconic pyramids, <u>and that had once sustained a population of some two million people, had vanished</u>.

(A) and that had once sustained a population of some two million people had vanished
(B) and that had at one time sustained a population of some two million people has vanished
(C) and that once sustained a population of some two million people, would vanish
(D) and once to sustain a population of some two million people had vanished
(E) and once sustaining a population of some two million people, had vanished

14. The court of Versailles was the center of political power in France from 1682, when Louis XIV moved from Paris, until the beginning of the French Revolution; not until the royal family was forced to return to the capital in October 1789 <u>that Paris again became</u> the seat of government.

(A) that Paris again became
(B) when Paris again became
(C) that Paris would again become
(D) has Paris again become
(E) did Paris again become

15. The Battle of Waterloo marked the final defeat of French military leader and emperor Napoleon Bonaparte, which took place in Belgium on June 18, 1815.

    (A) The Battle of Waterloo marked the final defeat of French military leader and emperor Napoleon Bonaparte, which took place in Belgium on June 18, 1815
    (B) The Battle of Waterloo marked the final defeat of French military leader and emperor Napoleon Bonaparte, and taking place in Belgium on June 18, 1815
    (C) The Battle of Waterloo, which took place in Belgium on June 18, 1815, marked the final defeat of French military leader and emperor Napoleon Bonaparte
    (D) The Battle of Waterloo, which marked the final defeat of French military leader and emperor Napoleon Bonaparte, and which took place in Belgium on June 18, 1815
    (E) The Battle of Waterloo marked the final defeat of French military leader and emperor Napoleon Bonaparte; and this took place in Belgium on June 18, 1815

## *Chapter Thirteen*

# SHORTER IS BETTER –
# EXCEPT WHEN IT ISN'T

One of the major guiding principles of GMAT Sentence Corrections is that clear, concise constructions are preferable to wordy and convoluted ones. As a result, the shortest answer that is both grammatically and stylistically acceptable will usually be correct.

That principle does not imply, however, that the shortest answer—or even the second shortest answer—will usually be right. It simply means that on the whole, longer answers are somewhat less likely to be correct than are shorter answers. If you are experiencing significant difficulty identifying the error in a particular sentence, you may therefore find it helpful to work through the answer choices in order of shortest to longest. If nothing else, this approach will allow you to work methodically and strategically, and to exploit a common pattern to your advantage.

Note that because answer choices do not vary too widely in length, and the differences that do exist are often obscured by strategic spacing, you may need to look very closely in order to determine which answer is shortest.

For example, consider the following:

> Lyme disease <u>causes muscle aches in its early stages</u>
> <u>and nervous system problems in its later ones, and</u> it
> is so named because the first cases occurred in the town
> of Lyme, Connecticut.
>
> (A)  causes muscle aches in its early stages and nervous
>       system problems in its later ones, and
> (B)  which causes muscle aches in its early stages and
>       nervous system problems in their later ones, and
> (C)  causes muscle aches in its early stages and
>       has led to nervous system problems in their later
>       ones, being
> (D)  had caused muscle aches in its early stages and
>       led to nervous system problems in its later
>       ones, while
> (E)  is caused as muscle aches in its early stages and
>       nervous system problems in its later ones, and

At first glance, the answer choices look like an undifferentiated mass of information. While they clearly do not all end in the same place, they all seem reasonably similar in length; nothing stands out as overwhelmingly longer or shorter than anything else.

Upon closer inspection, however, some differences begin to emerge. First, (A), (B), and (E) only take up two lines, while (C) and (D) run onto a third line. That immediately suggests that (A), (B), and (E) should be considered first. Moreover, (E) runs all the way to the end of the second line, while (B) only takes up most of the line and (A) is slightly shorter.

At this point, you might be thinking that these differences are too minor to be important; however, given that answers must always fall within a general range of length and cannot differ from each other too obviously, seemingly minor differences can actually turn out to be quite significant.

Our working assumption, until proven otherwise, is therefore that (A), (B), or (E) is most likely correct.

> Lyme disease <u>causes muscle aches in its early stages</u>
> <u>and nervous system problems in its later ones, and</u> it
> is so named because the first cases occurred in the town
> of Lyme, Connecticut.

(A)  causes muscle aches in its early stages and nervous
system problems in its later ones, and

(B)  causes muscle aches in its early stages and nervous
system problems in their later ones, and

(E)  is caused as muscle aches in its early stages and
nervous system problems in its later ones, and

Let's go in order of length, which in this case just happens to be alphabetical order.

(A) is a perhaps a bit awkward, but there are no glaring errors. The two appearances of *its* are parallel, and that pronoun correctly refers back to the singular noun *Lyme Disease*.

(B) is almost identical to (A), but there's a pronoun shift: *its* to *their*. As established in (A), the pronoun must refer back to the singular noun *Lyme Disease*, so *their* is incorrect. (B) is out.

(E) doesn't work when it's plugged back in. The phrase *Lyme Disease is caused as muscle aches…* is both illogical and idiomatically unacceptable. A disease can *cause* a symptom (muscle aches), but it cannot *be caused as* a symptom. So (E) can be eliminated as well.

If you're still not sure about (A), you can check (C) and (D).

> Lyme disease <u>causes muscle aches in its early stages</u>
> <u>and nervous system problems in its later ones, and</u> it
> is so named because the first cases occurred in the town
> of Lyme, Connecticut.

(C)  causes muscle aches in its early stages and
has led to nervous system problems in their later
ones, being

(D)  had caused muscle aches in its early stages and
led to nervous system problems in its later
ones, while

(C) has the same problem as (B); it uses *their* instead of *its*. (D) contains two verbs in different tenses (*had caused, led*), and an illogical transition (*while*).

So the answer is (A) after all. As it turned out, that small difference in spacing between (A) and the next shortest option was important after all.

To be sure, most GMAT questions will not obey the "shorter is better" rule this strictly. The point of this exercise was to show you how to analyze answer choices visually, as well as to work more strategically and efficiently when you're not immediately certain of what you're looking for.

## Wordiness

As you work through Sentence Corrections, you should constantly be on the lookout for unnecessarily wordy constructions.

Verbs are preferable to noun/gerund phrases when the latter only serves to make sentences longer.

    Incorrect:    Speed bumps, which are used in many countries around the world, are found most frequently in places where **the imposition/imposing of speed limits occurs legally**.

    Correct:    Speed bumps, which are used in many countries around the world, are found most frequently in places where **speed limits are legally imposed**.

Likewise, modifiers should be kept to as few words as possible.

    Incorrect:    Widely used by the ancient Greeks, copper was **a type of metal of significance** because of its association with Cyprus, which was considered a sacred island.

    Correct    Widely used by the ancient Greeks, copper was **a significant type of metal** because of its association with Cyprus, which was considered a sacred island.

Sometimes, however, short can be too short. In certain instances, the construction *noun + of + noun* may be more idiomatically correct than the possessive (apostrophe) version.

In general, concrete nouns such as names and places can be paired with possessive nouns, whereas abstract nouns (which often end in –MENT or –TION) cannot.

    Incorrect:    **Ceramics' production** in China began during the Neolithic period, an era characterized by the development of settled communities that relied primarily on farming and domesticated animals rather than hunting and gathering.

    Correct:    **The production of ceramics** in China began during the Neolithic period, an era characterized by the development of settled communities that relied primarily on farming and domesticated animals rather than hunting and gathering.

## Passive Voice

The passive voice is another potential source of wordiness. By definition, the passive (*y is done by x*) is longer than the active (*x does y*).

    Active:    As Roland Barthes bemoaned in *The Reality Effect*, a novel's realism is an illusion, a dollhouse in which a creator has impeccably decorated each room.

    Passive:    As Roland Barthes bemoaned in *The Reality Effect*, a novel's realism is an illusion, a dollhouse in which each room **has been** impeccably decorated **by** its creator.

Note, however, that in some passive constructions, the object is omitted (*y is done* rather than *y is done by x*).

    No object:    As Roland Barthes bemoaned in *The Reality Effect*, a novel's realism is an illusion, a dollhouse in which each room **has been** impeccably decorated.

# Redundancy

Redundant constructions, in which two synonymous words or phrases are included in a sentence, can also make answer choices unnecessarily long. While redundancy is not a major focus of the GMAT, questions testing this concept do appear.

This error can be difficult to catch if you are not paying close attention because it depends on meaning rather than grammar or sound. Answers that include it may strike your ear as perfectly acceptable; it is up to you to recognize that two different words or phrases have the same meaning.

The GMAT is particularly fond of redundancies involving **increasing** and **decreasing**.

Incorrect:   Over the past several months, property values in the city as well as in the surrounding suburbs have **risen by an increase of** nearly 5%, bringing them to their highest levels this year.

Since an increase is, by definition, something that has "risen," only one of these terms should be used.

Correct:   Over the past several months, property values in the city as well as in the surrounding suburbs have **risen** nearly 5%, bringing them to their highest levels this year.

It is also possible that you will encounter other types of redundancies.

Incorrect:   The upper basin of Utah's Lake Powell provides a minimum **annual** flow of eight million tons of water to states across the Southwest **each year**.

Correct:   The upper basin of Utah's Lake Powell provides a minimum **annual** flow of eight million tons of water to states across the Southwest.

Correct:   The upper basin of Utah's Lake Powell provides a minimum flow of eight million tons of water to states across the Southwest **each year**.

Since *annual* and *per year* mean exactly the same thing, it is unnecessary to include both in the sentence. Either one by itself is correct.

# Exercise: Wordiness

In the following sentences, identify passive and/or unnecessarily wordy constructions, and replace them with more concise ones. Some sentences may not contain an error. (Answers p. 199)

| | |
|---|---|
| 1. | Although Troy, as described by Homer in *The Illiad*, was long considered an imaginary city that did not exist, recent excavations have revealed remains consistent with some of the locations the poem depicts. |
| 2. | *Glengarry Glen Ross* earned David Mamet a Pulitzer Prize in 1984, eight years after a trio of off Broadway plays initially garnered him major acclaim for the first time. |
| 3. | Bongoyo Island, located off the coast of Tanzania, has become a popular vacation spot for both tourists and Tanzanians because of the closeness of its proximity to the mainland. |
| 4. | Technology companies have spent years developing better, cheaper devices to immerse people in digital worlds, yet they are still trying to determine how to make virtual reality into an indispensible technology that people cannot live without. |
| 5. | Although smartphone developers often attempt to reduce energy consumption by writing code that runs as quickly as possible, some instructions require more power than others, with the net result that energy consumption has actually risen by a nearly 25% increase over the last two decades. |
| 6. | Scuba divers usually move around underwater by using fins attached to their feet, but external propulsion can be provided from an outside source by a specialized propulsion vehicle or a sled pulled from the surface. |
| 7. | As the domestication of pack animals increased prehistoric peoples' capacity for carrying heavier loads over greater distances, cultural exchanges and trade developed rapidly. |
| 8. | Though it has now been banned in many countries, asbestos, formerly used in both industrial and domestic environments in the past, has left potentially dangerous material in many buildings. |
| 9. | It is hoped by physicists that within the next 50 years, string theory or other new theoretical work will provide a solid understanding of quantum gravity, including an explanation of how the universe began. |
| 10. | Although their work is highly stylized and depicts figures in contemporary dress, comic artists can be considered the inheritors of the classical tradition because they are universally concerned with the human form's representation. |
| 11. | People who live in cities tend to eat more processed foods than those who live in rural areas; consequently more health problems are experienced by the former. |
| 12. | Historically, only a small number of educated elites were taught to read and write, so surviving documents tend to reflect the assumptions and values of a limited range of individuals. |
| 13. | In response to a series of scandals, the governing council has adopted a handful of ethics rules, including one stating that members may not divulge confidential information acquired by their position's virtue. |
| 14. | As the cost of the installing of green technologies has declined by an 80 percent decrease between 2008 and 2015, solar panels have become an increasingly common accessory for middle-income and working-class households. |
| 15. | Faced with reports of an embezzlement scandal, company executives intentionally concealed the news from both shareholders and consumers with great deliberateness because they feared the inevitable financial consequences. |

| | |
|---|---|
| 16. | Vietnam became independent from Imperial China in 938 AD following the Battle of Bach Dang River, with consecutive Vietnamese royal dynasties flourishing one after the other as the nation expanded geographically and politically into Southeast Asia. |
| 17. | Province House, home to royal governors in seventeenth-century Massachusetts, was considered one of the grandest examples of American colonial architecture because of its possessing of beautiful Tudor-style chimneystacks. |
| 18. | Heart disease's high rates are often blamed on modern diets and sedentary habits, but mummies of ancient people, who ate "natural" food and stayed active, also reveal signs of arterial plaque. |
| 19. | People with more bodily awareness tend have reactions of a greater intensity to emotive pictures and to report being more affected by the images; they are also better at describing their feelings. |
| 20. | Although eighteenth century European sailors and naval surgeons were convinced that citrus fruits could cure scurvy, the evidence did not conform to current theories of disease and was therefore dismissed by classically trained physicians, who rejected it. |

# Official Guide Wordiness Questions

| Question # | Page | Question # | Page |
|---|---|---|---|
| **Official Guide** | | **Official Verbal Guide** | |
| 833 | 862 | 239 | 403 |
| 837 | 863 (Passive Required) | 244 | 404 |
| 852 | 866 | 248 | 405 |
| 853 | 866 | 250 | 405 |
| 857 | 867 | 254 | 406 |
| 858 | 867 | 244 | 404 |
| 861 | 867 | 248 | 405 |
| 863 | 868 | 254 | 406 |
| 865 | 868 | 259 | 407 |
| 878 | 870 | 272 | 410 |
| 885 | 872 | 287 | 414 |
| 887 | 872 | 306 | 418 (Shorter Isn't Better) |
| 889 | 873 | 307 | 418 |
| 890 | 873 | 312 | 419 |
| 893 | 873 | 314 | 420 (Passive Required) |
| 894 | 874 | 316 | 420 |
| 906 | 876 (Shorter Isn't Better) | 319 | 421 |
| 919 | 879 | 337 | 425 |
| 924 | 879 | | |
| 929 | 880 | | |
| 961 | 887 | | |
| 963 | 888 | | |
| 977 | 890 | | |
| 991 | 893 (Passive Required) | | |

*Chapter Fourteen*

# PARTICIPLES AND GERUNDS
# (GOOD –ING, BAD –ING)

Gerunds and present participles are created by adding –ING to verbs (*going, doing, occurring*). Although the two forms are identical in appearance, they have different functions.

**Gerund –** verb acting as a noun

**Participle –** verb acting as an adjective

Although you do not need to know the formal definitions of these parts of speech for the GMAT, you do need to have a practical understanding of them in order to identify common types of correct and incorrect answers.

**Gerunds** (particularly BEING) are often used to create awkward and un-idiomatic constructions, as well as fragments, and are frequently included in **incorrect answers**.

In contrast, **present participles** are often used to join clauses cleanly and concisely. They are frequently included in **correct answers**.

For example, consider the following two sentences.

Gerund:    Because meteorologists are predicting **of their being** fierce storms during the upcoming season, residents of coastal areas are bracing for floods by stockpiling sandbags and rushing to buy insurance.

Participle:    Meteorologists are predicting that there will be fierce storms during the upcoming season, **prompting** residents of coastal areas to brace for floods by stockpiling sandbags and rushing to buy insurance.

Although both of the above sentences contain –ING words, those words have different functions.

In the first version of the sentence, the gerund phrase *predicting of their being* is exceedingly awkward and un-colloquial. (The correct phrase is *predict that there will be*.)

In contrast, the participle *prompting* in the second sentence serves to join the two parts of the sentence cleanly, and is grammatically and idiomatically acceptable.

In the following pages, we're going to look more in-depth at errors involving gerunds and participles.

## A. Gerunds

Some constructions including gerunds are incorrect not for any grammatical reason, but simply because they are unnecessarily wordy. For example, compare the beginnings of the two sentences below.

Incorrect:   **Being that he was** a member of the first Viennese school, Mozart, along with Haydn and Beethoven, set the course for the development of classical music well into the nineteenth century.

Correct:   **As** a member of the first Viennese school, Mozart, along with Haydn and Beethoven, set the course for the development of classical music well into the nineteenth century.

Many common gerund phrases have clearer, more concise counterparts that should be used whenever possible.

| Wordy | Concise |
|---|---|
| Being that | Because/As |
| Because of (her/him) being | Because she/he was |
| Despite (her/him) being<br>In spite of (her/him) being | Although she/he was |
| For the purpose of going | (In order) to go |

In some instances, you may also need to replace a gerund with its more idiomatically correct noun form.

Incorrect:   Mobile phone manufacturers' **trying** to make their products more appealing by implementing new forms of technology has led to great innovations in phone development.

Correct:   Mobile phone manufacturers' **attempts** to make their products more appealing by implementing new forms of technology have led to great innovations in phone development.

### Conjunction + Gerund = Wrong

One favorite GMAT error involves placing a gerund rather than a conjugated verb after a conjunction (e.g., *and going, unless beginning, although increasing*).

While some of these constructions may sound acceptable to you, they are grammatically incorrect. In order to be considered a clause, either dependent or independent, a phrase that follows a conjunction must contain both a subject and a verb. To fix the error, it is therefore necessary to replace the gerund with *(pro)noun + verb*.

Incorrect:   John Breckinridge came close to winning the 1860 United States presidential election, **although holding** strong personal convictions that made it difficult for him to navigate a moderate course in an era of extremes.

Incorrect:   John Breckinridge came close to winning the 1860 United States presidential election, **in spite of his holding** strong personal convictions that made it difficult for him to navigate a moderate course in an era of extremes.

Correct:   John Breckinridge came close to winning the 1860 United States presidential election, **although he held** strong personal convictions that made it difficult for him to navigate a moderate course in an era of extremes.

Note that there are some conjunctions after which either a gerund or *(pro)noun + verb* is acceptable. In such cases, the distinction between the correct answer and the incorrect answers will depend on a separate issue.

Correct:       After **serving** as a volunteer in the Black Hawk War, Abraham Lincoln decided to pursue a political career and, in 1834, was elected to the Illinois state legislature.

Correct:       After **he served** as a volunteer in the Black Hawk War, Abraham Lincoln decided to pursue a political career and, in 1834, was elected to the Illinois state legislature.

For a list of common expressions that can acceptably include gerunds, see the chart on p. 134.

## That vs. "Of + Gerund"

Another GMAT error involves replacing *that + subject and verb* with *of + gerund*.

Incorrect:     Federal Reserve policy makers declined to offer a forecast for economic conditions, **arguing of its being** unclear whether market turmoil would impede growth.

Correct:       Federal Reserve policy makers declined to offer a forecast for economic conditions, **arguing that it was** unclear whether market turmoil would impede growth.

Although there is no way to predict which expressions will be tested, there are a handful of very common ones that you should know. Note that these expressions are generally related to **arguments, demands, and predictions**.

| Common Expressions with "That" | | |
|---|---|---|
| Agree/agreement that<br>Argue/argument that<br>Believe/belief that<br>Claim that<br>Clear that<br>Concerned/concern that<br>Confirm/confirmation that<br>Convince(d)/Conviction that | Decide/decision that<br>Demand that<br>Dictate that<br>Doubt/doubtful that<br>Emphasize/emphasis that<br>Ensure that<br>Estimate/estimation that<br>Explain/explanation that | Hypothesize/hypothesis that<br>Insist/insistence that<br>Predict/prediction that<br>Require/requirement that<br>Stipulate/stipulation that<br>Suggest/suggestion that<br>The reason is that |

Note that some of these verbs/nouns may be followed by various prepositions in different contexts (e.g., *insist* can be followed either by *that* or *on*); however, they should not be followed by *of + gerund*.

If you encounter a set of answer choices split between *that* and *of + gerund*, and are unable to identify the correct version by ear, you should work from the assumption that choices containing *that* are more likely to be correct.

## So when is it ok to use a gerund...?

When idiomatic usage requires one.

Incorrect: With the aid of 10,000 reinforcement troops, the Spanish city of Cádiz earned the distinction **to be** the only city in continental Europe to survive a siege by Napoleon.

Correct: With the aid of 10,000 reinforcement troops, the Spanish city of Cádiz earned the distinction **of being** the only city in continental Europe to survive a siege by Napoleon.

To preserve parallel structure.

Incorrect: Large fires, far from <u>destroying</u> forests and **to hinder** plant growth, can act as catalysts that simulate biodiversity and promote ecological health throughout an ecosystem.

Correct: Large fires, far from <u>destroying</u> forests and **hindering** plant growth, can act as catalysts that simulate biodiversity and promote ecological health throughout an ecosystem.

To indicate method or means.

Incorrect: The nineteenth century French author Gustave Flaubert attempted to achieve stylistic perfection in his **novels, and he rewrote** each sentence as many as 10 times.

Correct: The nineteenth century French author Gustave Flaubert attempted to achieve stylistic perfection in his novels **by rewriting** each sentence as many as 10 times.

## B. Present Participles

Present participles can be used in two main ways:

1) They can be placed **before a noun**.

2) They can **begin a participial phrase**.

Although the GMAT is primarily concerned with the latter usage, you should be familiar with the former simply to know that it is acceptable and does not affect whether an answer is correct or incorrect.

### Before a noun

Correct:    Although it lacks traditional circus elements such as animals and clowns, Cirque du Soleil is regarded by both audiences and critics as a **thrilling** spectacle.

In the above sentence, the participle *thrilling* modifies the noun *spectacle*. It acts exactly like a normal adjective and does nothing to make the sentence unnecessarily wordy.

To reiterate: the use of a participle in this way has no bearing on whether an answer choice is correct or incorrect.

### Begin a participial phrase

When a participial phrase occurs at the beginning of a sentence, it is typically used to describe the subject, as in the example below.

Correct:    **Rejecting** a quiet life in Norway, Roald Amundsen chose to seek his fortune at sea and became the first person to reach both the North and South Poles.

When a participial phrase appears in the middle of a sentence, it is often used to replace a pronoun that lacks a referent, or to replace a passive and awkward construction. (A participial phrase may also be used to correct a comma splice, but that error is rare on the GMAT.) **To reiterate, this usage tends to appear in correct answers.**

Incorrect:    In the fourteenth century, the bubonic plague devastated the working population of Europe, **which** caused wages to rise and the economic power of the middle class to increase.

To review, *which* must refer to the (pro)noun that immediately precedes it. Here, the noun (*Europe*) is not the logical referent of *which*. The devastation caused by the bubonic plague, not Europe itself, led to the rise of the middle class.

The problem is that the noun *devastation* does not appear, only the verb *devastated*. Because a verb cannot act as a referent, *which* has no referent.

It is possible to correct this error by replacing *which* with a participle.

Correct:    In the fourteenth century, the bubonic plague devastated the working population of Europe, **causing** wages to rise and the economic power of the middle class to increase.

Note that the transitions *thus* and *thereby* are also commonly placed before participles when the second clause describes a result of the first clause.

Correct:    In the fourteenth century, the bubonic plague devastated the working population of Europe, **thus/thereby causing** wages to rise and the economic power of the middle class to increase.

You should, however, be on the lookout for constructions that attempt to replace a main verb with a participle. Note that when sentences are long and complex (and often jumbled), you can easily get distracted trying to figure out just what is being said and overlook the fact that a main verb is missing.

Incorrect:     Beads from beauty products and other microplastic **debris, having** a detrimental effect on fish and other creatures that studies suggest such waste can affect animals higher up in the food chain as well.

Correct:       Beads from beauty products and other microplastic **debris have** a detrimental effect on fish and other creatures, and studies suggest that such waste can affect animals higher up in the food chain as well.

## Eliminate a Passive Construction

Incorrect:     The notion that Shakespeare did not revise his works is logical, **and an explanation is therefore provided** for his ability to direct, write, and perform in multiple plays each year.

Correct:       The notion that Shakespeare did not revise his works is logical, **providing** an explanation for his ability to direct, write, and perform in multiple plays each year.

## Eliminate a Comma Splice

To reiterate, this error appears rarely on the GMAT, but you may occasionally encounter answers that incorrectly use only a comma to separate two independent clauses.

Incorrect:     The notion that Shakespeare did not revise his works is logical, **it provides** an explanation for his ability to direct, write, and perform in multiple plays each year.

Correct:       The notion that Shakespeare did not revise his works is logical, **providing** an explanation for his ability to direct, write, and perform in multiple plays each year.

## Form a Progressive Tense

While progressive tenses (a form of *to be* + *participle*) tend to be less clean than simple tenses (verb only), there is nothing inherently wrong about them. If you are asked to choose between a progressive tense and a simple tense that is clearly unacceptable, the progressive tense will be correct.

Incorrect:     For centuries before the advent of movable type, woodblock printing **has been used** in Asia to create books, but it was not until the Edo period in Japan (1603-1868) that the technique became widespread.

Correct:       For centuries before the advent of movable type, woodblock printing **was being used** in Asia to create books, but it was not until the Edo period in Japan (1603-1868) that the technique became widespread.

The present perfect (*has been used*) can only be used to refer that an action that is currently occurring, and the sentence is describing an action that clearly occurred in the past (*centuries before the advent of moveable type*). The first version of the sentence is thus incorrect. The second version properly uses the past progressive (*was being used*) to emphasize an ongoing action in the past.

## C. To vs. –ING

On the GMAT, the –ING form of a verb (either participle or gerund) can be incorrectly used in place of the TO version.

In such cases you do not need to worry about the participle/gerund distinction; the question is whether –ING or TO is *idiomatically* correct in a given expression.

Note that TO/–ING errors do not depend on specific rules and must be identified by ear.

| | |
|---|---|
| Incorrect: | Though she was one of the few women of her time **gaining** international prominence, Clara Barton would not have described herself as a proponent of women's rights. |
| Correct: | Though she was one of the few women of her time **to gain** international prominence, Clara Barton would not have described herself as a proponent of women's rights. |

The TO version can also be incorrectly used in place of the –ING version. Note that when the –ING version is inserted to correct the sentence, a preposition must often be placed before it, as in the example below.

| | |
|---|---|
| Incorrect: | Deactivated viruses form the basis of many vaccines known for their effectiveness **to prevent** diseases that were once responsible for decimating entire populations. |
| Correct: | Deactivated viruses form the basis of many vaccines known for their effectiveness **at preventing** diseases that were once responsible for decimating entire populations. |

Only an –ING word should be used to set off a modifying clause. One GMAT error involves incorrectly placing a TO word at the beginning of a modifier.

| | |
|---|---|
| Incorrect: | For nearly a millennium, Egypt's early pharaohs presided over a prosperous state, **to build** countless temples and palaces, enormous public works, and the famous Giza pyramids. |
| Correct: | For nearly a millennium, Egypt's early pharaohs presided over a prosperous state, **building** countless temples and palaces, enormous public works, and the famous Giza pyramids. |

For an *Official Guide* example of this error, see question #877 on p. 870, answer choices (B) and (C).

When both versions are acceptable, the correct answer will usually depend on a separate factor.

| | |
|---|---|
| Correct: | In 1858, architects Frederick Law Olmsted and Calvert Vaux won the commission to improve and expand Manhattan's Central Park, and they <u>began</u> **to renovate** the park that same year. |
| Correct: | In 1858, architects Frederick Law Olmsted and Calvert Vaux won the commission to improve and expand Manhattan's Central Park, and they <u>began</u> **renovating** the park that same year. |

You should, however, note that the GMAT is more partial to TO than it is to –ING. If you are asked to decide between two seemingly acceptable answers on that basis alone, the TO form is typically cleaner and more correct.

The list on the following page provides some common idioms (fixed expressions) with TO and –ING. (Note that idioms in general are covered in the following chapter; idioms involving TO and –ING are discussed here for the sake of consistency.)

| Idioms with TO | Idioms with –ING |
|---|---|
| Able/ability to be | Accused of being |
| Agree to be | Accustomed to being |
| Allow to be | Admired for being |
| Appear to be | Admit to being |
| Arrange to be | After being |
| Attempt to be | Aimed at being |
| Choose to be | Avoid being |
| Claim to be | Banned from being |
| Consider (to be)* | Before being |
| Decide to be | Capable of being |
| Decline to be | Consider being |
| Deserve to be | Deny being |
| Desire to be | Describe being |
| Encourage to be | Discuss being |
| Expect to be | Effective in/at being |
| Fail to be | Enjoy being |
| Inclined to be | Goal of being |
| Inspire to be | Have difficulty being |
| Intend to be | Imagine being |
| Make an effort to be | In charge of being |
| Manage to be | In the hope(s) of being |
| Neglect to be | Insist on being |
| Offer to be | Likelihood of being |
| Prepare to be | Mind being |
| Promise to be | Postpone being |
| Refuse to be | Praised for being |
| Reluctant to be | Prevent from being |
| Require to be | Prohibit x from being y |
| Seek to be | Refrain from being |
| Seem to be | Regarded as (being) |
| Shown to be | Report being |
| Strive to be | Resent being |
| Struggle to be | Risk being |
| Tend to be | Seen as being |
| Threaten to be | Stop being |
| Try to be | Succeed in/at being |
| Want to be | Used to being |
| Wish to be | Viewed as (being) |
| | Without being |

*The infinitive after *consider* is optional. It is correct to say both, *He is <u>considered to be</u> one of the most important artists of the twentieth century* and *He is <u>considered</u> one of the most important artists of the twentieth century*. The GMAT is partial to the latter.

## Exercise: Participles and Gerunds

**Rewrite the following sentences to eliminate incorrectly used gerunds, participles, and infinitives. Some sentences may not contain an error. (Answers p. 200)**

| | |
|---|---|
| 1. | Having opened nearly a hundred years ago, the Panama Canal is hardly new, but the idea of a waterway connecting the Atlantic and Pacific Oceans is significantly older than the canal itself. |
| 2. | When the Stanford Artificial Intelligence Laboratory opened in 1963, its founders mistakenly predicted of their only needing a decade to create a thinking machine. |
| 3. | Although an array of government policies aim to support entrepreneurs through grants and tax breaks that facilitate the acquiring of capital, startup companies usually turn to private financing. |
| 4. | Ellsworth Kelly shaped a distinctive style of American painting, combining the solid shapes and brilliant colors of European abstraction with forms distilled from everyday life. |
| 5. | In response to be criticized for the poor nutritional value of its food, the restaurant chain has altered its menu to include a variety of more healthful options. |
| 6. | A new hybrid approach to environmentalism, combining existing public lands with private resources and a businesslike approach to land preservation, thus restoring wildlife and benefiting citizens. |
| 7. | In 1856, Norman Robert Pogson formalized the magnitude system of classifying stars by defining a first-magnitude star as one that is 100 times as bright as a sixth-magnitude star. |
| 8. | The depicting of ordinary, everyday subjects in art has a long history, although scenes from daily life were often squeezed into the edges of compositions or shown at a smaller scale. |
| 9. | In response to accusations that Internet companies are failing to inform consumers about data-sharing agreements, one data broker estimated that more than 250,000 web sites apprise consumers that personal data may be accessible to third parties. |
| 10. | Although big vine production of grapes is not economically feasible, it demonstrates the vine's naturally being able to produce fruit in an environmentally sustainable manner. |
| 11. | Being that he was one of the most powerful leaders of his era, Sultan Suleyman I, known as Suleyman the Magnificent, was responsible for the expansion of the Ottoman Empire from Asia Minor to North Africa. |
| 12. | The combination of spiritual fervor and close emotional self-scrutiny makes St. Augustine's *Confessions* read as if being the work of a great novelist or poet. |
| 13. | According to experts, people have the best chance of succeeding at their goals when having an incentive—a financial, social, or physical cost—not to fail. |
| 14. | Because of her experimenting with stream of consciousness narratives and the underlying psychological motives of her characters, Woolf is considered a major innovator in English literature. |
| 15. | California is able to supply a third of the United States' vegetables and two-thirds of its fruits and nuts because of having the cold, wet winters and dry, sunny summers that characterize a Mediterranean climate. |
| 16. | The Sherlock Holmes form of mystery novel, revolving around a baffling crime that is ultimately solved by an eccentric master detective and his assistant, who summarizes the most interesting cases for the public. |

| 17. | In his novel *Parallel Stories*, the Hungarian author Peter Nadas is concerned not only with historical events but also with their role to influence people's everyday lives and emotions. |
|-----|-----|
| 18. | Some planets that are very different from our own may have the potential of turning current theories of solar system formation upside down. |
| 19. | Although not publishing her first novel until she was 40 years old, Wharton became an exceptionally prolific writer: in addition to her seven novellas, 15 novels, and 85 short stories, she published poetry, books on design, travel, literary and cultural criticism, and a memoir. |
| 20. | Objectivity, one of the central values of science, is based on the idea that scientists must aspire to eliminate all of their personal biases in attempting to uncover truths about the natural world. |

# Official Guide Participle and Gerund Questions

| Question # | Page | |
|---|---|---|
| **Official Guide** | | |
| 824 | 860 | Participle Joins Clauses |
| 827 | 861 | Being (E) |
| 830 | 861 | Verb vs. –ING |
| 832 | 862 | Correct Use of Gerund |
| 839 | 863 | Gerund, Participle (Correct) |
| 840 | 864 | That vs. Of + Gerund |
| 841 | 864 | TO vs. -ING |
| 848 | 865 | Verb vs. –ING |
| 852 | 866 | Verb vs. -ING |
| 855 | 866 | Verb vs. -ING |
| 872 | 869 | Correct Use of Gerund |
| 876 | 870 | Verb vs. –ING |
| 877 | 870 | Participle Joins Clauses, To vs. –ING |
| 892 | 873 | Participle Joins Clauses |
| 908 | 877 | Verb vs. –ING |
| 920 | 917 | Incorrect Use of Participle (A) |
| 921 | 879 | Noun vs. -ING |
| 924 | 879 | TO vs. –ING |
| 927 | 880 | TO vs. –ING |
| 929 | 880 | TO vs. –ING |
| 930 | 881 | Verb vs. –ING, Noun vs. –ING |
| 931 | 881 | Participle Joins Clauses |
| 950 | 885 | Participle Joins Clauses |
| 957 | 886 | TO vs. –ING |
| 965 | 888 | Participle Joins Clauses |
| 974 | 890 | Verb vs. –ING (Conjunction) |
| 978 | 891 | Participle Joins Clauses |
| 979 | 891 | Being |
| **Official Verbal Guide** | | |
| 236 | 402 | Verb vs. -ING |
| 240 | 403 | Verb vs. –ING (Conjunction) |
| 246 | 404 | Participle Joins Clauses |
| 263 | 408 | Incorrect Use of Participle |
| 289 | 414 | TO vs. -ING |
| 293 | 415 | Participle Joins Clauses (C) |
| 320 | 421 | Incorrect Use of Participle (C) |
| 335 | 425 | Verb vs. –ING |
| 337 | 425 | Being (D) |
| 346 | 427 | Participle (Present Progressive) |

# *Chapter Fifteen*
# **IDIOMS AND DICTION**

## I. Transitions

The GMAT is not overly concerned with testing your ability to identify logical relationships between statements, but questions do occasionally target this concept from an idiomatic standpoint.

Although correct and incorrect answers to transition questions may not directly hinge on the (mis)use of a particular conjunction—that is, there may be additional, unrelated factors that make the correct answer right and the incorrect answers wrong—certain transitions are nonetheless likely to appear only in correct answers, whereas others are likely to appear only in incorrect answers.

### Cause-and-Effect: Because, Due To, When

In sentences involving causes and effects, you are likely to be asked to decide between *because* and *due to*. Note that it is unlikely (although not impossible) that you will encounter *due to* used correctly on the GMAT. **But because the misuse of this expression is so rampant, the GMAT is primarily concerned with your ability to recognize when it is <u>incorrect</u>.**

That said, the phrase *due to* can correctly be used before a noun, as a synonym for *caused by*. If you are not sure whether *due to* is appropriate, plug in *caused by* and check whether the phrase makes sense in context.

| | |
|---|---|
| Incorrect: | Most Tudor uprisings failed **due to (caused by)** the weakness of the rebels as well as the power of the reigning monarchs. |
| Correct: | The failures of most Tudor uprisings were **due to (caused by)** the weakness of the rebels as well as the power of the reigning monarchs. |

In addition, phrases including *due to* tend to be wordy and awkward, and often include gerunds. For example, consider the following sentences. The versions with *due to* are considerably less clean than those with *because*.

| | |
|---|---|
| Incorrect: | Completed in the 1860s, the Neuschwanstein castle in Germany is considered one of the seven wonders of the modern world **due to** <u>its representing/the fact that it represents</u> such an incredible feat of architecture. |
| Correct: | Completed in the 1860s, the Neuschwanstein castle in Germany is considered one of the seven wonders of the modern world **because** <u>it represents</u> such an incredible feat of architecture. |

**To reiterate:** GMAT answers containing *due to* may contain other, larger errors, but the appearance of *due to* in an answer choice is a pretty reliable tip-off that that answer is incorrect.

The primary **exception** to the "because is usually right" pattern involves the conjunction *for*, which can be used interchangeably with *because*.

Correct:        Insider trading is considered an illicit activity, **for** the market is based on the principle that investors can gain an advantage only through skill in analyzing and interpreting available information.

If you encounter a set of answer choices that contain both *because* and *for*, the correct answer will depend on a separate factor. The use of *for* rather than *because* is purely stylistic and serves only as a distraction.

You should also be careful with *because* and *because of*: the former is a conjunction used to begin a clause while the latter functions as a preposition and is a synonym for *as a result of*.

Although you may easily hear errors involving *because* and *because of*, they can be (as discussed in the introduction) easy to overlook on a screen.

Correct:        Insider trading is considered an illicit activity **because** the market is based on the principle that investors can gain an advantage only through skill in analyzing and interpreting available information.

Correct:        Insider trading is considered an illicit activity **because of** the fact that investors can gain an advantage only through skill in analyzing and interpreting available information.

*When* should not be used to indicate cause-and-effect. It should only be used to refer to times or time periods.

Incorrect:      The first astronauts were required to undergo mental evaluation before their flight **when** the psychological danger inherent in space travel was judged to be as important as the physiological one.

Correct:        The first astronauts were required to undergo mental evaluation before their flight **because** the psychological danger inherent in space travel was judged to be as important as the physiological one.

## So That

Another cause-and-effect transition you should be familiar with is *so that*. When this construction appears among the answer choices, you should give it serious consideration because it is likely to represent the clearest, most idiomatic way of indicating that an action was performed in order to achieve a given result.

Incorrect:      During the 1920s and 1930s, developers in Hawaii purchased excess sand leveled from California's Manhattan Beach **so as to turn** Waikiki's reef and rocky beaches into sandy ones.

Correct:        During the 1920s and 1930s, developers in Hawaii purchased excess sand leveled from California's Manhattan Beach **so that they could turn** Waikiki's reef and rocky beaches into sandy ones.

Correct:        During the 1920s and 1930s, developers in Hawaii purchased excess sand leveled from California's Manhattan Beach **so that** Waikiki's rocky beaches could be turned into sandy ones.

## With + Gerund

One less common conjunction involves the construction *with ... –ING*. Although this construction is a general synonym for *and*, it serves more specifically to suggest that two actions are occurring at the same time. If you are asked to choose between "*with ... –ING*" and the continuer *and*, the former is more likely to be correct because it generally creates a clearer, more precise meaning.

Iffy:        The increasingly global character of publishing has caused editors to be pulled in many different directions at once, **and** authors in multiple countries **make** competing demands.

Correct:      The increasingly global character of publishing has caused editors to be pulled in many different directions at once, **with** authors in multiple countries **making** competing demands.

Note, however, that this is a case in which only the gerund is correct. Answers in which the word *with* is followed by a conjugated verb (or *that* + conjugated verb) will almost certainly be incorrect.

Incorrect:    The increasingly global character of publishing has caused editors to be pulled in many different directions at once, **with** authors in multiple countries **that make** competing demands.

Note also that the construction *with...–ING* absolutely **cannot** be used interchangeably with a contradictor such as *but* or *yet*.

Incorrect:    Hobbits are often associated with fantasy novels, **with some such creatures existing** as *homo floriensis*, a long extinct species that once lived among human beings.

Correct:      Hobbits are often associated with fantasy novels, **but** some such creatures existed as *homo floriensis*, a long extinct species that once lived among human beings.

## In Addition vs. As Well As

Although these transitions have the same meaning and can both be used to join items in the middle of a sentence, only *in addition to* + gerund should be used to begin a sentence.

Note that while *as well as* can be acceptably used at the start of a sentence in British English, that construction is not normally used in American English. As a result, it is highly unlikely to appear in correct answers on the GMAT.

Incorrect:    **As well as** being considered the most sincere form of flattery, imitation may carry evolutionary benefits for both model and mimic alike.

Correct:      **In addition to** being considered the most sincere form of flattery, imitation may carry evolutionary benefits for both model and mimic alike.

## II. Idiomatic Phrases and Constructions

Idioms are fixed phrases that are not correct or incorrect for any logical reason; they simply reflect the fact that certain phrases have evolved to be considered standard usage. Although English contains hundreds of idioms, it is probably not worth your while to devote an excessive amount of time to memorizing long lists of them. At the very least, you should not do so until you are consistently able to answer every other type of question correctly.

In addition, **some questions that appear to be testing idioms may in fact be solvable by other means, although they may not be immediately obvious**. For example, consider #961 on p. 771.

Choice (A) contains *employed as*, whereas (B) and (D) use *employed to be*. If you don't know that *employed as* is standard, you cannot use the idiom to decide among these answers. If you look at the section of the sentence right <u>after</u> the underlined portion, however, you can notice that it refers to people *who initially promoted new and unfamiliar technology to female consumers*. Logically, the people doing the promoting were the *product demonstrators and publicists*, so to avoid a modification error, the right answer must end with this phrase. (A) is the only option that places it at the end. Approaching the question from this standpoint allows you to circumvent the idiom entirely.

That said, there are a handful of common constructions to which the GMAT is partial.

## A. Whether, If, and That

As a general rule, *whether* is switched both with *that* and *if*, but *that* and *if* are not switched with one another.

### Whether vs. If

**Right = the question is whether**
**Wrong = the question is if**

In situations that refer to a choice between alternatives, *whether* should be used.

| | |
|---|---|
| Incorrect: | Bees often behave in what appears to be an agitated manner, but according to naturalists, **a persistent question is if** they are truly capable of experiencing emotions such as annoyance and irritation or are reacting instinctively to unexpected stimuli. |
| Correct: | Bees often behave in what appears to be an agitated manner, but according to naturalists, **a persistent question is whether** they are truly capable of experiencing emotions such as annoyance and irritation or are reacting instinctively to unexpected stimuli. |

Note that this rule holds even when the alternatives are not spelled out.

| | |
|---|---|
| Incorrect: | Mesopotamian clay tablets recording interest-bearing loans have established that the concept of debt dates to the ancient world, but **the question of if** the medieval Venetians were truly the inventors of corporate stock remains unanswered. |
| Correct: | Mesopotamian clay tablets recording interest-bearing loans have established that the concept of debt dates to the ancient world, but **the question of whether** the medieval Venetians were truly the inventors of corporate stock remains unanswered. |

Although the second option—namely that the medieval Venetians were *not* truly the inventors of corporate stock—is only implied, the use of *whether* is still required.

This rule also applies to verbs such as *choose*, *decide*, and *determine*. When you see the word *if* paired with these verbs (or any synonyms) in a GMAT sentence, you should automatically cross out all of the options containing that construction before you consider any other information.

## Whether vs. That

*Whether* is used to emphasize the possibility of more than one alternative, whereas *that* is used to indicate the existence of a single option. As a result, *whether* tends to be used in cases of uncertainty, whereas *that* tends to be used in situations that are clear-cut. For example, consider the following sentences:

Incorrect:    During the Turing Test, an experiment devised by British mathematician Alan Turing, a panel of experts poses questions to unseen correspondents without knowing **that** they are <u>human beings or machines</u>.

Correct:    During the Turing Test, an experiment devised by British mathematician Alan Turing, a panel of experts poses questions to unseen correspondents without knowing **whether** they are <u>human beings or machines</u>.

Because two alternatives are clearly presented in the above version, *whether* should be used.

Now, consider this set of sentence:

Incorrect:    Although origins of the koala bear are unclear, naturalists do not doubt **whether** the species descended from terrestrial wombat-like animals millions of years ago.

Correct:    Although origins of the koala bear are unclear, naturalists do not doubt **that** the species descended from terrestrial wombat-like animals millions of years ago.

In this case, however, only one option is offered: the koala descended from terrestrial wombat-like animals. In addition, the phrase *do not doubt* indicates that the sentence is describing a settled matter rather than one that is still in question.

## B. Can it be Counted?

Some modifiers are used with nouns that are **countable** (or **quantifiable**). These words are used with **plural nouns**.

Other modifiers are used with nouns that are **not countable**. These words are used with **singular nouns**.

| Countable | Not Countable |
|-----------|---------------|
| Number | Amount |
| More | Much |
| Fewer | Less |

### Amount vs. Number

Correct:        Filled with office buildings dating back to the early 1900s, Los Angeles is also home to a vast **amount** of industrial space built from the turn of the twentieth century to the 1980s, a vestige of a once-robust manufacturing economy.

Because *space* is singular, *amount* should be used.

Correct:        Filled with office buildings dating back to the early 1900s, Los Angeles is also home to a vast **number** of industrial warehouses built from the turn of the twentieth century to the 1980s, a vestige of a once-robust manufacturing economy.

Because *warehouses* is plural, *number* should be used.

### Much vs. Many

Correct:        Moving between industries can be unsettling, but it offers workers **much** opportunity to learn new professional vocabularies, acquire new skills, and form new relationships.

Because *opportunity* is singular, *much* should be used.

Correct:        Moving between industries can be unsettling, but it offers workers **many** opportunities to learn new professional vocabularies, acquire new skills, and form new relationships.

Because *opportunities* is plural, *many* should be used

### Less vs. Few(er)

Correct:        Because Antarctica is characterized by extreme temperatures and harsh living conditions, it supports **less** animal life than any other continent does.

Because *animal life* is singular, *less* should be used.

Correct:        Because Antarctica is characterized by extreme temperatures and harsh living conditions, it supports **fewer** animal species than does any other continent.

Because *animal species* is plural, *fewer* should be used.

**Note:** as an alternative to *less*, the GMAT may test *little*, which is also used with singular nouns.

Correct:        Because Antarctica is characterized by extreme temperatures and harsh living conditions, it supports **little** animal life.

# C. Additional Top GMAT Idioms

**A means of (+ noun) = a type of**
**A means to  (+ verb) = a method of achieving (a goal)**

**Shortcut:** Because the GMAT is primarily concerned with the <u>misuse</u> of *a means of* (a rampantly misused expression), it is usually safe to work from the assumption that answers containing that phrase are incorrect.

> Correct: After the completion of the Erie Canal, manufacturers located in the Great Lakes region began to rely on water as **a means of** transport.

> Correct: Because large sections of the Great Lakes freeze in winter, manufacturers are unable to ship goods by water and are forced to find other **means to transport** their products.

**Appear as = appear in the form/role of**
**Appear to be = seem to be**

One way to decide between theses two idioms is to plug in the phrase *seem(s) to be*, which is a synonym for *appear(s) to be*. If *seem to be* makes sense, then *appear to be* is correct. Otherwise, *appear as* should be used.

> Incorrect: Although procrastination is a fundamental human drive, anxiety about it **appears as** a relatively recent phenomenon, one that arose only a few hundred years ago.

> Correct: Although procrastination is a fundamental human drive, anxiety about it **appears to be** a relatively recent phenomenon, one that arose only a few hundred years ago.

Because it would make sense to say ...*anxiety about it <u>seems</u> to be a recent phenomenon*, the phrase *appears to be* is correct. Conversely, it is illogical to interpret the sentence to mean that anxiety appeared in the form of a recent phenomenon.

Now consider these sentences.

> Incorrect: The senator will **appear to be** the keynote speaker at a benefit coordinated by a group of her supporters, a group that includes a number of prominent media personalities.

> Correct: The senator will **appear as** the keynote speaker at a benefit coordinated by a group of her supporters, a group that includes a number of prominent media personalities.

The use of *appear to be* in the incorrect version implies that the senator only gave the impression of being the keynote speaker but actually was not. A far more logical meaning, one conveyed by the use of *as*, is that the senator appeared in the role of keynote speaker.

**As such = as it is, in itself**
**Thus = that way**

> Correct: Camping is an inexpensive form of accommodation, and **as such (=as an inexpensive form of accommodation)**, it is popular among attendees of large open air events, including sporting matches and music festivals.

> Correct: Although they collaborated with other partners early in their careers, Richard Rodgers and Oscar Hammerstein became a team with the creation of *Oklahoma!* in 1943 and remained **thus (=a team)** for the duration of their professional lives.

**Between = two things**
**Among = three or more things**

> Correct: Carl Sagan attributed his sense of justice to his father, who helped sooth tensions **between** <u>workers</u> and <u>managers</u> in New York's turbulent garment industry.

> Correct: Carl Sagan attributed his sense of justice to his father, who helped sooth tensions **among** <u>workers</u>, <u>managers</u>, and <u>union leaders</u> in New York's turbulent garment industry.

**Different from = right**
**Different than = wrong**

> Incorrect: Scholars believe that lowland Mayan rituals were different **than** those of other ancient peoples because lowland Mayan culture developed in relative isolation.

> Correct: Scholars believe that lowland Mayan rituals were different **from** those of other ancient peoples because lowland Mayan culture developed in relative isolation.

**Is best + past participle**

> Correct: The distinctive Scottish tradition in political economy **is best understood** as a method that aims to understand order and progress from principles of human nature derived from experience.

**Known as = have an identity as**
**Known to be = understood as true**

In most cases, both are grammatically correct, and the use of one versus the other is too subtle to be tested on the GMAT. That said, there are some situations in which one connotation is clearly more appropriate.

> Correct: Although she was unable to obtain academic credentials comparable to those of her male colleagues, Austrian-born psychoanalyst Melanie Klein became **known as** an innovator for her work with young children.

*Known as* is correct because the sentence describes Klein's professional identity, not an accepted fact.

> Correct: The hormone FGF21, which is produced in response to high carbohydrate levels, is **known to be** responsible for the body's regulation of sugar intake.

*Known to be* is correct here because the sentence is describing an accepted fact, not an identity.

**Such as = set up example(s)**
**Like = comparison between nouns**

Use *such as* to introduce examples or lists.* *Like* should only be used to form comparisons.

> Incorrect: As one of the first screenwriters to include details **like** stage directions and physical settings in her work, June Mathis helped make film into an art form.

> Correct: As one of the first screenwriters to include **such** details **as** stage directions and physical settings in her work, June Mathis helped make film into an art form.

*Note that this rule is violated in the non-underlined portion of question #846 on p. 865 of the *Official Guide*. Despite this, if you are directly tested on *such as* vs. *like* in the context of introducing examples, you can assume *such as* will be correct.

**The reason is that = right**
**The reason is because = wrong**

By definition, a reason is "because," and so it is redundant to include that word.

> Incorrect:     **The reason** the Filipino government has outlawed certain kinds of fishing destructive to marine life **is because** most of the coral reefs off the coast of the Philippines have disappeared.

> Correct:       **The reason** the Filipino government has outlawed certain kinds of fishing destructive to marine life **is that** most of the coral reefs off the coast of the Philippines have disappeared.

**The term x refers to y = right**
**The term x is y = wrong**

A term can only *refer to* a particular thing/activity; it cannot actually *be* that thing or activity.

> Incorrect:     In the Middle Ages, **the term "arts" was a wide range of fields**, including geometry, grammar, and astronomy; not until the nineteenth century did it come to denote activities such as painting, drawing, and sculpting.

> Correct:       In the Middle Ages, **the term "arts" referred to a wide range of fields**, including geometry, grammar, and astronomy; not until the nineteenth century did it come to denote activities such as painting, drawing, and sculpting.

**Try to  = right**
**Try and = wrong**

> Incorrect:     In an effort to attract more patrons, the museum is venturing into the rapidly evolving field of "visitor engagement" in order to **try and** reach everyone from children to seasoned scholars.

> Correct:       In an effort to attract more patrons, the museum is venturing into the rapidly evolving field of "visitor engagement" in order to **try to** reach everyone from children to seasoned scholars.

**With the exception of = right**
**Excepting = wrong**

> Incorrect:     During the Spanish Civil War, many Catalan writers were forced into exile and, **excepting** Salvador Espriu, ceased to publish new works until after democracy had been reestablished.

> Correct:       During the Spanish Civil War, many Catalan writers were forced into exile and, **with the exception of** Salvador Espriu, ceased to publish new works until after democracy had been reestablished.

The chart on the following page lists a number of additional idioms for reference. But **to reiterate:** the chance that any given idiom will be tested on the GMAT is quite small, and I do not advocate devoting large amounts of time to memorizing idioms if there are other rule or logic-based question types you have not yet mastered.

# Additional Common Idioms

| | | |
|---|---|---|
| Bring about | Responsible for | Dwell on |
| Complain about | Strive for | Elaborate on |
| Concerned about | Substitute x for y | Expend x on y |
| Curious about | Tolerance for | Expert on |
| Excited about | Wait for | Focus on |
| Particular about | Watch for | Influence on |
| Think about | | Insist on |
| Wonder about | Apparent from | Reflect on |
| Worry about | Away from | Rely on |
| | Defend from | |
| Appear as | Differ(ent) from | Control over |
| Employed as | Far from | Mull over |
| Established as | Protect from | Power over |
| Known as | | |
| Regard as | Engage in | Allow x to do y |
| Think of x as | Enter into | Alternative to |
| | Have confidence in | Attribute to |
| Adept at | Insight into | Attuned to |
| Dated at | Interest in | Averse to |
| Successful at | Result in | Central to |
| | Succeed in/at | Decrease to |
| Connection between | Take pride in | Devoted to |
| Overlap between | | Exclusive to |
| Relationship between | Appreciation of | Flock to |
| | At the expense of | Immune to |
| Accompanied by | Characteristic of | Impervious to |
| Amazed by | Command of | In contrast to |
| Awed by | Composed of | In order to |
| Confused by | Comprised of | In relation to |
| Encouraged by | Conceive of | Increase to |
| Fascinated by | Consist of | Listen to |
| Followed by | Convinced of | Native to |
| Impressed by | Devoid of | Parallel to |
| Outraged by | (Dis)approve of | Prefer x to y |
| Perplexed by | In advance of | Recommend x to y |
| Puzzled by | In awe of | Similar to |
| Shocked by | In the hope(s) of | Subject to |
| Stunned by | In recognition of | Threat to |
| Surprised by | (In)capable of | Try to |
| x predates y by | Mastery of | Unique to |
| | Offer of | |
| Account for | Predecessor of | Biased toward |
| Celebrated for | Proponent of | Indifferent toward |
| Compensate for | Source of | Tendency toward |
| Criticize for | Suspicious of | |
| Endure for | Take advantage of | Associated with |
| Famous for | Typical of | Correlate with |
| In return for | Understanding of | (In)consistent with |
| Known for | Variety of | Identify with |
| Last for | With the exception of | Preoccupied with |
| Look out for | | Simultaneously with |
| Named for | Based on | Sympathize with |
| Necessary for | Do research on | (Un)familiar with |
| Prized for | Draw (up)on | x is contrasted with y |
| Recognized for/as | | |

# III. Commonly Confused Words

This type of diction error is not a focus of the GMAT, but questions involving it are not beyond the scope of the test. These errors are created by switching two identical- or similar-sounding but differently-spelled words. A list of commonly confused words is provided on the following page; however, the pairs below are somewhat more complicated than the others and require further explanation.

## Affect vs. Effect

This set can be exceptionally confusing because each word in the pair can function as both a verb and a noun. One set of rules governs their most common uses, and another set of rules governs their less common uses—uses that would not be out of bounds for the GMAT to test.

**Affect** is most often used as a verb meaning "to influence," or "to have an effect on."

| | |
|---|---|
| Correct: | Consumer advocates caution that even seemingly low error rates in credit score calculations can **affect** numerous customers because each credit bureau has hundreds of millions of files. |

Less commonly, it can be used as a noun meaning "to feign," or "to adopt in a pretentious manner."

| | |
|---|---|
| Correct: | Voiceover work often requires that quiz-show champion Arthur Chu **affect** a Chinese accent rather than speak in the meticulous American English that now comes naturally to him. |

**Effect** is most often used as a noun meaning "an impact."

| | |
|---|---|
| Correct: | Benjamin Franklin demonstrated his enthusiasm for inoculating people against smallpox by collaborating on numerous studies that demonstrated the procedure's protective **effects**. |

Less commonly, it can be used as a verb meaning "to bring about a change."

| | |
|---|---|
| Correct: | An executive's ability to **effect** a change within a company depends on his or her capacity to engage successfully with key members of the franchise community. |

## Lie vs. Lay

**Lie = recline or remain.** Not followed by a direct object (noun or pronoun).
**Lay = set down.** Followed by a direct object (noun or pronoun).

| Infinitive | Simple Past | Past Participle |
|---|---|---|
| Lie | Lay | Lain |
| Lay | Laid | Laid |

To determine whether *lie* or *lay* should be used, check to see whether the verb is followed by a noun or pronoun.

| | |
|---|---|
| Correct: | Some bacteria spores can **lie** dormant in soil for centuries because they have so thoroughly adapted to extreme weather conditions that neither intense heat nor bitter cold is capable of destroying them. |

Since the bolded verb is not followed by a noun or pronoun, *lie* is correct.

Now consider this sentence:

Correct:     Ancient communities created the first bridges by taking planks from fallen trees and **laying** <u>them</u> across ravines and small bodies of water.

Because the verb is followed by the (object) pronoun *them*, the correct form is *laying*.

Unfortunately, things get a bit more complicated. Although *lie* and *lay* look and sound different in the present tense, the simple past of *lie* is also *lay*.

Correct:     The bacteria spores **lay** dormant in the soil for centuries, having adapted so thoroughly to extreme weather conditions that neither intense heat nor bitter cold was capable of destroying them.

The **past participle** of *lie* (used after any form of *to be* or *to have*) is *lain*:

Correct:     The bacteria spores **had lain** dormant in the soil for centuries, having adapted so thoroughly to extreme weather conditions that neither intense heat nor bitter cold was capable of destroying them.

In contrast, the **simple past** and **past participle** of *lay* are the same: *laid*.

Correct:     Ancient communities created the first bridges when they took planks from fallen trees and **laid** <u>them</u> across ravines and small bodies of water.

Correct:     Ancient communities created the first bridges when they took planks from fallen trees and, having **laid** <u>them</u> across ravines and small bodies of water, proceeded to walk across.

| Commonly Confused Words | |
|---|---|
| Adverse – difficult, unfavorable<br>Averse (to) – inclined to avoid | Discreet – cautious, guarded<br>Discrete – distinct, separate |
| Allusion – reference<br>Illusion – not real | Elicit – evoke<br>Illicit – illegal |
| Appraise – assess the value of<br>Apprise – inform | Eminent – distinguished<br>Imminent – about to occur |
| Capital – (1) geographic seat of government; (2) wealth<br>Capitol – legislature building | Ensure – guarantee<br>Insure – obtain insurance for |
| Censor – suppress unacceptable/controversial works<br>Censure – punish, reprimand | Precede – come before<br>Proceed – continue |
| Council – noun, governing body<br>Counsel – verb, to give advice | Principal – most important<br>Principle – rule |

# Exercise: Idioms and Diction

In the following sentence, identify and correct any diction that appears. Some sentences may not contain an error. (Answers p. 201)

| | |
|---|---|
| 1. | For decades, scientist debated about if bears truly hibernate because the drop in body temperature of wintering bears is modest in comparison to the drop in body temperature of smaller hibernating animals. |
| 2. | Some eucalyptus species have attracted attention from the horticultural industry because they have such desirable traits as providing lumber and producing oils for cleaning. |
| 3. | Roman women could only exercise political power through men, the only people considered true citizens, for female participation in politics was forbidden throughout the Roman Empire. |
| 4. | Nijinsky's genius as a dancer laid in his capacity to express through movement the emotions and subtleties of thoughts that others could express only through speech. |
| 5. | Many of Mary Shelley's works contain the notion that cooperation between individuals, and more specifically cooperation between women, could represent a means to improve society. |
| 6. | Throughout the Romantic period, a significant amount of adventurous artists and writers flocked to Lake Geneva to savor its inspiring mountain scenery and serene atmosphere. |
| 7. | Culture has become a force that may accelerate human evolution due to people having no choice but to adapt to pressures and technologies of their own creation. |
| 8. | A rebellion from the rigid academic art that predominated during the nineteenth century, the Art Nouveau movement was inspired by natural forms and structures. |
| 9. | During the 1940s, French poet Victor Segalen was considered as a minor figure; however, his reputation later began to soar, first in France and then internationally. |
| 10. | If people spend time in a room with others who are yawning, it is almost certain whether those individuals will begin to yawn as well. |
| 11. | In creating psychoanalysis, Freud developed therapeutic techniques like free association and transference, establishing their central role in the analytic process. |
| 12. | After it was announced that the former president would appear to be the convention's keynote speaker, several thousand people registered to attend, more than twice as many as had been expected. |
| 13. | Even though oil prices have rebounded, bolstered by a variety of technical market factors and some optimistic forecasts from oil producers, analysts doubt that a significant price recovery is imminent. |
| 14. | Books, diaries, and newspapers recording African-American life during the Harlem Renaissance abound, but far less documents chronicling the lives of African Americans during the 1930s have been preserved. |
| 15. | With the exception of his Academy Award performance in the 1967 film *Cool Hand Luke*, actor George Kennedy was a peripheral player, a sidekick to the star or a foil for the comedian. |
| 16. | A consumer should approach a potential tax-preparations company with many questions, regardless of if the company's employees possess formal accounting credentials. |
| 17. | Although Korean lacquerware of the Goryeo period was highly prized throughout East Asia, it was also quite delicate, and only a small amount of pieces are known to have survived until the present day. |

| 18. | The term "Baroque" was originally the eccentric redundancy and noisy abundance of details that characterized seventeenth century artistic production—a sharp contrast to the clear and sober rationality of the Renaissance. |
|---|---|
| 19. | The ENIAC computer, contrasting with its predecessor, the EDVAC, ran on a binary rather than a decimal system and was able to store program instructions in its electronic memory. |
| 20. | Early in the nineteenth century, the last of the property restrictions that prevented white males from voting in the United States were abolished, but 50 years later, the question of if voting rights should be extended to other groups—particularly women and former slaves—remained controversial. |
| 21. | Modern chemistry prevents insects from ravaging crops, lifts stains from carpets, and saves lives, with the constant exposure to chemicals taking a toll on many people's health. |
| 22. | The words "based on a true story" give marketers a hook, one that appeals to movie-goers seeking something different than the established brands and pre-existing characters featured in the majority of films. |
| 23. | Although birds are not generally known for their intelligence, recent findings have established whether parrots often possess skills similar to those of human toddlers. |
| 24. | Some global banks show an alarming willingness to facilitate the flow of illegal money; in certain cases, they even counsel financial institutions about how to evade regulators' grasp. |
| 25. | Although many traits are governed by a group of genes acting in concert, genes often have multiple functions, and altering a large amount of genetic material could affect unforeseen changes in an organism. |
| 26. | Even though the idea of layering solar cells over plastic materials to capture energy from the sun is far from original, past attempts have been ineffective because problems involving low energy yields as well as the use of colored rather than transparent materials. |
| 27. | Elephants typically live in core, bond, and clan groups, with core groups that comprise close relatives and bond and clan groups including more distant ones. |
| 28. | John Dryden was removed from the post of British poet laureate—a post that was normally held for life— due to his staunchly refusing to swear an oath of allegiance to the king. |
| 29. | Chopin's charming and sociable personality attracted loyal groups of friends and admirers like Liszt and George Sand, but his private life was often painful and difficult. |
| 30. | The mineral azurite, a mineral produced by the weathering of copper deposits, has an exceptionally deep blue hue and thus has historically been associated with the color of winter skies. |

# Official Guide Idiom and Diction Questions

| Question # | Page | |
|---|---|---|
| **Official Guide** | | |
| 843 | 864 | Allowed x to do y |
| 848 | 865 | Due to vs. Because |
| 854 | 866 | Examination of |
| 861 | 867 | Do research on |
| 867 | 868 | Fewer vs. Less |
| 871 | 869 | Regard as |
| 872 | 869 | With…-ING |
| 873 | 870 | Much vs. Many |
| 881 | 871 | Attribute to |
| 893 | 873 | Expert on |
| 914 | 878 | Fewer vs. Less |
| 937 | 882 | Due to vs. Because |
| 944 | 884 | Appear as/to be |
| 953 | 885 | With…-ING |
| 957 | 886 | But vs. With…-ING |
| 958 | 886 | Employed as |
| 970 | 889 | Try to |
| 973 | 890 | With the exception of |
| 975 | 890 | Agree to be |
| 984 | 892 | In return for |
| 993 | 893 | Considered |
| 995 | 894 | Dated at |
| **Official Verbal Guide** | | |
| 238 | 403 | Like vs. Such as |
| 249 | 405 | Dependent on…as |
| 256 | 406 | Concern that |
| 265 | 408 | Link between |
| 274 | 410 | Fewer vs. Less |
| 278 | 411 | Due to |
| 282 | 412 | Overlap between, Between vs. Among |
| 285 | 413 | Fewer vs. Less |
| 304 | 417 | Fewer vs. Less |
| 316 | 420 | Influence on |
| 342 | 426 | Is best |
| 346 | 427 | Like vs. Such as |

## *Chapter Sixteen*

# PUTTING IT TOGETHER

Before you get too excited and start to dive into the practice questions in the next section, we're going to pause and look at some strategies for working through questions that can test any of the concepts covered in this book, in any combination.

As you may have noticed from your work with the *Official Guide*, the vast majority of GMAT Sentence Corrections test multiple rules simultaneously. As a result, it can be very difficult to know where to start and how to proceed.

If you are sufficiently familiar with common errors, however, many questions include a sort of "back door" that allows you to bypass distracting verbiage and quickly narrow down your options—or even jump straight to the right answer. This section is designed to give you some strategies for doing so.

Let's look at some examples.

## Example #1

Last month, the NASA probe Cassini <u>began a new phase of its mission, a phase that will end with the destruction of the spacecraft in the atmosphere of the planet they have studied</u> for the past 12 years.

- (A) began a new phase of its mission, a phase that will end with the destruction of the spacecraft in the atmosphere of the planet they have studied
- (B) has begun a new phase of their mission, a phase ending with the destruction of the spacecraft in the atmosphere of the planet it has studied
- (C) began a new phase of their mission, a phase that ends with the destruction of the spacecraft in the atmosphere of the planet having been studied
- (D) began a new phase of its mission, a phase that ends with the destruction of the spacecraft in the atmosphere of the planet they had studied
- (E) began a new phase of its mission, a phase that will end with the destruction of the spacecraft in the atmosphere of the planet it has studied

This is a great example of a question that looks very complicated but that can actually be answered very quickly. If you can zero in on the key information from the start, you can pretty much jump right to the answer.

At first glance, this might seem to be a tense question. The various answer choices include verbs in a variety of tenses, and you certainly could approach it very effectively from that angle. The problem with that approach is that you have to re-think through each tense, considering it in terms of meaning/logic as well as the other verbs in the sentence.

So we're actually going to skip that part and focus on something simpler: pronouns.

When you look through the choices, you can notice that each answer includes a different combination of *it* and *they*.

    (A)  its, they
    (B)  their, it
    (C)  their, no pronoun
    (D)  its, they
    (E)  its, it

That pattern is a flashing red light telling you that the question is testing pronoun agreement.

Furthermore, no two choices have the same combination of pronouns; if you find the right combination, you find the answer. You don't even have to think about tense, or anything else for that matter.

The next step is to identify the referent of each pronoun.

First, what began a new phase of the mission? The NASA probe Cassini. *Probe* is singular, so the first pronoun should be *its*. Eliminate (B) and (C).

Second, what has studied the atmosphere of a planet for the past 12 years? The spacecraft. *Spacecraft* is again singular, so the second pronoun must be *it* as well. That makes (E) the only possibility. Done.

Now, consider question #950 on p. 885 of the *Official Guide*. It tests singular vs. plural pronouns as well, but from a slightly different angle. The original version does not contain any pronouns at all, but if you look at the answers, you can notice that (B) contains *it*, whereas (C), (D), and (E) all contain *they*.

Again, the first step is to determine which noun that pronoun refers to, and whether it is singular or plural.

What will *rarely hold more than one percent of the shares of any particular corporation*? Logically, it must be *a mutual fund* (singular), the subject of the sentence. *Companies* (plural) does not make sense.

As a result, *they* is incorrect, allowing you to eliminate (C)-(E). Now, be careful with (B). The first warning sign is that this option is noticeably longer and more awkward than (A). True, (B) does contain *it*, but here that pronoun is used impersonally—it does not actually refer to *mutual funds*. In addition, the inclusion of both *at least* and *more* is redundant. So (A) is correct.

## Example #2

The development of increasingly accurate representations of the visual appearances of objects has a long history: in Europe, Upper Paleolithic art achieved remarkably lifelike depictions of animals, and Ancient Egyptian art developed conventions involving both stylization <u>as well as idealization that nevertheless allowed effective depictions being produced</u> widely and consistently.

    (A)  as well as idealization that nevertheless allowed effective depictions being produced
    (B)  and idealization nevertheless allowing effective depictions to be produced
    (C)  as well as idealization that nevertheless allowed the effective production of depictions
    (D)  and idealization that nevertheless allowed effective depictions to be produced
    (E)  and idealizing which had nevertheless allowed the production of effective depictions

The first thing to notice here is that the section of the sentence immediately preceding the underlined portion contains the word *both*. That word is a red flag because it's half of the word pair *both...and*. The correct answer must therefore join *stylization* and *idealization* using *and*.

Because (A) and (C) use *as well as* rather than *and*, both answers can be eliminated immediately.

Likewise, (E) contains *which* without a comma before it, a construction that is effectively guaranteed to signal an incorrect answer.

Note that these answers also contain additional errors that can be used to eliminate them.

(A) contains the gerund *being*, which almost invariably signals an incorrect answer. Here, the verb *allowed* must be followed by the infinitive (*to be*) rather than the gerund.

When (C) is plugged into the sentence, the adverb *widely*, which immediately follows the underlined portion, no longer modifies the verb *produced*. Instead, it incorrectly modifies the noun *depictions*.

(E) contains an unnecessary tense switch, from the simple past (*achieved, developed*) to the past perfect (*had allowed*). The past perfect must refer to an action that came before a second action, and that is not the case here. In addition, the noun *idealization* rather than the gerund *idealizing* should be used, because that word must be parallel to *stylization*.

**But focusing on the red flags allows you to eliminate those answers much, much faster.**

So now we're down to (B) and (D).

The shortcut: (B) contains an –ING word (*allowing*), whereas (D) contains a verb (*allowed*). That's a major tip-off that (D) is the answer.

And in fact, the correct construction is ...*Ancient Egyptian art developed conventions involving both stylization and idealization that nevertheless allowed*. A "that" clause with a verb (*allowed*) is required. In contrast, the gerund in (B) is unidiomatic and unacceptable. So (D) is right.

Note that even if you can't answer the question by ear, you can use the patterns of the test to your advantage and make a very educated guess that the version with the conjugated verb is correct.

For a similar *Official Guide* example, see question #830 on p. 861. The non-underlined portion of the question contains *both* (*as both a vaudeville performer...*), indicating that the correct answer must contain *and*. On that basis, (D) and (E) can be eliminated immediately.

(A) and (B) both contain the –ING form *enjoying*, whereas (C), the correct answer contains *subject + verb* (*he...enjoyed*).

**Example #3**

After conducting a review that lasted several months, <u>it was decided by officials to proceed with a broad investigation into accusations that the hospital submitted hundreds of millions of dollars worth of fraudulent claims</u>.

(A) it was decided by officials to proceed with a broad investigation into accusations that the hospital submitted hundreds of millions of dollars worth of fraudulent claims

(B) the decision was made by officials to proceed with a broad investigation into accusations that the hospital submitted hundreds of millions of dollars worth of fraudulent claims

(C) officials decided to proceed broadly with investigating hundreds of millions of dollars in fraudulent claims

(D) a broad investigation was decided on by officials into accusations of the hospital having submitted hundreds of millions of dollars in fraudulent claims

(E) officials decided to proceed with a broad investigation into accusations that the hospital had submitted hundreds of millions of dollars in fraudulent claims

Once again, don't get distracted by the length of the underlined portion. In reality, only a very small amount of information is relevant here. The key is not to overlook the non-underlined portion at the beginning of the sentence.

Notice that the sentence begins with a participial phrase (*After conducting*), which often signals a dangling modifier.

Who conducted a review that last several months? Officials. So *officials*, the subject, must be placed immediately after the comma, and must therefore be the first word of the correct answer. That eliminates (A), (B), and (D). You don't even have to read those answers.

In (C), the gerund *investigating* suggests that this answer is incorrect. Indeed, when you compare (C) and (E), *decided to proceed broadly with investigating* is far more awkward than *officials decided to proceed with a broad investigation*.

In addition, the officials didn't *proceed* broadly. Rather, their *investigation* was broad. So (C) contains a modification problem too. That makes the answer (E).

By the way, that whole *worth of fraudulent claims* vs. *in fraudulent claims* issue that you might have noticed? That was just a distraction. (Both are acceptable, although *in* is somewhat cleaner.) When you focus on what the question is really asking, you don't even need to think about it.

For *Official Guide* examples, question #976 on p. 890 is a stellar example of a question in which shortcuts can be used to quickly eliminate all but two answers. Logically, the introductory phrase (*The largest of all the planets*) refers to Jupiter, so the correct answer must begin with the word *Jupiter*. (A) and (B) can thus be eliminated immediately.

The word *as* in the remaining answer is a tip-off that the word pair *as...as* is being tested. (E) incorrectly pairs *as* with *so*, so that answer can be eliminated as well. To test out (C), cross out the non-essential clause *not only three times as large as Saturn*, and read what remains. You're left with nonsense, so (D) is correct.

Likewise, consider question #985 on p. 892. If you recognize that the phrase *Almost like clones in their similarity to one another* must refer to cheetahs, you can immediately eliminate (C) and (D).

Upon closer inspection, you can see that (A) uses a possessive version of the subject (*the cheetah species' homogeneity*), eliminating that answer as well. To decide between (B) and (E), notice that the pronoun *their* in the non-underlined portion is plural, whereas the noun *species* is singular. In contrast, the plural noun *members of the cheetah species* agrees with the plural pronoun *their*, making (E) the answer.

## Example #4

In the eighteenth century, the conservation ethic evolved to include the core principles that human activity can cause damage to the <u>environment and that people have a civic duty to maintain</u> the environment for future generations.

- (A) environment and that people have a civic duty to maintain
- (B) environment and people would have a civic duty to maintain
- (C) environment and people had a civic duty to maintain
- (D) environment, with people having a civic duty for maintaining
- (E) environment and people have a civic duty for the maintaining of

Like #1, this is a question that looks like it's testing verb tense but is really (primarily) testing something else. That's not to say that the tense issue is unimportant, just that there's a way to approach this question that doesn't involve thinking so much about tense.

The word *and* in the underlined portion is a pretty good tip-off that the question is testing parallel structure.

In addition, if you back up and read the whole sentence, you can notice the construction *the core principles that*. Recall that parallel structure with *that* is a GMAT favorite.

If *that* appears in the first item (*that human activity can cause damage to the environment*), then *that* must appear in the second item as well.

Thus, the correct answer must include *that*. Because (A) is the only option in which it appears, it must be the correct answer.

For a comparable *Official Guide* question, see #945 on p. 884. As in the above example, a clause beginning with *that* appears in the non-underlined portion of the sentence (*waves that originate in the earth's crust and ricochet around its interior*), suggesting that the correct answer is likely to contain a parallel construction. If you can pick up on that subtle clue, you can immediately jump to (E) as the only possibility. No other answer contains *that*.

One more.

## Example #5

A larger quantity of high value goods have been found at Delphi, home of the Delphic Oracle, <u>than at any other mainland sanctuary, which suggests that Delphi was a focus of attention for</u> a wide range of ancient Greek worshippers.

(A) than at any other mainland sanctuary, which suggests that Delphi was a focus of attention for
(B) than any other mainland sanctuary, and this suggests that Delphi was a focus of attention on
(C) than at any other mainland sanctuary, suggesting that Delphi was a focus of attention for
(D) as at any other mainland sanctuary, which suggests that Delphi was a focus of attention on
(E) as at any other mainland sanctuary and suggests that Delphi was a focus of attention for

To be sure, there's a lot going on in this set of answer choices, but once again, our goal is to identify and focus on its weak points, so to speak.

Whenever the word *which* appears in a GMAT, you should be suspicious—usually with good reason. In this case, it appears in two answers: (A) and (D).

If you recall, the rule is that *which* must refer to the noun that immediately precedes it. Would the sanctuary itself suggest that Delphi was a focus of attention for a wide range of ancient Greek worshipers? No.

Technically, the <u>fact</u> that a larger quantity of high value goods were found at Delphi than at any other mainland sanctuary is what suggests Delphi attracted a wide range of worshippers. But because the phrase *the fact that* does not appear in the sentence, *which* is incorrect. That eliminates (A) and (D).

As a shortcut, (B) can be eliminated because *this* should be followed by a noun. In the absence of one, the pronoun is vague and ambiguous.

(E) can be eliminated because *larger* must be paired with *than*. (You could also eliminate (D) this way.)

That leaves (C), which makes a classic correction to the pronoun/referent problem by substituting the participle *suggesting*. Sometimes, the –ING form is right after all.

Note also that the issue of *for* vs. *on* does not even need to be addressed. (You can, however, eliminate (B) and (D) if you know that *on* is unacceptable in this context.)

Now look at *Official Guide* question #986 on pp. 892. Notice the word *which* in answers (A) and (E). It does not refer to the noun *year*, which immediately precedes it, but rather to the <u>fact</u> that production is expected to double by the end of the year. As in the above example, the noun *fact* does not appear, so those answers can be eliminated.

Now things get a little trickier. (B) contains a similar correction to the one given above (replacement of *which* with the participle *providing*) but creates a misplaced modifier: *almost* should not modify *expected*.

(C) might seem reasonably acceptable on its own, but it creates nonsense when plugged back into the sentence (*…but production is expected that it will almost double…*).

That leaves (D), which correctly uses two infinitives (*to double…to provide*) to form a parallel construction.

# Multiple-Choice Practice Questions

........................................................................

**(Answers p. 203)**

1. Precipitation in California is often erratic, and when arriving, tends to fall in the mountainous northern and eastern parts of the state rather than the populous and fertile southern and western ones.

   (A) when arriving, tends to fall
   (B) when arriving, has a tendency of falling
   (C) when it arrives, it tends in falling
   (D) when it arrives, tending to fall
   (E) when it arrives, it tends to fall

2. Some people contend that the distinction between an extreme sport and a conventional one has as much to do with marketing as with the level of danger involved or how much adrenaline is generated.

   (A) with the level of danger involved or how much adrenaline is generated
   (B) with the level of danger that is involved or the adrenaline amount it generates
   (C) with the level of danger involved or the amount of adrenaline generated
   (D) to the danger level involved or the amount of adrenaline being generated
   (E) to the level of danger involved or the amount of adrenaline it generates

3. Just who inspired English painter John Constable's marvelously enigmatic cloud studies, much prized by collectors, have never been entirely clear.

   (A) studies, much prized by collectors, have
   (B) studies, much prized by collectors, has
   (C) studies, many of them prized by collectors, have
   (D) studies, many of which are prized by collectors,
   (E) studies, and many of them prized by collectors, has

4. James Joyce is best known for *Ulysses* (1922), a landmark work in which the episodes of Homer's *Odyssey* are paralleled in an array of contrasting literary styles, with the stream of consciousness narration most prominent among them.

   (A) in which the episodes of Homer's *Odyssey* are paralleled in an array of contrasting literary styles, with the stream of consciousness narration most prominent among them
   (B) where the episodes of Homer's *Odyssey* are a parallel array of contrasting literary styles, with the stream of consciousness narration being most prominent among these
   (C) where the episodes of Homer's *Odyssey* are paralleled in an array of contrasting literary styles, with the stream of consciousness narration is most prominent among these
   (D) in which the episodes of Homer's *Odyssey* is paralleled in an array of contrasted literary styles, and the stream of consciousness narration is most prominent among these
   (E) in which the episodes of Homer's *Odyssey* are paralleled in a contrasting array of literary styles, with the stream of consciousness narration most prominent among it

5. By day, hippos enjoy bathing in water to cool themselves down, which might have contributed to their reputation for being relatively sluggish and sedentary.

   (A) which might have contributed to their reputation for being
   (B) which might contribute to its reputation for being
   (C) and this might have contributed to their reputation to be
   (D) a preference that might contribute to their reputation for being
   (E) a preference which might have contributed to their reputation to be

6. The starling, a bird mentioned in one of Shakespeare's plays, <u>was first introduced in the United States in 1890 and has since become</u> a significant pest species.

(A) was first introduced in the United States in 1890 and has since become
(B) were first introduced in the United States in 1890 and has since become
(C) was first introduced to the United States in 1890 and would since become
(D) was first introduced to the United States in 1890 and since became
(E) were first introduced to the United States in 1890 and since has become

7. The outsourcing of hospital workers has become relatively common in the last decade, driven by a combination of factors including <u>a desire for efficiency gains as well as the growing pressure on hospitals to measure quality and keeping</u> people healthy after they are discharged.

(A) a desire for efficiency gains as well as the growing pressure on hospitals to measure quality and keeping
(B) a desire for efficiency gains as well as the growing pressure on hospitals to measure quality and they keep
(C) a desire for gains in efficiency as well as the growing pressure on hospitals to measure quality and keep
(D) a desire for gains in efficiency as well as the growing pressure on hospitals in measuring quality and to keep
(E) a desire for gains in efficiency as well as the growth of pressure on hospitals that measure quality and keep

8. <u>Contrasting with the works of the rationalists,</u> Hume held that passion rather than reason governs human behavior and postulated that humans can have knowledge only of the objects of experience.

(A) Contrasting with the works of the rationalists,
(B) In contrast with the rationalists' work,
(C) In contrast to those of the rationalists,
(D) Unlike those of the rationalists,
(E) Unlike the rationalists,

9. Categorized as a "red" volcano as a result of the lava that periodically spews from its crater, a depression measuring 2,100 feet across and 750 feet deep, <u>many cataclysmic explosions have been associated with Mt. Vesuvius since the volcano's most famous eruption in 79 A.D.</u>

(A) many cataclysmic explosions have been associated with Mt. Vesuvius since the volcano's most famous eruption in 79 A.D.
(B) they have associated many cataclysmic explosions with Mt. Vesuvius since its most famous eruption in 79 A.D.
(C) and many cataclysmic explosions were associated with Mt. Vesuvius since its most famous eruption in 79 A.D.
(D) Mt. Vesuvius has exploded cataclysmically many times since its most famous eruption in 79 A.D.
(E) Mt. Vesuvius has erupted cataclysmically many times since its most famous one in 79 A.D.

10. The wandering albatross, the first albatross ever to be described by naturalists, is a large seabird that belongs to the albatross family <u>and found primarily in the seas around Antarctica.</u>

(A) and found primarily in the seas around Antarctica
(B) and that is found primarily in the seas around Antarctica
(C) and primarily found in the Antarctic seas
(D) being found primarily in the seas around Antarctica
(E) and are found primarily in the seas around Antarctica

11. All of the country's political parties <u>agree as to whether constitutional reform is necessary to address</u> chronic instability and other pressing issues, but when it comes to deciding what kind of reform, they can only agree to disagree.

(A) agree as to whether constitutional reform is necessary to address
(B) agree that constitutional reform is necessary to address
(C) have an agreement of constitutional reform being necessary to address
(D) agree that constitutional reform is necessary for the addressing of
(E) agree about whether constitutional reform is necessary to address

12. Even an act as apparently benign as <u>eliminating mosquitoes could have serious ecological affects because they interact</u> with other species in ways that scientists do not yet fully understand.

(A) eliminating mosquitoes could have serious ecological affects because they interact

(B) the elimination of mosquitoes can have serious ecological affects because mosquitoes interact

(C) eliminating mosquitoes could have serious ecological affects because they interact

(D) to eliminate mosquitoes can have serious ecological effects because they interact

(E) eliminating mosquitoes could have serious ecological effects because mosquitoes interact

13. One historical theory posits that an important effect of the Industrial Revolution was that living standards for the general population began to increase consistently for the first time in history, <u>while an opposing theory holds that it did not begin</u> to improve meaningfully until the late 1800s.

(A) while an opposing theory holds that it did not begin

(B) while an opposing theory holds that they have not begun

(C) but an opposing theory holds that it did not begin

(D) but an opposing theory holds that they did not begin

(E) with an opposing theory holding that it did not begin

14. Customized electric cargo bicycles can use specialized cycle lanes to travel around congested cities, <u>to outpace their fuel-driven four-wheel rivals, and delivers</u> a variety of goods and services.

(A) to outpace their fuel-driven four-wheeled rivals, and delivers

(B) to outpace their fuel-driven four-wheeled rivals, and deliver

(C) outpacing their fuel-driving four-wheeled rivals, and to deliver

(D) outpacing their fuel-driven four-wheel rivals, and delivered

(E) outpacing their fuel-driven four-wheel rivals and delivering

15. In general, the design of automotive spaces such as highways and parking lots <u>are overseen by traffic engineers, whose decisions heavily influence</u> drivers' behavior in those surroundings.

(A) is overseen by traffic engineers, whose decisions heavily influence

(B) are overseen by traffic engineers, whose decisions are heavily influencing

(C) are overseen by traffic engineers, whose decisions heavily influence

(D) is overseen by traffic engineers, which heavily influences

(E) is overseen by traffic engineers, of whom the decision influence heavily

16. Arthur Conan Doyle, the creator of Sherlock Holmes, was himself a physician, <u>and there is evidence that he is modeled on one of the leading doctors of the day,</u> Joseph Bell of the Royal Edinburgh Infirmary.

(A) and there is evidence that he is modeled on one of the leading doctors of the day,

(B) and evidence exists that he is modeled on one of the leading doctors of the day,

(C) with evidence existing that he is modeled after one of the leading doctors of the day,

(D) and there is evidence that Holmes was modeled on one of the leading doctors of the day,

(E) and evidence exists that one of the day's leading doctors was a model for Holmes,

17. Normally associated with airplane construction, wind-tunnel testing has also been applied to automobiles, not so much to calculate aerodynamic forces as <u>determining ways to reduce the power required to move vehicles on roadways</u> at a given speed.

(A) determining ways to reduce the power required to move vehicles on roadways

(B) to determine ways to reduce the power required to move vehicles on roadways

(C) to determine ways to reduce the power required for the moving of vehicles on roadways

(D) it has determined ways to reduce the power required to move roadways' motor vehicles

(E) in the determination of ways to reduce the power required to move vehicles on roadways

18. One study has indicated that if the marriage patterns of 1960 were imported into 2005, the American economy's Gini coefficient—the standard measure of income inequality—would fall to 0.34 from 0.43, a considerable drop given that the scale runs from zero to one.

(A) Gini coefficient—the standard measure of income inequality—would fall to 0.34 from 0.43, a considerable drop
(B) Gini coefficient, the standard measure of income inequality, falls to 0.34 from 0.43, a considerable drop
(C) Gini coefficient—the standard measure of income inequality—will fall to 0.34 from 0.43, a considerable drop
(D) Gini coefficient—the standard measure of income inequality—will fall to 0.34 from 0.43, dropping considerably
(E) Gini coefficient, the standard measure of income inequality, would fall to 0.34 from 0.43, a drop of consideration

19. Internet usage has become so pervasive in virtually every aspect of daily life, and many psychologists are beginning to turn their attention to the impact of constant exposure to screens on the lives of children and adolescents.

(A) so pervasive in virtually every aspect of daily life, and many psychologists are beginning
(B) so pervasive in virtually every aspect of daily life, many psychologists are beginning
(C) so pervasive in daily life's virtually every aspect, so many psychologists are beginning
(D) of such pervasiveness in virtually every aspect of daily life that many psychologists are beginning
(E) so pervasive in virtually every aspect of daily life that many psychologists are beginning

20. In 1294 Boniface VIII began his papacy, replacing Celestine V, who, having declared that it was permissible for a Pope to resign, and promptly did.

(A) who, having declared that it was permissible for a Pope to resign, and promptly did
(B) who declared that it was permissible for a Pope to resign, which he promptly did
(C) who had declared that it could be permitted that a Pope resign and then promptly did so
(D) who had declared that it was permissible for a Pope to resign and then promptly did so
(E) who, having declared it permissible for a Pope to resign, then promptly doing so

21. Neuroscientists of today, unlike 30 years ago, have access to sophisticated instrumentation that has only become possible as a result of recent technological advances.

(A) Neuroscientists of today, unlike 30 years ago,
(B) Today's neuroscientists, unlike those of 30 years ago,
(C) Neuroscientists who are conducting research today, unlike 30 years ago,
(D) Neuroscientists conducting research today, in contrast to 30 years ago,
(E) Neuroscientists who conduct research today, differing from that of 30 years ago,

22. SpaceX was founded in June 2002 by Elon Musk, whose goal was to build a simple and relatively inexpensive reusable rocket which returns into space on multiple occasions.

(A) which returns
(B) that returns
(C) which will return
(D) that could return
(E) having returned

23. Because the country has made significant progress in reducing its budget deficit, economic authorities are recommending that its development aid payments, each of which is worth tens of millions of dollars, are restored by the beginning of next year.

(A) each of which is worth tens of millions of dollars, are restored
(B) each worth tens of millions of dollars, are restored
(C) each of these worth tens of millions of dollars, should be restored
(D) each worth tens of millions of dollars, be restored
(E) each of which are worth tens of millions of dollars, be restored

24. The choice and treatment of subject matter, rather than careful attention to visual appearance, defines Realism as an artistic movement.

(A) defines Realism as an artistic movement
(B) define Realism as an artistic movement
(C) define Realism to be an artistic movement
(D) define Realism as being an artistic movement
(E) defines the artistic movement that is Realism

25. Cicero's influence on the Latin language was so immense that the subsequent history of prose in not only Latin but also European languages up until the nineteenth century was said to be either a reaction against or a return to his style.

(A) but also European languages up until the nineteenth century was said to be either a reaction against
(B) but also European languages up until the nineteenth century were said to be either a reaction
(C) and European languages up until the nineteenth century was said to be either a reaction against
(D) but European languages up until the nineteenth century were also said to be either a reaction
(E) but also European languages up until the nineteenth century was said to be either a reaction

26. The Chinese zokor, a small rodent with a stocky build and conical tail, lives solitarily underground in extensive burrows that they excavate to leave evidence of its presence in the form of mounds of material on the surface of the ground.

(A) that they excavate to leave evidence of its presence
(B) that they excavate to leave evidence of their presence
(C) that they excavate, leaving evidence of its presence
(D) that are excavated and left evidence of its presence
(E) that it excavates, leaving evidence of its presence

27. At the urging of aviation industry leaders, who believed that the airplane can only reach its full commercial potential if federal action were taken to improve and maintain safety standards, the Air Commerce Act was passed into law on May 20, 1926.

(A) can only reach their full commercial potential if federal action were taken to improve
(B) could only reach its full commercial potential if federal action is taken to improve
(C) could only reach full commercial potential if taking federal action to improve
(D) could only reach its full commercial potential if federal action were taken to improve
(E) could only reach its full commercial potential if federal action would be taken to improve

28. As an animal develops from a fertilized egg into an embryo, their cells may diversify into a seemingly limitless range of types and tissues, from tusks to feathers to brains.

(A) their cells may diversify into a seemingly limitless range of
(B) its cells may diversify into a seeming limitless range of
(C) its cells may diversify into a seemingly limitless range from
(D) their cells may diversify into a seeming limitless range from
(E) its cells may diversify into a seemingly limitless range of

29. Excepting programs like Betamax, which in the 1970s outperformed VHS as a result of exceptional marketing strategies, inferior technologies and the stocks associated with them tend to perform poorly in the global market.

(A) Excepting programs like Betamax,
(B) Programs like Betamax being excepted,
(C) Except for programs such as Betamax
(D) With the exception of programs such as Betamax
(E) As an exception to programs such as Betamax

30. Like when scientists turn from experiments on animals to ones on humans, the results of the new study are provocative but hardly clear-cut.

(A) Like when
(B) As is often the case when
(C) In such a way as
(D) Just as if
(E) Similar to when

31. In 1789, the Confederation Congress formed after the American Revolution rejected the Articles of Confederation in favor of the Constitution due to their lack of provision for the creation of either executive agencies or judiciary institutions.

(A) due to their lack of provision
(B) due to their lack of providing
(C) because they did not provide
(D) because of their lack of providing
(E) when they have not provided

32. Genetics-based drugs, an emerging class of medications, are likely be tailored at least in part to individuals; as a result, drug companies will probably try and charge patients made-to-measure prices.

(A) will probably try and charge
(B) will probably try to charge
(C) probably try and charge
(D) probably try charging
(E) have probably tried to charge

33. Film studies, an academic discipline that deals with various theoretical, historical, and critical approaches to movie-making, is less concerned with advancing proficiency in film production than to explore the cultural, economic, and political implications of the cinema.

(A) than to explore
(B) than in the exploring of
(C) than with the exploration of
(D) than it is with exploring
(E) than in the exploration of

34. Shigeru Miyamoto joined Nintendo in the late 1970s and became known as the creator of some of the best-selling video games of all time, a period when the company was beginning its foray into electronic entertainment and abandoning the production of playing cards, which it had manufactured since 1889.

(A) Shigeru Miyamoto joined Nintendo in the late 1970s and became known as the creator of some of the best-selling video games of all time,
(B) Shigeru Miyamoto joined Nintendo in the late 1970s, becoming known as the creator of some of the best-selling video games of all time,
(C) Shigeru Miyamoto joined Nintendo in the late 1970s to become known as the creator of some of the best-selling video games of all time,
(D) Shigeru Miyamoto, who became known as the creator of some of the best-selling video games of all time, and joined Nintendo in the late 1970s,
(E) Shigeru Miyamoto, who became known as the creator of some of the best-selling video games of all time, joined Nintendo in the late 1970s,

35. During the Renaissance, glass products made on the island of Murano could only be crafted according to traditional techniques, and local artisans were forbidden to leave and sell their creations elsewhere.

(A) During the Renaissance, glass products made on the island of Murano could only be crafted according to traditional techniques, and local artisans were forbidden to leave and sell their creations elsewhere.
(B) Glass products, which were made on the island of Murano, could only be crafted during the Renaissance according to traditional techniques, and it was forbidden that local artisans leave and sell their creations elsewhere.
(C) The crafting of glass products could only be done according to traditional techniques during the Renaissance on the island of Murano, and local artisans were forbidden in leaving and selling their creations elsewhere.
(D) Local artisans, forbidden to leave the island of Murano, could not sell their creations elsewhere during the Renaissance, glass products only being crafted according to techniques of tradition.
(E) Only traditional techniques could be used during the Renaissance that crafted glass products on the island of Murano, so local artisans were forbidden to leave and sell their creations elsewhere.

36. Once common across southwest Asia, the Indian cheetah was driven nearly to extinction during the late 1900s, and only a small amount of animals now presently reside in their remaining original habitat.

(A) and only a small amount of animals now presently reside in their remaining original habitat
(B) only a small number of animals are now residing in their remaining original habitat
(C) and only a small number of animals now reside in what remains of their original habitat
(D) with only a small number of animals that now reside in their present remaining habitat
(E) and only a small amount of animals reside in their original habitat that presently remains

37. Even after leaving their posts, some diplomats <u>may continue to act like intermediaries</u> between conflicting groups, using their negotiation skills to smooth over disagreements and reconcile opposing interests.

(A) may continue to act like intermediaries
(B) could continue acting like intermediaries
(C) continue to act as intermediaries
(D) would continue acting as intermediaries
(E) are continuing to act like intermediaries

38. Popular cold-weather activities such as skiing on fresh snow and skating on reflective ice often expose people to more harmful ultraviolet rays than a day at the beach <u>is</u>.

(A) is
(B) does
(C) has
(D) will
(E) can

39. Because the Helicobacter pylori bacterium is transmitted only through intimate contact and <u>is distributed around the world in a way that matches almost perfectly the distribution of human populations, its genetic variations are used to supplement human genetics as a means to track</u> ancient human migrations.

(A) is distributed around the world in a way that matches almost perfectly the distribution of human populations, its genetic variations are used to supplement human genetics as a means to track
(B) is distributed around the world in a way that matches almost perfectly the distribution of human populations, their genetic variations are used to supplement human genetics as a means of tracking
(C) are distributed around the world in a way that matches almost perfectly the distribution of human populations, its genetic variations are used to supplement human genetics as a means of tracking
(D) is distributed around the world in a way that almost perfectly matches the distribution of human populations, their genetic variations are used like a supplement to human genetics as a means to track
(E) are distributed around the world in a way such that the distribution of human populations is almost perfectly matched, and its genetic variations are used to supplement human genetics as a means to track

40. If the current market trends persist as projected, the majority of mobile phone manufacturers <u>go out of business rather than continue to lose</u> money and customers to a small number of competitors.

(A) go out of business rather than continue to lose
(B) would go out of business rather than continue losing
(C) will go out of business rather than continued to lose
(D) will go out of business rather than continue to lose
(E) would go out of business rather than continue to lose

41. Found in the depths of all the world's oceans, the vampire squid lives in a twilight zone that contains extremely low levels of dissolved oxygen <u>such to be uninhabitable by most other sea creatures</u>.

(A) such to be uninhabitable by most other sea creatures
(B) such that it is uninhabitable to most other sea creatures
(C) that cannot be inhabited by most other sea creatures
(D) and that cannot be inhabited by most other sea creatures
(E) making them uninhabitable by most other sea creatures

42. The black-backed woodpecker lives almost exclusively in severely burned forests, <u>thrives on insects that are adapted to fire, and detecting heat up to 30 miles away</u>.

(A) thrives on insects that are adapted to fire, and detecting heat up to 30 miles away
(B) thriving on insects that have adapted to fire, and detects heat up to 30 miles away
(C) thrives on insects adapted to fire, and can detect heat up to 30 miles away
(D) thrives on insects to adapt them to fire, and detects heat up to 30 miles away
(E) thrives on insects, adapting to fire, and detecting heat up to 30 miles away

43. Passed in 1943 in order to make housing affordable for middle-class residents, <u>rents for some New York City apartments having remained stable for decades because of the existence of rent control laws</u>.

(A) rents for some New York City apartments having remained stable for decades because of the existence of rent control laws
(B) rents for some New York City apartments have remained stable because rent control laws exist
(C) rents for some New York City apartments have remained stable due to the existence of rent control laws
(D) some New York City apartments have rents that have remained stable for decades as a result of rent control laws
(E) rent control laws have kept rents for some New York City apartments stable for decades

44. Scholars have little doubt <u>whether the latter years of Egypt's Old Kingdom were marked</u> by economic decline and a breakdown in the centralized system of government, disasters likely brought about by changes in the flow of the Nile.

(A) whether the latter years of Egypt's Old Kingdom were marked
(B) as to whether the latter years of Egypt's Old Kingdom were marked
(C) that the latter years of Egypt's Old Kingdom were marked
(D) about the latter years of Egypt's Old Kingdom having been marked
(E) about whether the latter years of Egypt's Old Kingdom was marked

45. For centuries, <u>dolls dressed as witches have hung in Norwegian kitchens because they traditionally believe</u> that such figures have the power to keep pots from boiling over.

(A) dolls dressed as witches have hung in Norwegian kitchens because they traditionally believe
(B) dolls dressed as witches have been hung in Norwegian kitchens because of a traditional belief
(C) dolls dressed as witches hang in Norwegian kitchens because they traditionally believe
(D) dolls dressed as witches had hung in Norwegian kitchens because of it traditionally being believed
(E) dolls dressed as witches have hung in Norwegian kitchens because of traditionally believing

46. Chicago's Willis Tower, formerly the Sears Tower, was the tallest office building in the world <u>until losing that distinction to the completion of the Taipei 101 Tower</u> in 2004.

(A) until losing that distinction to the completion of the Taipei 101 Tower
(B) until it had lost that distinction upon the completion of the Taipei 101 Tower
(C) until that distinction was lost after the Taipei 101 Tower's being completed
(D) until it lost that distinction when the Taipei 101 Tower was completed
(E) until the loss of that distinction after the completion of the Taipei 101 Tower

47. Under the feudal system, which prevailed in Europe during the Middle Ages, the status of an individual and <u>his or her interactions with members of different social classes were rigidly specified</u>.

(A) his or her interactions with members of different social classes were rigidly specified
(B) his or her interacting with members of different social classes rigidly was specified
(C) their interactions with members of different social classes rigidly were specified
(D) their interactions with members of different social classes was rigidly specified
(E) there were rigid specifications for interactions with members of different social classes.

48. Coined by historian of science Robert Proctor, <u>the term "agnotology" is the study of acts intended deliberately to spread</u> confusion and deceit, usually to sell a product or win favor.

(A) the term "agnotology" is the study of acts intended deliberately  to spread
(B) the term "agnotology" is the study of acts deliberately intended to spread
(C) the term "agnotology" involves the study of acts having the deliberate intention to spread
(D) the term "agnotology" is the referral of the study of acts that have the deliberate intention to spread
(E) the term "agnotology" refers to the study of acts deliberately intended to spread

49. During warmer months, zooplankton, microscopic marine animals that drift in oceans and bodies of fresh water, sink from the water's surface when the sun rises to escape predators, ascending again to feed at night.

(A) sink from the water's surface when the sun rises to escape predators, ascending
(B) sink from the surface of the water at the sun's rise to escape predators, to ascend
(C) and sink from the water's surface when the sun rises, escaping predators and ascending
(D) sink from the water's surface in order to escape predators when the sun rises and ascend
(E) sink from the water's surface to escape predators at the sun's rising, and to ascend

50. In the late 1890s, Pacific trading companies ceased to place traders in residence on the islands where they conducted business; instead beginning to require that trading mangers negotiate directly with local inhabitants when company ships arrived in port.

(A) business; instead beginning to require
(B) business, instead beginning of the requirement
(C) business, but instead began to require
(D) business, beginning instead to be required
(E) business; it began to instead to require

51. The use of rooftop solar panels have spread rapidly over the past decade, but wind energy remains the province of industrial-scale operations providing power to utilities companies and large businesses.

(A) The use of rooftop solar panels have spread
(B) The use of rooftop solar panels has spread
(C) The use of rooftop solar panels having spread
(D) Although use of rooftop solar panels has spread
(E) The using of rooftop solar panels has spread

52. According to United Nations estimates, more than three percent of the world's population currently lives in a country other than where they were born.

(A) other than where they were born
(B) other than those of where they were born
(C) other than what they were born in
(D) other than the one in which they were born
(E) other than that of their birth country

53. Whether families living in economically disadvantaged neighborhoods spend more money on food than do families living in economically advantaged ones has become a recurring controversy because neither the government nor private industry routinely collects the type of detailed data necessary to resolve the matter fully.

(A) Whether
(B) Insofar as
(C) Were it to be that
(D) The question of if
(E) Should

54. When a corporation exploits loopholes in financial regulations in order to pay less taxes than it otherwise would owe, the government is forced to find alternate sources of revenue to compensate for the shortfall.

(A) less taxes than it otherwise would owe
(B) less taxes than what they otherwise owe
(C) less taxes than otherwise are owed
(D) less money in taxes than it would otherwise owe
(E) less tax money than what is otherwise to be owed

55. Ownership of the Arctic is governed by the 1958 United Nations Convention of the Law of the Sea, which had provided Arctic nations with an exclusive economic zone extending 200 nautical miles from land.

(A) which had provided Arctic nations with an exclusive economic zone extending
(B) which provides Arctic nations with an exclusive economic zone to extend
(C) a treatise that provides Arctic nations with an exclusive economic zone extending
(D) a treatise provided Arctic nations with an exclusive economic zone that extends
(E) which provides Arctic nations with an exclusive economic zone of extension

56. The manufacturing company has created an advisory board to oversee the implementing of their new safety regulations, several of which have already been put into effect.

(A) to oversee the implementing of their new safety regulations,
(B) to oversee the implementation of its new safety regulations,
(C) to oversee that its new safety regulations are implemented, and
(D) to oversee their new safety regulations being implemented,
(E) to oversee as to how its new safety regulations are implemented,

57. Augustus Caesar is known to have commissioned the Pantheon, a monument to all the deities of Rome, as part of a construction program undertaken in the aftermath of the Battle of Actium in 31 C.E.

(A) Augustus Caesar is known to have commissioned the Pantheon, a monument to all the deities of Rome, as part of a construction program undertaken
(B) The Pantheon, a monument to all of Rome's deities, is known to have been commissioned by Augustus Caesar and part of a construction program undertaking
(C) Augustus Caesar, who commissioned the Pantheon, a monument to all of the deities of Rome undertaken as part of a construction project
(D) A monument to all the deities of Rome, Augustus Caesar is known for having commissioned the Pantheon as part of a construction program to be undertaken
(E) The Pantheon, commissioned as a monument to all of the deities of Rome, was part of Augustus Caesar's construction project undertaking

58. Some leading pharmaceutical companies are joining forces in an effort to accelerate the testing of new types of cancer drugs that battle tumors when harnessing the body's natural defenses.

(A) that battle tumors when harnessing
(B) that battle tumors when it harnesses
(C) that battle tumors by harnessing
(D) by which tumors are battled to harness
(E) where they battle tumors by harnessing

59. Like other forms of physical activity, tai chi might help mitigate the risk of heart disease because it has such effects as reducing levels of harmful triglycerides while levels of "good" HDL cholesterol are increased.

(A) it has such effects as reducing levels of harmful triglycerides while levels of "good" HDL cholesterol are increased
(B) its effects include the reduction of levels of harmful triglycerides and levels of "good" HDL cholesterol increase
(C) it has such effects like the reducing of harmful levels of triglycerides while levels of "good" HDL cholesterol are increasing
(D) its effects are such that harmful triglyceride levels are reduced and increasing "good" HDL cholesterol levels
(E) its effects include a reduction in levels of harmful triglycerides and an increase in levels of "good" HDL cholesterol.

60. The security systems of small companies can often be hacked easier than large ones because small companies have a tendency to lack the financial resources to upgrade their software and set up protective barriers.

(A) easier than large ones because small companies have a tendency to lack
(B) easier than those of large ones because of small companies tending to lack
(C) more easily than large ones because small companies have a tendency of lacking
(D) more easily than those of large ones because small companies tend to lack
(E) more easily than large ones because small companies have tended to lack

61. Named for an Intel co-founder, Gordon Moore, Moore's Law is that computing power, as measured by the density in transistors on a microchip, typically doubles every 18 to 24 months.

(A) Moore's Law is that computing power, as measured by the density in transistors on a microchip, typically doubles
(B) Moore's Law states that computing power, as measured by the density of transistors on a microchip, typically doubles
(C) Moore's Law is that computing power, as measured in transistors' microchip density, will double typically
(D) Moore's Law states that computing power, as measured by the density of transistors on a microchip, which typically doubles
(E) Moore's Law states that the measurement of the power of computing by the density of transistors on a microchip typically doubled

62. Born in the Macedon capital of Pella in 356 B.C.E., Alexander the Great spent most of his ruling years on an unprecedented military campaign through Asia and northeast Africa, and by the age of 30 he had created one of the largest empires in the ancient world.

(A) and by the age of 30 he had created one of the largest empires in the ancient world
(B) and one of the largest empires of the ancient world had been created by the age of 30
(C) and has created one of the ancient world's largest empires by 30 years of age
(D) having created one of the largest empires in the ancient world by 30 years old
(E) and creating one of the largest empires of the ancient world by the age of 30

63. Although politicians have a longstanding reputation for dishonesty, many of their falsehoods emerge as much from a sincere belief in their promises as because they want to appeal to their constituents.

(A) as because they want to appeal to their constituents
(B) as having the desire to appeal to their constituents
(C) as from their desire to appeal to their constituents
(D) as because of wanting to appeal to their constituents
(E) as in the desire of appealing to their constituents

64. Although many children want to read digital books and read for fun more frequently if they could obtain this with ease, an even larger percentage claim that they do not want to give up traditional print books completely.

(A) and read for fun more frequently if they could obtain this with ease,
(B) and will read for fun more frequently if they could obtain these easily,
(C) and read it for fun more frequently if they can be easily obtained,
(D) and would read for fun more frequently if they could obtain such books with ease,
(E) and would read for fun more frequently if they can obtain such books easily,

65. Although Artie Shaw, a clarinetist and popular big band leader during the 1930s, spent far more of his life writing prose than making music, a careful look at his compositions reveal that he was a musician of genius.

(A) a careful look at his compositions reveal that he was a musician of genius
(B) looking carefully at his compositions reveal that he was a genius as a musician
(C) a careful look at his compositions reveals of his being a genius musician
(D) a careful look at his compositions are a revelation of his genius in music
(E) a careful look at his compositions reveals that he was a musical genius

66. The status of photography as an art form was initially unclear: at the International Exhibition of 1862, for example, organizers debated over if photographs should be exhibited with the machines or with the paintings and sculptures.

(A) over if photographs should be exhibited
(B) whether photographs should be exhibited
(C) that the photographs should be exhibited
(D) as to the exhibiting of photographs
(E) about the photograph's exhibition

67. Prepaid bank cards, which are issued by a wide range of operators, are different compared to debit and credit cards because they need to be loaded before payments can be made but can carry substantial amounts of money.

(A) are different compared to debit and credit cards because they need to be

(B) are different when compared to debit and credit cards because they need to be

(C) differ from debit and credit cards because bank cards must be

(D) are different than debit and credit cards, for these must be

(E) different from debit and credit cards because they need to be

68. According to *The Stock Trader's Almanac*, the performance of stocks in January foretells how the market performs throughout the year, but statistics experts warn that causation is impossible to prove.

(A) how the market performs throughout the year,

(B) the market's performing throughout the year,

(C) the performance of the year's market

(D) what the market will perform like in the year

(E) how the market will perform during the year

69. Unlike his contemporaries, whose work he considered conventional and uninspiring, Le Corbusier insisted on using modern industrial techniques to construct buildings.

(A) Unlike his contemporaries, whose work he considered

(B) Unlike that of his contemporaries, whose work he considered to be

(C) Unlike his contemporaries, whom he considered their work to be

(D) Unlike his contemporaries, where he considered that their work was

(E) In contrast to the work of his contemporaries, which he considered it to be

70. Grace Hopper, who in 1944 became one of the first programmers of Harvard University's Mark I computer, was reported for popularizing the term "debugging" as a synonym for "fixing computer glitches" after she had removed a moth from one.

(A) was reported for popularizing the term "debugging" as a synonym for "fixing computer glitches" after she had removed a moth from one

(B) was reported to popularize the term "debugging" as a synonym that meant "fixing computer glitches" after the removal of a moth from a computer by her

(C) is reported to have popularized the term "debugging" as a synonym for "fixing computer glitches" after she removed a moth from a computer

(D) is reported for popularizing the term "debugging" as a synonym to mean "fixing computer glitches" after removing a moth from a computer

(E) was reported for popularizing the term "debugging" to mean "fixing computer glitches" after the removal of moth from a computer

71. An important stylistic element in Dostoevsky's novels is polyphony, the simultaneous presence of multiple narrative voices and perspectives first identified by the critic M. M. Bakhtin.

(A) novels is polyphony, the simultaneous presence of multiple narrative voices and perspectives

(B) novels are polyphony, multiple narrative voices and perspectives' being simultaneously present

(C) novels is polyphony, whose simultaneous presence of multiple narrative voices and perspectives were

(D) novels is polyphony, in which multiple narrative voices and perspectives are present simultaneously

(E) novels are polyphony, the simultaneous presence of the multiplicity of narratives and perspectives

72. Having for years recommended that customers protect their electronic accounts by creating strong passwords, many people nevertheless fail to heed security experts' advice.

(A) Having for years recommended that customers protect their electronic accounts by creating strong passwords, many people nevertheless fail to heed security experts' advice.
(B) For years, security experts, who have recommended that customers protect their electronic accounts by creating strong passwords, but many people nonetheless fail to heed their advice.
(C) While security experts recommend for years that customers protect their electronic accounts through the creation of strong passwords, there is a failure to heed that advice by many people.
(D) Although security experts have for years recommended that customers protect their electronic accounts by creating strong passwords, many people nevertheless fail to heed that advice.
(E) Having for years recommended for customers to protect their electronic accounts through creating strong passwords, many people are nonetheless failing to heed security experts' advice.

73. In comparison to people, elephants are capable of perceiving a much wider variety of sounds; in fact, an elephant's ears can pick up frequencies more than 20 Hertz lower than what human ears can hear.

(A) lower than what human ears can hear
(B) lower as opposed to humans' hearing
(C) lower in opposition to range that human ears have
(D) lower than those perceptible to human ears
(E) lower than those by human ears

74. Many design movements have political or philosophical  beginnings or intentions, with the art deco style being invented for purely decorative purposes.

(A) with the art deco style being invented
(B) with the invention of the art deco style
(C) but the art deco style was invented
(D) but the art deco style invented
(E) but the inventing of the art deco style was

75. In response to their critics, proponents of genetically modified foods typically insist that such crops grow at a faster rate, are less vulnerable to disease, and reduce the amount of stress placed on natural resources.

(A) grow at a faster rate, are less vulnerable to disease, and reduce the amount of stress placed on natural resources
(B) grow at a faster rate, being less vulnerable to disease and a reduction in the amount of stress placed on natural resources
(C) grow at a faster rate, less vulnerable to disease, and would reduce the amount of stress placed on natural resources
(D) are growing at a faster rate, they are less vulnerable to disease, and reduce the amount of stress they place on natural resources
(E) grow at a faster rate, have less vulnerability to disease, and to reduce how much stress is placed on natural resources

76. If his longevity claim would be confirmed, Carmelo Flores Laura, a former rancher from Bolivia, would have the longest verified lifespan of anyone in human history.

(A) If his longevity claim would be confirmed,
(B) Should his longevity's claim be confirmed,
(C) Had his longevity claim been confirmed,
(D) That his claim to longevity was confirmed,
(E) Were his longevity claim confirmed,

77. In an era when the economies of many European countries were fueled by their overseas possessions, the American colonies were to the British Empire as the islands of Martinique and Guadeloupe related to France.

(A) as the islands of Martinique and Guadeloupe related to France
(B) what that of the islands of Martinique and Guadeloupe were to France
(C) just like the islands of Martinique and Guadeloupe belonged to France
(D) much the same as Martinique and Guadeloupe with France
(E) what the islands of Martinique and Guadeloupe were to France

78. An initial public offering (IPO) or stock market launch is a type of public offering <u>where shares of a company are sold to institutional investors that, in turn, are sold to the general public</u> on a securities exchange for the first time.

    (A) where shares of a company are sold to institutional investors that, in turn, are sold to the general public
    (B) where shares of a company are sold to institutional investors who, in turn, sell these to the general public
    (C) in which shares of a company are sold to institutional investors who, in turn, sell to the general public
    (D) in which a company's shares are sold to institutional investors and, in turn, sell it to the general public
    (E) whereby shares of a company are sold to institutional investors that are sold to the general public in turn

79. In the 1880s new steamships made it possible to bring cheap wheat and meat to Europe, <u>which bankrupted family farms and aristocratic estates, and sent</u> a flood of rural refugees into cities.

    (A) which bankrupted family farms and aristocratic estates, and sent
    (B) a development that bankrupted family farms and aristocratic estates, sending
    (C) a development bankrupting family farms and aristocratic estates and sending
    (D) which bankrupted family farms as well as aristocratic estates, sending
    (E) a development which bankrupted family farms and aristocratic estates, to send

80. Traditional methods of salmon farming have led to homogeneity <u>rather than the diversity that make a species more capable to survive</u> myriad natural challenges, including predators and disease.

    (A) rather than the diversity that make a species more capable to survive
    (B) rather than to the diversity that makes a species more capable of surviving
    (C) rather than the diversity that make a species more capable in surviving
    (D) rather than for the diversity which makes a species more capable of surviving
    (E) rather than the diversity making a species more capable to survive

81. Clinical trials are the key to obtaining information about the safety and efficacy of new medications, and <u>without volunteers to take part in it, there will be no new treatments for serious diseases like cancer, multiple sclerosis and arthritis</u>.

    (A) without volunteers to take part in it, there will be no new treatments for serious diseases like cancer, multiple sclerosis and arthritis
    (B) with volunteers to take part in these being absent, there would be no new treatments for serious diseases like cancer, multiple sclerosis and arthritis
    (C) in the absence of the participation by volunteers, there will be no new serious disease treatments, including cancer, multiple sclerosis and arthritis
    (D) without volunteers to participate in them, there would be no new treatments for serious diseases such as cancer, multiple sclerosis and arthritis
    (E) without voluntary participating, there are no new treatments for serious diseases such as cancer, multiple sclerosis and arthritis

82. One of the earliest environmentalists, <u>it was prohibited to burn sea coal by King Edward I of England in 1306 because the smoke it created was becoming</u> a health hazard.

    (A) it was prohibited to burn sea coal by King Edward I of England in 1306 because the smoke it created was becoming
    (B) they were prohibited from burning sea coal by King Edward I of England in 1306 because the smoke created by it
    (C) the prohibition by King Edward I against burning sea coal was made in 1306, after its smoke became
    (D) the smoke created by the burning of sea coal led in 1306 to its prohibition by King Edward I because it had become a
    (E) King Edward I of England prohibited the burning of sea coal in 1306 because the smoke it created had become

83. Three million years ago, the creation of the Panama Isthmus wreaked ecological havoc not just by triggering large-scale extinctions but divert ocean currents and transforming the climate.

(A) not just by triggering large-scale extinctions but divert
(B) not just by triggering large-scale extinctions but by the diversion of
(C) not just by triggering large-scale extinctions but also by diverting
(D) not just because they trigger large-scale extinctions but also to divert
(E) not just in triggering large-scale extinctions but because they are diverting

84. The paintings of Caravaggio (Michelangelo Merisi da Caravaggio) combines a realistic observation of the human state, both physical and emotional, with a dramatic use of lighting, had a formative influence on Baroque painting.

(A) Caravaggio) combines a realistic observation of the human state, both physical and emotional, with a dramatic use of lighting,
(B) Caravaggio), which combine a realistic observation of the human state, both physical and emotional, with a dramatic use of lighting,
(C) Caravaggio), which combines a realistic observation of the human state, physical as well as emotional, to dramatically used lighting,
(D) Caravaggio) combine a realistic observing of the human state, both physical and emotional, with a dramatic use of lighting,
(E) Caravaggio), which combine a realistic observation of the human state, physical as well as emotional, with a dramatic use of lighting and

85. The First Industrial Revolution evolved into the Second Industrial Revolution in the transition years between 1840 and 1870, when technological and economic progress continued with the adoption of steam transport, machine tools being manufactured on a large scale, and the use of machinery increasing in steam-powered factories.

(A) the adoption of steam transport, machine tools being manufactured on a large scale, and the use of machinery increasing in steam-powered factories
(B) adopting steam transport, manufacturing machine tools on a large scale, and the use of machinery increasing in steam-powered factories
(C) the adoption of steam transport, the large-scale manufacture of machine tools, and the increasing use of machinery in steam-powered factories
(D) the adopting of steam transport, the manufacture of machine tools on a large scale, and the use of machinery in steam-powered factories increased
(E) the adoption of steam transport, to manufacture machine tools on a large scale, and an increase in machinery use in steam-powered factories

86. In 1963, Lina Wertmüller directed her first film, *I Basilischi* (*The Lizards*), whose theme—the lives of impoverished inhabitants of southern Italy—would become a recurring motif in her later works.

(A) whose theme – the lives of impoverished inhabitants of southern Italy – would become
(B) whose theme, the lives of impoverished inhabitants of Italy's south, becoming
(C) of which the theme, the lives of southern Italy's impoverished inhabitants, have become
(D) where the theme – the lives of impoverished inhabitants in the south of Italy – would become
(E) its theme – the lives of impoverished inhabitants in Italy's south – became

87. As part of a mandatory 30-day "cooling-off" period between loans, a reform intended to prevent borrowers from taking out fresh loans to cover their outstanding debts, <u>a bank will not be permitted to extend a new loan to a customer until receiving full payment from existing ones</u>.

(A) a bank will not be permitted to extend a new loan to a customer until receiving full payment from existing ones
(B) a bank will not be permitted to extend a new loan to a customer until they have received full payment for existing ones
(C) and banks will be prohibited to extend new loans to customers that have not fully repaid their existing ones
(D) banks will be prohibited from extending new loans to customers who have not fully repaid their existing ones
(E) a bank will be prohibited from extending new loans to a customer that has not fully repaid its existing ones

88. Researchers have suggested that soft music and gentle humming <u>is perceived as soothing because humans, like many social animals, are predisposed in interpreting</u> silence as a sign of danger.

(A) is perceived as soothing because humans, like many social animals, are predisposed in interpreting
(B) has been perceived to be soothing because humans, like many social animals, have the predisposition to interpret
(C) are perceived as soothing because humans, like many social animals, are predisposed to interpret
(D) is perceived to be soothing because humans, just as many social animals, are predisposed in the interpretation of
(E) are perceived as soothing due to humans, like many social animals, having the predisposition to interpret

89. Urban gardens and farming initiatives <u>not only recycle and transform old lots in many formerly crumbling cities, but also address</u> pressing quality-of-life issues.

(A) not only recycle and transform old lots in many formerly crumbling cities, but also address
(B) are not only recycling and transforming old lots in many formerly crumbling cities, but also are addressing to
(C) not only recycle and transform old lots in many formerly crumbling cities, but also addressing
(D) not only recycle and transform old lots in many cities that formerly were crumbling, but also addresses
(E) not only recycle and transform old lots in many cities that crumbled formerly, and also address to

90. Studies have shown that naps lasting 20-30 minutes can boost job performance by up to 34 <u>percent by the enhancement of attention to detail, decreasing stress, and an improvement</u> in overall cognitive abilities.

(A) percent by the enhancement of attention to detail, decreasing stress, and an improvement
(B) percent, for they enhance attention to detail, decrease stress, and improve
(C) percent in that it enhances attention to detail, decreasing stress, and to improve
(D) percent because of their enhancing attention to detail, decrease of stress, and improve
(E) percent, enhancing attention to detail, decreasing stress, and improves

91. Although many consumers frequent their local farmers market because they believe that the foods sold there are safer than foods sold in traditional supermarkets, there is a positive correlation between the number of farmers markets per capita <u>to the amount of per capita reported outbreaks of food-borne illness</u>.

(A) to the amount of per capita reported outbreaks of food-borne illness
(B) with how many reported outbreaks of food-borne illness per capita are reported
(C) and per capita reports of the amount of food-borne illnesses
(D) or the number of per capita reported outbreaks of food-borne illness being reported
(E) and the number of reported outbreaks of food-borne illness per capita

92. The 16.5-ton bell known as "Great Paul," <u>rang traditionally at one o'clock each day, was the largest bell in the British Isles until the casting of the Olympic Bell</u> for the 2012 London Olympics.

(A) rang traditionally at one o'clock each day, was the largest bell in the British Isles until the casting of the Olympic Bell
(B) traditionally rang at one o'clock daily, was the largest bell in the British Isles until casting the Olympic Bell
(C) traditionally rung at one o'clock each day, was the largest bell of the British Isles until the Olympic Bell had been cast
(D) traditionally rung at one o'clock each day, was the largest bell in the British Isles until the Olympic Bell was cast
(E) rang at one o'clock each day by tradition, and was the largest bell in the British Isles until the Olympic Bell was cast

93. <u>Although naturally ranging from Western Europe to the Persian shores of the Caspian Sea, *Vitis vinifera*, the common grape vine, has demonstrated</u> high levels of adaptability and can sometimes mutate to accommodate a new environment.

(A) Although naturally ranging from Western Europe to the Persian shores of the Caspian Sea, *Vitis vinifera*, the common grape vine, has demonstrated
(B) Although its habitat ranges naturally from Western Europe to the Persian shores of the Caspian Sea, but *Vitis vinifera*, the common grape vine, has demonstrated
(C) Even though it has a natural range from Western Europe to the Persian shores of the Caspian Sea, *Vitis vinifera*, the common grape vine, having demonstrated
(D) Despite its naturally ranging from Western Europe to the Persian shores of the Caspian Sea, *Vitis vinifera*, the common grape vine, demonstrates
(E) Although the natural habitat of *Vitis vinifera*, the common grape vine, ranges from Western Europe to the Persian shores of the Caspian Sea, the plant has demonstrated

94. <u>Galileo, who is depicted generally as a strict proponent for rationalism and scientific thought, also derived</u> much of his inspiration from works of art, particularly Dante's *Divine Comedy*.

(A) Galileo, who is depicted generally to be a strict proponent for rationalism and scientific thought, also derived
(B) Galileo, whom they generally depicted as a strict proponent of rationalism and scientific thought, also derived
(C) Generally depicted as a strict proponent of rationalism and scientific thought, Galileo also derived
(D) Depicted generally to be strict proponent for rationalism and scientific thought, Galileo would also derive
(E) Galileo generally depicted as a strict proponent of rationalism and scientific thought, but he also derived

95. <u>In addition to being</u> the second smallest country in the world, Monaco, which has a land border of just 2.7 miles, is also the second smallest monarchy as well as the most densely populated country.

(A) In addition to being
(B) Adding to its being
(C) As long as it is
(D) As well as being
(E) Additionally being

96. <u>Having received a subpoena to appear in court like a witness, a person must either comply with the directive or face</u> arrest and possible sequestration for the duration of a trial.

(A) Having received a subpoena to appear in court like a witness, a person must either comply with the directive or face
(B) Having received a subpoena to appear in court to be a witness, a person must either comply to the directive or else they face
(C) Having received a subpoena to appear in court as a witness, it is necessary that a person either comply with the directive or face
(D) When a subpoena is received to appear in court as a witness, a person must either comply with the directive or face
(E) A person who has received a subpoena to appear in court as a witness must either comply with the directive or face

97. While small banks are still passing some of their loans off to larger institutions, it is now the big banks that are most active in what is known as the loan sub-participation market.

(A) it is now the big banks that are most active in what is known as the loan sub-participation market
(B) what is known as the loan sub-participation market counts the big banks among its most active participants
(C) the greatest activity in what is known as the loan sub-participation market comes from the big banks
(D) the loan sub-participation market draws its greatest activity from big banks
(E) big banks are most active in what is known as the loan sub-participation market

98. Choreographer and dancer Savion Glover aims to restore the African roots of tap dance by eliminating hand gestures and he returns to a focus on the feet as the primary source of movement.

(A) he returns to a focus on the feet
(B) return to a focus on the feet
(C) returning to the feet's focusing
(D) returned to the feet as a focus
(E) returning that the feet be the focus

99. Introduced in 1678, the term "conscious" acquired at least five different definitions in the space of 50 years, and its ambiguity had not faded in more recent times.

(A) acquired at least five different definitions in the space of 50 years, and its ambiguity had not faded
(B) would acquire at least five different definitions within 50 years, of which the ambiguity has not faded
(C) acquired at least five different definitions within 50 years, and its ambiguity has not faded
(D) acquired at least five differing definitions within 50 years, and their ambiguity did not fade
(E) acquired within 50 years at least five separate definitions, its ambiguity not fading

100. Much of the experiments performed by cognitive psychologist Elizabeth Spelke have been designed to test how much babies and young children understand about the world around them.

(A) Much of the experiments performed by cognitive psychologist Elizabeth Spelke have been designed
(B) Much of the experiments that cognitive psychologist Elizabeth Spelke performs are designed
(C) Many of the experiments that cognitive psychologist Elizabeth Spelke performs is designed
(D) Many of the experiments performed by cognitive psychologist Elizabeth Spelke are designed
(E) Many of the experiments that are performed by cognitive psychologist Elizabeth Spelke designed

101. Far from being a modern dietary invention, salad has a long and distinguished history: food historians claim that the Romans ate mixed greens with dressing, and the Babylonians are known to douse lettuce with oil and vinegar more than 2,000 years ago.

(A) are known to douse
(B) are known to have doused
(C) were knowing to douse
(D) have been known to douse
(E) who were known to douse

102. The *Oxford English Dictionary* was completed in the early nineteenth century, before which Samuel Johnson's *Dictionary of the English Language* was the most comprehensive British lexicon.

(A) century, before which Samuel Johnson's *Dictionary of the English Language* was the most comprehensive British lexicon
(B) century, and Samuel Johnson's *Dictionary of the English Language* was before this the most comprehensive lexicon in Britain
(C) century, before that Samuel Johnson's *Dictionary of the English Language* was the most comprehensive British lexicon
(D) century, Samuel Johnson's *Dictionary of the English Language* being the most comprehensive lexicon in Britain before this
(E) century, before which Samuel Johnson's *Dictionary of the English Language* has been the most comprehensive lexicon in Britain

103. The Hale–Bopp comet received so much media coverage when it returned in 1997, becoming one of the highest observed astronomical bodies in history.

(A) when it returned in 1997, becoming one of the highest observed
(B) when returning in 1997 to become one of the highest observed
(C) upon its 1997 return and became one of the highest observed
(D) when it returned in 1997 that it became one of the most highly observed
(E) on its return in 1997, thus becoming one of the most highly observed

104. Because the lemur shares some traits also possessed by other primates, it is frequently mistaken for an ancestor of modern monkeys and chimpanzee.

(A) Because the lemur shares some traits also possessed by other primates, it is frequently mistaken for
(B) Because the lemur shares some traits with other primates, it is frequently mistaken for
(C) Because the lemur shares some traits that other primates also have, it is frequently mistaken to be
(D) Because some of the lemurs traits are shared with other primates, they are frequently mistaken for
(E) Because of its sharing some traits that other primates possess as well, the lemur is frequently mistaken as

105. During the 1970s, the demand for long-lasting staple foods prompted the adding of preservatives to dishes that previously were simple, whereby the quality of their flavors was reduced.

(A) prompted the adding of preservatives to dishes that previously were simple, whereby the quality of their flavors was reduced
(B) prompted the addition of preservatives to previously simple dishes, so the quality of their flavors were reduced
(C) prompted them to add preservatives to previously simple dishes, reducing the food's flavor quality
(D) prompted the addition of preservatives to previously simple dishes, a change that reduced the quality of the food's flavors
(E) prompted them to add preservatives to previously simple dishes, which reduced the quality of the food's flavors

106. What an advertising agency chooses to focus on for their major campaigns depends upon the interests and strengths of the executives responsible for overseeing the projects.

(A) What an advertising agency chooses to focus on for their major campaigns depends
(B) What an advertising agency chooses to focus on for its major campaigns are dependent
(C) What an advertising agency chooses to focus on for its major campaigns depends
(D) What an advertising agency should choose to focus on for its major campaigns depend
(E) For an advertising agency to choose to focus on for their major campaigns depends

107. Nikola Tesla's inventions, which include fluorescent lighting and the modern radio, are still considered equally important to Thomas Edison.

(A) equally important to Thomas Edison
(B) important like that of Thomas Edison
(C) of an importance as great as Thomas Edison
(D) of equal importance as Thomas Edison
(E) just as important as those of Thomas Edison

108. In 1983, geneticist Barbara McClintock was awarded the Nobel Prize in Physiology or Medicine for discovering the process whereby chromosomes, the thread-like structures that are located inside a cell's nucleus and that contain an organism's DNA, exchange information during cell division.

(A) for discovering the process whereby chromosomes, the thread-like structures that are located
(B) for her discovering of the process where chromosomes, the thread-like structures located
(C) for her discovery of the process by which chromosomes, and these are the thread-like structures located
(D) that she discovered the process through which chromosomes, these being the thread-like structures which are located
(E) for her discovery of the chromosomes' process, the thread-like structures that locate

109. A 2007 federal law mandated that all pharmaceutical companies, universities and hospitals conducting clinical trials must disclose study results and adverse events on ClinicalTrials.gov, a website used by a large amount of doctors and patients.

(A) a website used by a large amount of doctors and patients
(B) a website that a large amount of doctors and patients use
(C) a website that many doctors and patients use
(D) and a website that a large number of doctors and patients use
(E) a website of use by many doctors and patients

110. The Zika and dengue viruses, like virtually all mosquito-borne disease, does not occur in mosquito larvae but rather are transmitted by female mosquitoes, who become carriers by biting infected humans.

(A) does not occur in mosquito larvae but rather are transmitted by female mosquitoes, who become carriers by biting
(B) do not occur in mosquito larvae but rather are transmitted by female mosquitoes, who become carriers after biting
(C) do not occur in mosquito larvae but transmitted by female mosquitoes, who become carriers after biting
(D) does not occur in mosquito larvae transmitted by female mosquitoes, becoming carriers when biting
(E) do not occur in mosquito larvae yet are transmitted by female mosquitoes and become carriers after biting

111. The French Revolution of 1830, also known as the July Revolution or the Second French Revolution, saw the overthrow of King Charles X, the French Bourbon monarch, and the ascent of his cousin Louis-Philippe, who himself would be deposed after 18 precarious years on the throne.

(A) and the ascent of his cousin Louis-Philippe, who himself would be deposed after 18 precarious years on the throne
(B) the ascent of his cousin Louis-Philippe, whose deposition himself would come after 18 precarious years on the throne
(C) and Louis-Philippe's ascent, his cousin who, after 18 precarious years on the throne, was deposed
(D) the ascent of Louis-Philippe, his cousin had himself been deposed after 18 precarious years on the throne
(E) and his cousin Louis-Philippe's ascent, which would himself be deposed after 18 precarious years on the throne

112. As is the case for other volcanoes in the Cascade Range, Mount St. Helens consists of a large eruptive cone containing lava rock interlayered with ash, pumice, and other deposits, is part of the Pacific Ring of Fire, the ring of volcanoes and associated mountains around the Pacific Ocean.

(A) As is the case for other volcanoes in the Cascade Range, Mount St. Helens consists of a large eruptive cone containing
(B) Similar to other volcanoes in the Cascade Range, Mount St. Helens consists in a large eruptive cone that contains
(C) Like other volcanoes in the Cascade Range, Mount St. Helens consists of a large eruptive cone that contains
(D) Like other volcanoes in the Cascade Range, Mount St. Helens, which consists of a large eruptive cone containing
(E) Like other volcanoes in the Cascade Range, Mount St. Helens, which consists in a large eruptive cone and contain

113. The cubist movement was founded by Pablo Picasso along with his colleague, the French artist Georges Braque, in 1909, a movement that would revolutionize longstanding ideas about art.

    (A) The cubist movement was founded by Pablo Picasso along with a colleague, the French artist Georges Braque in 1909,

    (B) In 1909, Pablo Picasso, along with a colleague, the French artist Georges Braque, founded the cubist movement,

    (C) The cubist movement was founded by Pablo Picasso in 1909 along with a colleague, the French artist Georges Braque,

    (D) Pablo Picasso founded the cubist movement in 1909, along with the French artist Georges Braque, his colleague,

    (E) The founding of the cubist movement occurred in 1909 by Pablo Picasso, along with a colleague, the French artist Georges Braque,

114. Economist George Akerlof has argued that procrastination reveals the limits of rational thinking and can teach useful lessons about phenomena as diverse as overeating, to save money, and the purchasing of automobiles.

    (A) phenomena as diverse as overeating, to save money, and the purchasing of automobiles

    (B) phenomena as diverse as overeating, to save money, and to purchase automobiles

    (C) such diverse phenomena as overeating, saving money, and purchasing automobiles

    (D) diverse phenomena, including to overeat, to save money, and the purchasing of automobiles

    (E) diverse phenomena like overeating, the saving of money, and the purchasing of automobiles

115. New mortgage rules, which do not require down payments from borrowers, are intended to encourage lending, but some real estate analysts insist of their ineffectiveness to prevent high levels of default.

    (A) insist of their ineffectiveness to prevent high levels of default

    (B) insist on its ineffectiveness at preventing high levels of default

    (C) insist that they are ineffective in preventing high default levels

    (D) insist that such regulations are ineffective at preventing high levels of default

    (E) insist that this is ineffective to prevent high levels of default

116. When faced with drought conditions, farmers must survive by pumping groundwater at a furious rate, causing water tables to drop precipitously by as much as a 75% decline.

    (A) causing water tables to drop precipitously by as much as a 75% decline

    (B) causing a drop precipitously in water tables by as much as a 75% decline

    (C) causing water tables to drop precipitously by as much as 75%

    (D) precipitously dropping water tables by as much as 75%

    (E) causing as much as a 75% decline in the drop of water tables

117. Before they became a team, Richard Rogers and Oscar Hammerstein wrote a series of hit musicals in the 1950s and collaborating with other partners: Rogers with Lorenz Hart and Hammerstein with Jerome Kern.

    (A) Richard Rogers and Oscar Hammerstein wrote a series of hit musicals in the 1950s and collaborating

    (B) Richard Rogers and Oscar Hammerstein, whose series of hit musicals in the 1950s had collaborated

    (C) Richard Rogers and Oscar Hammerstein, who wrote a series of hit musicals in the 1950s, collaborating

    (D) Richard Rogers and Oscar Hammerstein, who wrote a series of hit musicals in the 1950s and had collaborated

    (E) Richard Rogers and Oscar Hammerstein, who wrote a series of hit musicals in the 1950s, had collaborated

118. Although the Concorde's development required a significant economic loss for both France and Great Britain, it became increasingly profitable as a customer base developed for what then had been the fastest form of commercial air travel in the world.

    (A) it became increasingly profitable as a customer base developed for what then had been

    (B) they became increasingly profitable as a customer base developed for what was then

    (C) its profitability increased after the development of a customer base, which was then

    (D) this became increasingly profitable as a customer base developed for the aircraft, then

    (E) the Concorde became increasingly profitable as a customer base developed for what was then

119. Higher education in the United States has undergone radical changes over the past century, having evolved from a system that consisted primarily of rote memorization of classics to one covering a vast number of disciplines.

(A) having evolved from a system consisting primarily of rote memorization of classics to one covering
(B) having evolved from a system consisting primarily of rote memorization of classics and one that covers
(C) having evolved from a system consisting primarily of classics' rote memorization with one covering
(D) which has evolved from a system consisting primarily in rote memorization of classics to one covering
(E) which had evolved from a system consisting primarily of rote memorization of classics to one that covers

120. Analysis of ancient thigh bones, discovered in 1989 along with other remains at a site known as Maludong, or Red Deer Cave, indicate that an early hominid species might have survived as late as 14,000 years ago in southwest China.

(A) indicate that an early hominid species might have survived
(B) indicate that a species of early hominid has survived
(C) indicates that a species of early hominid might have survived
(D) indicate that an early hominid species could have survived
(E) indicates an early species of hominid's possible surviving

121. According to a recent consumer report, some borrowers do not realize that they have been sued by a lender until receiving notification of their guilt by default.

(A) until receiving notification of their guilt by default
(B) until they receive notification of their guilt that is by default
(C) until they receive notification that their guilt is by default
(D) until they receive notification of having defaulted on their guilt
(E) until they receive notification that they have been found guilty by default

122. Henri Becquerel, who shared in the 1903 Nobel Prize in Nuclear Physics, is credited with the discovery that the radiation emitted by uranium salts depended not on an external source of energy but were emanating spontaneously from the uranium itself.

(A) depended not on an external source of energy but were emanating spontaneously
(B) depended not on an external energy source but had emanated spontaneously
(C) has not depended on an external energy source but rather spontaneously emanated
(D) does not depend on an external source of energy but spontaneously emanates
(E) did not depend on an external energy source but emanate spontaneously

123. The lands of the ancient Near East did not develop as a single entity because they were divided into individual states, each with their own distinct identity and culture.
(A) each with their own distinct identity and culture
(B) each with its own distinct identity and culture
(C) each of their own distinct identity and culture
(D) each of its own distinction of identity and culture
(E) and each had their own distinct identity and culture

124. The classification "novel" is a long fictional work, while the category "graphic novel" is applied broadly and includes fiction, non-fiction, and anthologized works.

(A) The classification "novel" is a long fictional work, while the category "graphic novel" is applied broadly
(B) The classification "novel" is a long fictional work, while the application of the category of "graphic novel" is to apply broadly
(C) The classification "novel" is given to long works of fiction, whereas the category "graphic novel" is applied broadly
(D) The classification "novel" given to long works of fiction while the category "graphic novel" has broad applications
(E) Long works of fictions are classified as novels, whereas the category "graphic novel" applies broadly to

125. High-pressure sales techniques practiced by timeshare representatives have prompted multiple lawsuits and lead to predictions that regulators increase oversight of the industry.

(A) lead to predictions that regulators increase oversight of the industry
(B) lead to predictions that regulators will increase oversight of the industry
(C) have lead to predictions the regulators should increase oversight of the industry
(D) led to predictions that the industry's oversight would be increased by regulators
(E) led to predictions that regulators will increase oversight of the industry

126. With his theories of relativity and gravity long confirmed and his Nobel Prize was a decade old, Einstein was, in 1931, by far the most famous scientist in the world.

(A) his Nobel Prize was a decade old,
(B) his Nobel Prize a decade old,
(C) his Nobel Prize being a decade old,
(D) a Nobel Prize of a decade's age,
(E) a Nobel Prize aged of a decade,

127. Because economists cannot reliably prevent, or even predict, recessions or other economic events, some skeptics claim that it is based not so much on empirical observation and rational analysis as on ideology.

(A) some skeptics claim that it is based not so much on empirical observation and rational analysis as on ideology
(B) some skeptics claim that economics is based not so much on empirical analysis as on
(C) some skeptics claim of an ideological basis in economics rather than empirical observation and rational analysis
(D) some skeptics claim that they have a basis not so much in empirical observation and rational analysis as in ideology
(E) it is claimed by some skeptics that economics is based not so much on observation and rational analysis but on

128. Foreign-language instruction, when taught by the direct method, standing in contrast to traditional grammar and translation methods, emphasizes teaching through the target language only—the rationale being that students will be able to work out grammatical rules from the language provided.

(A) Foreign-language instruction, when taught by the direct method, standing in contrast to traditional grammar and translation methods,
(B) When taught by the direct method, standing in contrast to traditional grammar and translation methods, foreign-language instruction
(C) The direct method of foreign-language instruction, which stands in contrast to traditional grammar and translation methods,
(D) When taught by the direct method, foreign-language instruction, in contrast to traditional grammar and translation methods,
(E) Instructing foreign languages by the direct method, which stands in contrast to traditional grammar and translation methods,

129. Modeling the formation of the terrestrial and gas giants is relatively straightforward and uncontroversial because the terrestrial planets of the Solar System are widely understood to have formed through the collision of micro-planets within the newly formed disk of gas surrounding the sun.

(A) is relatively straightforward and uncontroversial because the terrestrial planets of the Solar System are widely understood to have formed through the collision of micro-planets
(B) is relatively straightforward and uncontroversial because the terrestrial planets of the Solar System widely understood to have formed through micro-planets' colliding
(C) are relatively straightforward and uncontroversial because the terrestrial planets of the Solar System are widely understood to have formed through the colliding of micro-planets
(D) are relatively straightforward and uncontroversial because the Solar System's terrestrial planets are understood widely to have formed through the colliding of micro-planets
(E) is relatively straightforward and uncontroversial because of the wide understanding that the formation of the terrestrial planets of the Solar System were caused by the collision of micro-planets

130. Most bird species sing despite lacking vocal cords, compensating with their throat muscles and membranes for their absence by vibrating and generating sound waves when air from the lungs passes over them

(A) compensating with their throat and membranes for their absence by vibrating
(B) to compensate with their throat muscles and membranes by vibrating for their absence
(C) their throat muscles and membranes being compensated for their absence when they vibrate
(D) their throat muscles and membranes compensating for the absence by vibrating
(E) with compensation from their throat muscles and membranes for their absence that vibrates

131. However promptly the company responds to the recent decline in sales, they will need to reduce prices by at least 10% so as to remain competitive with its traditional rivals.

(A) However promptly the company responds to the recent decline in sales, they will need to reduce prices by at least 10% so as to remain
(B) However promptly the company responds to the recent decline in sales, it will need to reduce prices by at least 10% to remain
(C) Even if the company should respond promptly to the recent decline in sales, they will need to reduce prices by a minimum of 10% in remaining
(D) Even if the company promptly responded to the the recent decline of sales, it will need to reduce prices by a minimum of 10% to remain
(E) Regardless of if the company responds promptly to the recent decline in sales, it will need to reduce prices by at least 10%

132. Before the raising of chickens became industrial, they were far less important to human diets; researchers estimate that the birds were first eaten in significant numbers only about 2,200 years ago.

(A) Before the raising of chickens became industrial, they were far less important to
(B) Before the raising of chickens became industrial, they were of a far lesser importance in
(C) Before the industrial raising of chickens, their importance was far less important to
(D) Before chickens had been raised industrially, they were far less important to
(E) Before chickens were raised according to an industrial model, they were far less important to

133. One important aspect of Haydn's genius lays in his sense of the energy latent in his material—or maybe it was his invention of material that gave him the requisite energy to sustain such remarkable musical compositions.

(A) lays in his sense of the energy latent in his material—or maybe it was his invention of material that gave
(B) lays in his sense of the energy latent in his material—or maybe it was his inventing of material that gave
(C) lies in his sense of the energy latent in his material—or perhaps in his invention of material that gave
(D) lies in his sense of his material's latent energy—or maybe his invention of material to give
(E) lay in his sense of the latent energy of his material—or perhaps his invention of material which would give

134. Plunging prices are revealing the extent to which nations, hailed in recent years as having outgrown their roots in natural resources, still rely heavily on those commodities.

(A) as having outgrown their roots in natural resources, still rely heavily
(B) to have outgrown their roots in natural resources, are still heavily reliant
(C) as an outgrowth of their roots in natural resources, still rely heavily
(D) to outgrow their roots in natural resources, are still relying heavily
(E) as outgrowing their roots in natural resources, still heavily reliant

135. After Henry Ford established the Ford Motor Company in Detroit in 1903, the city rapidly became the United States' automotive capital and so remaining for more than seven decades.

(A) capital and so remaining
(B) capital and so to remain
(C) capital and had remained as such
(D) capital, remaining thus
(E) capital, which it will remain

136. A tablet containing one of the most famous mathematical texts from ancient Mesopotamia proves that the Babylonians had derived the formula that came later to be called the Pythagorean theorem long before the Greek philosopher Pythagoras would.

(A) had derived the formula that came later to be called the Pythagorean theorem long before the Greek philosopher Pythagoras would

(B) derived the formula later called the Pythagorean theorem long before the Greek philosopher Pythagoras did

(C) derived what was later called the Pythagorean theorem long before the time where the Greek philosopher Pythagoras was

(D) derived the formula later called the Pythagorean theorem long before the Greek philosopher Pythagoras has

(E) derived from the formula later called the Pythagorean theorem long before its derivation by the Greek philosopher Pythagoras

137. Many economists argue that the dollar's continued rise will help Europe and Japan overcome economic weaknesses by making their products cheaper in world markets and are boosting overall global growth.

(A) markets and are boosts overall global growth
(B) markets and that it will boost overall global growth
(C) markets, and global growth is boosted overall
(D) markets, and that global growth overall is boosted
(E) markets, with a boost overall in global growth

138. In his third book, *The Court and the World*, Supreme Court justice Stephen Breyer suggests that the court should not be willing to look abroad for guidance but should in some instances be encouraged to do it because about 20% of its cases involve events occurring outside the United States.

(A) but should in some instances be encouraged to do it
(B) but sometimes should be also encouraged to do this
(C) but should sometimes also be encouraged to do so
(D) and in some instances it should be encouraged to do this
(E) whereas in some instances it should be encouraged that it do so

139. When the Cooper Union for the Advancement of Science and Art opened its doors in 1859, the school represented for Peter Cooper the realization of an idea that had occupied his imagination for nearly three decades.

(A) the realization of an idea that had occupied his imagination
(B) the realization of an idea that was occupied by his imagination
(C) the realizing of an idea that would occupy his imagination
(D) that an idea which had occupied his imagination was realized
(E) an idea whose occupation of his memory was realized

140. Although it is estimated that more than 15% of adults are afraid of flying, a condition known as aviophobia, modern air travel is widely acknowledged to be safer than almost any form of transportation—far safer, for example, than automotive travel.

(A) widely acknowledged to be safer than almost any form of transportation
(B) acknowledged widely as safer than almost any transportation form
(C) widely acknowledged as being safer than almost any form of transportation
(D) widely acknowledged to be safer than almost any other form of transportation
(E) widely acknowledged that it is safer than almost any other form of transportation

141. Azurite, a carbonate mineral also known as Chessylite, has an exceptionally deep blue hue that has been described to be reminiscent of the color of winter skies since antiquity.

(A) hue that has been described to be reminiscent of the color of winter skies since antiquity
(B) hue that since antiquity described as reminiscent of the color that winter skies have
(C) hue, whose descriptions since antiquity are reminiscent of the color of winter skies
(D) hue, of which the descriptions have reminisced since antiquity about winter skies' color
(E) hue, which since antiquity has been described as reminiscent of the color of winter skies

142. Should the Albert Bridge be demolished, as some city planners regularly urge, Tower Bridge will become the only bridge in London to exist in its original form.

(A) Should the Albert Bridge be demolished,
(B) If the Albert Bridge were demolished,
(C) Had the Albert Bridge been demolished,
(D) Were the Albert Bridge to be demolished,
(E) The Albert Bridge, having been demolished,

143. Cumulus clouds, clouds that produce little or no precipitation, cool the earth and reflecting the incoming solar radiation to come in many distinct sub-forms.

(A) clouds that produce little or no precipitation, cool the earth and reflecting the incoming solar radiation to come
(B) clouds producing little or no precipitation, cooling the earth and reflecting the incoming solar radiation, which comes
(C) clouds that produce little or no precipitation and that cool the earth by reflecting the incoming solar radiation, come
(D) clouds that produce little or no precipitation to cool the earth, and the incoming solar radiation is reflected, come
(E) clouds that produce little or no precipitation, cooling the earth and reflecting the incoming solar radiation, comes

144. In the Southern Hemisphere, mild and rainy winters produce ideal breeding conditions for locusts, which creates a surge in population outpacing authorities' ability to control their spread.

(A) which creates a surge in population outpacing authorities' ability to control their spread
(B) which creates a population surge that outpaces authorities' ability to control their spread
(C) whose surge in population creates an outpacing of the ability to control their spread by authorities
(D) creating a surge in population that outpaces the ability of authorities to control the insects' spread
(E) and creates a surge in population which outpaces the ability of authorities to control their spread

145. The Must Farm archaeological site in Cambridgeshire, England, is considered so rich in Bronze age ruins that it has been compared to Pompeii, the Roman town buried by the eruption of Mount Vesuvius in the first century B.C.E.

(A) is considered so rich in Bronze age ruins
(B) is considered of such richness in Bronze age ruins
(C) is considered to have a great richness in Bronze age ruins
(D) considered to be so rich in Bronze age ruins
(E) which is considered to be so rich in Bronze age ruins

146. Even though individuals with Highly Superior Autobiographical Memory (HSAM) can remember details from their own lives' events in extraordinary detail, they appear to be no better than average to recall impersonal information like random lists of words.

(A) they appear to be no better than average to recall impersonal information like random lists of words
(B) they appear to be no better than average at recalling impersonal information such as random lists of words
(C) they appear as no better than average in recalling impersonal information such as random lists of words
(D) they appear to be no better than average when recalling impersonal information like random word lists
(E) but they appear to be no better than average when they recall impersonal information such as random lists of words

147. Parrots are not only capable of mimicking human speech but on some occasions also demonstrate their being able to form associations between words with their meanings.

(A) demonstrate their being able to form associations between words with their meanings
(B) demonstrate being able to form associations between words to their meanings
(C) demonstrate the ability of forming associations between words to their meanings
(D) demonstrate its ability to form associations between words and their meanings
(E) demonstrate the ability to form associations between words and their meanings

148. Alvin Ailey Dance Theater became a resident company of New York City's Clark Center for the Performing Arts in 1960, and having established a permanent home for his troupe, _Revelations, Ailey's famous character dance accompanied by traditional spirituals and gospel songs, was choreographed_.

(A) _Revelations_, Ailey's famous character dance accompanied by traditional spirituals and gospel songs, was choreographed
(B) Ailey's famous character dance _Revelations_, accompanied by traditional spirituals and gospel songs, was choreographed
(C) Ailey choreographed his famous work _Revelations_, a character dance accompanied by traditional spirituals and gospel songs
(D) _Revelations_ was choreographed, which was Ailey's famous character dance accompanied by traditional spirituals and gospel songs,
(E) the choreography of _Revelations_, Ailey's famous character dance, was accompanied by traditional spirituals and gospel songs

149. Professional liability insurance, also known as professional indemnity insurance, focuses on the alleged error in the performance or financial loss from a product sold by the policyholder.

(A) error in the performance or financial loss from
(B) error in the performance of or financial loss from
(C) error in the performance or financial loss
(D) error in the performance and financial loss of
(E) error of the performance and financial loss from

150. Although female authors were permitted to publish under their own names in England during the Victorian era, Mary Ann Evans (George Eliot) nevertheless elected to use a pseudonym so as to escape the stereotype of the female romance novelist.
(A) so as to escape
(B) for the escape from
(C) in order that she could escape
(D) so that she could escape
(E) in escaping

# Answer Key

## Identifying Non-Essential Words and Phrases, p. 26

1.  Over the next 50 million years, the cesium fountain atomic clock, **considered the most precise form of timekeeper ever created,** is expected to become inaccurate by less than a single second.

2.  Each year, the field of fluid dynamics, **a field that is as mathematically demanding and challenging to the nonscientist as any field of physics,** produces compelling and beautiful videos by capturing motion and movement that cannot be seen with the naked eye.

3.  More than any other recent innovation in entertainment, Internet streaming has the **potential, even the likelihood,** to create an entirely new narrative genre: one with elements of television, film and the novel.

4.  Used in some martial arts, the Red Belt, **one of several colored belts intended to denote a practitioner's skill level and rank,** originated in Japan and Korea.

5.  Patients who receive anesthesia during surgery are put into a semi-comatose state, not, **as many people assume,** a deep state of sleep.

6.  Because dams supply relatively little water, **independent experts and most environmental groups argue, aggressive** modern methods of water storage and management are required.

7.  Centered in Nantucket, Massachusetts, whaling, **a risky pursuit that led sailors halfway across the world and sometimes to the bottom of the sea,** was a lucrative business during the early nineteenth century.

8.  Human "computers," **once responsible for performing basic numerical analysis for laboratories,** were behind the calculations for everything from the first accurate prediction of the return of Halley's Comet to the success of the Manhattan Project.

9.  Entertainment sources such as movies and books are not, **some critics claim,** responsible for shaping a culture, only for reflecting it.

10.  The Environmental Protection Agency's Clean Power Plan, **a major component of governmental efforts to push electricity generators away from coal and toward natural gas,** provides businesses with incentives for renewable-power generation.

11.  Illegal logging has declined in recent years, but the practice, **which was once nearly responsible for destroying the monarch butterfly's winter habitat,** persists in a number of regions.

12.  Norman Rockwell's intricately conceived narrative paintings, **reproduced widely in magazines,** appealed to a vast audience of readers who recognized themselves in the stories the images told.

13.  Unlike programs created for online distribution, network television shows, **which produce new episodes while the seasons air,** can alter their storylines midseason if ratings drop or a new character is rejected.

14.  The right and left portions of the amygdala, **two almond-shaped groups of nuclei located deep and medially within the temporal lobes of the brain,** have independent memory systems but work together to store, encode, and interpret emotion.

15.  Forensic biology, **the application of biology to law enforcement,** has been used for a wide range of purposes, including identifying illegal products from endangered species and preventing collisions between birds and wind turbines.

## Sentences and Fragments, p. 34

1.  Fragment: The pyramids of ancient Egypt, constructed as monuments to the Pharaohs' **greatness, were** built with the help of immense armies of slaves.

2.  Fragment: Although the painter has earned praise for his ironic depictions of everyday life, neither humor nor self-awareness is apparent in his **work; rather, it appears** to rely predominantly on cliché.

3.  Sentence

4.  Fragment: Quasars, the most energetic and distant members of a class of objects called active galactic nuclei, **are** often caused by collisions of galaxies, with the galaxies' central black holes merging to form either a supermassive black hole or a binary black hole system.

5.    Fragment: A recent trend of advertisers treating major awards ceremonies as platforms for new ads that will elicit an audience response **seems** to be intensifying, with a variety of well-known companies planning to introduce new campaigns.

6.    Sentence

7.    Fragment: Recent findings from research on moose **suggest** that the development of arthritis in human beings may be linked to nutritional deficits as well as to the natural consequences of aging.

8.    Fragment: Although photovoltaic (PV) cells, first discovered in the 1950s, have long been the dominant source for solar **power, concentrated** solar power (CSP) technology has been rising in popularity in recent years as well.

OR: Photovoltaic (PV) cells, first discovered in the 1950s, have long been the dominant source for solar **power, but concentrated** solar power (CSP) technology has been rising in popularity in recent years as well.

9.    Fragment: A popular novelist and playwright, George Barr McCutcheon **is** best known for the series of novels set in Graustark, a fictional country in Eastern Europe.

10.   Sentence

11.   Fragment: Brunei is the only sovereign state located entirely on the island of **Borneo; the** remainder of the island's territory is divided between the nations of Malaysia and Indonesia.

12.   Fragment: Although Rodin purposely omitted crucial elements such as arms from his sculptures, his consistent use of the human figure **attested** to his respect for artistic tradition.

13.   Correct

14.   Fragment: When companies move from a traditional office model to an open office **model, discrete** offices placed along a central corridor are removed in order to make way for large communal rooms.

15.   Fragment: In 1763, the signing of the Treaty of Paris marked the end of the Seven Years' War, also known as the French and Indian **War, ushering in (or: War, and ushered in)** a period of British dominance outside of Europe.

**Subject-Verb Agreement, p. 44**

1.    First described by Aristotle in his *Poetics* (c. 335 B.C.E.), the process of living vicariously through a fictional character in order to purge one's emotions **is** known as catharsis.

2.    On the border between China and Tibet **lie** the Himalaya Mountains, which rise to more than 25,000 ft. above sea level and include some of the highest peaks in the world.

3.    The buildings of Frank Gehry, including Gehry's private residence, **attract** thousands of visitors annually because critics frequently praise his designs for embodying the most important principles of contemporary architecture.

4.    Although Andrew Carnegie and Cornelius Vanderbilt eventually became two of  most powerful figures in business during the late nineteenth century, neither **was** born into a wealthy family.

5.    Correct

6.    Playboating, a discipline of whitewater rafting or canoeing in which players stay in one spot while performing a series of complex maneuvers, **involves** specialized canoes designed specifically for the sport.

7.    Often found in plastic drinking bottles **are** substantial amounts of a substance known as Bisphenol A, a potentially toxic chemical that may affect the brains and behaviors of infants and young children.

8.    Louise Glück's seemingly straightforward language and unadorned style **give** her poems an air of accessibility that masks the intensity of their content.

9.    Among the finds from a recent archaeological dig in London **were** earthenware knobs originally used for "pay walls," boxes into which Elizabethan theater-goers deposited their admission fees.

10.   One of the animal kingdom's best jumpers **is** the flea, whose ability to leap up to 200 times its own body length is virtually unsurpassed among either insects or other land-dwelling creatures.

11.   Correct

12. The patent for the first mechanical pencils **was** granted to Sampson Morgan and John Hawkins in England during the early nineteenth century, a time when fountain pens were the most commonly used writing implement.

13. Each of the Taino's five chiefdoms, which inhabited the Bahamas before the arrival of Europeans during the late fifteenth century, **was** ruled by a leader known as a *cacique*.

14. Writing about scientific matters **poses** a problem because it requires the adoption of imprecise metaphors that allow new findings to be put in perspective for readers with minimal expertise.

15. Possible explanations for the suspicion surrounding Shakespeare's Macbeth **include** the superstition that the witches' song is an actual incantation and the belief that theaters only mount the play when they are in need of money.

16. *Saint Maybe*, the twelfth novel by Pulitzer prize-nominated author Anne Tyler, revolves around a protagonist whose efforts to compensate for a single thoughtless act **dictate** the shape of his entire life.

17. The Hebrides islands have been continuously occupied since the Mesolithic period, and the culture of their inhabitants **has** been shaped by the successive influences of Celtic, Norse, and English-speaking peoples.

18. Found throughout England, stiles, structures that **provide** people with a passage through or over a fence, are often built in rural areas or along footpaths in order to prevent farm animals from moving between enclosures while allowing path users to travel freely.

19. Correct

20. Opposition to rodeos from animal-rights workers **centers** primarily on the poor treatment and living conditions of the horses that are ridden in competitions.

21. Because planes have been grounded and flights eliminated from schedules, the number of airplane tickets available to passengers **has** declined, causing prices to rise.

22. Preliminary studies of the new drug **suggest** that adverse effects are unlikely and, moreover, that any reactions that do occur will probably be minor.

23. Correct

24. Dry stone structures, structures built from stones not bound together by mortar, **achieve** stability because of their unique construction method, which is characterized by load-bearing façades of carefully selected interlocking stones.

25. A landmark 2015 report that cast doubt on the results of dozens of published psychology studies has exposed deep divisions in the field, but neither the report itself nor the critique published in response **has** found evidence of data fraud or manipulation.

## Cumulative Review 1: Chapters 1-4, p. 47

1. B
2. C
3. A
4. B
5. E
6. D
7. C
8. D
9. A
10. E

## Verb Exercise 1, p. 52

1. Correct

2. After traveling widely through Russia, where he discovered many previously unknown artistic masterpieces, Diaghilev **mounted** a massive exhibition of Russian portraiture in St. Petersburg.

3. Correct

4. In 1915, the Dutch government approved the proposal for new ships to protect its holdings in the East Indies, not realizing that the request **had been/was** withdrawn because of the start of the First World War.

5. Correct

6. By the time Pearl Buck was awarded the Nobel Prize for Literature in 1938, she **had been** a best-selling author in the United States for nearly a decade.

7. Correct

8.   During the 1950s, the Detroit area emerged as a metropolitan region with the construction of an extensive freeway system that **expanded** in the following decades.

9.   Correct

10.  In 1309, Pope Clement V moved the papacy from Rome to the French city of Avignon and **left** Rome prey to the ambitions of local overlords.

**Verb Exercise 2, p. 57**

1.   By the time suffragist Elizabeth Cady Stanton narrowed her political focus to women's rights, she **had been** an active member of the abolitionist movement for several decades.

2.   In 1498, the Dutch scholar Erasmus of Rotterdam moved from Paris to England, where he **would** eventually be appointed as a professor of ancient languages at Cambridge.

3.   Were an earthquake to strike, the bridge's concrete piers **would** sway and absorb the majority of the shock, thus limiting the amount of damage sustained by areas that lack additional steel reinforcements.

OR: **Should an earthquake strike/If an earthquake strikes**, the bridge's concrete piers will sway and absorb the majority of the shock, thus limiting the amount of damage sustained by areas that lack additional steel reinforcements.

4.   Correct

5.   Correct

6.   Mahatma Gandhi, who was born in India, studied law in London and in 1893 moved to South Africa, where he **spent** twenty years opposing discriminatory legislation.

7.   Over the last century, several dozen boats are known to have sunk off of the French Frigate Shoals, part of an enormous protected zone that covers nearly 150,000 square miles in the Pacific Ocean.

8.   The country's economists speculate that thousands of additional jobs would have been lost if consumer demand for domestically manufactured products **had** continued to decline.

9.   Correct

10.  Since the 1950s, computer scientists **have struggled** to create a machine capable of responding to human language, but despite their many attempts, they have achieved only limited success.

11.  Correct

12.  Should it be proven, the researchers' theory **will confirm** that the first life evolved on Earth shortly after the Late Heavy Bombardment, a period during which thousands of asteroids slammed into the young planet.

13.  After Great Britain achieved a decisive victory in the Seven Years' War, several successive ministries **implemented** reforms in an attempt to achieve more effective administrative control and raise more revenue in the colonies.

14.  Correct

15.  Hot air balloons **have been made** in every shape imaginable for over 40 years, although the traditional form remains most popular for both commercial and non-commercial uses.

16.  Correct

17.  Several members of the arts council have suggested that the sculpture, commissioned to mark the bicentennial of the city's founding, **be** placed in the city's main square.

18.  Morgan Stanley Chairman Robert Baldwin predicted that hundreds of brokerage firms would go out of business if fixed commissions **were** eliminated, a prophecy that was often quoted as its accuracy became increasingly apparent.

19.  Correct

20.  Since landing in a 96-mile-wide depression known as Gale Crater, Curiosity, the Mars rover, **has** made a number of discoveries, most notably that the crater once held lakes of fresh water.

21.  Hardly a stranger to self-censorship, Mark Twain never hesitated to change his prose if he believed that the alterations **would improve** the sales of his books.

22.  A Federal Aviation Administration task force has recommended that drone operators **be** required to register their aircrafts, paving the way for regulations intended to help reverse a surge in rogue drone flights.

23. Harold Sheldon was a scientist ahead of his time: in 1929, he wrote the original introduction to The Conquest of Space, the first English-language book to suggest that human beings **would** one day visit other planets.

24. Passed in response to widespread calls for financial reform, the 2010 Dodd-Frank Wall Street Reform and Consumer Protection Act, commonly referred to as simply "Dodd-Frank," stipulates that markets **be** restrained by a set of comprehensive regulations.

25. When former space shuttle commander Pamela Melroy retired from NASA in 2009, more than a decade after being selected for its astronaut training program, she **had** successfully logged close to 40 days in orbit.

26. Before playwright Lynn Nottage **was** awarded a Pulitzer Prize for Ruined in 2009, seven of her plays were successfully produced in off-Broadway theaters. OR: Before playwright Lynn Nottage **was** awarded a Pulitzer Prize for Ruined in 2009, seven of her plays **had been** successfully produced in off-Broadway theaters.

27. More than 6,000 languages are now spoken around the world, but nearly half of them will be extinct by the end of the twenty-first century if current trends **continue**.

28. Although some oil industry experts warn of dire consequences if rules to prevent another catastrophic oil spill in the Gulf of Mexico go into effect, regulators project that such laws **will** actually save money by preventing costly oil spills and saving lives.

29. Since Benjamin Franklin's invention of the lightning rod in 1752, the weather **has resisted** numerous efforts at manipulation by meteorologists, physicists, and amateur scientists alike.

30. Ergonomic experts predict that workers **will face** a greater risk of injury as they begin to communicate on more electronic devices in a wider range of professional situations.

**Noun and Pronoun Agreement, p. 68**

1. In the nineteenth century, Albany, the capital of New York State, became one of the first cities in the world to install public natural gas lines and electricity in the homes of **its** citizens.

2. Japan's status as an island country means that **the Japanese** must rely heavily on other countries for the supply of natural resources that are indispensable to national existence.

3. When the fossil of an enormous ancient penguin was unearthed in Peru, archaeologists discovered that **its (or: the penguin's)** feathers were brown and gray rather than black and white.

4. Correct

5. The jewel beetle, along with the fire-chaser beetle, **is an insect** that can thrive in trees scorched by wildfires or destroyed by other natural disasters.

6. Poor sleep habits among employees takes a heavy economic toll because workers who fall asleep on the job or are tired to the point of incompetence can lose significant amounts of money for **their** employers as well as for the broader economy.

7. The chariot, together with the horse itself, was introduced to the Egyptians by the Hyksos in the sixteenth century B.C. and undoubtedly contributed to **the Egyptians'/Hyksos'** military success.

8. Freemasonry consists of fraternal organizations that trace **their** origins to local guilds of stonemasons, which from the end of the fourteenth century regulated stonemasons' qualifications as well as their interactions with authorities and clients.

9. Correct

10. Some demographers predict that the world's population could climb to 10.5 billion by 2050, **raising** questions about how many people the Earth can support.

11. Apollo's sacred precinct in Delphi was a panhellenic sanctuary where every four years, beginning in the sixth century B.C., **athletes** gathered to compete in the Pythian Games, which served as precursors to the modern Olympics.

12. The grasslands of northeastern Montana have become a priority for the conservation movement because of **their** extraordinary biodiversity and high percentage of intact native prairie.

13. Although the two books include the same characters and recount the same series of events, they do **so** from different perspectives and are not intended to be read in any particular order.

14. Correct

15. A *BusinessWeek* analysis has found that companies can cause their existing clientele significant anguish when they merge, leading **them** to experience a loss in profits and persistent declines in trust and satisfaction.

16. The ability of an executive to effect a change within a company depends on **his or her** capacity to engage successfully with key members of the franchise community.

17. Consumer advocates caution that even seemingly low error rates in credit score calculations can affect numerous customers because each credit bureau has hundreds of millions of files in **its** possession.

18. Correct

19. Financial plans are valuable for a number of reasons, but perhaps the most significant one is that **they** can help people understand how to react to volatile markets.

20. Small population sizes and selective breeding have caused the number of changes in the DNA of domesticated dogs to increase, **leaving/a phenomenon that has left** the animals less able to reproduce.

21. Initially, the Ford Motor Company produced no more than a few cars a day, but within a decade **it** led the world in the expansion and refinement of the assembly line concept.

22. The secret behind the *Mona Lisa* lies in the matter of which retinal cells pick up the image of the iconic figure's enigmatic smile and how **they/those cells channel** the information to the brain.

23. Correct

24. Munich is situated at a high altitude and in close proximity to the northern edge of the Alps, **making** large amounts of precipitation common in both the city and its surrounding regions.

25. Though the federal income tax is progressive in principle, the dizzying provisions of the tax code make **it** less transparent, less efficient, and probably more regressive in practice.

**Relative Pronouns, p. 74**

1. In classical Athenian democracy, citizens **who** failed to pay their debts were barred from attending assembly meetings and appearing in court in virtually any capacity.

2. Correct

3. The poet's works are unusual for the period **when/in which** they were written because they frequently include elements such as short lines and unconventional punctuation.

4. Supercells, the massive thunderstorms with rotating hearts **that** form the most intense tornadoes, contain winds that increase in strength and change direction with height, generating horizontal tubes of rotating air parallel to the earth's surface.

5. Correct

6. When readers who obtain their news from electronic rather than printed sources send articles to their friends, they tend to choose ones **that** contain intellectually challenging topics.

7. Correct

8. Alexander von Humboldt resurrected the word "cosmos" from the ancient Greek and assigned it to his multi-volume treatise *Kosmos*, **in which** he sought to unify diverse branches of scientific knowledge and culture.

9. In an era **when/in which** women painters were not easily accepted by the artistic community or patrons, Artemisia Gentileschi (1593-1656), who painted many pictures of strong and suffering women from myth and the Bible, became the first female member of the Accademia di Arte del Disegno in Florence.

10. Correct

11. There are more than 200 known Upanishads, **of which** the first dozen are considered particularly important; consequently, they are referred to as the principal or main Upanishads.

12. Correct

13.   William Etty's *The Wrestler* was painted at a time **when/in which** sports were becoming increasingly popular, and the work is both a reflection of that trend and a part of the English tradition of copying poses from classical Hellenistic works.

14.   Correct

15.   Correct

**Adjectives vs. Adverbs, p. 78**

1.   Both bizarre and familiar, fairy tales are intended to be spoken rather than read, and they possess a **truly** inexhaustible power over children and adults alike.

2.   Correct

3.   Examined under a microscope, a glass of apparently crystalline water can reveal a hodgepodge of microscopic drifters that appear quite **different** from other aquatic creatures.

4.   Though few people believe that human beings are entirely rational, a world governed by Voltaire and Locke would, in all probability, operate **more fairly** than one governed by anti-Enlightenment principles.

5.   Italian nobleman Cesare Borgia was ruthless and vain, but he was also a brilliant Renaissance figure who was **exceedingly** well-educated in the Greek and Latin classics.

6.   Surrounded by a well-known racing circuit that was created in the 1960s Lake Pergusa, the only **naturally** occurring lake in Sicily, has in recent years hosted a number of international sporting events.

7.   When Mt. Vesuvius first began to show signs of eruption, many of the people living at the base of the volcano **hastily** abandoned their villages in order to seek cover in nearby forests.

8.   Correct

9.   More is known about Augustine, Bishop of Hippo, than is known about any other figure from the ancient world, and his personality and perceptiveness shine **more brightly** than those of his contemporaries.

10.   Tests on the germination rates of *Salsola imbricata*, a shrub known for its salt tolerance, show that the plant sprouts **more quickly** at 20°C than at higher temperatures and that it shows higher germination rates at low salinity levels than at high ones.

**Cumulative Review 2: Chapters 1-8, p. 80**

1. D
2. C
3. E
4. B
5. A
6. C
7. B
8. C
9. E
10. E
11. A
12. D
13. E
14. A
15. C

**Dangling Modifiers (suggested corrections), p. 86**

1.   Once known to live throughout much of Europe and North America, the **gray wolf** declined in population as a result of the destruction of its habitat.

2.   Widely considered to be among the greatest pianists of her age, **Clara Wieck** began her musical studies when she was five years old; by the age of twelve she was renowned as both a performer and a composer.

3.   Precise, unforgiving, and frequently unnatural, **the form of classical ballet developed at the French court in the 1700s and perfected in Russia two centuries later** is more physically or mentally demanding than any other artistic pursuit.

4.   Correct

5.   A recipient of the Presidential Medal of Freedom, **Barbara Jordan** became one of the most politically accomplished African-American women in the United States when she was elected to Congress.

6.   Subject to Moorish rule until the twelfth century, **many Spaniards** still spoke Arabic when their cities first came under the control of European monarchs.

7.   Historically based on the carving of walrus ivory, which was once found in abundance, **Inuit art** has been characterized by the inclusion of prints and figures made from soft stone since the mid-twentieth century.

8. Correct

9. Predicting renewed interest in their country's natural resources, **political leaders** have established a plan to create mines in the most underdeveloped regions.

10. Raised in Hong Kong and Shanghai before he moved to the United States in 1935, **I.M. Pei** designed buildings that were immediately recognizable because of their characteristic glass exteriors and use of geometrical forms.

11. Since the 1970s, plastic bags have a been a staple in grocery stores; environmentalists now estimate that close to a trillion such bags are distributed worldwide each year.

12. Recent studies have shown that by consuming a small amount of dark chocolate daily, **most people** can improve their overall health.

13. Correct

14. Often spending their time hidden under submerged ledges or in crevices within reefs, **many nurse sharks** exhibit a preference for specific resting sites, returning to them each day after the night's hunting.

15. Drawn in black and white, **Marjane Satrapi's graphic novel Persepolis**, a combination of comic-strip form and astute political commentary, was written as a semi-autobiographical depiction of Satrapi's childhood and adolescence in Tehran and Vienna.

**Misplaced Modifiers (suggested corrections), p. 87**

1. Investors and executives in startup companies typically receive **preferred stock, a class of shares** that is often accompanied by a guaranteed payout when the companies go public.

2. In the mid-fifteenth century, **the printing press was introduced in Europe by Johannes Gutenberg, a goldsmith** who devised a hand mold to create metal movable type and adapted screw presses and other existing technologies to create a printing system.

3. When economic activity weakens, monetary policymakers can push interest rate targets below the economy's natural rate, **temporarily** lowering the real cost of borrowing.

4. Some of the gold-diggers known as "forty-niners" traveled alone to California during the gold rush of 1849, but most formed companies that enabled them to share expenses and supplies **with other miners** during the long journey.

5. Born in Jamaica and first educated by his older brother, who possessed a considerable library of novels, poetry, and scientific texts, Claude McKay, **who became one of the most important poets of the Harlem Renaissance, moved to New York after studying agronomy in Kansas**.

6. Thousands of forged stamps, some very similar to their authentic counterparts, have been produced over the years, and **only** a thorough knowledge of philately offers any hope of detecting the fakes.

7. Throughout the Middle Ages, **fortresses protected cities across Europe from** bands of invaders that roamed in search of settlements to plunder.

8. The trees and rivers of the Ardenne provided the charcoal industry with assets that enabled **Wallonia, arguably the second most important industrial region of the world, to experience its great industrial period** during the late 1700s and early 1800s.

9. Correct

10. A recent discovery by astronomers suggests that for the past 2.5 billion years, a black hole located 250 million light years from Earth has been continuously emitting **a B-flat, the lowest note ever detected**.

11. Prohibition movements in Europe and the United States coincided with the advent of women's suffrage; newly politically empowered women often **strongly** supported policies that curbed alcohol consumption.

12. Bioluminescence, a phenomenon occurring primarily among sea-dwelling creatures but occasionally found among land-dwelling ones, is light created by **a chemical reaction produced within a living organism**.

13. Only after joining Miles Davis's Second Great Quintet did Herbie Hancock, who had performed **professionally** as a musician since the age of seven, succeed in finding his voice as a pianist.

14. Correct

15.  Praised by consumer magazines for being both versatile and affordable, the food processor performs a wide range of functions, including chopping, dicing, and pureeing, when **a switch is flipped.**

## Word Pairs, p. 95

1.  When a white dwarf takes on enough mass from a neighboring star, the pressure becomes so great at its center **that** runaway fusion occurs and the star detonates in a thermonuclear supernova.

2.  Correct

3.  It was not until the late seventeenth century **that** some English writers began to challenge the traditional view of commerce, which held that money-making was a source of moral corruption to be avoided at all cost.

4.  Correct

5.  India's natural resources, which range from the frigid lakes of the Himalaya Mountains **to** the tropical forests that lie hundreds of miles to the south, are home to an astounding variety of birds and other animals.

6.  The original British settlements in Australia, chosen exclusively for their strategic locations, had rocky soil and produced scarcely **any** food to support their inhabitants.

7.  Correct

8.  So great was the surplus of food created by the ancient Mesopotamians **that** it led to the establishment of the first complex civilization in human history.

9.  Obedience to authority is not only a way for rulers to keep order in totalitarian states, **but it is also** the foundation on which such states exist.

10.  Normally associated with airplane construction, wind-tunnel testing has also been applied to automobiles, not so much to determine aerodynamic forces **as** to determine ways to reduce the power required to move the vehicle on roadways at a given speed.

11.  The time devoted to books by publishing companies, experts suggest, has been reduced by both financial constraints **and** an increased emphasis on sales and marketing considerations.

12.  A leading figure in the Pop Art movement, Andy Warhol was at once celebrated for his depictions of everyday objects **and** denounced for his embrace of consumerist culture.

13.  New Zealand has been so geographically isolated throughout its history **that** unique forms of fauna have arisen there, making the island nation one of the most ecologically distinctive places on Earth.

14.  Between the early 1870s **and** the 1910s, when his health began to fail, Thomas Eakins painted exactingly from life, choosing as his subject the people of his hometown of Philadelphia.

15.  One of the main effects of industrialization was the shift from a society in which women worked at home **to** one in which women worked in factories and brought home wages to their families.

## Parallel Structure, p. 106

1.  Seeing the Grand Canyon, standing in front of a beautiful piece of art, and **listening** to a beautiful symphony are all experiences that may inspire awe.

2.  The most important reforms introduced by France in the Rhineland during Napoleon's reign resulted from the abolition of all feudal privileges and historic taxes, **the introduction of legal reforms through** the Napoleonic Code, and the reorganization of the judicial and local administrative systems.

3.  The Delphic Oracle exerted considerable influence throughout the Greek world as well as in its peripheral regions, and she was consulted before major undertakings such as battles and **the establishment of colonies**.

4.  Correct

5.  In addition to providing badly needed space in cramped cities, skyscrapers fulfill an important social role because they connect people and **foster creativity**.

6.  The Euphrates River receives most of its water in the form of rainfall and melting snow, resulting in peak volumes during the spring months and **low volumes** during the summer and autumn ones.

7. Because human behavior is erratic and driven by emotion as well as **logic**, it is exceedingly difficult to predict the short-term directions of major markets, even when events would seem to be entirely predictable.

8. Except in very rare cases, photographers and artists seem to instinctively arrange compositions in order to make the experience of looking at the images dramatic, impressive and, above all, **engaging** to viewers.

9. It is almost as difficult to find consistent information about the Fort Pillow incident, which took place in Tennessee during the American Civil War, as (it is) **to determine** the significance of its outcome.

10. Correct

11. There is evidence of vast economic disparity in Viking society as early as the first century A.D., with some people living with animals in barns and others **dwelling** nearby in large, prosperous homes.

12. The title role of Bellini's opera *Norma*, one of the most difficult roles in the soprano repertoire, calls for a wide vocal range, dynamic control, and **the ability** to convey a wide range of emotions.

13. Taking actions without fully considering their risks is a form of wishful thinking known as exaggerated expectation—a phenomenon that is known as "reaching for yield" and **that has been** observed in many areas of life.

14. The term "single family house" describes how a house is built and who is intended to live in it, but it does not indicate the house's size, shape, or **location**.

15. Among Marie Curie's most significant achievements were the development of the theory of radioactivity, **the invention of** techniques for isolating radioactive isotopes, and the discovery of polonium and radium.

16. Although 68 of the female delegates at the Seneca Falls convention signed the Declaration of Sentiments, a document that included demands for many basic rights for women, only 32 of the male delegates **did**.

17. Listings by the Fish and Wildlife Service treat lions in different regions as genetically distinct subspecies, a division that echoes international classifications and **is** supported by scientific data.

18. Correct

19. In contemporary education, there is a disturbing contrast between the enormous popularity of certain pedagogical approaches and **the lack of** credible evidence for their effectiveness.

20. Antiques are typically objects that show some degree of craftsmanship or attention to design, and they are considered desirable because of their beauty, rarity, or **usefulness**.

21. Correct

22. Correct

23. Correct

24. Known for her musical compositions as well as for her poems and letters, Hildegard of Bingen was just as renowned in the twelfth century as **in** the twentieth.

25. Drawing on a wide range of influences and ideas, including modernist and avant-garde developments, Stanislavsky's work was as important to the creation of socialist realism in the Soviet Union as it was to **the development of** psychological realism in the United States.

26. Experiments on animals have in recent years challenged conventional thinking about heredity, suggesting that environmental factors play nearly as important a role in determining an individual's appearance and personality as genetic ones **do**.

27. The development of identity was one of psychologist Erik Erikson's greatest interests, dominating his own life as well as ~~in~~ his theoretical writings.

28. Correct

29. Though no longer a household name, nineteenth century English biologist Richard Owens published more than 600 articles and made discoveries that were nearly as important as Darwin's **were**.

30. Hans Holbein was one of the most exquisite draftsmen of all time, renowned for the precise rendering of his drawings **and the compelling realism of his portraits**.

## Faulty Comparisons, p. 116

1.  The writings of John Locke, unlike **those of** Thomas Hobbes, emphasize the idea that people are by nature both reasonable and tolerant.

2.  **Like** bears, coyotes are expanding into new habitats in recent decades because human settlements have encroached upon the wooded areas where they once lived.

3.  Doctors in Norway prescribe fewer antibiotics than **do doctors in any other country (or: than doctors in any other country do)**, so people do not have a chance to develop resistance to many kinds of drug-resistant infections.

4.  Gustave Caillebotte was a both a member and a patron of the circle of painters known as the Impressionists, although his works were much more realistic than **those/the works of** many other artists in the group.

5.  **Like** modern joint-stock companies, the Roman publicani were legal bodies independent of their members, whose ownership was divided into shares known as parties.

6.  Correct

7.  **In contrast to** merchants in coastal regions of central Asia, merchants in landlocked regions had fewer trade options because of their distance from maritime routes of commerce and because the aridness of the steppes made agriculture difficult.

8.  Even though the university has been wracked by recent administrative scandals, its reputation is still significantly better than **those/the reputations of** most other schools of comparable size and location.

9.  During the period between 1870 and 1900, the United States saw an influx of millions of European immigrants because wages in the United States were at that time much higher than **(they were) in** Europe.

10. Unlike motor vehicles, which run on a prepared flat surface but can move in any direction, **rail vehicles** are directionally guided by the tracks on which they run.

11. Archaeologists have long been far more puzzled by members of the Saqqaq culture, the oldest known inhabitants of Greenland, than by **those** of other prehistoric North American cultures.

12. A source of intense fascination for both art historians and museum patrons, the *Mona Lisa*, which has been exhibited continuously at the Louvre since 1797, is perhaps more famous than **any other** work of art in Europe.

13. At an apparent magnitude of 8.4, a brightness comparable to **that of** Saturn's moon Titan, the Crab Nebula is not visible to the naked eye but can be perceived with binoculars under favorable conditions.

14. Correct

15. The reproduction of ciliates, **in contrast to reproduction** in other organisms, takes place when a specimen splits in half and grows a completely new individual from each piece.

## Cumulative Review 3: Chapters 1-12, p. 118

1. C
2. D
3. B
4. D
5. B
6. A
7. C
8. C
9. E
10. B
11. D
12. A
13. B
14. E
15. C

## Wordiness*, p. 125

1.  Although Troy, as described by Homer in The Illiad, was long considered an imaginary city, recent excavations have revealed remains consistent with some of the locations the poem depicts.

2.  *Glengarry Glen Ross* earned David Mamet a Pulitzer Prize in 1984, eight years after a trio of off Broadway plays **initially** garnered him major acclaim ~~for the first time~~.

3.  Bongoyo Island, located off the coast of Tanzania, has become a popular vacation spot for both tourists and Tanzanians because of **its proximity** to the mainland.

*When there is more than one possible correction, the most concise version is given.

4. Technology companies have spent years developing better, cheaper devices to immerse people in digital worlds, yet they are still trying to determine how to make virtual reality into an **indispensible technology** ~~that people cannot live without~~.

5. Although smartphone developers often attempt to reduce energy consumption by writing code that runs as quickly as possible, some instructions require more power than others, with the net result that energy consumption has actually **risen by nearly 25%** over the last two decades.

6. Scuba divers usually move around underwater by using fins attached to their feet, but **external propulsion** can be provided ~~from an outside source~~ by a specialized propulsion vehicle or a sled pulled from the surface.

7. Correct

8. Though it has now been banned in many countries, asbestos, **formerly** used in both industrial and domestic environments ~~in the past~~, has left potentially dangerous material in many buildings.

9. **Physicists hope** that within the next 50 years, string theory or other new theoretical work will provide a solid understanding of quantum gravity, including an explanation of how the universe began.

10. Although their work is highly stylized and depicts figures in contemporary dress, comic artists can be considered the inheritors of the classical tradition because they are universally concerned with the **representation of the human form**.

11. People who live in cities tend to eat more processed foods than those who live in rural areas; consequently, **the former experience more health problems**.

12. Correct

13. In response to a series of scandals, the governing council has adopted a handful of ethics rules, including one stating that members may not divulge confidential information acquired by **virtue of their positions**.

14. As the cost of the installing of green technologies has declined by **80 percent** between 2008 and 2015, solar panels have become an increasingly common accessory for middle-income and working-class households.

15. Faced with reports of an embezzlement scandal, company executives **intentionally** concealed the news from both shareholders and consumers ~~with great deliberateness~~ because they feared the inevitable financial consequences.

16. Vietnam became independent from Imperial China in 938 AD following the Battle of Bach Dang River, with **consecutive** Vietnamese royal dynasties flourishing ~~one after the other~~ as the nation expanded geographically and politically into Southeast Asia.

17. Province House, home to royal governors in seventeenth-century Massachusetts, was considered one of the grandest examples of American colonial architecture because **it possessed** beautiful Tudor-style chimneystacks.

18. **High rates of heart disease** are often blamed on modern diets and sedentary habits, but mummies of ancient people, who ate "natural" food and stayed active, also reveal signs of arterial plaque.

19. People with more bodily awareness tend to have **more intense reactions** to emotive pictures and report being more affected by the images; they are also better at describing their feelings.

20. Although eighteenth century European sailors and naval surgeons were convinced that citrus fruits could cure scurvy, the evidence did not conform to current theories of disease and was therefore **dismissed** by classically trained physicians, ~~who rejected it~~.

### Participles and Gerunds, p. 136

1. Correct

2. When the Stanford Artificial Intelligence Laboratory opened in 1963, its founders mistakenly predicted **that they would only need** a decade to create a thinking machine.

3. Although an array of government policies aim to support entrepreneurs through grants and tax breaks that facilitate the **acquisition** of capital, startup companies usually turn to private financing.

4. Correct

5. In response to **being** criticized for the poor nutritional value of its food, the restaurant chain has altered its menu to include a variety of more healthful options.

6.  A new hybrid approach to environmentalism **combines** existing public lands with private resources and a businesslike approach to land preservation, thus restoring wildlife and benefiting citizens.

7.  Correct

8.  The **depiction** of ordinary, everyday subjects in art has a long history, although scenes from daily life were often squeezed into the edges of compositions or shown at a smaller scale.

9.  Correct

10.  Although big vine production of grapes is not economically feasible, it demonstrates the vine's natural **ability** to produce fruit in an environmentally sustainable manner.

11.  **(As) one** of the most powerful leaders of his era, Sultan Suleyman I, known as Suleyman the Magnificent, was responsible for the expansion of the Ottoman Empire from Asia Minor to North Africa.

12.  The combination of spiritual fervor and close emotional self-scrutiny makes St. Augustine's *Confessions* read **as if they were** the work of a great novelist or poet.

13.  According to experts, people have the best chance of succeeding at their goals when **they have** an incentive — a financial, social, or physical cost — not to fail.

14.  Because **she experimented (or: because of her experiments)** with stream of consciousness narratives and the underlying psychological motives of her characters, Woolf is considered a major innovator in English literature.

15.  California is able to supply a third of the United States' vegetables and two-thirds of its fruits and nuts because **it has** the cold, wet winters and dry, sunny summers that characterize a Mediterranean climate.

16.  The Sherlock Holmes form of mystery novel **revolves** around a baffling crime that is ultimately solved by an eccentric master detective and his assistant, who summarizes the most interesting cases for the public.

17.  In his novel *Parallel Stories*, the Hungarian author Peter Nadas is concerned not only with historical events but also with their role **in influencing** people's everyday lives and emotions.

18.  Some planets that are very different from our own may have the potential **to turn** current theories of solar system formation upside down.

19.  Although **she did not publish** her first novel until she was 40 years old, Wharton became an exceptionally prolific writer: in addition to her seven novellas, 15 novels, and 85 short stories, she published poetry, books on design, travel, literary and cultural criticism, and a memoir.

20.  Correct

**Idioms and Diction, p. 151**

1.  For decades, scientist debated **whether** bears truly hibernate because the drop in body temperature of wintering bears is modest in comparison to the drop in body temperature of smaller hibernating animals.

2.  Correct

3.  Correct

4.  Nijinsky's genius as a dancer **lay** in his capacity to express through movement the emotions and subtleties of thoughts that others could express only through speech.

5.  Correct

6.  Throughout the Romantic period, a significant **number** of adventurous artists and writers flocked to Lake Geneva to savor its inspiring mountain scenery and serene atmosphere.

7.  Culture has become a force that may accelerate human evolution **because people have** no choice but to adapt to pressures and technologies of their own creation.

8.  A rebellion **against** the rigid academic art that predominated during the nineteenth century, the Art Nouveau movement was inspired by natural forms and structures.

9.  During the 1940s, French poet Victor Segalen was **considered a** minor figure; however, his reputation later began to soar, first in France and then internationally.

10.  If people spend time in a room with others who are yawning, it is almost certain **that** those individuals will begin to yawn as well.

11.   In creating psychoanalysis, Freud developed therapeutic techniques **such as** free association and transference, establishing their central role in the analytic process.

12.   After it was announced that the former president would appear **as** the convention's keynote speaker, several thousand people registered to attend, more than twice as many as had been expected.

13.   Correct

14.   Books, diaries, and newspapers recording African-American life during the Harlem Renaissance abound, but far **fewer** documents chronicling the lives of African Americans during the 1930s have been preserved.

15.   Correct

16.   A consumer should approach a potential tax-preparations company with many questions, regardless of **whether** the company's employees possess formal accounting credentials.

17. Although Korean lacquerware of the Goryeo period was highly prized throughout East Asia, it was also quite delicate, and only a small **number** of pieces are known to have survived until the present day.

18.   The term "Baroque" originally **referred to** the eccentric redundancy and noisy abundance of details that characterized seventeenth century artistic production—a sharp contrast to the clear and sober rationality of the Renaissance.

19.   The ENIAC computer, **unlike (or: in contrast to)** its predecessor, the EDVAC, ran on a binary rather than a decimal system and was able to store program instructions in its electronic memory.

20.   Early in the nineteenth century, the last of the property restrictions that prevented white males from voting in the United States were abolished, but 50 years later, the question of **whether** voting rights should be extended to other groups—particularly women and former slaves—remained controversial.

21.   Modern chemistry prevents insects from ravaging crops, lifts stains from carpets, and saves lives, **but** the constant exposure to chemicals **takes** a toll on many people's health.

22.   The words "based on a true story" give marketers a hook, one that appeals to movie-goers seeking something different **from** the established brands and pre-existing characters featured in the majority of films.

23.   Although birds are not generally known for their intelligence, recent findings have established **that** parrots often possess skills similar to those of human toddlers.

24.   Correct

25.   Although many traits are governed by a group of genes acting in concert, genes often have multiple functions, and altering a large amount of genetic material could **effect** unforeseen changes in an organism.

26.   Even though the idea of layering solar cells over plastic materials to capture energy from the sun is far from original, past attempts have been ineffective **because of** problems involving low energy yields as well as the use of colored rather than transparent materials.

27.   Elephants typically live in core, bond, and clan groups, with core groups **comprising** close relatives and bond and clan groups including more distant ones.

28.   John Dryden was removed from the post of British poet laureate—a post that was normally held for life—**because he staunchly refused** to swear an oath of allegiance to the king.

29.   Chopin's charming and sociable personality attracted loyal groups of friends and admirers **such as (or: including)** Liszt and George Sand, but his private life was often painful and difficult.

30.   Correct

# Answers and Explanations: Multiple-Choice Practice Questions

### 1. E: Sentence vs. fragment; Idiom: gerund vs. infinitive

Precipitation in California is often erratic, and <u>when</u> <u>arriving, tends to fall</u> in the mountainous northern and eastern parts of the state rather than the populous and fertile southern and western ones.

(A) when arriving, tends to fall
(B) when arriving, has a tendency of falling
(C) when it arrives, it tends in falling
(D) when it arrives, tending to fall
**(E) when it arrives, it tends to fall**

A subject + conjugated verb should follow the conjunction *when*; the gerund is not idiomatically acceptable. (A) and (B) include the gerund *arriving* and thus can be eliminated.

(C) is incorrect because the verb *tend* should be followed by the infinitive (*to fall*) rather than the gerund (*falling*).

(D) is incorrect because the main clause is a fragment that lacks a subject + conjugated verb: *tending to fall in the mountainous northern and eastern parts of the state rather than the populous and fertile southern and western ones* is not a complete sentence.

**(E) is correct** because it supplies a subject and verb (*it tends*) for the main clause, and uses the infinitive (*to fall*) after the verb *tends*.

### 2. C: Parallel structure

Some people contend that the distinction between an extreme sport and a conventional one has as much to do with marketing as <u>with the level of danger involved or how much adrenaline is generated</u>.

(A) with the level of danger involved or how much adrenaline is generated
(B) with the level of danger that is involved or the adrenaline amount it generates
**(C) with the level of danger involved or the amount of adrenaline generated**
(D) to the danger level involved or the amount of adrenaline being generated
(E) to the level of danger involved or the amount of adrenaline it generates

This question requires that you deal with two types of parallel structure simultaneously. The first clue is the presence of the word pair *as much…as*. Because the preposition *with* is used after the first half of the word pair, it must be used after the second half as well: *as much to do with x as with y*. Don't get distracted by *to*; it's part of the infinitive *to do* and doesn't affect the parallel structure.

Based on that information, you can eliminate (D) and (E).

Now look at the second type of parallel structure: the constructions on either side of the word *or* must match as well.

(A) is not parallel because the first side starts with a noun (*the level*) and the second side contains a pronoun (*how*).

(B) does contain two nouns (*level...the adrenaline amount*), but the structure is not parallel. The first item is active whereas the second is passive.

(C) is correct because the two sides match: each contains the structure *noun + of + noun* immediately followed by a past participle (*involved, generated*).

### 3. B: Subject-verb agreement

Just who inspired English painter John Constable's marvelously enigmatic cloud <u>studies, much prized by collectors, have</u> never been entirely clear.

(A) studies, much prized by collectors, have
(B) studies, much prized by collectors, has
(C) studies, many of them prized by collectors, have
(D) studies, many of which are prized by collectors,
(E) studies, and many of them prized by collectors, has

The fact that (A) and (C) contain the plural verb *have*, while (B) and (E) contain the singular verb *has* tells you that this question is testing subject-verb agreement.

The sentence contains a non-essential clause; even though the end of it is underlined, you may want to cross it out in order to simplify the sentence: *Just who inspired English painter John Constable's marvelously enigmatic cloud studies...have never been entirely clear.*

The key to answering the question is to recognize that the subject is not the plural noun *cloud studies*, which is located closest to the verb, but rather *Just who*. When *who* is used as a subject this way, it is always singular and requires a singular verb. That eliminates (A) and (C).

(B) is correct because the phrase *much prized by collectors* correctly functions as a non-essential clause describing the noun *cloud studies*, and the sentence makes sense when the non-essential clause is removed (*Just who inspired English painter John Constable's marvelously enigmatic cloud studies...has never been entirely clear*).

(D) is incorrect because this version is missing a main verb (*has*); the sentence no longer makes grammatical sense when the non-essential clause is removed.

(E) is incorrect because the construction *and many of them prized by collectors* is awkward and rhetorically unacceptable; a non-essential clause that describes a noun should not normally begin with *and*.

**4. A: Relative pronoun; Pronoun Agreement; Subject-verb agreement; Misplaced modifier**

James Joyce is best known for *Ulysses* (1922),
a landmark work <u>in which the episodes of Homer's</u>
<u>*Odyssey* are paralleled in an array of contrasting</u>
<u>literary styles, with the stream of consciousness</u>
<u>narration most prominent among them</u>.

- (A) **in which the episodes of Homer's *Odyssey* are**
  **paralleled in an array of contrasting literary**
  **styles, with the stream of consciousness**
  **narration most prominent among them**
- (B) where the episodes of Homer's *Odyssey* are
  a parallel array of contrasting literary styles, with
  the stream of consciousness narration being
  most prominent among these
- (C) where the episodes of Homer's *Odyssey* are
  paralleled in an array of contrasting literary
  styles, with the stream of consciousness
  narration is most prominent among these
- (D) in which the episodes of Homer's *Odyssey* is
  paralleled in an array of contrasted literary
  styles, and the stream of consciousness
  narration is most prominent among these
- (E) in which the episodes of Homer's *Odyssey* are
  paralleled in a contrasting array of literary styles,
  with the stream of consciousness narration most
  prominent among it

Don't get too distracted by the fact that the original version of the sentence is awkward. If you look at the answer choices, you'll notice that some answer choices contain *where* while others contain *in which*. If you remember that *where* should only be used to refer to places, then you can eliminate (B) and (C).

**(A) is correct** because it uses the plural pronoun *them* to refer to the plural noun *styles*. The use of *with* after the comma is also idiomatically acceptable.

(D) is incorrect because the plural noun *episodes* is the subject of the singular verb *is*; the singular noun *Odyssey* is part of the prepositional phrase *of Homer's Odyssey*. In addition, the pronoun *these*, which appears at the end of the sentence, should be followed by a noun.

(E) is incorrect because the singular pronoun *it* is used to refer to the plural noun *styles*. In addition, *contrasting* modifies *literary styles* and should be placed next to that phrase rather than next to *array* (the styles are contrasting, not the array itself).

### 5. D: Pronoun: missing referent; Idiom: gerund vs. infinitive

By day, hippos enjoy bathing in water to cool
themselves down, <u>which might have contributed
to their reputation for being</u> relatively sluggish and
sedentary.

- (A) which might have contributed to their
  reputation for being
- (B) which might contribute to its reputation for
  being
- (C) and this might have contributed to their
  reputation to be
- **(D) a preference that might contribute to their
  reputation for being**
- (E) a preference which might have contributed to
  their reputation to be

The pronoun *which* must refer to the noun that comes immediately before it. In this case, however, there is no noun, only a verb (*cool themselves down*), and a verb cannot act as a referent. That eliminates (A) and (B).

(C) is incorrect because *this* should be followed by a noun, and *reputation* should be followed by *for* + gerund rather than by an infinitive.

Logically, *which* must refer to the fact that hippos enjoy bathing to cool themselves, and both (D) and (E) correctly convey that idea by supplying the noun *preference*.

**(D) is correct** because the correct idiom is *reputation for* + gerund.

(E) is incorrect because *which* should only be used after a comma; *that* should be used after *preference*. In addition, *reputation to be* is idiomatically incorrect; *reputation for being* should be used instead.

### 6. A: Verb form; Subject-verb agreement

The starling, a bird mentioned in one of
Shakespeare's plays, <u>was first introduced in the
United States in 1890 and has since become</u> a
significant pest species.

- **(A) was first introduced in the United States in 1890
  and has since become**
- (B) were first introduced in the United States in 1890
  and has since become
- (C) was first introduced to the United States in 1890
  and would since become
- (D) was first introduced to the United States in 1890
  and since became
- (E) were first introduced to the United States in 1890
  and since has become

The sentence contains a non-essential clause, so you might want to start by crossing it out in order to simplify the sentence: *The starling…was first introduced in the United States in 1890 and has since become a significant pest species.*

Next, the word *since* is a tip-off that the present perfect (*has/have* + *past participle*) is required—the sentence is describing an action that began in the past (1890) and that is continuing into the present. Based on that information, you can eliminate (C) and (D).

(B) and (E) can be eliminated because the subject is the singular noun *the starling*, whereas the verb *were* is plural. Notice how this error becomes apparent when the non-essential clause is removed.

That leaves **(A), which is correct** because it uses the present perfect (*has become*) and the singular verb *was*.

Notice that the preposition issue (*of* vs. *to*) is a distractor here; either is acceptable.

### 7. C: Parallel structure; Logical construction

The outsourcing of hospital workers has become relatively common in the last decade, driven by a combination of factors including <u>a desire for efficiency gains as well as the growing pressure on hospitals to measure quality and keeping</u> people healthy after they are discharged.

(A)  a desire for efficiency gains as well as the growing pressure on hospitals to measure quality and keeping
(B)  a desire for efficiency gains as well as the growing pressure on hospitals to measure quality and they keep
**(C)  a desire for gains in efficiency as well as the growing pressure on hospitals to measure quality and keep**
(D)  a desire for gains in efficiency as well as the growing pressure on hospitals in measuring quality and to keep
(E)  a desire for gains in efficiency as well as the growth of pressure on hospitals that measure quality and keep

The phrase *as well as* indicates that this question is testing parallel structure; the constructions on either side of must match. The first item begins with a noun (*desire*), a construction that is retained in all of the answer choices. As a result, the second item must begin with a noun as well.

That line of reasoning might prompt you to start with (E); however, that answer does not really make sense. The sentence indicates that the hospitals being pressured are ones that are *already* measuring quality and keeping people healthy after they are discharged. Given the context of the sentence, a more logical meaning is that the hospitals are being pressured to start measuring quality and keeping people healthy. So even though (E) is grammatically correct, it's wrong.

If you look at the other answers carefully, you can notice that they don't actually contain parallel construction errors. *Growing* simply acts as an adjective that modifies the noun *pressure*, so the two sides are parallel after all.

When you look at (A)-(D), remember that the constructions on either side of the transition *and* must be parallel too.

(A) is incorrect because *measure* and *keeping* are not parallel.

(B) is incorrect because *to measure* and *they keep* are not parallel.

**(C) is correct** because *to measure* and *keep* can be considered parallel. The word *to* "applies" to *keep*; it is not necessary to repeat it.

(D) is incorrect because *in measuring* and *to keep* are not parallel.

## 8. E: Faulty comparison; Idiom

<u>Contrasting with the works of the rationalists,</u> Hume held that passion rather than reason governs human behavior and postulated that humans can have knowledge only of the objects of experience.

(A) Contrasting with the works of the rationalists,
(B) In contrast with the rationalists' work,
(C) In contrast to those of the rationalists,
(D) Unlike those of the rationalists,
**(E) Unlike the rationalists,**

The original version of the sentence incorrectly compares the works of the rationalists (things) to Hume (person). In addition, the phrase *contrasting with* is not idiomatic; the correct idiom is *in contrast to*. Since the non-underlined part of the comparison involves a person, the underlined portion must be changed to refer to people.

(B) contains the same error as (A), comparing the rationalists' work to Hume. In addition, the phrase *in contrast with* is not idiomatic.

(C) and (D) are both incorrect because they simply replace the noun *works* with pronouns (*that* and *those*). Grammatically, they re-create the original error.

**(E) is correct** because it compares the rationalists to Hume.

## 9. D: Dangling modifier; Pronoun agreement: missing referent

Categorized as a "red" volcano as a result of the lava that periodically spews from its crater, a depression measuring 2,100 feet across and 750 feet deep, <u>many cataclysmic explosions have been associated with Mt. Vesuvius since the volcano's most famous eruption in 79 A.D.</u>

(A) many cataclysmic explosions have been associated with Mt. Vesuvius since the volcano's most famous eruption in 79 A.D.
(B) they have associated many cataclysmic explosions with Mt. Vesuvius since its most famous eruption in 79 A.D.
(C) and many cataclysmic explosions were associated with Mt. Vesuvius since its most famous eruption in 79 A.D.
**(D) Mt. Vesuvius has exploded cataclysmically many times since its most famous eruption in 79 A.D.**
(E) Mt. Vesuvius has erupted cataclysmically many times since its most famous one in 79 A.D.

The key to recognizing what this question is testing is to cross out the non-essential clause, which is strategically placed to obscure the error: *Categorized as a "red" volcano as a result of the lava that periodically spews from its crater…many cataclysmic explosions have been associated with Mt. Vesuvius since the volcano's most famous eruption in 79 A.D.*

What is *categorized as a red volcano as a result of the lava that periodically spews from its crater*? Logically, Mt. Vesuvius. Since *Mt. Vesuvius* does not appear at the beginning of the clause in question, the modifier is dangling. In order to fix the error, *Mt. Vesuvius* must be placed at the beginning of the clause. That eliminates (A), (B), and (C).

**(D) is correct** because it places *Mt. Vesuvius* after the comma and uses the singular pronoun *its* to refer to Vesuvius.

(E) is incorrect because the pronoun *one* should logically refer to the noun *eruption*; however, only the verb *erupted* appears, and a verb cannot act as a referent.

## 10. B: Parallel structure

The wandering albatross, the first albatross ever to be described by naturalists, is a large seabird that belongs to the albatross family <u>and found primarily in the seas around Antarctica</u>.

(A)  and found primarily in the seas around Antarctica
**(B)  and that is found primarily in the seas around Antarctica**
(C)  and primarily found in the Antarctic seas
(D)  being found primarily in the seas around Antarctica
(E)  and are found primarily in the seas around Antarctica

The key to understanding how this question functions is to recognize that the underlined portion of the sentence is part of the clause beginning with *that,* and that the correct version must be parallel to the non-underlined portion of that clause, and that clause only. The rest of the sentence is effectively irrelevant.

(A) and (C) are incorrect because *found primarily* should be *is found primarily*. The albatross is not *a large seabird that found around Antarctica*. Rather, it is *a large seabird that is found around Antarctica.*

**(B) is correct** because it supplies the verb *is* before *found,* creating the passive construction that makes the sentence logical. In addition, the word *that* makes this version parallel to the beginning of the clause: *that belongs…that is found.*

(D) is incorrect because the gerund *being* is not parallel to the verb *belongs* in the non-underlined portion of the clause.

(E) is incorrect because the plural verb *are* does not agree with the singular subject, *a large seabird.*

## 11. B: Idiom

All of the country's political parties <u>agree as to whether constitutional reform is necessary to address</u> chronic instability and other pressing issues, but when it comes to deciding what kind of reform, they can only agree to disagree.

(A)  agree as to whether constitutional reform is necessary to address
**(B)  agree that constitutional reform is necessary to address**
(C)  have an agreement of constitutional reform being necessary to address
(D)  agree that constitutional reform is necessary for the addressing of
(E)  agree about whether constitutional reform is necessary to address

The correct idiom is *agree that,* eliminating (A), (C), and (E).

(D) is incorrect because *necessary* should be followed by the infinitive rather than the gerund.

That leaves **(B), which is correct** because it places the infinitive *to address* after *necessary*.

**12. E: Diction; Pronoun: ambiguous referent**

Even an act as apparently benign as <u>eliminating</u>
<u>mosquitoes could have serious ecological affects</u>
<u>because they interact</u> with other species in ways
that scientists do not yet fully understand.

(A) eliminating mosquitoes could have serious
ecological affects because they interact
(B) the elimination of mosquitoes can have serious
ecological affects because mosquitoes interact
(C) eliminating mosquitoes could have serious
ecological affects because they interact
(D) to eliminate mosquitoes can have serious
ecological effects because they interact
**(E) eliminating mosquitoes could have serious**
**ecological effects because mosquitoes interact**

If you look through the answer choices, you can notice that (A), (B), and (C) contain *affects* whereas (D) and (E) contain *effects*. The word in question functions as a noun, so *effects* is the correct version. That eliminates (A)-(C).

(D) is incorrect because the gerund *eliminating* rather than the infinitive *to eliminate* is more idiomatic here. *Can* should be *could*: the phrase *scientists do not yet fully understand* indicates that the sentence is describing a hypothetical situation. Finally, *they* is ambiguous because there are two plural nouns to which this pronoun could potentially refer: *mosquitoes* and *ecological effects*.

**(E) is correct** because it uses the gerund *eliminating* (in this case grammatically equivalent to a noun) to refer to "an act," and the conditional *could* to refer to a hypothetical situation. In addition, the inclusion of the noun *mosquitoes* removes the ambiguity created by the pronoun *they*.

**13. D: Pronoun agreement; Tense; Transition**

One historical theory posits that an important effect of
the Industrial Revolution was that living standards for the
general population began to increase consistently
for the first time in history, <u>while an opposing theory</u>
<u>holds that it did not begin</u> to improve meaningfully
until the late 1800s.

(A) while an opposing theory holds that it did not
begin
(B) while an opposing theory holds that they have
not begun
(C) but an opposing theory holds that it did not
begin
**(D) but an opposing theory holds that they did**
**not begin**
(E) with an opposing theory holding that it did
not begin

The easiest way to approach this question is to focus on the word *it*. When this pronoun appears in the underlined portion of a sentence, the question will often test pronoun agreement. Furthermore, the answer choices alternately include *it* and *they*, confirming that pronoun agreement is the focus of the question.

The next step is to determine which noun *it* refers to, and whether that noun is singular or plural. If you back up and read from the beginning of the sentence, you can see that the logical referent is the plural noun *living standards*. (What did not begin to increase meaningfully until the late 1800s? Living standards.) The plural pronoun *they* is therefore required, eliminating (A), (C), and (E). (E) is also incorrect because the sentence describes two opposing ideas, and the construction *with…-ING* conveys two similar ideas.

(B) is incorrect because the sentence describes a completed action in the past, as indicated by the mention of *Industrial Revolution* and *1800s*. The present perfect (*have not begun*) is incorrect because this tense should only be used to describe events continuing into the present.

**(D) is correct** because it correctly uses the plural pronoun *they* to refer to the plural noun *living standards*.

**14. E: Parallel structure; Participle**

Customized electric cargo bicycles can use specialized cycle lanes to travel around congested cities, <u>to outpace their fuel-driven four-wheel rivals, and delivers</u> a variety of goods and services.

- (A)  to outpace their fuel-driven four-wheeled rivals, and delivers
- (B)  to outpace their fuel-driven four-wheeled rivals, and deliver
- (C)  outpacing their fuel-driving four-wheeled rivals, and to deliver
- (D)  outpacing their fuel-driven four-wheel rivals, and delivered
- **(E)  outpacing their fuel-driven four-wheel rivals and delivering**

This is a parallel structure question with a twist. The original version appears to be testing a list with three items, two of which are underlined. The reasonable assumption is to work from the first, non-underlined item. Because that item is an infinitive (*to travel*), the other two items should presumably be infinitives as well.

(A) is incorrect because although the second item is an infinitive (*to outpace*), the third is a conjugated verb (*delivers*).

(B) is incorrect for the same reason as (A); the only difference is that the verb is plural (*deliver*).

(C) creates a different version of the original problem. Here, the first and third items are infinitives (*to travel, to deliver*), but the second item (*outpacing*) is not.

(D) is incorrect because each item in the list is presented in a different format.

**(E) is correct**, even though it changes the three-item list to a two-item. The two items are both participles *outpacing* and *delivering* that serve to modify the preceding clause and describe what electronic cargo bicycles do.

### 15. A: Subject-verb agreement; Relative pronoun

In general, the design of automotive spaces such as highways and parking lots <u>are overseen by traffic engineers, whose decisions heavily influence</u> drivers' behavior in those surroundings.

(A) **is overseen by traffic engineers, whose decisions heavily influence**
(B) are overseen by traffic engineers, whose decisions are heavily influencing
(C) are overseen by traffic engineers, whose decisions heavily influence
(D) is overseen by traffic engineers, which heavily influences
(E) is overseen by traffic engineers, of whom the decision influence heavily

If you look at the answer choices, you'll notice that they begin with a combination of singular (*is*) and plural (*are*) verbs. That pattern tells you that the question is testing subject-verb agreement, and that your next step is to determine the subject of that verb.

Don't be fooled by the plural noun *lots*, which appears immediately before the verb. It's part of the prepositional phrase *of automotive spaces such as highways and parking lots*. The actual subject is the singular noun *the design*. (What is overseen by traffic engineers? The design of automotive spaces.) A singular verb is therefore required, eliminating (B) and (C).

Now, look at the second part of each answer choice; notice that (A) includes *whose* whereas (D) includes *which*. Answers with *which* are frequently wrong, so you can start by assuming **(A) is correct**. That answer is in fact right because the singular verb *is* agrees with the subject *design* and the possessive pronoun *whose* accurately refers to traffic engineers.

(D) is incorrect because the pronoun *which* is missing a referent. Logically, *which* refers to the fact that the design of automotive spaces is overseen by traffic engineers, but the noun *fact* does not actually appear.

(E) is incorrect because the phrase *of whom the decisions influence heavily* is awkward and un-idiomatic. *Whose* rather than *of whom* should be used to indicate possession. Standard usage also requires that the adverb *heavily* be placed before *influence*.

### 16. D: Pronoun agreement: ambiguous referent

Arthur Conan Doyle, the creator of Sherlock Holmes, was himself a physician, <u>and there is evidence that he is modeled on one of the leading doctors of the day,</u> Joseph Bell of the Royal Edinburgh Infirmary.

(A) and there is evidence that he is modeled on one of the leading doctors of the day,
(B) and evidence exists that he is modeled on one of the leading doctors of the day,
(C) with evidence existing that he is modeled after one of the leading doctors of the day,
(D) **and there is evidence that Holmes was modeled on one of the leading doctors of the day,**
(E) and evidence exists that one of the day's leading doctors was a model for Holmes,

The most straightforward way to answer this question is to recognize that the underlined pronoun *he* is ambiguous because the beginning of the sentence includes two male names: Arthur Conan Doyle and Sherlock Holmes. Even though it is logical that *he* would refer to Holmes, the sentence does not actually make that association explicit. (A)-(C) contain the same problem and can therefore be eliminated.

**(D) is correct** because it repeats Holmes' name and because the phrase *one of the leading doctors of the day* correctly refers to Joseph Bell, whose name follows.

(E) is incorrect because it creates a misplaced modifier when it is plugged back into the sentence: the name *Holmes* does not logically modify *Joseph Bell of the Royal Edinburgh Infirmary*.

### 17. B: Parallel structure

Normally associated with airplane construction, wind-tunnel testing has also been applied to automobiles, not so much to calculate aerodynamic forces as <u>determining ways to reduce the power required to move vehicles on roadways</u> at a given speed.

(A) determining ways to reduce the power required to move vehicles on roadways
(B) to determine ways to reduce the power required to move vehicles on roadways
(C) to determine ways to reduce the power required for the moving of vehicles on roadways
(D) it has determined ways to reduce the power required to move roadways' motor vehicles
(E) in the determination of ways to reduce the power required to move vehicles on roadways

The fastest way to answer this question is to spot the word pair *not so much...as*. The underlined portion of the sentence, which follows the second half of the word pair, must match the non-underlined construction that follows the first half of the pair. Because an infinitive (*to calculate*) follows *not so much*, an infinitive must also follow *as*. That eliminates (A), (D), and (E).

**(B) is correct** because it begins with the infinitive *to determine* and also correctly uses infinitives after *ways* and *required*. Although the string of three infinitives may sound somewhat clumsy, it is grammatically and idiomatically acceptable.

(C) is incorrect because the gerund phrase *for the moving of vehicles* is awkward and un-idiomatic. According to standard usage, the infinitive should be used after *required*.

## 18. A: Verb form

One study has indicated that if the marriage patterns of 1960 were imported into 2005, the American economy's <u>Gini coefficient—the standard measure of income inequality—would fall to 0.34 from 0.43, a considerable drop</u> given that the scale runs from zero to one.

- (A) Gini coefficient—the standard measure of income inequality—would fall to 0.34 from 0.43, a considerable drop
- (B) Gini coefficient, the standard measure of income inequality, falls to 0.34 from 0.43, a considerable drop
- (C) Gini coefficient—the standard measure of income inequality—will fall to 0.34 from 0.43, a considerable drop
- (D) Gini coefficient—the standard measure of income inequality—will fall to 0.34 from 0.43, dropping considerably
- (E) Gini coefficient, the standard measure of income inequality, would fall to 0.34 from 0.43, a drop of consideration

The key to answering this question is to recognize that the non-underlined portion of the sentence includes an "if" clause (*One study has indicated that if the marriage patterns of 1960 were imported into 2005…*). That clause contains a verb in the past tense: *were*.

Recall the formula: "if" clause = past, main clause = conditional (*would* + *verb*). So the correct answer must include *would*.

**(A) is correct** because it includes the conditional (*would fall*) and begins the appositive at the end of the sentence with a noun phrase (*a considerable drop*) that refers back to the "fall."

(C) and (D) include the future (*will*) and can therefore be eliminated. (B) includes the present (*falls*) and can be eliminated as well.

(E) is incorrect despite the appropriate use of the conditional because the phrase *a drop of consideration* is not idiomatically acceptable; *considerable drop* is standard usage.

## 19. E: Word pair (so...that)

Internet usage has become <u>so pervasive in virtually</u> <u>every aspect of daily life, and many psychologists are</u> <u>beginning</u> to turn their attention to the impact of constant exposure to screens on the lives of children and adolescents.

(A) so pervasive in virtually every aspect of daily life, and many psychologists are beginning
(B) so pervasive in virtually every aspect of daily life, many psychologists are beginning
(C) so pervasive in daily life's virtually every aspect, so many psychologists are beginning
(D) of such pervasiveness in virtually every aspect of daily life that many psychologists are beginning
**(E) so pervasive in virtually every aspect of daily life that many psychologists are beginning**

The easiest way to answer this question is to recognize that the word *so*, which appears at the start of the sentence, must be paired with *that*. That eliminates (A), (B), and (C). Note that the use of different tenses (present vs. present perfect) is a distraction here; both are acceptable and have no effect on the correct answer. Only the word pair is relevant.

(D) is incorrect because the phrase *of such pervasiveness* is unnecessarily wordy, awkward, and idiomatically unacceptable.

**(E) is correct** because *so* is correctly paired with *that*, and no additional error is created.

## 20. D: Sentence vs. fragment; Non-essential clause; Pronoun agreement

In 1294 Boniface VIII began his papacy, replacing Celestine V, <u>who, having declared that it was</u> <u>permissible for a Pope to resign, and promptly did</u>.

(A) who, having declared that it was permissible for a Pope to resign, and promptly did
(B) who declared that it was permissible for a Pope to resign, which he promptly did
(C) who had declared that it could be permitted that a Pope resign and then promptly did this
**(D) who had declared that it was permissible for a Pope to resign and then promptly did so**
(E) who, having declared it permissible for a Pope to resign, then promptly doing so

Begin by crossing out the non-essential clause: *In 1294, Boniface VIII began his papacy, replacing Celestine V, who...and promptly did.*

Clearly, that does not make sense. (A) can therefore be eliminated. Note that if you skip this step, you risk not noticing that the original version is not a complete sentence.

(B) is incorrect because *which* is missing a referent. Logically, that pronoun refers to Celestine V's resignation, but the noun *resignation* does not appear—only the infinitive *to resign*. Because an infinitive cannot act as a referent, this version is incorrect.

(C) is incorrect because the phrase *that it could be permitted that a Pope resign* is awkward and not idiomatic, and because the pronoun *this* should be followed by a noun.

215

**(D) is correct** because it uses the past perfect to refer to a completed action (Celestine V's declaration that a Pope could resign) that occurred before a second action (Celestine V's resignation), and because it fixes the missing-referent problem in (C) by using the expression *did so*.

(E) is incorrect because it repeats the error in (A). If the non-essential clause is eliminated, the sentence does not make sense: *In 1294, Boniface VIII began his papacy, replacing Celestine V, who...then promptly doing so.*

### 21. B: Faulty comparison

Neuroscientists of today, unlike 30 years ago, have access to sophisticated instrumentation that has only become possible as a result of recent technological advances.

(A)  Neuroscientists of today, unlike 30 years ago,
**(B)  Today's neuroscientists, unlike those of 30 years ago,**
(C)  Neuroscientists who are conducting research today, unlike 30 years ago,
(D)  Neuroscientists conducting research today, in contrast to 30 years ago,
(E)  Neuroscientists who conduct research today, differing from that of 30 years ago,

The original version of the sentence compares today's neuroscientists (people) to 30 years ago (time). To fix the sentence, people must either be compared to people, or a time must be compared to a time.

**(B) is correct** because it compares people to people, appropriately replacing the singular noun *neuroscientists* with the singular pronoun *those*.

(C) and (D) create the same error as (A), just using wordier constructions.

(E) is incorrect because the pronoun *that* is singular, whereas *neuroscientists* is plural. In addition, the use of *differing from* is awkward and not idiomatic; the GMAT prefers *unlike*.

### 22. D: Relative pronoun; Verb form

SpaceX was founded in June 2002 by Elon Musk, whose goal was to build a simple and relatively inexpensive reusable rocket <u>which returns</u> into space on multiple occasions.

(A)  which returns
(B)  that returns
(C)  which will return
**(D)  that could return**
(E)  having returned

*Which* should only follow a comma, and there is no comma here, so (A) and (C) can be eliminated.

(B) is incorrect because the sentence is describing a hypothetical event, as indicated by the word *goal*. The present tense (*returns*) cannot be used to convey that meaning.

**(D) is correct** because the condition *could return* should be used to describe a hypothetical event.

(E) creates a grammatically unacceptable and illogical fragment: *having returned* indicates that an event has already happened, and the sentence is referring to an event that has not yet occurred.

## 23. D: Subjunctive, Subject-verb agreement

Because the country has made significant progress
in reducing its budget deficit, economic authorities
are recommending that its development aid
payments, <u>each of which is worth tens of millions of dollars,</u>
<u>are restored</u> by the beginning of next year.

  (A)  each of which is worth tens of millions of dollars,
        are restored
  (B)  each worth tens of millions of dollars, are restored
  (C)  each of these worth tens of millions of dollars,
        should be restored
  **(D)  each worth tens of millions of dollars, be restored**
  (E)  each of which are worth tens of millions of dollars,
        be restored

Start by eliminating the non-essential clause to simplify the sentence: *Because the country has made significant progress in reducing its budget deficit, economic authorities are recommending that its development aid payments, ...are restored by the beginning of next year.*

Now the relevant information becomes more apparent. The major structure tested in this question is the subjunctive, which is used for recommendations and commands. Here, the word *recommend* is a tip-off that the subjunctive (*be*) rather than the indicative (*are*) is required.

On that basis, (A) and (B) can be eliminated.

(C) is incorrect because *should* is unnecessary/redundant—by definition something that is recommended is something that "should" be done—and because *these* should be followed by a noun.

**(D) is correct** because the subjunctive *be* is correctly used with *recommend*.

(E) is incorrect because the plural verb *are* disagrees with the singular subject *each*.

## 24. B: Subject-verb agreement; Idiom

The choice and treatment of subject matter, rather
than careful attention to visual appearance, <u>defines</u>
<u>Realism as an artistic movement.</u>

  (A)  defines Realism as an artistic movement
  **(B)  define Realism as an artistic movement**
  (C)  define Realism to be an artistic movement
  (D)  define Realism as being an artistic movement
  (E)  defines the artistic movement that is Realism

The answer choices contain a mix of singular (*defines*) and plural (*define*) verbs, indicating that the sentence is testing subject-verb agreement.

The sentence also contains a non-essential clause that can be removed to simplify the sentence: *The choice and treatment of subject matter...defines Realism as an artistic movement.*

The sentence contains a compound subject (*choice and treatment*), which is plural. A plural verb (*define*) is therefore required. (A) and (E) contain singular verbs and can thus be eliminated.

**(B) is correct** because it provides the plural form of the verb (*define*) as well as the correct idiom—*define as* is standard usage.

217

(C) is incorrect because *define to be* is idiomatically unacceptable.

(D) is incorrect because the inclusion of the gerund *being* is awkward and unnecessary. It also creates an illogical meaning: read this way, the sentence implies that the choice and treatment of subject matter are responsible for making Realism an artistic movement. In contrast, a more logical interpretation is that the choice and treatment of subject matter are defining characteristics of the Realist movement.

**25. A: Word pair; Parallel structure; Subject-verb agreement**

> Cicero's influence on the Latin language was so immense that the subsequent history of prose in not only Latin <u>but also European languages up until the nineteenth century was said to be either a reaction against</u> or a return to his style.

(A) **but also European languages up until the nineteenth century was said to be either a reaction against**
(B) but also European languages up until the nineteenth century were said to be either a reaction against
(C) and European languages up until the nineteenth century was said to be either a reaction against
(D) but European languages up until the nineteenth century were also said to be either a reaction
(E) but also European languages up until the nineteenth century was said either to be a reaction

This is a fairly complicated sentence, so examine it in pieces. The key is to understand the underlined portion in relation to the sentence as a whole; if you focus only on the underlined portion, you will have no way to determine the answer.

The first piece is the word pair: the phrase *not only*, which appears right before the start of the underlined portion, indicates that the underlined portion must contain *but also*. That eliminates (C).

Now, look at the verbs: (A) and (E) include *was*, whereas (B) and (D) include *were*. That pattern indicates that the question is testing subject-verb agreement. The next step, therefore, is to back up and figure out which noun is the subject, taking the entire sentence into account.

What was said to be either *a reaction against or a return to his style*? Logically, *the subsequent history (of prose)*, which is singular. Note that if you only consider the underlined portion, you risk mistaking *European languages* (plural) for the subject.

Because the subject is singular, (B) and (D) can be eliminated.

**(A) is correct** because it contains the appropriate verb form (*was*) and supplies the preposition *against*, which clearly conveys the idea that certain types of European writing were created in opposition to Cicero's style.

(E) is incorrect because the word *either* modifies *reaction* and should be placed next to it, and because the omission of the preposition *against* makes the meaning of the sentence less clear. Although the preposition *to*, which follows *return*, could technically "apply" to *reaction* as well, the contrast between the ideas of *reaction* and *return* would be less clear.

The idea is not simply that some writing was produced in reaction *to* Cicero's style, but rather that it was produced as a reaction *against* it. In contrast, other writing was produced as an emulation of Cicero's style.

## 26. E: Pronoun agreement; Parallel structure

The Chinese zokor, a small rodent with a stocky build and conical tail, lives solitarily underground in extensive burrows <u>that they excavate to leave evidence of its presence</u> in the form of mounds of material on the surface of the ground.

(A)  that they excavate to leave evidence of its presence
(B)  that they excavate to leave evidence of their presence
(C)  that they excavate, leaving evidence of its presence
(D)  that are excavated and left evidence of its presence
**(E)  that it excavates, leaving evidence of its presence**

The *it/they* split in the various answer choices indicates that this question is testing pronoun agreement.

What is the referent of the pronouns in question? *The Chinese zokor* (singular). If you have any uncertainty just from looking at the name, you can see that it is defined in the non-underlined portion as *a small rodent*, and that it is referred to by the singular verb *lives*.

Since both pronouns in the underlined portion logically refer to the zokor, not to the "extensive burrows," both pronouns should be singular. Any choice that includes a plural pronoun can therefore be eliminated. That takes care of (A), (B), and (C).

(D) is incorrect because the phrase *that are excavated* can logically refer to the burrows, but the phrase *and left evidence of its presence* clearly must refer to the zokor. The second phrase is trying to act as a parallel continuation of the first, but in context of the referent *burrows*, it makes no sense.

**(E) is correct** because the singular pronoun *it* agrees with *zokor*, and the participial phrase *leaving evidence of its presence* is appropriately used to modify the preceding clause.

## 27. D: Verb tense; Parallel structure; Pronoun agreement

At the urging of aviation industry leaders, who believed that the airplane <u>can only reach its full commercial potential if federal action were taken to improve</u> and maintain safety standards, the Air Commerce Act was passed into law on May 20, 1926.

(A)  can only reach their full commercial potential if federal action were taken to improve
(B)  could only reach its full commercial potential if federal action is taken to improve
(C)  could only reach full commercial potential if taking federal action to improve
**(D)  could only reach its full commercial potential if federal action were taken to improve**
(E)  could only reach its full commercial potential if federal action would be taken for the improvement

Question #27 tests a number of concepts simultaneously, and there are a number of ways it can be approached. One possibility is to work through it as follows:

If you look through the answer choices, you can notice that (A) includes *their*, whereas (B)-(E) include *its*. That pattern indicates that pronoun agreement is in part being tested. What is the logical referent of the pronoun in question? *The airplane*. That is singular, so (A) can be eliminated.

Next, consider the end of the underlined portion. Because *improve* is paired with *maintain* in the non-underlined portion, the two must be parallel (*to improve and maintain*). When plugged in, (E) does not preserve parallel structure (*...for the improvement and maintain*), so that answer can be eliminated as well.

Now, consider the fact that the sentence contains a date: *1926*. That's a date firmly in the past, so it indicates that the correct answer will contain verbs in the past tense.

(B) is incorrect because it contains the present-tense verb *is*.

(C) is incorrect for a reason unrelated to tense. Although it eliminates the tense issue by using the gerund *taking*, it creates a different problem: the phrase *who believed that the airplane could only reach its full commercial potential if taking federal action* implies that the airplane itself could take federal action. In this case, that is a nonsense implication; the passive construction *federal action were taken* is much more logical.

**(D) is correct** because it applies the formula discussed in the chapter on tense: "if" clause = past, main clause = conditional (*the airplane <u>could</u> only reach its full commercial potential if federal action <u>were</u> taken*).

### 28. E: Pronoun agreement; Adjective vs. adverb; Idiom

As an animal develops from a fertilized egg into an embryo, <u>their cells may diversify into a seemingly limitless range of</u> types and tissues, from tusks to feathers to brains.

(A)  their cells may diversify into a seemingly limitless range of
(B)  its cells may diversify into a seeming limitless range of
(C)  its cells may diversify into a seemingly limitless range from
(D)  their cells may diversify into a seeming limitless range from
**(E)  its cells may diversify into a seemingly limitless range of**

The fact that some answer choices contain *its* and others contain *their* indicates that the question is testing pronoun agreement. The first step is therefore to determine which noun the pronoun in question refers to.

Logically, the referent is *an animal* (singular), making *its* correct. (A) and (D) contain *their* and can both be eliminated.

Now be careful. If you look closely, you can see that (B) contains the adjective *seeming* while (C) and (E) contain the adverb *seemingly*. That word modifies the adjective *limitless*, so the adverb is required. That eliminates (B).

(C) is incorrect because *range* should be followed by the preposition *of*. Although it is idiomatically correct to say *range from x to y*, that is not the case in the underlined phrase.

**(E) is correct** because *range* is followed by one noun, making *of* the correct preposition.

## 29. D: Idiom

Excepting programs like Betamax, which in the
1970s outperformed VHS as a result of exceptional
marketing strategies, inferior technologies and the
stocks associated with them tend to perform poorly in
the global market.

(A) Excepting programs like Betamax,
(B) Programs like Betamax being excepted,
(C) Except for programs such as Betamax
**(D) With the exception of programs such as Betamax**
(E) As an exception to programs such as Betamax

The correct idiom is *with the exception of*. (D) is the only option to contain it in the appropriate form, so it is the only possible answer.

## 30. B: Comparison: like vs. as

Like when scientists turn from experiments on
animals to ones on humans, the results of the new
study are provocative but hardly clear-cut.

(A) Like when
**(B) As is often the case when**
(C) In such a way as
(D) Just as if
(E) Similar to when

Recall the rule for *like vs. as: like* is used to compare nouns, whereas *as* is used to compare clauses. At the simplest level, that means *(un)like* is probably correct only if it's followed by a noun. In the original version, *like* is followed by *when* rather than a noun, so (A) is incorrect.

**(B) is correct** because the sentence compares two clauses rather than two nouns, making *as + clause* the appropriate start to the sentence. This option also creates the most logical meaning: the new study is typical because its results are intriguing but not straightforward—a common situation when studies are first conducted using humans rather than animals.

All of the other options are awkward and idiomatically unacceptable.

## 31. C: Because vs. due to; Gerund

In 1789, the Confederation Congress formed after
the American Revolution rejected the Articles of
Confederation in favor of the Constitution due to their
lack of provision for the creation of either executive
agencies or judiciary institutions.

(A) due to their lack of provision
(B) due to their lack of providing
**(C) because they did not provide**
(D) because of their lack of providing
(E) when they have not provided

**Shortcut:** start by assuming that any answer that includes *due to* will be incorrect, and that the correct answer will contain *because*. That's usually the case on the GMAT. By that logic, everything except (C) and (D) can be eliminated, and (D) can be crossed out because it includes the wordy and awkward gerund phrase *their lack of providing*. In contrast, (C) includes a subject + conjugated verb (*they did not provide*) and is therefore correct.

**Longer version:** Recall that *due to* is a synonym for *caused by*. To check it out, plug in *caused by*, and see whether the sentence still makes sense: *In 1789, the Confederation Congress formed after the American Revolution rejected the Articles of Confederation in favor of the Constitution* <u>*caused by*</u> *their lack of provision for the creation of either executive agencies or judiciary institutions.* No, that does not work grammatically, so (A) and (B) are out.

**(C) is correct** because it replaces *due to* with *because* and provides a subject + conjugated verb (*they did not provide*).

(D) is incorrect because it includes the wordy and awkward gerund phrase *their lack of providing*.

(E) is incorrect because *when* should be used only to refer to times, not to indicate cause-and-effect.

**32. B: Idiom: try and vs. try to; Verb form**

> Genetics-based drugs, an emerging class of medications, are likely be tailored at least in part to individuals; as a result, drug companies <u>will probably try and charge</u> patients made-to-measure prices.

    (A)  will probably try and charge
    **(B)  will probably try to charge**
    (C)  probably try and charge
    (D)  probably try charging
    (E)  have probably tried to charge

The phrases *emerging class of medications* and *are likely to be tailored* indicates that the sentence is referring to events that have not yet occurred; as a result, the future tense should be used to create the most logical meaning.

(A) and (C) are incorrect because the correct idiom is *try to*, not *try and*.

**(B) is correct** because it uses both the future tense and the correct idiom, *try to*.

(D) is incorrect because it uses the present rather than the future tense, even though *try + gerund* is idiomatically acceptable.

(E) is incorrect because the present perfect (*have + past participle*) refers to an action that began in the past and that continues into the present, and here the future tense should be used.

## 33. D: Parallel structure

Film studies, an academic discipline that deals with various theoretical, historical, and critical approaches to movie-making, is less concerned with advancing proficiency in film production <u>than to explore</u> the cultural, economic, and political implications of the cinema.

(A) than to explore
(B) than in the exploring of
(C) than with the exploration of
**(D) than it is with exploring**
(E) than in the exploration of

The key to answering #33 is to recognize the word pair *less…than*. The first half of the word pair is followed by the construction *with + gerund* (*less concerned <u>with</u> advancing*), so the second half of the word pair must be followed by *with + gerund* as well. That makes **(D)** the only possible answer.

## 34. E: Misplaced modifier; Non-essential clause

<u>Shigeru Miyamoto joined Nintendo in the late 1970s and became known as the creator of some of the best-selling video games of all time,</u> a period when the company was beginning its foray into electronic entertainment and abandoning the production of playing cards, which it had manufactured since 1889.

(A) Shigeru Miyamoto joined Nintendo in the late 1970s and became known as the creator of some of the best-selling video games of all time,
(B) Shigeru Miyamoto joined Nintendo in the late 1970s, becoming known as the creator of some of the best-selling video games of all time,
(C) Shigeru Miyamoto joined Nintendo in the late 1970s to become known as the creator of some of the best-selling video games of all time,
(D) Shigeru Miyamoto, who became known as the creator of some of the best-selling video games of all time, and joined Nintendo in the late 1970s,
**(E) Shigeru Miyamoto, who became known as the creator of some of the best-selling video games of all time, joined Nintendo in the late 1970s,**

Although this sentence is quite long, the question can actually be answered very quickly if you identify the relevant information. Doing so requires that you consider the underlined portion in context of the information that follows.

The appositive that comes immediately after the underlined portion begins with the words *a period when*. That appositive must modify whatever came right before it, so logically, the underlined portion must end with a reference to a time period. The only answers that places the date *1970s* at the end are (D) and (E); (A), (B), and (C) can all be eliminated.

(D) is incorrect because it creates a fragment, a fact that becomes apparent when the non-essential clause is removed: *Shigeru Matsumoto…and joined Nintendo in the late 1970s.*

**(E) is correct** because it ends with *1970s*, fixing the misplaced modification, and places a verb (*joined*) after the non-essential clause.

## 35. A: Modification; Idiom: gerund vs. infinitive; Non-essential clause

> During the Renaissance, glass products made on the island of Murano could only be crafted according to traditional techniques, and local artisans were forbidden to leave and sell their creations elsewhere.

(A) **During the Renaissance, glass products made on the island of Murano could only be crafted according to traditional techniques, and local artisans were forbidden to leave and sell their creations elsewhere.**

(B) Glass products, which were made on the island of Murano, could only be crafted during the Renaissance according to traditional techniques, and it was forbidden that local artisans leave and sell their creations elsewhere.

(C) The crafting of glass products could only be done according to traditional techniques during the Renaissance on the island of Murano, and local artisans were forbidden in leaving and selling their creations elsewhere.

(D) Local artisans, forbidden to leave the island of Murano, could not sell their creations elsewhere during the Renaissance, glass products only being crafted according to techniques of tradition.

(E) Only traditional techniques could be used during the Renaissance that crafted glass products on the island of Murano, so local artisans were forbidden to leave and sell their creations elsewhere.

If you read through the original version and cannot find an error but are unsure whether (A) is correct, the simplest approach is to work through the answers in order. Because the entire sentence is underlined, it is difficult to identify one or two things to focus on as a shortcut.

**(A) is correct** because the clauses proceed in a logical order, and because all of the modification/idiom errors that appear in other answers are absent here.

(B) is incorrect because *according to traditional techniques* modifies *crafted* and should be placed next to that word. In addition, the use of *that* + subjunctive after *forbidden* is not idiomatic; the passive voice is considered standard usage with that verb (local artisans *were* forbidden).

(C) is incorrect because the phrase *The crafting of glass products* is wordy and employs a gerund unnecessarily. In addition, standard usage requires that *forbidden* be followed by an infinitive (*to leave*) rather than a gerund (*in leaving*).

(D) is incorrect because the sentence does not make the cause-and-effect relationship clear: local artisans were forbidden to leave Murano is a *result* of the fact that glass products could only be crafted on the island and according to traditional techniques. In addition, the use of multiple sub-clauses and the gerund *being* makes this version wordy and awkward, and the phrase *techniques of tradition* is not idiomatic.

(E) is incorrect because it contains a misplaced modifier: the phrase *Renaissance that crafted glass products on the island of Murano* implies that the time period itself was responsible for crafting glass—clearly an illogical implication.

## 36. C: Idiom: number vs. amount; Redundancy

Once common across southwest Asia, the Indian cheetah was driven nearly to extinction during the late 1900s, <u>and only a small amount of animals now presently reside in their remaining original habitat</u>.

- (A) and only a small amount of animals now presently reside in their remaining original habitat
- (B) only a small number of animals are now residing in their remaining original habitat
- **(C) and only a small number of animals now reside in what remains of their original habitat**
- (D) with only a small number of animals that now reside in their present remaining habitat
- (E) and only a small amount of animals reside in their original habitat that presently remains

If you look through the answer choices, the fact that some options include the word *number* while others include *amount* tells you in part what this question is testing.

Recall the rule for *number vs. amount*: *number* is used with plural (quantifiable) nouns, whereas *amount* is used with singular nouns (non-quantifiable). Because *animals* is plural, *number* is correct. That eliminates (A) and (E).

(B) is incorrect because the omission of the word *and* after the comma creates a comma splice. If you don't pay attention to exactly what is and isn't underlined, you can easily overlook that error.

**(C) is correct** because that answer correctly uses *number* to modify *animals* and the phrase *what remains of their original habitat* is idiomatically acceptable. Missing from this answer are the redundancy problems that characterize (D) and (E).

(D) is incorrect because the use of both *now* and *present* is redundant. In addition, *with* should be used with a gerund (*remaining*) rather than *that + verb*.

## 37. C: Idiom: Like vs. as

Even after leaving their posts, some diplomats <u>may continue to act like intermediaries</u> between conflicting groups, using their negotiation skills to smooth over disagreements and reconcile opposing interests.

- (A) may continue to act like intermediaries
- (B) could continue acting like intermediaries
- **(C) continue to act as intermediaries**
- (D) would continue acting as intermediaries
- (E) are continuing to act like intermediaries

*Act like* means "behave in a manner similar to," whereas *act as* means "act in the capacity of." Only the second meaning makes sense here, eliminating (A), (B), and (E).

**(C) is correct** because the present tense *continue* is logical here; the sentence describes an ongoing state of affairs.

(D) is incorrect because the use of the condition (*would continue*) does not make sense in context; there is nothing to suggest that the sentence is describing a hypothetical situation.

**38. B: Parallel structure: verb**

Popular cold-weather activities such as skiing on
fresh snow and skating on reflective ice often expose
people to more harmful ultraviolet rays than a day at
the beach <u>is</u>.

(A) is
**(B) does**
(C) has
(D) will
(E) can

Normally, when parallel structure is involved, the construction in the underlined portion must match the construction in the non-underlined portion. If you look at the sentence as a whole, however, you'll notice that it does not contain any of the verbs that appear in the answer choices.

In this case, the correct answer must be parallel to *expose*, the only verb in the sentence.

Recall that there is one verb that can be used to substitute for a different verb while still maintaining parallel structure: *to do*. That makes *does* the only option, so **(B) is correct**.

**39. A: Idiom: means of vs. means to; Subject-verb agreement; Pronoun agreement**

Because the Helicobacter pylori bacterium is
transmitted only through intimate contact and <u>is
distributed around the world in a way that matches
almost perfectly the distribution of human
populations, its genetic variations are used to
supplement human genetics as a means to track</u>
ancient human migrations.

**(A) is distributed around the world in a way that
matches almost perfectly the distribution of
human populations, its genetic variations are used
to supplement human genetics as a means to track**
(B) is distributed around the world in a way that
matches almost perfectly the distribution of
human populations, their genetic variations are
used to supplement human genetics as a means
of tracking
(C) are distributed around the world in a way that
matches almost perfectly the distribution of
human populations, its genetic variations are used
to supplement human genetics as a means of
tracking
(D) is distributed around the world in a way that
almost perfectly matches the distribution of
human populations, their genetic variations are
used like a supplement to human genetics as a
means to track
(E) are distributed around the world in a way such
that the distribution of human populations is
almost perfectly matched, and its genetic variations
are used to supplement human genetics as a means
to track

Don't get overwhelmed by the amount of information underlined in Question #39; the answer is actually very straightforward if you can identify the relevant information.

If you're well-versed in favorite GMAT idioms, the inclusion of *a means of/to* in the various answer choices should immediately leap out at you. Recall that *a means of* is a synonym for "a type of" (noun), whereas *a means to* refers to a method for achieving. Since the "means" used here clearly refers to the latter, *a means to* is correct. (B) and (C) can thus be eliminated.

Now look at the beginnings of the remaining answer choices. (A) and (D) begin with *is*, whereas (E) begins with *are*. If you back up to the beginning of the sentence, you can see that the subject of the verb in question is the singular noun *Helicobacter pylorium bacterium*; in addition, the singular verb *is* appears next to the subject in the non-underlined portion, and the underlined verb must be parallel to that verb. (E) can therefore be eliminated.

**(A) is correct** because that answer includes the singular verb *is*, the singular pronoun *its*, and the correct idiom, *a means to*.

(D) is incorrect because the plural pronoun *their* disagrees with the singular referent *bacterium*, and because the *as* rather than *like* should follow the verb *used*. *Used like* means "used in a way that is similar to," whereas *used as* means "used in the capacity of." The second meaning is more logical here.

## 40. D: Tense

If the current market trends persist as projected, the majority of mobile phone manufacturers <u>go out of business rather than continue to lose</u> money and customers to a small number of competitors.

(A) go out of business rather than continue to lose
(B) would go out of business rather than continue losing
(C) will go out of business rather than continued to lose
**(D) will go out of business rather than continue to lose**
(E) would go out of business rather than continue to lose

The key phrase is *persist as projected*, which indicates that the sentence is describing an action that is expected to take place. The future tense is therefore required.

(A) is incorrect because it includes the present tense (*go*) rather than the future.

(B) and (E) are incorrect because they contain the condition (*would go*) rather than the future. Note that both *to continue* and *continuing* are acceptable here. The gerund vs. infinitive issue is only a distractor here.

(C) is incorrect despite its use of the future (*will go*) because there is an unnecessary switch to the past tense for the second verb (*continued*).

**(D) is correct** because it puts the first verb in the future tense (*will go*) and keeps the second verb in the present tense (*continue*).

## 41. D: Parallel structure; Pronoun agreement

Found in the depths of all the world's oceans, the vampire squid lives in a twilight zone that contains extremely low levels of dissolved oxygen <u>such to be uninhabitable by most other sea creatures</u>.

(A) such to be uninhabitable by most other sea creatures
(B) such that it is uninhabitable to most other sea creatures
(C) that cannot be inhabited by most other sea creatures
**(D) and that cannot be inhabited by most other sea creatures**
(E) making them uninhabitable to most other sea creatures

Although you might be able to tell that (A) is unlikely to be correct because the phrase *such to be uninhabitable* is so awkward, it is difficult to tell from the original version what the exact error is and thus what correction to look for. It therefore makes the most sense to work through the answers in order.

(B) is incorrect for the same reason as (A): the phrase *such that it is uninhabitable* is awkward and un-idiomatic.

(C) is incorrect because it creates a misplaced modifier. Because it follows the word *oxygen*, the phrase *that cannot be inhabited by most other sea creatures* implies that most other sea creatures are unable to inhabit *oxygen* — not the "twilight zone," as would be logical.

**(D) is correct** because it creates a parallel structure between two clauses in the sentence: *the vampire squid lives in a twilight zone that contains…and that cannot be inhabited*.

(E) is incorrect because the use of the plural pronoun *them* creates a disagreement with the logical referent, the singular noun *twilight zone*.

## 42. C: Parallel structure

The black-backed woodpecker lives almost exclusively in severely burned forests, <u>thrives on insects that are adapted to fire, and detecting heat up to 30 miles away</u>.

(A) thrives on insects that are adapted to fire, and detecting heat up to 30 miles away
(B) thriving on insects that have adapted to fire, and detects heat up to 30 miles away
**(C) thrives on insects adapted to fire, and can detect heat up to 30 miles away**
(D) thrives on insects to adapt them to fire, and detects heat up to 30 miles away
(E) thrives on insects, adapting to fire, and detecting heat up to 30 miles away

This is a straightforward "list" parallel structure question: the two underlined items must match the non-underlined first item. The first item begins with a verb (*lives*), so the other two items must begin the same way.

(A) is incorrect because the second item begins with a verb, but the third begins with a gerund.

(B) is incorrect because it reverses the error in (A): the second item is a gerund, and the third item is a verb.

**(C) is correct** because it includes both the second and third items in verb form, making them parallel to the first item.

(D) is incorrect because the phrase *thrive on insects to adapt them to fire* is illogical: it implies that the black-backed woodpecker's feasting on insects causes those insects to become adapted to fire.

(E) is incorrect because it turns the three-part list into four parts, the first two of which begin with verbs and the second two of which begin with gerunds.

### 43. E: Dangling modifier

Passed in 1943 in order to make housing affordable for middle-class residents, <u>rents for some New York City apartments having remained stable for decades because of the existence of rent control laws</u>.

(A)  rents for some New York City apartments having remained stable for decades because of the existence of rent  control laws
(B)  rents for some New York City apartments have remained stable because rent control laws exist
(C)  rents for some New York City apartments have remained stable due to the existence of rent control laws
(D)  some New York City apartments have rents that have remained stable for decades as a result of rent control laws
**(E)  rent control laws have kept rents for some New York City apartments stable for decades**

What was passed in 1943 in order to make housing affordable for middle-class residents? Rent control laws. So *rent control laws*, the subject, must appear immediately after the comma. That makes **(E)** the only possible answer.

### 44. C: Idiom: whether vs. that

Scholars have little doubt <u>whether the latter years of Egypt's Old Kingdom were marked</u> by economic decline and a breakdown in the centralized system of government, disasters likely brought about by changes in the flow of the Nile.

(A)  whether the latter years of Egypt's Old Kingdom were marked
(B)  as to whether the latter years of Egypt's Old Kingdom were marked
**(C)  that the latter years of Egypt's Old Kingdom were marked**
(D)  about the latter years of Egypt's Old Kingdom having been marked
(E)  about whether the latter years of Egypt's Old Kingdom was marked

According to standard usage, the verb *doubt* should be followed by *that*. (In contrast, *the question is* should be followed by *whether*). On that basis, **(C)** is the only possible answer.

**45. B: Tense; Pronoun agreement: missing referent**

For centuries, <u>dolls dressed as witches have hung in Norwegian kitchens because they traditionally believe</u> that such figures have the power to keep pots from boiling over.

(A)  dolls dressed as witches have hung in Norwegian kitchens because they traditionally believe

**(B)  dolls dressed as witches have been hung in Norwegian kitchens because of a traditional belief**

(C)  dolls dressed as witches hang in Norwegian kitchens because they traditionally believe

(D)  dolls dressed as witches had hung in Norwegian kitchens because of it traditionally being believed

(E)  dolls dressed as witches have hung in Norwegian kitchens because of traditionally believing

The phrase *For centuries* is a tip-off that the present perfect (*has/have* + past participle) is required. (C) and (D) can thus be eliminated.

(A) is incorrect because the pronoun *they* is missing its true referent: logically, it refers to *the Norwegians*, but here the word *Norwegian* acts as an adjective modifying *kitchens*, and an adjective cannot function as a referent.

**(B) is correct** because this answer eliminates the pronoun-referent problem entirely by replacing the pronoun with the unambiguous noun *traditional belief.*

(E) is incorrect for two reasons. First, the conjunction *because* should be followed by a subject + conjugated verb rather than a gerund; second, the wording of the sentence implies that the dolls themselves have been the ones believing that they have the power to keep pots from boiling over—clearly an illogical meaning.

**46. D: Gerund; Verb form**

Chicago's Willis Tower, formerly the Sears Tower, was the tallest office building in the world <u>until losing that distinction to the completion of the Taipei 101 Tower</u> in 2004.

(A)  until losing that distinction to the completion of the Taipei 101 Tower

(B)  until it had lost that distinction upon the completion of the Taipei 101 Tower

(C)  until that distinction was lost after the Taipei 101 Tower's being completed

**(D)  until it lost that distinction when the Taipei 101 Tower was completed**

(E)  until the loss of that distinction after the completion of the Taipei 101 Tower

The conjunction *until* should be followed by a subject + verb; the original version provides only the gerund *losing*, making (A) incorrect.

(B) is incorrect because it uses the past perfect to refer to an action that clearly came *after* a second action: the Willis Tower could only have lost the distinction of being the world's tallest building <u>after</u> being the world's tallest building.

(C) is incorrect because the phrase *after the Taipei 101 Tower's being completed* is wordy and awkward, and contains an unnecessary gerund.

**(D) is correct** because it provides both a subject (*it*) and a verb (*lost*) and uses the simple past tense.

(E) is incorrect because the conjunction *until* is followed only by a noun, and a verb is also required to create a clause. In addition, the first clause begins with the subject (*Chicago's Sears Tower*), so the second clause should begin with a pronoun renaming the subject (*it*) in order to maintain parallel structure.

**47. A: Subject-verb agreement; Pronoun-agreement; Modification; Parallel structure**

Under the feudal system, which prevailed in Europe during the Middle Ages, the status of an individual and <u>his or her interactions with members of different social classes rigidly were specified</u>.

(A) **his or her interactions with members of different social classes were rigidly specified**
(B) his or her interacting with members of different social classes rigidly was specified
(C) their interactions with members of different social classes rigidly were specified
(D) their interactions with members of different social classes was rigidly specified
(E) there were rigid specifications for interactions with members of different social classes.

If you look through the answer choices, you can see that (B) and (D) contain *was*, whereas (A), (C), and (E) contain *were*. That pattern indicates that the question is testing subject-verb agreement.

What is the subject of the verb in question? *the status of an individual* <u>*and*</u> *his or her interactions with members of different social classes*. It's a compound subject, so a plural verb is required. (B) and (D) can thus be eliminated.

**(A) is correct** because the singular noun *an individual* is referred to by the singular *his or her*. Recall that the entire phrase is used when the gender of a singular subject is not specified. In addition, the adverb *rigidly* is correctly placed next to the verb it modifies (*specified*).

(C) is incorrect because the singular noun *an individual* disagrees with the plural pronoun *their*. In addition, the adverb *rigidly* is not placed next to the verb it modifies (*specified*).

(E) is incorrect because the two items paired by *and* should be parallel. The first item begins with a noun, *the status*, but the second item begins with *there were*.

## 48. E: Logical construction

Coined by historian of science Robert Proctor,
the term "agnotology" is the study of acts intended
deliberately to spread confusion and deceit, usually to
sell a product or win favor.

(A)  the term "agnotology" is the study of acts
     intended deliberately to spread
(B)  the term "agnotology" is the study of acts
     deliberately intended to spread
(C)  the term "agnotology" involves the study of acts
     having the deliberate intention to spread
(D)  the term "agnotology" is the referral of the
     study of acts that have the deliberate intention
     to spread
**(E)  the term "agnotology" refers to the study of acts
     deliberately intended to spread**

A term cannot *be* something — it can only *refer to* something. That eliminates every answer except **(E)**.

## 49. D: Logical predication; Non-essential clause

During warmer months, zooplankton, microscopic
marine animals that drift in oceans and bodies of
fresh water sink from the water's surface when the
sun rises to escape predators, ascending again to
feed at night.

(A)  sink from the water's surface when the sun rises
     to escape predators, ascending
(B)  sink from the surface of the water at the sun's
     rise to escape predators, to ascend
(C)  and sink from the water's surface when the sun
     rises, escaping predators and ascending
**(D)  sink from the water's surface in order to escape
     predators when the sun rises and ascend**
(E)  sink from the water's surface to escape predators
     at the sun's rising, and to ascend

The sentence contains a non-essential clause that can be crossed out to simplify the sentence: *During warmer months, zooplankton…sink from the water's surface when the sun rises to escape predators, ascending again to feed at night.*

(A) is incorrect because it implies that the sun rises in order to escape predators. In fact, *to escape predators* explains why zooplankton *sink from the water's surface,* so the two phrases should be placed next to one another.

(B) The phrase *at the sun's rise* is not idiomatic, and the repetition of *to escape predators, to ascend* is awkward.

(C) is incorrect because it creates a nonsense construction by placing *and* rather than a verb after the non-essential clause: *During warmer months, zooplankton…and sink from the water's surface when the sun rises, escaping predators and ascending…*

**(D) is correct** because it is the clearest and most logical option. This version makes apparent that zooplankton, not the sun, must escape from predators. In addition, the verb *ascend* is correctly made parallel to *sink*.

(E) is incorrect because the parallel construction of *to escape* and *to ascend* creates an illogical meaning: it implies that zooplankton sink from the surface in order to ascend. In addition, the phrase *at the sun's rising* is not idiomatic.

**50. C: Sentence vs. fragment; Pronoun agreement**

In the late 1890s, Pacific trading companies ceased to place traders in residence on the islands where they conducted <u>business; instead beginning to require</u> that trading mangers negotiate directly with local inhabitants when company ships arrived in port.

(A)  business; instead beginning to require
(B)  business, instead beginning of the requirement
**(C)  business, but instead began to require**
(D)  business, beginning instead to be required
(E)  business; it began to instead to require

(A) is incorrect because a semicolon should only be placed between two complete sentences, and the information after the semicolon is not a complete sentence because it lacks a subject and a verb.

(B) is incorrect because the gerund phrase *beginning of the requirement* is awkward and not idiomatic.

**(C) is correct** because it removes the semicolon, replacing it with a comma for the sake of clarity, and makes the verb *began* parallel to *ceased* (*Pacific trading companies ceased to place traders in residence…but instead began to require*).

(D) is incorrect because the construction *beginning instead to be required* is awkward and illogical. The trading companies began to require direct negotiation with local inhabitants; they were not required to begin doing so by an outside entity, as the passive voice implies.

(E) is incorrect despite the correct use of a semicolon to separate two complete sentences. The singular pronoun *it* disagrees with the plural referent *Pacific trading companies*.

**51. B: Subject-verb agreement; Grammatical construction; Gerund**

<u>The use of rooftop solar panels have spread</u> rapidly over the past decade, but wind energy remains the province of industrial-scale operations providing power to utilities companies and large businesses.

(A)  The use of rooftop solar panels have spread
**(B)  The use of rooftop solar panels has spread**
(C)  The use of rooftop solar panels having spread
(D)  Although use of rooftop solar panels has spread
(E)  The using of rooftop solar panels has spread

The presence of both singular and plural forms of the verb *to have* indicate that this question is in part testing subject-verb agreement.

What is the subject of the verb in question? *The use* (singular). So a singular verb is required. *Have* is plural, so (A) can be eliminated.

**(B) is correct** because it provides the singular verb *has* and creates an independent clause. Because the remainder of the sentence consists of the FANBOYS conjunction *but* + independent clause, the first clause must be independent as well.

(C) is incorrect because the gerund *having* turns the first clause into a fragment, and that clause must be independent.

(D) is incorrect because the second clause already begins with *but*; it is both redundant and grammatically unacceptable to begin the first clause with *although*. Two consecutive clauses should not both begin with conjunctions that have the same meaning.

(E) is incorrect because the gerund *using*, is not idiomatic; the noun *use* should appear instead.

## 52. D: Faulty comparison

According to United Nations estimates, more than three percent of the world's population currently lives in a country <u>other than where they were born</u>.

(A) other than where they were born
(B) other than those of where they were born
(C) other than what they were born in
**(D) other than the one in which they were born**
(E) other than that of their birth country

The phrase *other than* is a tip-off that this question is testing the formation of a comparison. The first step is thus to identify the items being compared and determine whether they are parallel. Because the non-underlined side of the comparison contains a noun (*country*), the underlined portion of the comparison must contain a noun or equivalent pronoun.

(A) is incorrect because the noun *country* is not equivalent to the relative pronoun *where*.

(B) is incorrect because it creates the same error as (A). In addition, the first side of the comparison is not possessive, making *those of* unnecessary.

(C) is incorrect because it again compares a noun (*country*) to a relative pronoun (*what*).

**(D) is correct** because the pronoun *one* can appropriately substitute for the noun country, making the construction parallel: *...three percent of the world's population currently lives in a country other than the country (= the one) in which they were born.*

(E) is incorrect because *country* is not possessive in the first side of the comparison. The phrase *that of* is therefore unnecessary.

## 53. Grammatical construction

<u>Whether</u> families living in economically disadvantaged neighborhoods spend more money on food than do families living in economically advantaged ones has become a recurring controversy because neither the government nor private industry routinely collects the type of detailed data necessary to resolve the matter fully.

**(A) Whether**
(B) Insofar as
(C) Were it to be that
(D) The question of if
(E) Should

234

Although the sentence in Question #53 is long and complicated you can eliminate one choice immediately: phrases involving *the question* should always include *whether*, not *if*, so (D) can be eliminated without being plugged in.

**(A) is correct** because it is the only answer that creates a logical meaning: It is unclear *whether* families living in poor neighborhoods spend more money on food than families living in wealthier neighborhoods because not enough data exists to judge. If you're not sure about this answer, remember that when *whether* is used as a subject, it's actually a shortened version of *the question is whether*. If you plug in the entire phrase *the question is whether*, you may find it easier to make sense out of the sentence. In addition, *controversy* and *not enough information to resolve the matter fully* are both tip-offs that the sentence is describing a matter than is uncertain, i.e. questionable.

All of the other options create ungrammatical nonsense when plugged back into the sentence.

## 54. D: Comparison; Verb form

When a corporation exploits loopholes in financial regulations in order to pay <u>less taxes than it otherwise would owe</u>, the government is forced to find alternate sources of revenue to compensate for the shortfall.

(A) less taxes than it otherwise would owe
(B) less taxes than what they otherwise owe
(C) less taxes than otherwise are owed
**(D) less money in taxes than it would otherwise owe**
(E) less tax money than what is otherwise to be owed

The appearance of the word *less* is a big clue to what this question is testing. Recall that *less* is used with singular (non-quantifiable) nouns. Any answer that uses *less* to modify a plural (quantifiable) noun is therefore incorrect. (A), (B), and (C) can all be eliminated because *less* is used to modify the plural noun *taxes*.

**(D) is correct** because it pairs *less* with the singular noun *money* and appropriately uses the conditional to refer to a hypothetical situation. (A corporation *would owe* more money in taxes if it did not exploit loopholes in financial regulations.)

(E) is incorrect because the construction *is otherwise to be owed* is equivalent to the future tense. Here, the conditional is required because the sentence is referring to a hypothetical situation.

## 55. C: Verb form; Grammatical construction

Ownership of the Arctic is governed by the 1958 United Nations Convention of the Law of the Sea, <u>which had provided Arctic nations with an exclusive economic zone extending</u> 200 nautical miles from land.

(A) which had provided Arctic nations with an exclusive economic zone extending
(B) which provides Arctic nations with an exclusive economic zone to extend
**(C) a treatise that provides Arctic nations with an exclusive economic zone extending**
(D) a treatise provided Arctic nations with an exclusive economic zone that extends
(E) which provides Arctic nations with an exclusive economic zone of extension

If you look through the answer choices to Question #55, you can notice that they contain the same verb (*provide*) in various forms, a pattern that indicates that the question is testing tense.

Notice also that although the underlined portion of the sentence includes the date *1958*, it also includes a verb in the present tense (*Ownership of the Arctic is governed*), indicating that the United Nations Convention of the Law of the Sea is still in effect.

(A) is incorrect because the use of the past perfect (*had provided*) implies that the treatise is no longer in effect—and as discussed above, the sentence clearly implies that it is still valid.

(B) is incorrect because the exclusive economic zone *extends*. The infinitive *to extend* could either be interpreted as meaning *in order to extend* or *that will extend*, neither of which makes sense in context.

**(C) is correct** because the present tense verb *provides* reflects the fact that the treatise is still in effect, and because the participle *extending* appropriately modifies *exclusive economic zone*.

(D) is incorrect because the construction *a treatise provided* is ungrammatical. The word *that* is required for the phrase to make logical sense.

(E) is incorrect because the phrase *economic zone of extension* is not idiomatic and does not appropriately convey the idea that the zone itself extends.

## 56. B: Pronoun agreement: collective noun; Grammatical construction; Gerund

The manufacturing company has created an advisory board <u>to oversee the implementing of their new safety regulations,</u> several of which have already been put into effect.

(A) to oversee the implementing of their new safety regulations,
**(B) to oversee the implementation of its new safety regulations,**
(C) to oversee that its new safety regulations are implemented, and
(D) to oversee their new safety regulations being implemented,
(E) to oversee as to how its new safety regulations are implemented,

The word *company* is a tip-off that the question is testing collective nouns. These nouns are always singular, so answer choices that include the plural pronoun *they* are incorrect. (A) and (D) can thus be eliminated.

**(B) is correct** because the noun *implementation* rather than the gerund *implementing* is used. In addition, the last word of the underlined portion is *regulations*, which is modified by the phrase *several of which* in the following clause.

(C) and (E) are incorrect because the verb *oversee* should be followed by a noun; *that* and *as to how* are not idiomatic. The use of *and* to begin a relative clause after the comma is also grammatically unacceptable.

## 57. A: Verb form; Non-essential clause; Modification

Augustus Caesar is known to have commissioned the
Pantheon, a monument to all the deities of Rome, as
part of a construction program undertaken in the
aftermath of the Battle of Actium in 31 C.E.

**(A)** **Augustus Caesar is known to have commissioned
the Pantheon, a monument to all the deities of
Rome, as part of a construction program
undertaken**

(B) The Pantheon, a monument to all of Rome's
deities, is known to have been commissioned by
Augustus Caesar and part of a construction
program undertaking

(C) Augustus Caesar, who commissioned the
Pantheon, a monument to all of the deities of
Rome undertaken as part of a construction project

(D) A monument to all the deities of Rome, Augustus
Caesar is known for having commissioned the
Pantheon as part of a construction program to be
undertaken

(E) The Pantheon, commissioned as a monument to
all of the deities of Rome, was part of Augustus
Caesar's construction project undertaking

To simplify the original version of the sentence, cross out the non-essential clause: *Augustus Caesar is known to have commissioned the Pantheon...as part of a construction program undertaken in the aftermath of the Battle of Actium in 31 C.E.*

The sentence is clearly describing events in the past, and the construction *known to have commissioned* is an acceptable way to refer to current knowledge about past events. Otherwise, there is no glaring error, so you can move on to checking the non-essential clause itself. It consists of an appositive that correctly uses the noun *a monument* to refer back to the Pantheon. If you're still not sure, you can leave (A) and check the other answers.

(B) is incorrect because it creates a nonsense fragment. The verb *was* must be placed before *part of a construction* in order for the sentence to make sense.

(C) is incorrect because the sentence clearly does not make sense when the non-essential clause is removed: *August Caesar...a monument to all the deities of Rome undertaken as part of a construction project in the aftermath of the Battle of Actium in 31 C.E.*

(D) is incorrect because it creates a dangling modifier. What was a monument to all the deities of Rome? The Pantheon. So *the Pantheon*, the subject, must immediately follow the comma. Because the subject does not appear in that place, the modification is dangling.

(E) is incorrect because past participle (*undertaken*) rather than the present participle (*undertaking*) is required here. The program was *undertaken* by Augustus Caesar. *Undertaking* implies that the construction program was itself initiating an activity.

That leaves **(A), which is correct.**

## 58. C: Gerund

Some leading pharmaceutical companies are joining
forces in an effort to accelerate the testing of new
types of cancer drugs that battle tumors when harnessing
the body's natural defenses.

(A)  that battle tumors when harnessing
(B)  that battle tumors when it harnesses
**(C)  that battle tumors by harnessing**
(D)  by which tumors are battled to harness
(E)  where they battle tumors by harnessing

(A) is incorrect because the conjunction *when* should be followed by a subject + verb. *When* + gerund does not create a clause.

(B) is incorrect because the singular pronoun *it* disagrees with its referent, the plural noun *cancer drugs*.

(C) **is correct** because it uses the construction *by* + gerund to indicate method/means.

(D) is incorrect because it reverses the sequence cause-and-effect: logically, the cancer drugs are able to battle tumors *because* they harness the body's natural defenses. This answer, however, implies that the tumors are battled in order to harness the body's natural defenses—the opposite of what occurs. In addition, the phrase *by which* is wordy and awkward; there is a cleaner option here.

(E) is incorrect because *where* should only be used to refer to places, and cancer drugs are not places.

## 59. E: Parallel structure

Like other forms of physical activity, tai chi might help
mitigate the risk of heart disease because it has such
effects as reducing levels of harmful triglycerides
while levels of "good" HDL cholesterol are increased.

(A)  it has such effects as reducing levels of harmful
     triglycerides while levels of "good" HDL
     cholesterol are increased
(B)  its effects include the reduction of levels of
     harmful triglycerides and levels of "good" HDL
     cholesterol increase
(C)  it has such effects like the reducing of harmful
     levels of triglycerides while levels of "good" HDL
     cholesterol are increasing
(D)  its effects are such that harmful triglyceride levels
     are reduced and increasing "good" HDL
     cholesterol levels
**(E)  its effects include a reduction in levels of harmful
     triglycerides and an increase in levels of "good"
     HDL cholesterol**

The sentence is presenting two effects of tai chi, using the basic structure of x goes up, y goes down. When two items are listed this way, you can assume that the question is testing parallel structure and that the correct answer will present the items on either side of the conjunction in the same format.

To simplify the process of working through the answers, focus on the beginning of each item. Only if the beginnings match should you check the rest of the answer. Although there may be secondary errors, you should not worry about them at this point—the goal is to make the process of eliminating answers are simple as possible.

(A) and (C) are incorrect because the first item begins with a gerund (*reducing*) whereas the second item begins with a noun (*levels*).

(D) has the opposite problem: the first item begins with a noun (*harmful triglyceride levels*) whereas the second item begins with a gerund (*increasing*).

Now consider (B) and (E). In both answer choices, the two items begin with nouns: *reduction…levels* in (B), and *reduction…increase* in (E). Even without any additional information, you can make a reasonable assumption that (E) is correct: *reduction* and *increase* are direct opposites, whereas *reduction* and *levels* are not.

Looking more closely, you can see that indeed the two items in (E) are perfectly parallel: reduction in levels of x = increase in levels of y.

In contrast, the two items in (B) are not truly parallel: the first item contains nouns only (*reduction of levels of harmful triglycerides*) whereas the second contains a full clause, with a subject + verb (*levels of "good" HDL cholesterol increase*).

**(E) is therefore correct.**

### 60. D: Adjective vs. adverb; Faulty comparison; Idiom: gerund vs. infinitive

The security systems of small companies can often be hacked <u>easier than large ones because small companies have a tendency to lack</u> the financial resources to upgrade their software and set up protective barriers.

(A) easier than large ones because small companies have a tendency to lack
(B) easier than those of large ones because of small companies tending to lack
(C) more easily than large ones because small companies have a tendency of lacking
**(D) more easily than those of large ones because small companies tend to lack**
(E) more easily than large ones because small companies have tended to lack

(A) and (B) begin with *easier* whereas (C), (D), and (E) begin with *more easily*, indicating that the question is testing in part adjective vs. adverb usage.

What word is the adjective/adverb in question intended to modify? *Hacked.* That's a verb, so the adverb *more easily* is required, and (A) and (B) can be eliminated.

(C) is incorrect because *tendency* should be followed be an infinitive; *of* + gerund is idiomatically unacceptable.

**(D) is correct** because *those of* replaces the plural noun *security systems*, and *tend* is followed by the infinitive *to lack*.

(E) is incorrect because this answer creates a faulty comparison between security systems and small companies (*small ones*). The shift from the present to the present perfect (*have tended*) is also unnecessary.

**61. B: Non-essential clause; Logical construction**

Named for an Intel co-founder, Gordon Moore,
<u>Moore's Law is that computing power, as measured
by the density in transistors on a microchip, typically
doubles</u> every 18 to 24 months.

(A) Moore's Law is that computing power, as
    measured by the density in transistors on a
    microchip, typically doubles
**(B) Moore's Law states that computing power, as
    measured by the density of transistors on a
    microchip, typically doubles**
(C) Moore's Law is that computing power, as
    measured in transistors' microchip density,
    will double typically
(D) Moore's Law states that computing power, as
    measured by the density of transistors on a
    microchip, which typically doubles
(E) Moore's Law states that the measurement of
    the power of computing by the density of
    transistors on a microchip typically doubled

A law cannot *be* x—it can only *state* x. As a result, (A) and (C) can both be eliminated.

**(B) is correct** because the sentence still makes sense when the non-essential clause is removed: *Named for an Intel co-founder, Gordon Moore, Moore's Law states that computing power…typically doubles every 18 to 24 months.*

(D) is incorrect because a fragment is created when the non-essential clause is removed: *Named for an Intel co-founder, Gordon Moore, Moore's Law states that computing power…which typically doubles every 18 to 24 months.* The subject of the verb *doubles* is no longer *computing power* but rather *which*.

(E) is incorrect because the phrase *the measurement of the power of computing by the density of transistors* is wordy and awkward, and because there is an unnecessary tense switch to the past tense with the verb *doubled*.

**62. A: Verb form**

Born in the Macedon capital of Pella in 356 B.C.E.,
Alexander the Great spent most of his ruling years on
an unprecedented military campaign through Asia
and northeast Africa, <u>and by the age of 30 he had
created one of the largest empires in the ancient
world</u>.

**(A) and by the age of 30 he had created one of the
    largest empires in the ancient world**
(B) and one of the largest empires of the ancient world
    had been created by the age of 30
(C) and has created one of the ancient world's largest
    empires by 30 years of age
(D) having created one of the largest empires in the
    ancient world by 30 years old
(E) and creating one of the largest empires of the
    ancient world by the age of 30

The word *by*, which appears in every answer choice, is a tip-off that the past perfect (*had created*) is required.

**(A) is correct** because it uses the past perfect appropriately and uses the pronoun *he* to make it clear that Alexander was responsible for creating one of the largest empires in the world.

(B) is incorrect because the phrase *one of the largest empires in the world had been created by the age of 30* implies that the empire itself was 30 years old when it became the largest empire in the world. Clearly it was Alexander, not the empire, who turned 30.

(C) is incorrect because the use of the present perfect (*has created*) is inconsistent with the historical topic of the sentence. This tense should only be used for actions that continue into the present.

(D) is incorrect because the gerund *having* creates a fragment.

(E) is incorrect because the gerund *creating* creates a fragment and disrupts parallel structure.

### 63. C: Word pair; Parallel structure

Although politicians have a longstanding reputation for dishonesty, many of their falsehoods emerge as much from a sincere belief in their promises <u>as because they want to appeal to their constituents</u>.

(A) as because they want to appeal to their constituents
(B) as having the desire to appeal to their constituents
**(C) as from their desire to appeal to their constituents**
(D) as because of wanting to appeal to their constituents
(E) as in the desire of appealing to their constituents

The simplest way to approach this question is to recognize the word pair *as much...as*. The first half of the word pair, in the non-underlined portion of the sentence, is followed by the preposition *from*, so the correct answer must contain the construction *as from* as well. Although all of the answers begin with *as*, only (C) contains *from*. That makes **(C)** the only possible answer.

### 64. D: Verb form; Pronoun agreement

Although many children want to read digital books <u>and read for fun more frequently if they could obtain this with ease</u>, an even larger percentage claim that they do  not want to give up traditional print books completely.

(A) and read for fun more frequently if they could obtain this with ease,
(B) and will read for fun more frequently if they could obtain these easily,
(C) and read it for fun more frequently if they can be easily obtained,
**(D) and would read for fun more frequently if they could obtain such books with ease,**
(E) and would read for fun more frequently if they can obtain such books easily,

The presence of an "if" clause (*if they could obtain this with ease*) in the underlined portion of the sentence is a tip-off that the question is testing tense. In addition, consider the most logical meaning: children want to read digital books but are unable to obtain them easily. That is, children *would read* for fun more frequently if they *could* obtain digital books more easily. The conditional is the most likely tense for the first verb (main clause), meaning that the past should be used for the second verb ("if" clause).

(A) is incorrect because the conditional *would read*, rather than the present tense *read*, should be used. Even though the underlined *read* is parallel to the *read* that appears earlier in the non-underlined portion of the sentence, the tense switch is required to create a logical meaning.

(B) is incorrect because the future tense (*will read*) in a main clause should only be paired with an "if" clause that uses a present-tense verb, and here the "if" clause uses a past-tense verb (*could*).

(C) is incorrect because the singular pronoun *it* disagrees with the plural referent *books*.

**(D) is correct** because it places the first verb in the conditional (*would read*) and the second in the past (*could*), creating the most logical meaning.

(E) is incorrect because it pairs the conditional (*would read*) in a main clause with the present (*can*) in an "if" clause.

**65. E: Subject-verb agreement; Idiom: of vs. that**

> Although Artie Shaw, a clarinetist and popular big band leader during the 1930s, spent far more of his life writing prose than making music, <u>a careful look at his compositions reveal that he was a musician of genius</u>.

(A)  a careful look at his compositions reveal that he was a musician of genius
(B)  looking carefully at his compositions reveal that he was a genius as a musician
(C)  a careful look at his compositions reveals of his being a genius musician
(D)  a careful look at his compositions are a revelation of his genius in music
**(E)  a careful look at his compositions reveals that he was a musical genius**

If you look carefully at the answer choices, you can see that some options include the singular verb *reveals* and other include the plural verb *reveal*, a pattern that indicates the question is testing subject-verb agreement.

(A) is incorrect because the plural verb *reveal* disagrees with the singular subject *a careful look*. The plural noun *compositions* is part of the prepositional phrase *at his compositions*.

(B) is incorrect because the plural verb *reveal* disagrees with the singular subject *looking*. Remember that when a gerund is used as a subject, it is always singular.

(C) is incorrect even though the singular verb *reveals* agrees with the singular subject *a careful look*. The correct idiom is *reveal + that*, not *reveal of* + gerund.

(D) is incorrect because the plural verb *are* disagrees with the singular subject *a careful look*. As in (A), the plural noun *compositions* is part of the prepositional phrase *at his compositions*.

**(E) is correct** because the singular verb *reveals* agrees with the singular subject *a careful look*, and *reveals* is appropriately followed by *that*.

### 66. B: Idiom: if vs. whether

The status of photography as an art form was initially unclear: at the International Exhibition of 1862, for example, organizers debated <u>over if photographs should be exhibited</u> with the machines or with the paintings and sculptures.

(A)  over if photographs should be exhibited
**(B)  whether photographs should be exhibited**
(C)  that the photographs should be exhibited
(D)  as to the exhibiting of photographs
(E)  about the photograph's exhibition

Expressions involving questions and debates typically use *whether* rather than *if*, so **(B)** is the only possible answer.

### 67. C: Idiom; Grammatical construction

Prepaid bank cards, which are issued by a wide range of operators, <u>are different compared to debit and credit cards because they need to be</u> loaded before payments can be made but can carry substantial amounts of money.

(A)  are different compared to debit and credit cards because they need to be
(B)  are different when compared to debit and credit cards because they need to be
**(C)  differ from debit and credit cards because bank cards must be**
(D)  are different than debit and credit cards, for these must be
(E)  different from debit and credit cards because they need to be

The correct idiom is *differ(ent) from*; both *different (when) compared to* and *different than* are incorrect. On that basis, (A), (B), and (D) can all be eliminated.

**(C) is correct** because it uses the appropriate preposition after *differ* and because it repeats *bank cards* to distinguish that plural noun from the other plural nouns in the sentence. (In contrast, the use of *they/these* in other answer choices is problematic because the referent is unclear. Is it prepaid bank cards? Debit and credit cards?)

(E) is incorrect because the verb *are* must be placed before the adjective *different*; this version lacks a main verb.

### 68. E: Verb form

According to *The Stock Trader's Almanac*, the performance of stocks in January foretells <u>how the market performs throughout the year</u>, but statistics experts warn that causation is impossible to prove.

(A)  how the market performs throughout the year,
(B)  the market's performing throughout the year,
(C)  the performance of the year's market
(D)  what the market will perform like in the year
**(E)  how the market will perform during the year**

The key word is *foretells*, which indicates that the sentence is describing a future action. The correct answer must therefore include a verb in the future tense.

(A) is incorrect because the verb *performs* is in the present tense.

(B) is incorrect because the phrase *the market's performing* is not idiomatic; the noun *performance* should be used instead.

(C) is incorrect because the phrase *the performance of the year's market* is not idiomatically acceptable.

(D) is incorrect because the phrase *what the market will perform like* is awkward and unacceptable for formal writing. In addition, the preposition *in* is idiomatically questionable; either *throughout* or *during* is preferable.

**(E) is correct** because it uses the future tense (*will perform*) and is otherwise grammatically/idiomatically acceptable.

### 69. A: Faulty comparison; Grammatical construction

<u>Unlike his contemporaries, whose work he
considered</u> conventional and uninspiring,
Le Corbusier insisted on using modern industrial
techniques to construct buildings.

- **(A)  Unlike his contemporaries, whose work he
  considered**
- (B)  Unlike that of his contemporaries, whose work
  he considered to be
- (C)  Unlike his contemporaries, whom he considered
  their work to be
- (D)  Unlike his contemporaries, where he considered
  that their work was
- (E)  In contrast to the work of his contemporaries,
  which he considered it to be

The word *unlike* at the beginning of the sentence is an immediate tip-off that the sentence is testing comparisons. The original version also contains a non-essential clause, which can be crossed out to simplify the sentence. The fact that part of the clause is included in the underlined portion is irrelevant—the clause is simply there for description, and removing it allows you to see the comparison more clearly.

Crossed out: *Unlike his contemporaries… Le Corbusier insisted on using modern industrial techniques to construct buildings.*

Yes, the original version correctly compares Le Corbusier (person) to *his contemporaries* (people). So (A) can stay.

(B) and (E), however, compare Le Corbusier to his contemporaries' work, so those answers can be eliminated. Note that in (B), the pronoun *that* replaces the noun *work*.

Now consider the non-essential clause.

**(A) is correct** because the possessive pronoun *whose* is appropriately used to refer to Le Corbusier's contemporaries.

(C) is incorrect because the phrase *whom he considered their work to be* is both awkward and grammatically unacceptable. It is correct to say either *he considered their work to be* or *whose work he considered (to be)*, but the forms cannot be combined.

(D) is incorrect because *where* should only be used to refer to places, and *contemporaries* are people, not places.

244

## 70. C: Verb Form; Logical Construction

Grace Hopper, who in 1944 became one of the first programmers of Harvard University's Mark I computer, <u>was reported for popularizing the term "debugging" as a synonym for fixing computer glitches after she had removed a moth from one</u>.

.

(A) was reported for popularizing the term "debugging" as a synonym for "fixing computer glitches" after she had removed a moth from one

(B) was reported to popularize the term "debugging" as a synonym that meant "fixing computer glitches" after the removal of a moth from a computer by her

**(C) is reported to have popularized the term "debugging" as a synonym for "fixing computer glitches" after she removed a moth from a computer**

(D) is reported for popularizing the term "debugging" as a synonym to mean "fixing computer glitches" after removing a moth from a computer

(E) was reported for popularizing the term "debugging" to mean "fixing computer glitches" after the removal of moth from a computer

(A) is incorrect because the construction *was reported for doing x* is used to indicate that a person's wrongdoing was revealed, and that is not a logical implication here. In addition, the pronoun *one* at the end of the sentence lacks a referent. Logically, it must refer to "a computer," but the word *computer* does not appear in the sentence as a noun. Rather, *computer* functions as an adjective in the phrase *computer glitches*.

(B) is incorrect because *reported to popularize* should be *reported to have popularized* and because the word *synonym* should be followed by *for*: the idiom is *x is a synonym for y*. In addition, the passive construction *the removal of a moth from a computer by her* is awkward and wordy.

**(C) is correct** because the phrase *is reported to have popularized* conveys the fact that the sentence is describing an event in the past (as indicated by the date *1944*). This version also uses two gerunds *debugging* and *fixing* to create a parallel structure, and supplies the noun *computer* at the end of the sentence.

(D) is incorrect because the phrase *is reported for popularizing* does not convey the fact that the sentence is describing an event in the past. The word *synonym* should also be followed by *for*.

(E) is incorrect for the same reason as (A); *was reported for popularizing* should be *was reported to have popularized*.

## 71. A: Subject-verb agreement

An important stylistic element in Dostoevsky's <u>novels</u> <u>is polyphony, the simultaneous presence of multiple</u> <u>narrative voices and perspectives</u> first identified by the critic M. M. Bakhtin.

**(A)** **novels is polyphony, the simultaneous presence of** **multiple narrative voices and perspectives**

(B)  novels are polyphony, multiple narrative voices and perspectives' being simultaneously present

(C)  novels is polyphony, whose simultaneous presence of multiple narrative voices and perspectives were

(D)  novels is polyphony, in which multiple narrative voices and perspectives are present simultaneously

(E)  novels are polyphony, the simultaneous presence of the multiplicity of narratives and perspectives

The answer choices contain a mix of singular (*is*) and plural (*are*) verbs, indicating that the question is testing subject-verb agreement. The first step is therefore to identify the subject of the verb in question.

What is the logical subject? *An important stylistic element* (singular). The plural noun *novels* is part of the prepositional phrase *in Dostoevsky's novels*. A singular verb is thus required, eliminating (B) and (E).

**(A) is correct** because it correctly provides a singular verb (*is*) and uses an appositive after the comma to define the word *polyphony*.

(C) is incorrect because it creates a new subject-verb disagreement: the subject of the plural verb *were* is the singular noun *presence*. The plural noun *perspectives* is part of the prepositional phrase *of multiple narrative voices and perspectives*.

(D) is incorrect because this version creates an ungrammatical construction when it is plugged back into the sentence: *...in which multiple narrative voices and perspectives are present simultaneously first identified by the critic M. M. Bakhtin*. The phrase *first identified by the critic M. M. Bakhtin* can only modify a noun, not an adverb.

## 72. D: Dangling modifier; Non-essential clause; Verb form

Having for years recommended that customers
protect their electronic accounts by creating strong
passwords, many people nevertheless fail to heed
security experts' advice.

(A) Having for years recommended that customers
protect their electronic accounts by creating strong
passwords, many people nevertheless fail to heed
security experts' advice.

(B) For years, security experts, who have
recommended that customers protect their
electronic accounts by creating strong passwords,
but many people nonetheless fail to heed their
advice.

(C) While security experts recommend for years that
customers protect their electronic accounts
through the creation of strong passwords, there is
a failure to heed that advice by many people.

**(D) Although security experts have for years
recommended that customers protect their
electronic accounts by creating strong passwords,
many people nevertheless fail to heed that advice.**

(E) Having for years recommended for customers to
protect their electronic accounts through creating
strong passwords, many people are nonetheless
failing to heed security experts' advice.

(A) is incorrect because it creates a dangling modifier. Logically, who has for years recommended that customers protect their electronic accounts by creating strong passwords? *Security experts*, not *many people*. Because *security experts* does not appear immediately after the comma, the modifier is dangling.

(B) is incorrect because this version creates an ungrammatical fragment, as becomes apparent when the non-essential clause is removed: *For years, security experts…but many people nonetheless fail to heed their advice.*

(C) is incorrect because the word *for* is a tip-off that the present perfect is required; *recommend* should be *have recommended*. In addition, the passive construction *there is a failure to heed that advice by many people* is wordy and awkward.

**(D) is correct** because it uses the present perfect tense (*have for years recommended*) to describe an action that is continuing into the present, and because it clearly sets up the opposition between security experts' recommendation and people's actual behavior.

(E) is incorrect because it creates a dangling modifier. The phrase *Having for years recommended for customers to protect their electronic accounts through creating strong passwords* clearly refers to *security experts*, but those words do not appear after the comma. In addition, *recommended for customers to protect* should be *recommended that customers protect*.

**73. D: Word pair; Faulty comparison; Grammatical construction**

In comparison to people, elephants are capable
of perceiving a much wider variety of sounds; in fact,
an elephant's ears can pick up frequencies more than
20 Hertz lower than what human ears can hear.

(A)  lower than what human ears can hear
(B)  lower as opposed to humans' hearing
(C)  lower in opposition to range that human ears
     have
**(D)  lower than those perceptible to human ears**
(E)  lower than those by human ears

Because the comparative *lower* must be paired with *than*, both (B) and (C) can be eliminated immediately.

(A) is incorrect because two parallel items are not compared: this version compares *frequencies* (noun) to *what human ears can hear* (relative clause).

**(D) is correct** because it maintains parallel constructions on either side of the comparison: the noun *frequencies* on the first side of the comparison is appropriately replaced with the pronoun *those* on the second side.

(E) is incorrect because *those* must be followed by a verb (*perceived* or *picked up*) in order to make the constructions parallel. The omission of a verb before *by* is grammatically unacceptable: x must be *done* by y.

**74. C: Transition**

Many design movements have political or
philosophical beginnings or intentions, with the art
deco style being invented for purely decorative
purposes.

(A)  with the art deco style being invented
(B)  with the invention of the art deco style
**(C)  but the art deco style was invented**
(D)  but the art deco style invented
(E)  but the inventing of the art deco style was

The construction *with* + gerund is generally equivalent to *and*; it is used to indicate that a sentence is continuing in the direction it began. The two clauses in this sentence, however, express opposing ideas: Many design movements have political or philosophical origins vs. art deco style was invented only to look nice. As a result, *but* is a more appropriate transition to use between the clauses. (A) and (B) can thus be eliminated.

**(C) is correct** because the transition *but* indicates the contrast between the two clauses, and because the passive construction *was intended* is used to create a logical meaning.

(D) is incorrect because *the art deco style invented* should be *the art deco style was invented*; a passive construction is required here because the art deco style itself did not invent anything.

(E) is incorrect because *the inventing of* should be *the invention of*; the noun form is standard usage. In addition, a stronger verb such as *occurred* should be used in place of *was*.

## 75. A: Parallel structure

In response to their critics, proponents of genetically modified foods typically insist that such crops <u>grow at a faster rate, are less vulnerable to disease, and reduce the amount of stress placed on natural resources</u>.

(A) **grow at a faster rate, are less vulnerable to disease, and reduce the amount of stress placed on natural resources**
(B) grow at a faster rate, being less vulnerable to disease and a reduction in the amount of stress placed on natural resources
(C) grow at a faster rate, less vulnerable to disease, and would reduce the amount of stress placed on natural resources
(D) are growing at a faster rate, they are less vulnerable to disease, and reduce the amount of stress they place on natural resources
(E) grow at a faster rate, have less vulnerability to disease, and to reduce how much stress is placed on natural resources

This is a parallel structure question, as indicated by the list. As always, the easiest way to check the answers is to focus on the beginnings of the items and see whether they match.

**(A) is correct** because each item in the list begins with a verb: *grow, are,* and *reduce*

(B) is grammatically acceptable, if somewhat awkward; however, it creates an illogical meaning. By setting up *reduction* as parallel to *disease*, this version implies that genetically modified foods are less vulnerable to a *reduction* in stress placed on natural resources. That, however, does not make sense. A reduction in stress would be a good thing, and the phrase "vulnerable to" is used to indicate something negative.

(C) is incorrect because the items in the list are not parallel. *Less vulnerable* should be *are less vulnerable*—only a passive construction makes sense. There is also an unnecessary switch to the conditional (*would reduce*) in the last item.

(D) is incorrect because the first item begins with a verb, the second with a pronoun, and the third with a verb.

(E) is incorrect because the first two items begin with conjugated verbs, whereas the third begins with an infinitive.

## 76. E: Verb form

<u>If his longevity claim would be confirmed,</u> Carmelo Flores Laura, a former rancher from Bolivia, would have the longest verified lifespan of anyone in human history.

(A) If his longevity claim would be confirmed,
(B) Should his longevity's claim be confirmed,
(C) Had his longevity claim been confirmed,
(D) That his claim to longevity was confirmed,
(E) **Were his longevity claim confirmed,**

The presence of the word *if* in the underlined portion is a tip-off that this question is testing tense.

(A) is incorrect because the conditional (*would* + *verb*) should not be used in an "if" clause.

(B) is incorrect because the phrase *longevity's claim* is idiomatically unacceptable and illogical: the use of the possessive implies that the longevity itself is making a claim.

(C) is incorrect because when a main clause contains the conditional (*would have*), the "if" clause must contain the past, not the conditional.

(D) is incorrect because the use of the conditional (*would have*) in the main clause indicates that the previous clause must describe a hypothetical situation, and *that* is used to refer to actual situations.

**(E) is correct** because the construction *Were his longevity claim confirmed* is grammatically equivalent to *If his longevity claim were confirmed*, and is thus appropriately used to convey a hypothetical situation. In addition, the past tense in the hypothetical clause is correctly paired with the conditional in the main clause.

**77. E: Word pair: were to…what**

In an era when the economies of many European countries were fueled by their overseas possessions, the American colonies were to the British Empire <u>as the islands of Martinique and Guadeloupe related to France</u>.

(A)  as the islands of Martinique and Guadeloupe
        related to        France
(B)  what that of the islands of Martinique and
        Guadeloupe were to France
(C)  just like the islands of Martinique and Guadeloupe
        belonged to France
(D)  much the same as Martinique and Guadeloupe
        with France
**(E)  what the islands of Martinique and Guadeloupe
        were to France**

Although this question might seem complicated, you can actually answer it very quickly if you identify the relevant information upfront. The words *were to* in the non-underlined portion of the sentence are a tip-off that this is a word pair question. *Were to* must be paired with *what* to form an analogy: *A is to B what C is to D*. Because (B) and (E) are the only option that contain *what*, (A), (C), and (D) can all be eliminated immediately.

(B) is incorrect because the construction on the first side of the word pair is *A is to B*, not *that of A is to B* or *A's is to B*. As a result, the possessive is unnecessary on the second side.

**(E) is correct** because it makes the construction after *what* parallel to the construction after *were to*, a construction that indicates the relationships between the two sets of countries were analogous. If it were set up like a formal analogy, it would read: *American colonies : British Empire : : Martinique and Guadeloupe : France*).

## 78. C: Relative pronoun; Logical construction

An initial public offering (IPO) or stock market launch is a type of public offering <u>where shares of a company are sold to institutional investors that, in turn, are sold to the general public</u> on a securities exchange for the first time.

(A) where shares of a company are sold to institutional investors that, in turn, are sold to the general public

(B) where shares of a company are sold to institutional investors who, in turn, sell these to the general public

**(C) in which shares of a company are sold to institutional investors who, in turn, sell to the general public**

(D) in which a company's shares are sold to institutional investors and, in turn, sell it to the general public

(E) whereby shares of a company are sold to institutional investors that are sold to the general public in turn

*Where* should only be used to refer to a place, and a public offering is not a place, so both (A) and (B) can be eliminated.

**(C) is correct** because *in which* is appropriately used to refer to a public offering, and because *who* is used to refer to investors. In addition the phrase *on a securities exchange for the first time* logically follows the end of the underlined portion.

(D) is incorrect because *and* should be *who* or *that*, and *sell* should be *sold*. As it is, this version implies that a company's shares themselves, not the institutional investors, sell to the general public—clearly an illogical meaning because shares cannot sell anything.

(E) is incorrect because *that are sold* should be *who sell*. This version contains a misplaced modifier: the phrase *institutional investors that are sold to the general public* illogically implies that the investors, not the company shares, are sold. In addition, the placement of *in turn* at the end of the underlined portion is awkward when this version is plugged into the sentence.

## 79. B: Pronoun agreement: missing referent

In the 1880s new steamships made it possible to bring cheap wheat and meat to Europe, <u>which bankrupted family farms and aristocratic estates, and sent</u> a flood of rural refugees into cities.

(A) which bankrupted family farms and aristocratic estates, and sent

**(B) a development that bankrupted family farms and aristocratic estates, sending**

(C) a development bankrupting family farms and aristocratic estates and sending

(D) which bankrupted family farms as well as aristocratic estates, sending

(E) a development which bankrupted family farms and aristocratic estates, to send

Whenever you see *which* underlined, the first thing you should do is back up and check whether the noun immediately before it (*Europe*) is the logical referent. In this case, it is reasonable to assume that Europe itself was not responsible for bankrupt[ing] family farms and aristocratic estates.

In fact, *which* refers to the fact that new steamships allowed cheap wheat and meat to be brought to Europe. Because the words *the fact* do not appear, *which* is missing a referent. (A) and (D) can thus be eliminated.

**(B) is correct** because it replaces *which* with the noun *a development*, eliminating the problem of the missing referent. In addition, the participial phrase *sending a flood of rural refugees into cities* is appropriately used to modify the previous clause. Note that this construction is just as correct as *a development that bankrupted family farms and aristocratic estates, and sent...*

(C) is incorrect because *a development bankrupting* should be *a development that bankrupted*; the gerund is idiomatically unacceptable here and also deprives the clause begun by *a development* of a main verb.

(E) is incorrect because *a development which bankrupted* should be *a development that bankrupted*. In addition, either *and sent* or *sending* can be used after the comma; the infinitive *to send* implies a cause-and-effect relationship (the development bankrupted farms and estates in order to send rural refugees into cities) that is illogical in context.

### 80. B: Subject-verb agreement; Parallel structure; Idiom: gerund vs. infinitive

Traditional methods of salmon farming have led to homogeneity <u>rather than the diversity that make a species more capable to survive</u> myriad natural challenges, including predators and disease.

(A) rather than the diversity that make a species more capable to survive
**(B) rather than to the diversity that makes a species more capable of surviving**
(C) rather than the diversity that make a species more capable in surviving
(D) rather than for the diversity which makes a species more capable of surviving
(E) rather than the diversity making a species more capable to survive

If you look through the answers, you can see that some choices contain *makes* (singular) while others contain *make* (plural). That pattern indicates that the question is testing subject-verb agreement, so the first step is to determine the subject of the verb in question.

In this case, you don't have to look very far. When a clause begins with *that* or *which*, the subject comes right before the pronoun. Here, that noun is *diversity* (singular). (A) and (C) can thus be eliminated.

Now consider the underlined portion in context of the information before it: the phrase *rather than* is a big clue that parallel structure is being tested. The basic construction of the non-underlined portion is *x has led to y*. As a result, the underlined portion should contain an equivalent construction.

When the question is considered from that angle, (B) is the only option because it is the only answer that contains the preposition *to* after *rather than*. It also correctly uses the idiomatically correct phrase *of* + gerund after *capable*.

(D) is incorrect because *for the diversity* should be *to the diversity*, and because *which* should be *that*.

(E) is incorrect because the preposition *to* is omitted, and because *the diversity making* should be *the diversity that makes*.

## 81. D: Verb form; Pronoun agreement; Like vs. such as

Clinical trials are the key to obtaining information about the safety and efficacy of new medications, and <u>without volunteers to take part in it, there will be no new treatments for serious diseases like cancer, multiple sclerosis and arthritis</u>.

(A) without volunteers to take part in it, there will be no new treatments for serious diseases like cancer, multiple sclerosis and arthritis

(B) with volunteers to take part in these being absent, there would be no new treatments for serious diseases like cancer, multiple sclerosis and arthritis

(C) in the absence of the participation by volunteers, there will be no new serious disease treatments, including cancer, multiple sclerosis and arthritis

**(D) without volunteers to participate in them, there would be no new treatments for serious diseases such as cancer, multiple sclerosis and arthritis**

(E) without voluntary participating, there are no new treatments for serious diseases such as cancer, multiple sclerosis and arthritis

Even though there is no "if" clause in this sentence, the phrase *without volunteers to take part* indicates that the sentence is describing an alternative or a hypothetical situation—something that *would* occur. The conditional is therefore required.

(A) is incorrect because it uses the future tense (*there will be no new treatments*); because the singular pronoun *it* disagrees with the plural referent *clinical trials*; and because *such as* rather than *like* should be used to set up the examples of diseases.

(B) is incorrect despite its use of the conditional because the phrase *with volunteers to take part in these being absent* is wordy and awkward; because *these* should be followed by a noun; and because *such as* rather than *like* should be used to set up the examples of diseases.

(C) is incorrect because *the participation by volunteers* should be *the participation of volunteers*, and because the future tense (*will be*) rather than the conditional is used.

**(D) is correct** because the conditional (*would be*) is used, and because the plural pronoun *them* agrees with its referent, the plural noun *clinical trials*.

(E) is incorrect because the gerund *participating* should be the noun *participate*, and because the present tense (*are*) rather than the conditional is used.

## 82. E: Dangling modifier

One of the earliest environmentalists, <u>it was prohibited to burn sea coal by King Edward I of England in 1306 because the smoke it created was becoming</u> a health hazard.

(A)  it was prohibited to burn sea coal by King Edward I of England in 1306 because the smoke it created was becoming
(B)  they were prohibited from burning sea coal by King Edward I of England in 1306 because the smoke created by it
(C)  the prohibition by King Edward I against burning sea coal was made in 1306, after its smoke became
(D)  the smoke created by the burning of sea coal led in 1306 to its prohibition by King Edward I because it had become a
**(E)  King Edward I of England prohibited the burning of sea coal in 1306 because the smoke it created had become**

Who was *one of the earliest environmentalists*? Logically, it could only have been King Edward I. *King Edward I*, the subject, must therefore appear immediately after the comma, at the beginning of the underlined portion. That makes **(E)** the only possible answer.

## 83. C: Word pair; Parallel structure

Three million years ago, the creation of the Panama Isthmus wreaked ecological havoc <u>not just by triggering large-scale extinctions but divert</u> ocean currents and transforming the climate.

(A)  not just by triggering large-scale extinctions but divert
(B)  not just by triggering large-scale extinctions but by the diversion of
**(C)  not just by triggering large-scale extinctions but also by diverting**
(D)  not just because they trigger large-scale extinctions but also to divert
(E)  not just in triggering large-scale extinctions but because they are diverting

Although the most common form of the word pair is *not only…but also*, in this case *not just* is used as an alternative to *not only*.

The preposition *by* follows the first half of the word pair, so the same preposition must follow the second half of the word pair. (A), (D), and (E) can thus be eliminated.

(B) is incorrect because the two sides of the word pair are not parallel: the first side contains a gerund (*triggering*), whereas the second side contains a noun (*diversion*). In addition, *but* should be *but also*.

**(C) is correct** because *by* + *gerund* (*triggering, diverting*) follows each side of the word pair.

### 84. B: Subject-verb agreement; Non-essential clause; Grammatical construction

The paintings of Caravaggio (Michelangelo Merisi da
<u>Caravaggio) combines a realistic observation of the
human state, both physical and emotional, with a
dramatic use of lighting,</u> had a formative influence on
Baroque painting.

(A)  Caravaggio) combines a realistic observation of the
    human state, both physical and emotional, with a
    dramatic use of lighting,
**(B)  Caravaggio), which combine a realistic observation
    of the human state, both physical and emotional,
    with a dramatic use of lighting,**
(C)  Caravaggio), which combines a realistic
    observation of the human state, physical as well as
    emotional, to dramatically used lighting,
(D)  Caravaggio) combine a realistic observing of the
    human state, both physical and emotional, with a
    dramatic use of lighting,
(E)  Caravaggio), which combine a realistic observation
    of the human state, physical as well as emotional,
    with a dramatic use of lighting and

If you look through the answers, you can see that some choices contain *combines* (singular) while others contain *combine* (plural). That pattern indicates that the question is testing subject-verb agreement, so the first step is to determine the subject of the verb in question.

What combines *a realistic observation of the human state with a dramatic use of lighting?* The *paintings* of Caravaggio (plural). So a plural verb, *combine*, is required. (A) and (C) can thus be eliminated.

**(B) is correct** because it begins the underlined portion with *which*, creating a non-essential clause. The construction works because the sentence makes sense when the clause is removed: *The paintings of Caravaggio (Michelangelo Merisi da Caravaggio)…had a formative influence on Baroque painting.* In addition, *combine* is correctly paired with the preposition *with*.

(D) is incorrect because it creates a fragment when plugged back into the sentence. At the beginning of the underlined portion, the pronoun *which* is required to create a non-essential clause; without it, the sentence makes no grammatical sense.

(E) is incorrect because the placement of *and* before the verb *had* creates a fragment by depriving the sentence of a main verb: *The paintings of Caravaggio, which combine a realistic observation of the human state…with a dramatic use of lighting and had a formative influence on Baroque painting.*

## 85. C: Parallel structure

The First Industrial Revolution evolved into the Second Industrial Revolution in the transition years between 1840 and 1870, when technological and economic progress continued with <u>the adoption of steam transport, machine tools being manufactured on a large scale, and the use of machinery increasing in steam-powered factories</u>.

(A) the adoption of steam transport, machine tools being manufactured on a large scale, and the use of machinery increasing in steam-powered factories

(B) adopting steam transport, manufacturing machine tools on a large scale, and the use of machinery increasing in steam-powered factories

**(C) the adoption of steam transport, the large-scale manufacture of machine tools, and the increasing use of machinery in steam-powered factories**

(D) the adopting of steam transport, the manufacture of machine tools on a large scale, and the use of machinery in steam-powered factories increased

(E) the adoption of steam transport, to manufacture machine tools on a large scale, and an increase in machinery use in steam-powered factories

The presence of a list signals that this question is testing parallel structure. Each item in the list is fairly long, however, and there is a considerable amount of information to deal with. To simplify the question, start by looking at the beginning of each item—but note that because the beginnings of some items contain modifiers, you will need to look at the first few words rather than the first word only. Otherwise, you can consider the specifics of the individual constructions afterward.

(A): *the adoption* (noun), *machine tools* (noun), *the use* (noun). Leave it.

(B): *adopting* (gerund), *manufacturing* (gerund), *the use* (noun). Eliminate it.

(C): *the adoption* (noun), *the large-scale manufacture* (noun), *the increasing use* (noun). Leave it.

(D): *the adopting* (gerund), *the manufacture* (noun), *the use* (noun). Eliminate it.

(E): *the adoption* (noun), *to manufacture* (infinitive), *an increase* (noun). Eliminate it.

So now you're down to (A) and (C), and you can take a closer look at each one.

(A) is incorrect because items one and three contain the construction *x of y*, whereas the second item contains the construction *x being y*.

**(C) is correct** because all three items contain the construction *x of y*. Again, notice that *increasing* is an adjective that modifies *use*; it is not a gerund that disrupts parallel structure. The basic structure is still *noun, noun, noun*.

### 86. A: Verb form; Subject-verb agreement; Relative pronoun

In 1963, Lina Wertmüller directed her first film,
*I Basilischi* (*The Lizards*), <u>whose theme—the lives of
impoverished inhabitants of southern Italy—would
become</u> a recurring motif in her later works.

(A) **whose theme—the lives of impoverished
inhabitants of southern Italy—would become**
(B) whose theme, the lives of impoverished
inhabitants of Italy's south, becoming
(C) of which the theme, the lives of southern Italy's
impoverished inhabitants, have become
(D) where the theme—the lives of impoverished
inhabitants in the south of Italy—would become
(E) its theme—the lives of impoverished
inhabitants in Italy's south—became

Don't get distracted by the fact that some versions use dashes and others use commas to form the non-essential clause. The two types of punctuation are grammatically identical, and the alternation is nothing more than a distraction tool! The fact that different answers contain the same verbs in different forms indicates that you should focus on the verbs.

**(A) is correct** because the condition (*would become*) is used to refer to an action that, from the perspective of the past (*1963*), has not yet occurred, and because the resulting sentence is logical and grammatically acceptable.

(B) is incorrect because the use of the gerund *becoming* after the non-essential clause creates a fragment: *In 1963, Lina Wertmüller directed her first film, I Basilischi (The Lizards), whose theme...becoming a recurring motif in her later works.*

(C) is incorrect first because the present perfect (*have become*) does not make sense: there is no tip-off word such as *for* or *since* to indicate that the sentence is referring to a situation that continues into the present. In addition, the plural verb *have* disagrees with its subject, the singular noun *theme*. The plural noun *inhabitants*, which immediately precedes the verb, is part of the non-essential clause *the lives of southern Italy's impoverished inhabitants*.

(D) is incorrect because *where* should only be used to refer to places, and a theme is not a place.

(E) is incorrect because the use of *its* after the comma creates a comma splice—two complete sentences separated by a comma.

## 87. D: Gerund; Pronoun agreement

As part of a mandatory 30-day "cooling-off" period between loans, a reform intended to prevent borrowers from taking out fresh loans to cover their outstanding debts, <u>a bank will not be permitted to extend a new loan to a customer until receiving full payment from existing ones</u>.

(A) a bank will not be permitted to extend a new loan to a customer until receiving full payment from existing ones

(B) a bank will not be permitted to extend a new loan to a customer until they have received full payment for existing ones

(C) and banks will be prohibited to extend new loans to customers that have not fully repaid their existing ones

**(D) banks will be prohibited from extending new loans to customers who have not fully repaid their existing ones**

(E) a bank will be prohibited from extending new loans to a customer that has not fully repaid its existing ones

(A) is incorrect because the conjunction *until* should be followed by a subject and verb rather than a gerund (*receiving*). In addition, *from a loan* should be *for a loan*; the use of *from* implies that the loan itself is paying.

(B) is incorrect because the plural pronoun *they* disagrees with the singular referent *a bank*.

(C) is incorrect because the placement of *and* at the beginning of the underlined portion creates an ungrammatical construction, a situation that becomes apparent when the non-essential clause is removed: *As part of a mandatory 30-day "cooling-off" period between loans…and banks will be prohibited to extend new loans to customers that have not fully repaid their existing ones.*

**(D) is correct** because the plural pronoun *their* agrees with the plural noun *customers*, which clearly and logically acts as the referent.

(E) is incorrect because the singular pronoun *its* cannot refer to a person, only a thing; *his or her* should be used instead. The only singular noun, *bank*, cannot be the referent of *its* because logically, a customer is responsible for paying off loans, not a bank.

## 88. C: Subject-verb agreement

Researchers have suggested that soft music and gentle humming <u>is perceived as soothing because humans, like many social animals, are predisposed in interpreting</u> silence as a sign of danger.

(A) is perceived as soothing because humans, like many social animals, are predisposed in interpreting

(B) has been perceived to be soothing because humans, like many social animals, have the predisposition to interpret

**(C) are perceived as soothing because humans, like many social animals, are predisposed to interpret**

(D) is perceived to be soothing because humans, just as many social animals, are predisposed in the interpretation of

(E) are perceived as soothing due to humans, like many social animals, having the predisposition to interpret

If you look through the answers, you can see that some choices contain *is* (singular) while others contain *are* (plural). That pattern indicates that the question is testing subject-verb agreement, so the first step is to determine the subject of the verb in question.

Don't get fooled by the formatting! Notice that if you start by focusing on the part of the sentence in which the underlined portion appears, you could miss the complete subject. The underlined portion begins at the second word of the second line, and if you look only at that line, you risk thinking that the subject is only the singular noun *humming*, which appears right before the underlined portion begins. Instead, you need to back up and read from the beginning of the sentence.

If you do so, you'll find the sentence contains a compound subject (*soft music and gentle humming*) that is by definition plural. So a plural verb is required, eliminating (A), (B) and (D). Note that the tense switch in (B) is a distraction; the real issue is the agreement.

**(C) is correct** because the plural verb *are* agrees with the compound subject; because *perceived* is appropriately followed by *as*; and because *predisposed* is followed by an infinitive (*to interpret*).

(E) is incorrect because *due to* should be *because*; if you plug in *caused by* in place of *due to*, the sentence does not make sense. In addition, the gerund phrase *having the predisposition* is unnecessarily wordy; *are predisposed* is cleaner and more concise.

**89. A: Word pair; Parallel structure; Idiom**

Urban gardens and farming initiatives <u>not only recycle and transform old lots in many formerly crumbling cities, but also address</u> pressing quality-of-life issues.

(A) **not only recycle and transform old lots in many formerly crumbling cities, but also address**
(B) are not only recycling and transforming old lots in many formerly crumbling cities, but also are addressing to
(C) not only recycle and transform old lots in many formerly crumbling cities, but also addressing
(D) not only recycle or transform old lots in many cities that formerly were crumbling, but also addresses
(E) not only recycle or transform old lots in many cities that crumbled formerly, and also address to

*Not only* must be paired with *but also*, so (E) can be eliminated immediately because it pairs *not only* with *and*.

**(A) is correct** because it maintains parallel structure on both sides of the word pair: the verb *address* is parallel to *recycle* and *transform*. In addition, it correctly omits the prepositions after *addressed*.

(B) is incorrect because *addressing* should not be followed by *to*. In some situations, this construction is permissible (e.g., to address a letter *to* someone), but when the verb *address* is used to mean "to deal with or discuss," the preposition is incorrect.

(C) is incorrect because *addressing* is not parallel to *recycle* and *transform*.

(D) is incorrect because the singular verb *addresses* is not parallel to the plural verbs *recycle* and *transform*. In addition, the phrase *cities that formerly were crumbling* is wordy and awkward; *formerly* modifies *crumbling* and should also be placed next to that adjective.

Note that the issue of *recycle and transform* in (A), (B), and (C) vs. *recycle and transform* in (D) and (E) is a distraction; it has no bearing whatsoever on the answer.

**90. B: Parallel structure; Pronoun agreement**

Studies have shown that naps lasting 20-30 minutes can boost job performance by up to 34 <u>percent by the enhancement of attention to detail, decreasing stress, and an improvement</u> in overall cognitive abilities.

(A) percent by the enhancement of attention to detail, decreasing stress, and an improvement
(B) **percent, for they enhance attention to detail, decrease stress, and improve**
(C) percent in that it enhances attention to detail, decreasing stress, and to improve
(D) percent because of their enhancing attention to detail, decrease of stress, and improve
(E) percent, enhancing attention to detail, decreasing stress, and improves

The presence of a list signals that Question #90 is testing parallel structure. To simplify the question, start by looking at the beginning of each item.

(A) is incorrect because the first item contains a noun (*enhancement*), the second contains a gerund (*decreasing*), and the third contains a noun (*improvement*). Note that at this point, you may be tempted to fix the sentence yourself by making each item a gerund, but unfortunately no option with that construction appears.

**(B) is correct** because all three items are verbs (*enhance, decrease, improve*) that agree with the plural subject *they*. The conjunction *for* is appropriately used as a synonym for *because*.

(C) is incorrect because the first item contains a verb (*enhances*), the second contains a gerund (*decreasing*), and the third contains an infinitive (*to improve*). The singular pronoun *it* also disagrees with the plural referent *naps*.

(D) is incorrect because the first item contains a gerund (*enhancing*), the second contains a noun (*decrease*), and the third contains a verb (*improve*).

(E) is incorrect because first two items contains gerunds (*enhancing, decreasing*) whereas the third contains a verb (*improve*).

**91. E: Word pair: between…and; Number vs. amount**

Although many consumers frequent their local farmers market because they believe that the foods sold there are safer than foods sold in traditional supermarkets, there is a positive correlation between the number of farmers markets per capita <u>to the amount of per capita reported outbreaks of food-borne illness</u>.

(A)   to the amount of per capita reported outbreaks of food-borne illness
(B)   with how many reported outbreaks of food-borne illness per capita are reported
(C)   and per capita reports of the amount of food-borne illnesses
(D)   or the number of per capita reported outbreaks of food-borne illness being reported
**(E)   and the number of reported outbreaks of food-borne illness per capita**

This question is somewhat easier than it might initially appear, provided that you are able to identify the most relevant information. The key is to consider the underlined portion in context of the non-underlined portion, which contains the word *between*. *Between* must be paired with *and*, so the correct answer must begin with the word *and*. That eliminates (A), (B), and (D).

(C) is incorrect because *amount* should only be used to refer to singular (non-quantifiable) nouns, and *food-borne illnesses* is plural.

**(E) is correct** because this version completes the word pair with *and*; it also uses *number* to refer to the plural (quantifiable) noun *outbreaks*.

## 92. D: Verb form

The 16.5-ton bell known as "Great Paul," <u>rang traditionally at one o'clock each day, was the largest bell in the British Isles until the casting of the Olympic Bell</u> for the 2012 London Olympics.

(A) rang traditionally at one o'clock each day, was the largest bell in the British Isles until the casting of the Olympic Bell
(B) traditionally rang at one o'clock daily, was the largest bell in the British Isles until casting the Olympic Bell
(C) traditionally rung at one o'clock each day, was the largest bell of the British Isles until the Olympic Bell had been cast
**(D) traditionally rung at one o'clock each day, was the largest bell in the British Isles until the Olympic Bell was cast**
(E) rang at one o'clock each day by tradition, and was the largest bell in the British Isles until the Olympic Bell was cast

If you look through the answer choices, you'll notice that some contain the past participle *rung* while others contain the simple past *rang*, a pattern that indicates that this question is testing verb form.

If you can't hear this error, there is a way to figure it out logically: the verb in question is used to begin a non-essential clause, which can only be set off by a past participle, not the simple past. That's part one.

Part two is that the ending –UNG or –UNK denotes a past participle (*sung, wrung, stung*), whereas –ANG or –ANK denotes the simple past (*sang, rang, drank*). The "u" is therefore a tip-off that *rung* is the correct form. That eliminates (A), (B), and (E).

(C) is incorrect because when a sentence refers to two events in the past, the past perfect (*had been cast*) should be used to refer to the event that came first. Logically, however, the Olympic Bell must have been cast *after* Great Paul had established itself as the largest bell in the British Isles.

**(D) is correct** because it uses the past participle *rung* to begin the non-essential clause, and because it keeps the verb tense consistent: *was the largest bell…was cast*.

## 93. E: Gerund

Although naturally ranging from Western Europe to the Persian shores of the Caspian Sea, *Vitis vinifera*, the common grape vine, has demonstrated high levels of adaptability and can sometimes mutate to accommodate a new environment.

(A) Although naturally ranging from Western Europe to the Persian shores of the Caspian Sea, *Vitis vinifera*, the common grape vine, has demonstrated

(B) Although its habitat ranges naturally from Western Europe to the Persian shores of the Caspian Sea, but *Vitis vinifera*, the common grape vine, has demonstrated

(C) Even though it has a natural range from Western Europe to the Persian shores of the Caspian Sea, *Vitis vinifera*, the common grape vine, having demonstrated

(D) Despite its naturally ranging from Western Europe to the Persian shores of the Caspian Sea, *Vitis vinifera*, the common grape vine, demonstrates

**(E) Although the natural habitat of *Vitis vinifera*, the common grape vine, ranges from Western Europe to the Persian shores of the Caspian Sea, the plant has demonstrated**

Even though the non-essential clause contained in this sentence is short, crossing it out may help you to better understand the structure of the sentence: *Although naturally ranging from Western Europe to the Persian shores of the Caspian Sea, Vitis vinifera...has demonstrated high levels of adaptability and can sometimes mutate to accommodate a new environment.*

(A) is incorrect because *Although naturally ranging* should be *Although it naturally ranges*. The conjunction *although* must be followed by a subject + verb, not a gerund (*ranging*) in order for a clause to be created.

(B) is incorrect because *although* and *but* cannot be used to begin two consecutive clauses. The use of both conjunctions is redundant and grammatically unacceptable.

(C) is incorrect because the gerund *having* creates a fragment; the sentence lacks a main verb.

(D) is incorrect because the phrase *Despite its naturally ranging* is wordy and awkward, and contains a gerund; *Although it naturally ranges* is preferable because it contains a subject + conjugated verb.

**(E) is correct** because this version correctly supplies a subject and conjugated verb after *although* (*the natural habitat...ranges*) and makes sense when the non-essential clause is removed: *Although the natural habitat of Vitis vinifera...ranges from Western Europe to the Persian shores of the Caspian Sea, the plant has demonstrated high levels of adaptability and can sometimes mutate to accommodate a new environment.*

Note that the switch from the present perfect (*has demonstrated*) to present (*can*) is acceptable here because the sentence still makes logical sense.

**94. C: Idiom; Pronouns: missing referent; Logical construction**

Galileo, who is depicted generally as a strict
proponent for rationalism and scientific thought, also
derived much of his inspiration from works of art,
particularly Dante's *Divine Comedy*.

(A)  Galileo, who is depicted generally to be a strict
     proponent for rationalism and scientific thought,
     also derived
(B)  Galileo, whom they generally depicted as a
     strict proponent of rationalism and scientific
     thought, also derived
**(C)  Generally depicted as a strict proponent of
     rationalism and scientific thought, Galileo also
     derived**
(D)  Depicted generally as a strict proponent for
     rationalism and scientific thought, Galileo would
     also derive
(E)  Galileo generally depicted as a strict proponent of
     rationalism and scientific thought, but he also
     derived

The fastest way to answer this question is to know that the correct idiom is *proponent of*, not *proponent for*. On that basis, you can immediately eliminate (A) and (D).

(B) is incorrect because the pronoun *they* lacks a referent; the sentence does not provide a plural noun that indicates who "they" could be.

**(C) is correct** because *depicted* is correctly followed by *as*, and the first clause (the information before the comma) logically describes Galileo, whose name immediately follows.

(E) is incorrect because *Galileo generally depicted* should be *Galileo is generally depicted*. Galileo does not depict anything himself but rather is depicted by others. The passive construction is necessary to create a logical meaning.

**95. A: Idiom; Grammatical construction**

In addition to being the second smallest country in the
world, Monaco, which has a land border of just 2.7
miles, is also the second smallest monarchy as well
as the most densely populated country.

**(A)  In addition to being**
(B)  Adding to its being
(C)  As long as it is
(D)  As well as being
(E)  Additionally being

Don't overthink this question. Even though (A) contains the gerund *being*, which typically signals a wrong answer, the construction *In addition to* + gerund is idiomatically correct and the only grammatically acceptable option. Note that although it is considered acceptable in British English to begin a sentence with *as well as*, as is the case in (D), this construction is not permitted in American English.

**96. E: Like vs. as; Modification; Logical construction; Pronoun agreement**

Having received a subpoena to appear in court like a witness, a person must either comply with the directive or face arrest and possible sequestration for the duration of a trial.

(A) Having received a subpoena to appear in court like a witness, a person must either comply with the directive or face

(B) Having received a subpoena to appear in court to be a witness, a person must either comply to the directive or else they face

(C) Having received a subpoena to appear in court as a witness, it is necessary that a person either comply with the directive or face

(D) When a subpoena is received to appear in court as a witness, a person must either comply with the directive or face

**(E) A person who has received a subpoena to appear in court as a witness must either comply with the directive or face**

(A) is incorrect because *appear like* should be *appear as*; *appear like* means "appear in a manner similar to," whereas *appear as* means "appear in the capacity of." Only the latter makes sense here.

(B) is incorrect because the plural pronoun *they* disagrees with the singular referent *a person*. *Appear to be* should be *appear as* because *appear to be* means "seem to be," a definition that does not make sense here.

(C) is incorrect because the introductory phrase *Having received a subpoena to appear in court as a witness* describes *a person*, the subject. Because *a person* does not appear immediately after the comma, a dangling modifier results.

(D) is incorrect because the phrase *When a subpoena is received to appear in court as a witness* implies that the subpoena itself is being asked to appear in court. That makes no sense: a subpoena is a summons ordering a person to appear in court.

**(E) is correct** because *appear* is appropriately followed by *as,* and the sentence is otherwise clear and logical.

**97. E: Parallel structure**

While small banks are still passing some of their loans off to larger institutions, it is now the big banks that are most active in what is known as the loan sub-participation market.

(A) it is now the big banks that are most active in what is known as the loan sub-participation market

(B) what is known as the loan sub-participation market counts the big banks among its most active participants

(C) the greatest activity in what is known as the loan sub-participation market comes from the big banks

(D) the loan sub-participation market draws its greatest activity from big banks

**(E) big banks are most active in what is known as the loan sub-participation market**

The sentence presents a contrast between two types of institutions: small banks and big banks. Small banks are described in the first clause, and big banks are described in the second. To make the sentence as clear and balanced as possible, the two clauses should have parallel constructions.

Because the first clause is not underlined and thus cannot be changed, the second clause must be changed (or not) to match the first.

As a result, the easiest way to approach this question is to look at the beginning of the first clause because the correct version of the second clause must begin the same way.

The first clause begins with *While* + *small banks,* so logically, the second clause must begin with *big banks* to form the basic construction *While small banks are x, big banks are y.*

The only option that begins with *big banks* is **(E)**, making that the only possible answer.

## 98. B: Parallel structure

Choreographer and dancer Savion Glover aims to restore the African roots of tap dance by eliminating hand gestures and <u>he returns to a focus on the feet</u> as the primary source of movement.

(A)   he returns to a focus on the feet
**(B)   return to a focus on the feet**
(C)   returning to the feet's focusing
(D)   returned to the feet as a focus
(E)   returning that the feet be the focus

**Note:** If you happen to recall the very tricky "music business" parallel structure question on p. 90, this one works the same way.

(A) is incorrect because the sentence indicates that Glover aims to restore the African roots of tap dance by doing two things, which should logically be presented in parallel form; however, *eliminating* and *he returns* are clearly not parallel.

When you read through the original sentence, your first inclination might be to fix it by replacing *he returns* with *returning.* Although that is a perfectly acceptable correction, it unfortunately does not appear among the answer choices—and that means you might need to reevaluate your assumption about how the sentence works.

**(B) is correct** because the verb *return* is parallel to the verb *restore* earlier in the sentence. The *to* in front of *restore* applies to both verbs: *Choreographer and dancer Savion Glover aims to restore the African roots of tap dance…and return to a focus on the feet as the primary source of movement.*

(C) is incorrect because the phrase *the feet's focusing* implies that the feet themselves are focusing; the correct construction is *focus on the feet.*

(D) is incorrect because the use of the past tense for the verb *returned* creates an unnecessary and illogical tense switch.

(E) is incorrect because the construction *returning that* is ungrammatical; *returning* should be followed by *to.*

### 99. C: Verb form; Pronoun agreement

Introduced in 1678, the term "conscious" <u>acquired at least five different definitions in the space of 50 years, and its ambiguity had not faded</u> in more recent times.

(A)  acquired at least five different definitions in the space of  50 years, and its ambiguity had not faded
(B)  would acquire at least five different definitions within 50 years, of which the ambiguity has not faded
**(C)  acquired at least five different definitions within 50 years, and its ambiguity has not faded**
(D)  acquired at least five differing definitions within 50 years, and their ambiguity did not fade
(E)  acquired within 50 years at least five separate definitions, its ambiguity not fading

If you look through the answer choices, you'll notice that they contain the same verb (*fade*) in a variety of tenses, indicating that the question is testing the correct form of that verb.

(A) is incorrect because when a sentence describes two completed actions in the past, the past perfect (*had not faded*) is used to refer to the action that came first. In this case, the action in question must have come second, as indicated by the phrase *in more recent times*.

(B) is incorrect because *of which* must refer to the noun that immediately precedes it (*50 years*), and it does not make any sense to say that the ambiguity of 50 years has not faded. Clearly, it is the ambiguity of the term "conscious" that has not faded.

**(C) is correct** because it uses the simple past to refer to the first action (the term "conscious's" acquisition of at least five definitions), which occurred firmly in the past. The use of the present perfect to refer to the second action (the ambiguity of the term "conscious" not fading) is also logical, indicating that the action is continuing into the present.

(D) is incorrect because the plural pronoun *their* disagrees with its referent, the singular noun *the term*. The only plural noun is *50 years*, and logically, the pronoun in question cannot refer to it.

(E) is incorrect because *its ambiguity not fading* should be *its ambiguity has not faded*; the gerund is awkward and less precise than the present perfect.

## 100. D: Many vs. much; Subject-verb agreement; Passive

Much of the experiments performed by cognitive psychologist Elizabeth Spelke have been designed to test how much babies and young children understand about the world around them.

(A) Much of the experiments performed by cognitive psychologist Elizabeth Spelke have been designed
(B) Much of the experiments that cognitive psychologist Elizabeth Spelke performs are designed
(C) Many of the experiments that cognitive psychologist Elizabeth Spelke performs is designed
**(D) Many of the experiments performed by cognitive psychologist Elizabeth Spelke are designed**
(E) Many of the experiments that are performed by cognitive psychologist Elizabeth Spelke designed

Recall the rule for *many vs. much*: *much* refers to singular (non-quantifiable) nouns, whereas *many* refers to plural (quantifiable) nouns. The noun being modified here is the plural *experiments*, so *many* should be used. On that basis, (A) and (B) can be eliminated.

(C) is incorrect because the singular verb *is* disagrees with the plural subject *many*. The name *Elizabeth Spelke*, which immediately precedes the verb, is part of the relative clause *that cognitive psychologist Elizabeth Spelke performs.*

**(D) is correct** because *many* is correctly paired with the plural noun *experiments*, and because the plural verb *are* agrees with the subject *many*.

(E) is incorrect because *designed* should be *are designed*; the experiments themselves do not design anything. A passive construction is required for the sentence to make sense.

## 101. B: Verb form

Far from being a modern dietary invention, salad has a long and distinguished history: food historians claim that the Romans ate mixed greens with dressing, and the Babylonians are known to douse lettuce with oil and vinegar more than 2,000 years ago.

(A) are known to douse
**(B) are known to have doused**
(C) were knowing to douse
(D) have been known to douse
(E) who were known to douse

The time *2,000 years ago* clearly indicates that the sentence is referring to actions that took place a very long time ago, and that some sort of past-tense construction is required.

(A) is incorrect because *are known* is the present tense, and the past tense is required.

**(B) is correct** because the construction *to have* + verb is equivalent to a past tense construction. *The Babylonians are known to have doused = It is known that the Babylonians doused.* The use of *are* is acceptable because it implies present knowledge about a situation in the past.

(C) is incorrect because the past progressive *were knowing* is awkward and illogical, implying that it was the Romans who knew to douse lettuce with oil and vinegar rather than that people now recognize that the Romans doused lettuce with oil and vinegar. The second meaning is supported by the phrase *food historians claim* at the beginning of the clause—the sentence is describing what is now known about the use of greens in ancient times.

(D) is incorrect because the present perfect *have been* indicates that the ancient Romans are still dousing lettuce with oil and vinegar, clearly an illogical implication.

(E) is incorrect because the inclusion of *who* at the beginning of the underlined portion creates a fragment; the verb *were* takes *who* rather than *the Babylonians* as its subject, depriving the clause of a main verb.

## 102. A: Relative pronoun; Comma splice

The *Oxford English Dictionary* was completed in the early nineteenth <u>century, before which Samuel Johnson's *Dictionary of the English Language* was the most comprehensive British lexicon</u>.

(A) **century, before which Samuel Johnson's** ***Dictionary of the English Language*** **was the most comprehensive British lexicon**

(B) century, and Samuel Johnson's *Dictionary of the English Language* was before this the most comprehensive lexicon in Britain

(C) century, before that Samuel Johnson's *Dictionary of the English Language* was the most comprehensive British lexicon

(D) century, Samuel Johnson's *Dictionary of the English Language* being the most comprehensive lexicon in Britain before this

(E) century, before which Samuel Johnson's *Dictionary of the English Language* has been the most comprehensive lexicon in Britain

The fastest way to answer this question is to know that the pronouns *this* and *that* must be followed by a noun, and that answer not containing *this* or *that* without a noun is virtually guaranteed to be incorrect. On that basis, (B), (C), and (D) can all be eliminated.

**(A) is correct** because the construction *before which* logically refers to the noun that immediately precedes it (*nineteenth century*), and because the past tense *was* is used to refer to a situation in the past. Note that although the past perfect (*had been the most comprehensive lexicon*) can also be used here to emphasize that one action took place before the other, the simple past is equally acceptable.

(E) is incorrect because *has been* should be *was*; the present perfect indicates an action that is continuing into the present, and the sentence clearly indicates that Johnson's dictionary ceased to be the most comprehensive lexicon in Britain in the early nineteenth century.

**103. D: Word pair; Adjective vs. adverb**

The Hale–Bopp comet received so much media coverage <u>when it returned in 1997, becoming one of the highest observed</u> astronomical bodies in history.

(A)  when it returned in 1997, becoming one of the highest observed
(B)  when returning in 1997 to become one of the highest observed
(C)  upon its 1997 return and became one of the highest observed
**(D)  when it returned in 1997 that it became one of the most highly observed**
(E)  on its return in 1997, thus becoming one of the most highly observed

This question can be answered very quickly if you know what information to focus on. The word *so* in the non-underlined portion of the sentence is a tip-off: *so* must be paired with *that*. **(D) is the only answer to contain that word, so it must be the correct answer by default.**

Note that if you approach the question this way, the adjective vs. adverb issue becomes irrelevant. That said, *highest observed* is incorrect because *highest* is an adjective but *observed* is a verb. Only an adverb can modify a verb, so *most highly observed* is the correct construction.

**104. B: Idiom/redundancy; Pronoun agreement**

<u>Because the lemur shares some traits also possessed by other primates, it is frequently mistaken for</u> an ancestor of modern monkeys and chimpanzee.

(A)  Because the lemur shares some traits also possessed by other primates, it is frequently mistaken for
**(B)  Because the lemur shares some traits with other primates, it is frequently mistaken for**
(C)  Because the lemur shares some traits that other primates also have, it is frequently mistaken to be
(D)  Because some of the lemurs traits are shared with other primates, they are frequently mistaken for
(E)  Because of its sharing some traits that other primates possess as well, the lemur is frequently mistaken as

(A) is incorrect because the idiom is *share x with y*. In addition to being idiomatically incorrect, the phrase *...shares some traits also possessed by other primates* is redundant because if the traits are "shared" with other primates, then by definition the other primates possess those traits as well.

**(B) is correct** because the preposition *with* is used after *share*, and because the singular pronoun *its* agrees with the singular referent *the lemur*.

(C) is incorrect for the same reason as (A): *share* should be followed by *with*, and the phrase *that other primates also have* is redundant. If lemurs share a trait with other primates, then the other primates possess that trait by definition.

(D) is incorrect because the pronoun *they* is ambiguous—does it refer to *the lemur's traits* or to *other primates*? In the case of the former, the meaning is illogical: the lemur, not the traits themselves, is mistaken for an ancestor of monkeys and chimpanzees.

(E) is incorrect because the phrase *Because of its sharing* is wordy and made unnecessarily awkward by the use of the gerund *sharing*. In addition, the phrase *that other primates possess as well* is redundant: if other primates share the traits, they possess the traits by definition. Finally, *mistaken as* should be *mistaken for*.

### 105. D: Gerund; Pronoun agreement: missing referent; Subject-Verb agreement

During the 1970s, the demand for long-lasting staple foods prompted <u>the adding of preservatives to dishes that previously were simple, whereby the quality of their flavors was reduced</u>.

- (A) prompted the adding of preservatives to dishes that previously were simple, whereby the quality of their flavors was reduced
- (B) prompted the addition of preservatives to previously simple dishes, so the quality of their flavors were reduced
- (C) prompted them to add preservatives to previously simple dishes, reducing the food's flavor quality
- **(D) prompted the addition of preservatives to previously simple dishes, a change that reduced the quality of the food's flavors**
- (E) prompted them to add preservatives to previously simple dishes, which reduced the quality of the food's flavors

If you look through the answer choices, you can see that some choices contain the gerund *adding*, whereas others contain the noun *addition*. That is a pretty good clue that the question is testing the use of nouns vs. gerunds, and that an answer containing the noun form is more likely to be correct.

(A) is incorrect because *the adding* should be *the addition*; the noun form is standard usage. In addition, the phrase *whereby the quality of their flavors was reduced* is wordy and awkward, and contains a passive construction.

(B) is incorrect because the plural verb *were* disagrees with its singular subject *quality*. The plural noun *flavors*, which appears immediately before the verb, is part of the prepositional phrase *of their flavors*.

(C) is incorrect because the pronoun *them* is missing a referent. Logically, we can assume that it refers to food manufacturers, but that noun does not actually appear in the sentence. In addition, *the food's flavor quality* should be *the quality of the food's flavors*; the former is idiomatically unacceptable.

**(D) is correct** because the noun *a change* is appropriately used to refer back to *the addition of preservatives* and to begin an appositive that modifies the previous clause.

(E) is incorrect because both *them* and *which* are missing referents. The sentence contains no plural noun to which *them* could reasonably refer. Although *which* logically refers to the addition of preservatives, the noun *addition* does not appear—only the verb *to add*, and a verb cannot act as a referent.

## 106. C: Subject-verb agreement Pronoun agreement: collective noun

What an advertising agency chooses to focus on for
their major campaigns depends upon the interests
and strengths of the executives responsible for
overseeing the projects.

(A)  What an advertising agency chooses to focus on
     for their major campaigns depends
(B)  What an advertising agency chooses to focus on
     for its major campaigns are dependent
**(C)  What an advertising agency chooses to focus on
     for its major campaigns depends**
(D)  What an advertising agency should choose to
     focus on for its major campaigns depend
(E)  For an advertising agency to choose to focus on
     for their major campaigns depends

If you look through the answer choices, you'll notice that some choices include *their*, whereas others include *its*. That pattern is a tip-off that the question is testing pronoun agreement.

(A) is incorrect because the pronoun *their* does not agree with the singular referent *advertising agency*. The word *agency* is a tip-off that the question is testing collective nouns, which are always singular.

(B) is incorrect because *are* should be *is*. The subject of that verb is *what*, which is always singular when it is used as a subject.

**(C) is correct** because *depends* agrees with its subject, *what*, and *its* agrees with its referent, *an advertising agency*.

(D) is incorrect because *depend* should be *depends*. A singular verb is required to agree with the subject *what*.

(E) is incorrect because *for* cannot be used to begin a subject; the entire construction is grammatically unacceptable.

## 107. E: Faulty comparison

Nikola Tesla's inventions, which include fluorescent
lighting and the modern radio, are still considered
equally important to Thomas Edison.

(A)  equally important to Thomas Edison
(B)  important like that of Thomas Edison
(C)  of an importance as great as Thomas Edison
(D)  of equal importance as Thomas Edison
**(E)  just as important as those of Thomas Edison**

Start by crossing out the non-essential clause to simplify the sentence: *Nikola Tesla's inventions...are still considered equally important to Thomas Edison.*

The sentence compares Nikola Tesla's inventions (things) to Thomas Edison (person). Because the portion of the sentence that refers to Tesla's inventions is not underlined, you must change the underlined portion of the sentence to refer to Edison's inventions: *Nikola Tesla's inventions...are still considered equally important to the inventions of Thomas Edison/Thomas Edison's inventions.*

(B) incorrectly replaces the plural noun *inventions* with the singular pronoun *that*. In addition, *important like* should be *as important as*.

**(E) is correct** because it simply replaces the word *inventions* with the pronoun *those* and creates an idiomatic comparison using *just as…as*.

Like (A), choices (C), and (D) use wordy and unidiomatic constructions to form the comparison and fail to compare inventions to inventions.

### 108. A: Non-essential clause

In 1983, geneticist Barbara McClintock was awarded the Nobel Prize in Physiology or Medicine <u>for discovering the process whereby chromosomes, the thread-like structures that are located</u> inside a cell's nucleus and that contain an organism's DNA, exchange information during cell division.

(A) **for discovering the process whereby chromosomes, the thread-like structures that are located**
(B) for her discovering of the process where chromosomes, the thread-like structures located
(C) for her discovery of the process by which chromosomes, and these are the thread-like structures located
(D) that she discovered the process through which chromosomes, these being the thread-like structures which are located
(E) for her discovery of the chromosomes' process, the thread-like structures that locate

Start by crossing out the non-essential clause to simplify the sentence.

(A): *In 1983, geneticist Barbara McClintock was awarded the Nobel Prize in Physiology or Medicine for discovering the process whereby chromosomes…exchange information during cell division.* Yes, that makes sense. Leave it.

At this point, you can either look at the sentence as a whole or repeat this process for each answer. The second option is outlined here in order to illustrate a potential method for working through questions when you do not see an error immediately.

(B): *In 1983, geneticist Barbara McClintock was awarded the Nobel Prize in Physiology or Medicine for her discovering of the process where chromosomes…exchange information during cell division.* No. *Where* refers to places, and a process is not a place. In addition, the noun *discovery* rather than the gerund *discovering* should be used.

(C): *In 1983, geneticist Barbara McClintock was awarded the Nobel Prize in Physiology or Medicine for her discovery of the process in which chromosomes…exchange information during cell division.* Yes, that makes sense. Keep it.

(D): *In 1983, geneticist Barbara McClintock was awarded the Nobel Prize in Physiology or Medicine that she discovered the process through which chromosomes…exchange information during cell division.* No, that makes no sense. Eliminate it.

(E): *In 1983, geneticist Barbara McClintock was awarded the Nobel Prize in Physiology or Medicine for her discovery of the chromosomes' process…exchange information during cell division.* No, that makes no sense. Eliminate it.

(C) is incorrect because the appositive (non-essential) clause should begin with a noun (*thread-like structures*), not a conjunction (*and*). In addition, the construction *and these are the thread-like structures* is wordy and awkward.

**(A) is correct** because *whereby* is appropriately used to refer to a process, and because the appositive (non-essential clause) begins with a noun, *the thread-like structures*, that refers to the noun that immediately precedes it (*chromosomes*).

**109. C: Idiom: number vs. amount; Passive vs. active**

A 2007 federal law mandated that all pharmaceutical companies, universities and hospitals conducting clinical trials must disclose study results and adverse events on ClinicalTrials.gov, <u>a website used by a large amount of doctors and patients</u>.

(A)  a website used by a large amount of doctors and patients
(B)  a website that a large amount of doctors and patients use
**(C)  a website that many doctors and patients use**
(D)  and a website that a large number of doctors and patients use
(E)  a website of use by many doctors and patients

*Doctors* and *patients* are plural nouns, so *number* rather than *amount* should be used. That eliminates (A) and (B). In addition, the passive construction *by a large amount of doctors and patients* is unnecessary and wordy.

**(C) is correct** because it appropriately uses *many* to modify *doctors and patients*.

(D) is incorrect because it creates a nonsense construction. The phrase after the comma should be an appositive describing ClinicalTrials.gov, and should begin with the noun *a website*. An appositive should not begin with *and*.

(E) is incorrect because the phrase *of use* is not idiomatic, and because the passive construction *by many doctors and patients* is unnecessary and wordy.

**110. B: Subject-verb agreement; Logical construction**

The Zika and dengue viruses, like virtually all mosquito-borne disease, <u>does not occur in mosquito larvae but rather are transmitted by female mosquitoes, who become carriers by biting</u> infected humans.

(A)  does not occur in mosquito larvae but rather are transmitted by female mosquitoes, who become carriers by biting
**(B)  do not occur in mosquito larvae but rather are transmitted by female mosquitoes, who become carriers after biting**
(C)  do not occur in mosquito larvae but transmitted by female mosquitoes, who become carriers after biting
(D)  does not occur in mosquito larvae transmitted by female mosquitoes, becoming carriers when biting
(E)  do not occur in mosquito larvae yet are transmitted by female mosquitoes and become carriers after biting

Start by crossing out the non-essential clause to simplify the sentence. *The Zika and dengue viruses…does not occur in mosquito larvae but rather are transmitted by female mosquitoes, who become carriers by biting infected humans.*

You can also notice that the answers are split between singular (*does*) and plural (*do*) verbs. That pattern tells you that the question is testing subject-verb agreement, and that your next step is to determine the subject of that verb.

What is the subject? *The Zika and dengue viruses* (plural). So the correct answer must contain a plural verb. On that basis, (A) and (D) can be eliminated.

**(B) is correct** because the verb *do* agrees with its plural subject, *the Zika and dengue viruses*, and because it expresses the contrast most clearly using the structure *not x but rather y*.

(C) is incorrect because *but transmitted* should be *but are transmitted*. A noun cannot "transmitted by"—it can only "*be* transmitted by." The passive construction is required for the sentence to make sense.

(E) is incorrect because the phrase *yet are transmitted by female mosquitoes and become carriers* implies that the Zika and dengue viruses, not female mosquitoes, become carriers (of themselves) after biting infected humans—a thoroughly nonsensical meaning.

**111. A: Non-essential clause**

The French Revolution of 1830, also known as the July Revolution or the Second French Revolution, saw the overthrow of King Charles X, the French Bourbon monarch, <u>and the ascent of his cousin Louis-Philippe, who himself would be deposed after 18 precarious years on the throne</u>.

(A) **and the ascent of his cousin Louis-Philippe, who himself would be deposed after 18 precarious years on the throne**
(B) the ascent of his cousin Louis-Philippe, whose deposition himself would come after 18 precarious years on the throne
(C) and Louis-Philippe's ascent, his cousin who, after 18 precarious years on the throne, was deposed
(D) the ascent of Louis-Philippe, his cousin had himself been deposed after 18 precarious years on the throne
(E) and his cousin Louis-Philippe's ascent, which would himself be deposed after 18 precarious years on the throne

Start by simplifying the sentence and crossing out the non-essential clauses—both of them: *The French Revolution of 1830...saw the overthrow of King Charles X...and the ascent of his cousin Louis-Philippe, who himself would be deposed after 18 precarious years on the throne.*

**(A) is correct** because the sentence still makes sense when stripped of its excess clauses. The construction *would* + verb is correctly used to refer to action that, from the perspective of the past (*1830*), has not yet occurred.

(B) is incorrect because *himself* must be used to refer to the noun that immediately precedes it (*deposition*). That, however, is illogical: a deposition is a thing, and *himself* can only refer to a person. Furthermore, this version implies that the deposition spent 18 years on the throne when it was clearly Louis-Philippe who did so.

(C) is incorrect because *his cousin who* should logically refer to Louis Philippe; however, *Louis Philippe* does not appear, only *Louis Philippe's ascent. Ascent* is therefore the actual referent, a construction that does not make sense.

(D) is incorrect because it creates a comma splice. The pronoun *his* after the comma creates a new sentence. In addition, the phrase *had himself deposed* can be interpreted to mean that Louis-Philippe was responsible for deposing himself—a highly illogical meaning.

(E) is incorrect because *himself* refers to *ascent*, not to Louis Philippe as would make sense.

## 112. D: Grammatical construction; Idiom

As is the case for other volcanoes in the Cascade
Range, Mount St. Helens consists of a large eruptive
cone containing lava rock interlayered with ash,
pumice, and other deposits, is part of the Pacific Ring
of Fire, the ring of volcanoes and associated
mountains around the Pacific Ocean.

(A)  As is the case for other volcanoes in the Cascade
     Range, Mount St. Helens consists of a large
     eruptive cone containing
(B)  Similar to other volcanoes in the Cascade Range,
     Mount St. Helens consists in a large eruptive cone
     that contains
(C)  Like other volcanoes in the Cascade Range, Mount
     St. Helens consists of a large eruptive cone that
     contains
**(D)  Like other volcanoes in the Cascade Range, Mount
     St. Helens, which consists of a large eruptive cone
     containing**
(E)  Like other volcanoes in the Cascade Range, Mount
     St. Helens, which consists in a large eruptive
     cone and contain

(A) is incorrect because it creates a nonsense fragment when it is read in context of the sentence as a whole. Be careful with this answer, though: even though it is somewhat wordy, it appears to be grammatically acceptable when read only in the context of the beginning of the sentence. The problem can be seen more easily if the sentence is stripped down to its basic components: *Mount St. Helens consists of a large eruptive cone…is part of the Pacific Ring of Fire.*

(B) is incorrect because it creates the same grammatical problem as (A). The use of *similar* to form the comparison is acceptable, but it is a distraction that does not address the underlying problem. In addition *consists in* should be *consists of.*

(C) is incorrect because it creates the same grammatical problem as (A) and (B). Even though *like* normally signals a correctly formed transition on the GMAT, in this case the formation of the comparison is secondary to the issue that the sentence does not make grammatical sense.

**(D) is correct** because the insertion of *which* creates a non-essential clause that, when removed, leaves a grammatically coherent sentence: *Like other volcanoes in the Cascade Range, Mount St. Helens…is part of the Pacific Ring of Fire.*

(E) is incorrect because of the formation of the non-essential clause: *consists in* should be *consists of*, and *contain* should be *contains* because the existing verb is not parallel to *consists* and disagrees with its subject, *Mount St. Helens.*

## 113. B: Misplaced modifier

The cubist movement was founded by Pablo Picasso along with his colleague, the French artist Georges Braque, in 1909, a movement that would revolutionize longstanding ideas about art.

(A) The cubist movement was founded by Pablo Picasso along with a colleague, the French artist Georges Braque in 1909,

**(B) In 1909, Pablo Picasso, along with a colleague, the French artist Georges Braque, founded the cubist movement,**

(C) The cubist movement was founded by Pablo Picasso in 1909 along with a colleague, the French artist Georges Braque,

(D) Pablo Picasso founded the cubist movement in 1909, along with the French artist Georges Braque, his colleague,

(E) The founding of the cubist movement occurred in 1909 by Pablo Picasso, along with a colleague, the French artists Georges Braque,

This question is actually much more straightforward than it might initially appear, but only if you can identify the relevant information before you wade through all the choices. The key is to consider the underlined information in context of the non-underlined information.

The last, non-underlined clause, begins with the words *a movement*, which in this context logically refer to the cubist movement. Because the final clause is an appositive that modifies the clause before it, the preceding information (the end of the underlined portion) must refer to the cubist movement.

The only answer that ends with a reference to the cubist movement is **(B)**, making it the only possible answer. All the other options end with information about something other than the cubist movement, creating misplaced modifiers.

## 114. C: Parallel structure

Economist George Akerlof has argued that procrastination reveals the limits of rational thinking and can teach useful lessons about phenomena as diverse as overeating, to save money, and the purchasing of automobiles.

(A) phenomena as diverse as overeating, to save money, and the purchasing of automobiles

(B) phenomena as diverse as overeating, to save money, and to purchase automobiles

**(C) such diverse phenomena as overeating, saving money, and purchasing automobiles**

(D) diverse phenomena, including to overeat, to save money, and the purchasing of automobiles

(E) diverse phenomena like overeating, the saving of money, and the purchasing of automobiles

The presence of a list indicates that Question #114 is testing parallel structure, so start by checking the beginning of each item.

(A) is incorrect because the first item is a gerund (*overeating*), the second is an infinitive (*to save money*), and the third is a gerund (*purchasing*).

(B) is incorrect because the first item is a gerund (*overeating*), the second is an infinitive (*to save money*), and the third is an infinitive (*to purchase*).

**(C) is correct** because all three items are gerunds (*overeating, saving,* and *purchasing*).

(D) is incorrect because the first two items are infinitives (*to overeat, to save money*) and the third is a gerund (*purchasing*).

(E) is incorrect for two reasons, despite the fact that all the answers contain gerunds. 1) The first item contains a gerund alone (*overeating*), while the other two contain *the* + gerund + *of*; and 2) *like* should not be used to introduce examples. *Such as* or *including* should be used instead.

**115. D: Idiom; Pronoun agreement**

New mortgage rules, which do not require down payments from borrowers, are intended to encourage lending, but some real estate analysts <u>insist of their ineffectiveness to prevent high levels of default</u>.

(A)  insist of their ineffectiveness to prevent high levels of default
(B)  insist on its ineffectiveness at preventing high levels of default
(C)  insist that they are ineffective in preventing high default levels
**(D)  insist that such regulations are ineffective at preventing high levels of default**
(E)  insist that this is ineffective to prevent high levels of default

(A) is incorrect because the idiom is *insist that*, not *insist of*.

(B) is incorrect even though *insist on* + noun is acceptable, because the singular pronoun *its* disagrees with the plural referent *rules*.

(C) is incorrect because the pronoun *they* is ambiguous. It could either refer to *real estate analysts* or to *new mortgage rules*.

**(D) is correct** because the phrase *such regulations* is used to refer to "new mortgage rules," eliminating the pronoun ambiguity problem in (C).

(E) is incorrect because *this* should be followed by a noun. *To prevent* should also be *at/in preventing*.

## 116. C: Redundancy

When faced with drought conditions, farmers must survive by pumping groundwater at a furious rate, <u>causing water tables to drop precipitously by as much as a 75% decline.</u>

(A) causing water tables to drop precipitously by as much as a 75% decline
(B) causing a drop precipitously in water tables by as much as a 75% decline
**(C) causing water tables to drop precipitously by as much as 75%**
(D) precipitously dropping water tables by as much as 75%
(E) causing as much as a 75% decline in the drop of water tables

Because a drop is by definition a decline, it is redundant to include both terms. (A), (B), and (E) can thus all be eliminated.

**(C) is correct** because it eliminates the redundancy by using only *drop* and creates a clear and concise construction.

(D) is incorrect because it is awkward and illogical, implying that farmers "drop" water tables by pumping water. A much more logical meaning is that the farmers' pumping of groundwater *causes* water tables to drop.

## 117. E: Verb form; Logical construction

Before they became a team, <u>Richard Rogers and Oscar Hammerstein wrote a series of hit musicals in the 1950s and collaborating</u> with other partners: Rogers with Lorenz Hart and Hammerstein with Jerome Kern.

(A) Richard Rogers and Oscar Hammerstein wrote a series of hit musicals in the 1950s and collaborating
(B) Richard Rogers and Oscar Hammerstein, whose series of hit musicals in the 1950s had collaborated
(C) Richard Rogers and Oscar Hammerstein, who wrote a series of hit musicals in the 1950s, collaborating
(D) Richard Rogers and Oscar Hammerstein, who wrote a series of hit musicals in the 1950s and had collaborated
**(E) Richard Rogers and Oscar Hammerstein, who wrote a series of hit musicals in the 1950s, had collaborated**

The fact that different answers include different tense/forms of the verb *collaborate* indicates that verb form is being tested.

(A) is incorrect because *collaborating* should be *collaborated*; the two verbs must be parallel.

(B) is incorrect because the phrase *whose series of hit musicals in the 1950s had collaborated* illogically implies that the musicals themselves rather than Rogers and Hammerstein worked with other partners.

(C) is incorrect because the sentence does not make sense when the non-essential clause is removed: *Before they became a team, Richard Rogers and Oscar Hammerstein...collaborating with other partners.*

(D) is incorrect because the sentence lacks a main verb: the verb *collaborated* belongs to the subject *who,* not to *Richard Rogers and Oscar Hammerstein.*

**(E) is correct** because the sentence makes sense when the non-essential clause is removed: *Before they became a team, Richard Rogers and Oscar Hammerstein...had collaborated with other partners.* In addition, the sentence describes two actions in the past (1: Rogers and Hammerstein worked with other partners; 2: Rogers and Hammerstein became a team), and the past perfect (*had collaborated*) is appropriately used for the action that came first.

### 118. E: Pronoun agreement: missing referent; Verb form

Although the Concorde's development required a significant economic loss for both France and Great Britain, it became increasingly profitable as a customer base developed for what then had been the fastest form of commercial of air travel in the world.

(A)  it became increasingly profitable as a customer base developed for what then had been
(B)  they became increasingly profitable as a customer base developed for what was then
(C)  its profitability increased after the development of a customer base, which was then
(D)  this became increasingly profitable as a customer base developed for the aircraft, then
**(E)  the Concorde became increasingly profitable as a customer base developed for what was then**

The answer choices contain both singular (*it/its*) and plural (*they*) pronouns, indicating that the question is in part testing pronoun agreement. The first step is thus to determine the pronoun's referent.

What noun does the pronoun in question most logically refer to? The Concorde. But the actual noun *the Concorde* does not appear in the sentence—only the possessive form, *the Concorde's development.* So *it(s)* is incorrect because the pronoun is missing its referent.

(A) is incorrect because *it* should refer to the Concorde, not its development, and because *had been* should be *was.* The sentence is describing two actions that took place at the same time, and the past perfect should only be used to emphasize that one action took place before another.

(B) is incorrect because *they* does not make sense: it could only refer to France and Great Britain, and logically it was the Concorde that became more profitable, not the nations that funded its development.

(C) is incorrect because *it* should refer to the Concorde, not its development, and this version creates a misplaced modifier when it is plugged into the sentence: the phrase *which was then the fastest commercial form of air travel in the world* does not logically refer to the "customer base."

(D) is incorrect because *this* should be followed by a noun.

**(E) is correct** because the insertion of the noun *Concorde* removes the ambiguity created by the various pronouns.

## 119. A: Parallel structure; Modification

Higher education in the United States has undergone radical changes over the past century, <u>having evolved from a system that consisted primarily of rote memorization of classics to one covering</u> a vast number of disciplines.

(A) **having evolved from a system that consisted primarily of rote memorization of classics to one covering**

(B) having evolved from a system consisting primarily of rote memorization of classics and one that covers

(C) having evolved from a system consisting primarily of classics' rote memorization with one covering

(D) which has evolved from a system consisting primarily in rote memorization of classics to one covering

(E) which had evolved from a system consisting primarily of rote memorization of classics to one that covers

The easiest way to narrow down the answers to this question is to spot the word pair: *from x to y*. The correct answer must include the word *to*, eliminating both (B) and (C).

**(A) is correct** because it includes *to*, the second half of the word pair, and because the participle *having* is appropriately used to begin a clause that modifies the previous one. Although *that consisted* and *covering* are not in the exact same format, the switch does not disqualify this answer because both modify *a system* in a grammatically acceptable way.

(D) and (E) are incorrect because *which* should be used to refer to the noun that immediately precedes it, and logically, the "last century" did not evolve from a system of rote memorization to one covering a vast number of disciplines.

## 120. C: Subject-verb agreement

Analysis of ancient thigh bones, discovered in 1989 along with other remains at a site known as Maludong, or Red Deer Cave, <u>indicate that an early hominid species might have survived</u> as late as 14,000 years ago in southwest China.

(A) indicate that an early hominid species might have survived

(B) indicate that a species of early hominid has survived

(C) **indicates that a species of early hominid might have survived**

(D) indicate that an early hominid species could have survived

(E) indicates an early species of hominid's possible surviving

To make the process of answering Question #120 as straightforward as possible, there are two pieces of information you should determine upfront.

The first thing to notice is that the sentence contains a non-essential clause, which you should start by crossing out in order to simplify the sentence: *Analysis of ancient thigh bones…indicate that a species of early hominid might have survived as late as 14,000 years ago in southwest China.*

Next, if you look at the answer choices, you'll notice that they begin with a combination of singular (*indicates*) and plural (*indicate*) verbs. That pattern tells you that the question is testing subject-verb agreement, and that your next step is to determine the subject of that verb.

What is the logical subject of the verb in question? Be very careful. The plural noun *bones*, which appears immediately before the non-essential clause, is part of the prepositional phrase *of thigh bones*. The actual subject is the singular noun *analysis*. A singular verb (*indicates*) is thus required. On that basis, (A), (B), and (D) can be eliminated.

**(C) is correct** because this version supplies the singular verb *indicates*, which agrees with the singular subject *analysis*, and because *indicates that* is idiomatically correct.

(E) is incorrect because the use of the gerund *surviving* makes this option awkward and less precise than the version that includes a conjugated verb.

**121. E: Gerund/grammatical construction; Idiom**

According to a recent consumer report, some borrowers do not realize that they have been sued by a lender <u>until receiving notification of their guilt by default</u>.

(A)   until receiving notification of their guilt by
      default
(B)   until they receive notification of their guilt that is
      by default
(C)   until they receive notification that their guilt is
      by default
(D)   until they receive notification of having defaulted
      on their guilt
**(E)   until they receive notification that they have been
      found guilty by default**

(A) is incorrect because the conjunction *until* should be followed by a subject + verb in order to create a clause; a gerund (*receiving*) is not acceptable.

(B) and (C) are incorrect because guilt can be "decided" or "determined" by default—it cannot "be" by default. Both of these options are exceedingly awkward and unidiomatic.

(D) is incorrect because this version creates an illogical meaning: *by default* has a different meaning from *default on*. One can default <u>on</u> (be unable to pay) a loan, or one can be found guilty <u>by</u> default (automatically). One cannot, however, default on one's guilt.

**(E) is correct** because it expresses the sentence's meaning most clearly and unambiguously. *Until* is appropriately followed by a subject and verb (*they receive*), and *notification* is followed by *that*.

## 122. D: Parallel structure

Henri Becquerel, who shared in the 1903 Nobel Prize in Nuclear Physics, is credited with the discovery that the radiation emitted by uranium salts <u>depended not on an external source of energy but were emanating spontaneously</u> from the uranium itself.

(A) depended not on an external source of energy
but were emanating spontaneously
(B) depended not on an external energy source
but had emanated spontaneously
(C) has not depended on an external energy source
but rather spontaneously emanated
**(D) does not depend on an external source of energy
but spontaneously emanates**
(E) did not depend on an external energy source but
emanate spontaneously

The original version of the sentence provides an important clue: the structure *not on x but...* indicates that the question is testing parallel structure. Logically, the construction after *but* should be the same as it is after *not*:

(A), (B), and (C) are incorrect because *not on x* should be reflected in the parallel construction *but on y*, and none of these answers includes the preposition *on*.

**(D) is correct** because the phrase *does not depend* is parallel to *but emanates*. Although the preposition *on* is still present in the first half of the comparison, the verbs are the focus here; the sentence is rearranged so that the preposition does not need to be repeated.

Note that even though the sentence describes an action in the past, the present tense is acceptable here because the situation it describes is a scientific fact that can reasonably be assumed to still hold true.

(E) is incorrect because *emanate* should be *emanated*; the verb should be parallel to *did*. It is acceptable to have both verbs in either the present or the past, but the two tenses cannot be mixed and matched.

## 123. B: Pronoun agreement

The lands of the ancient Near East did not develop as a single entity because they were divided into individual states, <u>each with their own distinct identity and culture</u>.

(A) each with their own distinct identity and culture
**(B) each with its own distinct identity and culture**
(C) each of their own distinct identity and culture
(D) each of its own distinction of identity and culture
(E) and each had their own distinct identity and
culture

The key to answering this question is to know that *each* is singular and must be paired with a singular pronoun (*its*). On that basis, (A), (C), and (E) can all be eliminated.

**(B) is correct** because *its* is paired with *each* and expresses the necessary information in a clear and idiomatic manner.

(D) is incorrect because the idiom is *each with...* The phrase *of its own distinction of identity and culture* is wordy and unidiomatic.

**124. C: Logical construction**

<u>The classification "novel" is a long fictional work, while the category "graphic novel" is applied broadly</u> and includes fiction, non-fiction, and anthologized works.

(A)  The classification "novel" is a long fictional work, while the category "graphic novel" is applied broadly

(B)  The classification "novel" is a long fictional work, while the application of the category of "graphic novel" is to apply broadly

**(C)  The classification "novel" is given to long works of fiction, whereas the category "graphic novel" is applied broadly**

(D)  The classification "novel" given to long works of fiction while the category "graphic novel" has broad applications

(E)  Long works of fictions are classified as novels, whereas the category "graphic novel" applies broadly to

The key to answering this question quickly is to recognize that a classification cannot logically a be "a long fictional work" — a classification is merely a tool for categorizing a work, not the work itself. On that basis, (A) and (B) can be eliminated immediately.

**(C) is correct** because the two clauses are parallel (*The classification is given = the category is applied*), and because *whereas* is used to clearly indicate the contrast between the two clauses.

(D) is incorrect because *given* should be *is given*. This version lacks a main verb, creating a fragment.

(E) is incorrect because the comparison is not presented in a parallel manner: *classification* and *category* are equivalent, so each should be used to begin a clause, as is the case in (C). Here, however, the first clause begins by referring to *long works of fiction* and uses the verb *classified* rather than the noun *classification*, whereas the second clause begins by referring to *the category*.

**125. E: Verb form**

High-pressure sales techniques practiced by timeshare representatives have prompted multiple lawsuits and <u>lead to predictions that regulators increase oversight of the industry</u>.

(A)  lead to predictions that regulators increase oversight of the industry

(B)  lead to predictions that regulators will increase oversight of the industry

(C)  have lead to predictions the regulators should increase oversight of the industry

(D)  led to predictions that the industry's oversight would be increased by regulators

**(E)  led to predictions that regulators will increase oversight of the industry**

The fact that different answers include different forms of the verb *increase* indicates that this question is testing verb form.

One way to approach this question is to use the key word *predictions*, which indicates that the sentence is referring to an action that has not yet occurred—the future tense (*will* + *verb*) is therefore required. On that basis, you can narrow the choices to (B) and (E), and (B) is incorrect because *lead* should be *led*.

Another way to work through this question is to use the *lead/led* distinction. The question plays on the fact that *lead* is pronounced the same as *led* when the former is used as a noun. As a verb, however, *lead* is the <u>present</u> tense form of *to lead* and is pronounced "leed."

The verb in question here must be a past participle because it must follow *have* in order to create the present perfect and maintain parallel structure: *have prompted…have led*. (The word *have* automatically "applies" to the second verb; it is unnecessary to repeat it.) The past participle of *to lead* is *led*, so (A), (B), and (C) can all be eliminated.

(D) is incorrect because *industry's oversight* should be *oversight of the industry*, and because *would* should be *will*.

**(E) is correct** because it uses the past participle *led* to maintain parallel structure with *prompted*, and because it uses *will increase* to refer to a predicted event.

## 126. B: Parallel structure

With his theories of relativity and gravity long confirmed and <u>his Nobel Prize was a decade old,</u> Einstein was, in 1931, by far the most famous scientist in the world.

(A)  his Nobel Prize was a decade old,
**(B)  his Nobel Prize a decade old,**
(C)  his Nobel Prize being a decade old,
(D)  a Nobel Prize of a decade's age,
(E)  a Nobel Prize aged of a decade,

The presence of the word *and* at the beginning of the underlined portion in (A)-(D) is a tip-off that this question is most likely testing parallel structure. The construction before the conjunction must match the construction after the conjunction. That means you need to work from the non-underlined portion of the sentence to the underlined portion.

(A) is incorrect because the non-underlined portion does not contain a conjugated verb, so the presence of the conjugated verb *was* disrupts parallel structure.

**(B) is correct** because it contains a construction parallel to that in the non-underlined portion: neither contains a conjugated verb, and both begin with *his* + *noun*.

(C) is incorrect because the non-underlined portion does not contain a gerund, so the presence of the gerund *being* disrupts parallel structure.

(D) is incorrect because *his* is used in the non-underlined portion and should be repeated in the underlined portion. In addition, *of a decade's age* should be *a decade old*; the former is not idiomatically acceptable.

(E) is incorrect because *his* is used in the non-underlined portion and should be repeated in the underlined portion. In addition, *aged of a decade* should be *a decade old*; the former is not idiomatically acceptable.

**127. B: Pronoun agreement: missing referent; Word Pair**

Because economists cannot reliably prevent, or
even predict, recessions or other economic events,
<u>some skeptics claim that it is based not so much on
empirical observation and rational analysis as on
ideology</u>.

(A)  some skeptics claim that it is based not so much
     on empirical observation and rational analysis as
     on ideology
**(B)  some skeptics claim that economics is based not
       so much on empirical analysis as on**
(C)  some skeptics claim of an ideological basis in
     economics rather than empirical observation and
     rational analysis
(D)  some skeptics claim that they have a basis not so
     much in empirical observation and rational
     analysis as in ideology
(E)  it is claimed by some skeptics that economics
     is based not so much on observation and rational
     analysis but on

When you look through the answer, you can notice that some choices include *it* while others include *they*. That pattern tells you that the question is in part testing pronouns, and that you need to make sure to determine the referent for each one.

(A) is incorrect because *it* lacks a referent. Logically, the pronoun refers to economics, but the noun *economics* does not appear in the sentence. In fact, there is no singular noun to which the pronoun could reasonably apply.

**(B) is correct** because it supplies the noun *economics*, eliminating the missing referent problem present in (A), and because the verb *claim* is appropriately followed by *that*.

(C) is incorrect because *claim of* is idiomatically unacceptable, and because the construction *an ideological basis in economics rather than empirical observation and rational analysis* is wordy, awkward, and confusing.

(D) is incorrect because the pronoun *they* is ambiguous—it could refer to either *some skeptics* or to *recessions or other economic events*.

(E) is incorrect because *not so much* must be paired with *as*, and because the passive construction *it is claimed by some skeptics* is wordy and awkward.

## 128. C: Non-essential clause; Logical construction; Redundancy

Foreign-language instruction, when taught by the
direct method, standing in contrast to traditional
grammar and translation methods, emphasizes
teaching through the target language only—the
rationale being that students will be able to work out
grammatical rules from the language provided.

(A) Foreign-language instruction, when taught by the
    direct method, standing in contrast to traditional
    grammar and translation methods,
(B) When taught by the direct method, standing in
    contrast to traditional grammar and translation
    methods, foreign-language instruction
**(C) The direct method of foreign-language instruction,
    which stands in contrast to traditional grammar
    and translation methods,**
(D) When taught by the direct method, foreign-
    language instruction, in contrast to traditional
    grammar and translation methods,
(E) Instructing foreign languages by the direct
    method, which stands in contrast to traditional
    grammar and translation methods,

Even though the non-essential clause is underlined you should start by removing it in order to simplify the sentence and reveal its structure more clearly: *Foreign-language instruction…standing in contrast to traditional grammar and translation methods, emphasizes teaching through the target language only.*

(A) is incorrect because the sentence does not make sense when the non-essential clause is eliminated. The non-essential clause should be followed by a verb rather than a gerund: *standing* should be *stands*.

(B) is incorrect because it does not make logical sense when the non-essential clause is removed: *When taught by the direct method…foreign-language instruction*. A foreign language can be taught—not foreign language *instruction*. Since *teach* and *instruct* have the same meaning, the inclusion of both is redundant.

**(C) is correct** because this version removes the redundancy, creates a clear, concise construction, and makes sense when the non-essential clause is removed: *The direct method of foreign-language instruction …emphasizes teaching through the target language only.*

(D) is incorrect because *foreign-language instruction* should be *foreign languages*. This answer contains the same redundancy as (B): foreign languages are taught, not foreign language *instruction*.

(E) is incorrect because it creates an illogical comparison: methods should be compared to methods, but here *instructing foreign languages* is compared to *traditional grammar and translation methods*.

### 129. C: Subject-verb agreement; Logical construction

Modeling the formation of the terrestrial and gas
giants is relatively straightforward and uncontroversial
because the terrestrial planets of the Solar System
are widely understood to have formed through the
collision of micro-planets within the newly formed disk
of gas surrounding the sun.

(A) **is relatively straightforward and uncontroversial**
    **because the terrestrial planets of the Solar System**
    **are widely understood to have formed through the**
    **collision of micro-planets**
(B) is relatively straightforward and uncontroversial
    because the terrestrial planets of the Solar System
    widely understood to have formed through
    micro-planets' colliding
(C) are relatively straightforward and uncontroversial
        because the terrestrial planets of the Solar System
    are widely understood to have formed through the
    colliding of micro-planets
(D) are relatively straightforward and uncontroversial
    because the Solar System's terrestrial planets
    are understood widely to have formed through
    the colliding of micro-planets
(E) is relatively straightforward and uncontroversial
    because of the wide understanding that the
    formation of the terrestrial planets of the Solar
    System were caused by the collision of micro-
    planets

Don't be thrown off by the length of the sentence/answer choices. You can simplify this question very easily.

If you look at the answer choices, you'll notice that they begin with a combination of singular (*is*) and plural (*are*) verbs. That pattern tells you that the question is testing subject-verb agreement, and that your next step is to determine the subject of that verb.

What is the subject? *Modeling*. The plural noun *giants*, which appears immediately before the verb, is part of the complete subject: *Modeling the formation of the terrestrial and gas giants*.

*Modeling* is a gerund, and gerunds are always singular, so a singular noun (*is*) is required. (C) and (D) can thus be eliminated.

**(A) is correct** because this version provides the passive construction necessary for the sentence to make sense (*the terrestrial planets of the Solar System are widely understood*), and because it uses the more idiomatic noun *collision* as opposed to the gerund *colliding*.

(B) is incorrect because the phrase *the terrestrial planets of the Solar System widely understood* should be *the terrestrial planets of the Solar System are widely understood*. The passive is required in order to make the sentence grammatically and logically acceptable; the terrestrial planets did not "understand" anything.

(E) is incorrect because in addition to being wordy, this version creates a new subject-verb disagreement: the plural noun *were* disagrees with the singular noun *formation*. The plural noun *planets*, which appears before the verb, is part of the prepositional phrase *of the terrestrial planets of the Solar System*.

### 130. D: Pronoun: ambiguous referent

Most bird species sing despite lacking vocal cords, <u>compensating with their throat muscles and membranes for their absence by vibrating</u> and generating sound waves when air from the lungs passes over them

(A) compensating with their throat and membranes for their absence by vibrating
(B) to compensate with their throat muscles and membranes by vibrating for their absence
(C) their throat muscles and membranes being compensated for their absence when they vibrate
**(D) their throat muscles and membranes compensating for the absence by vibrating**
(E) with compensation from their throat muscles and membranes for their absence that vibrates

(A) is incorrect because the pronoun *their* is ambiguous: it could refer to either *most birds* or to *throat muscles and membranes*. Even only the latter meaning makes sense, the sentence is still worded ambiguously, implying that the birds are responsible for their own absence.

(B) is incorrect because *their* is ambiguous in the same way as it is in (A). In addition, the phrase *vibrating for their absence* does not make sense. The birds' throat muscles and membranes vibrate to compensate for the absence of vocal cords. The existing construction implies that throat muscles and membranes vibrate for the purpose of their absence (the throat muscles and membranes' absence? the birds' absence?). Either way, the meaning is thoroughly illogical.

(C) is incorrect because *their* is ambiguous in the same way as it is in (A) and (B). In addition, the phrase *being compensated for their absence* is illogical: the throat muscles and membranes do not receive any compensation for vibrating.

**(D) is correct** because this version sidesteps the ambiguous referent problem entirely by replacing the pronoun *their* with the article *the*. The phrase *the absence* clearly refers to the fact that the birds lack vocal cords.

(E) is incorrect because this version contains a misplaced modifier: the phrase *for their absence that vibrates* implies that the absence, not the vocal cords, is vibrating—a thoroughly illogical meaning.

**131. B: Pronoun agreement: collective noun**

<u>However promptly the company responds to the recent decline in sales, they will need to reduce prices by at least 10% so as to remain</u> competitive with its traditional rivals.

(A) However promptly the company responds to the recent decline in sales, they will need to reduce prices by at least 10% so as to remain

**(B) However promptly the company responds to the recent decline in sales, it will need to reduce prices by at least 10% to remain**

(C) Even if the company should respond promptly to the recent decline in sales, they will need to reduce prices by a minimum of 10% in remaining

(D) Even if the company promptly responded to the the recent decline of sales, it will need to reduce prices by at least 10% to remain

(E) Regardless of if the company responds promptly to the recent decline in sales, it will need to reduce prices by at least 10%

If you look through the answer choices, you can notice that (A) and (C) include the pronoun *they*, whereas (B), (D), and (E) include *it*. That pattern indicates that pronoun agreement is in part being tested. What is the logical referent of the pronoun in question? *The company*. *Company* is a collective noun, and collective nouns are always singular, so (A) and (C) can be eliminated.

**(B) is correct** because the singular pronoun *it* is used to refer to the singular noun *company*, and because the combination of present tense (*responds*) and future (*will need*) is logical in context—the sentence is describing what the company must do in the future to address a current situation.

(D) is incorrect because the *will need* should be *would need*. The simple past (*responded*) should not be paired with the future (*will need*). A clause that begins with *even if* behaves like any other "if" clause: if that clause includes a verb in the past tense, the main clause must include a verb in the conditional (*would need*).

(E) is incorrect because the correct idiom is *regardless of whether*; *regardless of if* is unacceptable.

**132. E: Pronoun agreement: missing referent; Verb form**

<u>Before the raising of chickens became industrial, they were far less important to</u> human diets; researchers estimate that the birds were first eaten in significant numbers only about 2,200 years ago.

(A) Before the raising of chickens became industrial, they were far less important to

(B) Before the raising of chickens became industrial, they were of a far lesser importance in

(C) Before the industrial raising of chickens, their importance was far less important to

(D) Before chickens had been raised industrially, they they were far less important to

**(E) Before chickens were raised according to an industrial model, they were far less important to**

290

**Shortcut:** If you look at the answer choices, you can notice that (A)-(C) contain the gerund phrase *the raising of,* whereas (D) and (E) contain the verb *raised.* When you are given the option between a gerund and another part of speech, the latter will more often than not be correct. As a result, you can play the odds and start by checking (D) and (E). Otherwise, you can work through the answer in order:

(A) is incorrect because the pronoun *they* lacks a true referent. The noun *chickens* is part of the possessive phrase *the raising of chickens.* Even if the intended meaning is clear, only *raising* (singular) can function as a referent, and *they* is plural. In addition, *raising* would make no sense as the referent of *their;* only chickens, not the raising of chickens, could become part of the human diet.

(B) and (C) are incorrect because they contain the same problem as (A): the pronouns *they* and *their* lack a referent because *chickens* is part of the possessive phrase *raising of chickens.* Only *raising* (singular) can function as a referent, and *they* is plural.

(D) is incorrect because when a sentence describes two completed actions, the past perfect should be used to describe the first action. Here, the past perfect (*had been raised*) is used to refer to the action that came second (chickens were raised according to an industrial model) rather than the one that came first (chickens were less important to human diets). That sequence is indicated by the word *before.*

**(E) is correct** because the plural noun *chickens* in the first clause is logically referred to by the pronoun *they* in the second clause. This version replaces the gerund *raising* with the verb *raised,* creating a clear, concise construction.

### 133. C: Parallel structure; Diction

One important aspect of Haydn's genius <u>lays in his
sense of the energy latent in his material—or maybe
it was his invention of material that gave</u> him the
requisite energy to sustain such remarkable musical
compositions.

(A) lays in his sense of the energy latent in his
material—or maybe it was his invention of
material that gave
(B) lays in his sense of the energy latent in his
material—or maybe it was his inventing of
material that gave
**(C) lies in his sense of the energy latent in his
material—or perhaps in his invention of
material that gave**
(D) lies in his sense of his material's latent energy—
or maybe his invention of material to give
(E) lay in his sense of the latent energy of his
material—or perhaps his invention of material
which would give

Although this question may seem quite complicated, there is actually a shortcut, albeit one that is extremely subtle. The sentence describes two possibilities: Haydn's genius could come from the sense of energy in his material, or from his invention of material that gave him energy. Logically, the two options must be presented in parallel form.

In every single answer, the verb *lies* or *lays* is followed by the preposition *in,* so to make the two sides parallel, *in* should appear on the second side as well. The only option to contain that preposition is (C).

If that seems like too obscure an approach, you can work through the options from the perspective of the verb; the fact that some answers contain *lay* while others contain *lie* indicates that the *lay/lie* distinction is being tested.

The correct version is *lie* because *lay* must be followed by a noun (direct object), and this verb is followed by a preposition (*in*). (A), (B), and (E) can thus be eliminated.

**(C) is correct** because it includes the correct form of the verb, *lie*, and because its inclusion of the preposition *in* makes the construction after the dash parallel to the construction before the dash.

(D) is incorrect because the construction after the dash is not parallel to the construction before the dash. In addition, *material to give* should be *material that gave*—the sentence is describing a completed action in the past. *Maybe* is also slightly less formal than *perhaps* and is thus less preferable.

### 134. A: Idiom; Pronoun agreement; Grammatical construction

Plunging prices are revealing the extent to which
nations, hailed in recent years <u>as having outgrown
their roots in natural resources, still rely heavily</u> on
those commodities.

(A) **as having outgrown their roots in natural
resources, still rely heavily**
(B) to have outgrown their roots in natural resources,
are still heavily reliant
(C) as an outgrowth of their roots in natural resources,
still rely heavily
(D) to outgrow their roots in natural resources, are
still relying heavily
(E) as outgrowing their roots in natural resources, still
heavily reliant

If you know that the correct idiom is *hailed as*, then you can automatically eliminate (B) and (D).

**(A) is correct** because it uses the idiom *hailed as* + gerund and still makes sense when the non-essential clause is removed: *Plunging prices are revealing the extent to which nations...still rely heavily on those commodities.*

(C) is incorrect because it creates an illogical meaning: nations would not be "hailed" as *an outgrowth of their roots in natural resources*. Rather, they are hailed for having *outgrown* their natural resources, a meaning that sets up the contrast with the fact that in reality, they *still rely heavily on those resources*.

(E) is incorrect because *still heavily reliant* should be *are still heavily reliant*. The main verb (*are*) is missing, and the sentence no longer makes sense when the non-essential clause is removed: *Plunging prices are revealing the extent to which nations...still heavily reliant on those commodities.*

### 135. D: Parallel structure; Participle

After Henry Ford established the Ford Motor
Company in Detroit in 1903, the city rapidly became
the United States' automotive <u>capital and so
remaining</u> for more than seven decades.

(A) capital and so remaining
(B) capital and so to remain
(C) capital and had remained as such
(D) **capital, remaining thus**
(E) capital, which it will remain

(A), (B), and (C) are incorrect because they include verbs that are not parallel to *became*.

**(D) is correct** because the participle *remaining* is used to begin a new clause, eliminating the parallelism issue.

(E) is incorrect because *will remain* should be *would remain*. The underlined portion describes an action that, from the perspective of the past, has not yet occurred, so *would* should be used.

## 136. B: Parallel structure; Verb form; Logical construction

A tablet containing one of the most famous mathematical texts from ancient Mesopotamia proves that the Babylonians <u>had derived the formula that came later to be called the Pythagorean theorem long before the Greek philosopher Pythagoras would</u>.

(A) had derived the formula that came later to be called the Pythagorean theorem long before the Greek philosopher Pythagoras would

**(B) derived the formula later called the Pythagorean theorem long before the Greek philosopher Pythagoras did**

(C) derived what was later called the Pythagorean theorem long before the time where the Greek philosopher Pythagoras was

(D) derived the formula later called the        Pythagorean theorem long before the Greek philosopher Pythagoras has

(E) derived from the formula later called the Pythagorean theorem long before its derivation by the Greek philosopher Pythagoras

The presence of the verb *derived* in different forms, as well as the presence of different verbs at the end of different answer choices indicates that this question is testing both verb tense and parallel structure. The verb at the end of the sentence must be parallel to the verb at the beginning of the underlined portion.

(A) is incorrect because *had derived* is not parallel to *would*. In addition, *came later to be* should be *later came to be*. The adverb *later* modifies the entire clause *that came to be called the Pythagorean theorem*. Its placement in this version is ambiguous: does it modify *later* or *to be*?

If we were to write out the full correction, the sentence would read: *A tablet containing one of the most famous mathematical texts from ancient Mesopotamia proves that the Babylonians had derived the formula that later came to be called the Pythagorean theorem long before the Greek philosopher Pythagoras <u>derived it/the formula.</u>* The goal is to find the answer that matches it most closely.

**(B) is correct** because *did* is as an appropriate substitute for *derived*, and both verbs are placed in the simple past.

(C) and (D) are incorrect because *was* and *has* cannot substitute for *derived*, and because *where* in (C) cannot refer to a time.

(E) is incorrect because it is illogical. *Derived* should not be followed by a preposition: *x is derived from y*. The Babylonians derived the formula — they did not derive *from* the formula.

## 137. B: Parallel structure

Many economists argue that the dollar's continued rise will help Europe and Japan overcome economic weaknesses by making their products cheaper in world <u>markets and are boosting overall global growth</u>.

(A)  markets and are boosting overall global growth
**(B)  markets and that it will boost overall global growth**
(C)  markets, and global growth is boosted overall
(D)  markets, and that global growth overall is boosted
(E)  markets, with a boost overall in global growth

This is a question whose entire structure you must take into account in order to determine which answer creates a parallel construction; if you focus only on the underlined portion, you will have no way to determine the correct option. Your instinct may be to fix the sentence by turning the phrase *and are boosting overall global growth* into *and boosting overall global growth* in order to make it parallel to *by making*, but no such choice exists.

(A) is incorrect because *and are boosting* is not parallel to *by making*, or to any other construction in the sentence. It also cannot refer to the dollar's rise because *rise* is singular and *are* is plural.

**(B) is correct** because the phrase *that it will boost overall growth* is parallel to the phrase *that the dollar's continued rise* in the non-underlined portion of the sentence. When the excess verbiage is removed, the basic structure of the sentence is *Many economists argue that x…and that y*.

(C) is incorrect because the passive construction *and global growth is boosted overall* is not parallel to either the construction at the beginning of the sentence (*Many economists argue that the dollar's continued rise will help…*) or the one that immediately precedes the underlined portion (*by making their products cheaper*).

(D) is incorrect because the passive construction *growth is boosted* is not parallel to any other construction in the sentence, and because *overall* modifies *global growth* and should be placed before that phrase.

(E) is incorrect because the phrase *with a boost* is not parallel to any other construction in the sentence.

## 138. C: Pronouns: missing referent

In his third book, *The Court and the World*, Supreme Court justice Stephen Breyer suggests that the court should not only be willing to look abroad for guidance <u>but should in some instances be encouraged to do it</u> because about 20% of its cases involve events occurring outside the United States.

(A)  but should in some instances be encouraged to do it
(B)  but sometimes should be also encouraged to do this
**(C)  but should sometimes also be encouraged to do so**
(D)  and in some instances it should be encouraged to do this
(E)  whereas in some instances it should be encouraged that it do so

**Shortcut:** If you know that the phrase *do this* is pretty much guaranteed to be incorrect, and that the most likely correction for it is *do so*, then you can simply scan the answers for that construction. (C) and (E) are the only choices that contain it, so you can eliminate (A), (B), and (D) immediately.

A slightly longer shortcut involves knowing that any answer that contains *this* without a noun after it will almost certainly be wrong, and eliminating (B) and (D) on that basis.

(A) is incorrect because the pronoun *it* lacks a referent. Logically, it must refer to looking abroad for guidance, but the gerund *looking* does not appear. Only the infinitive *to look* appears, and an infinitive cannot be a referent.

**(C) is correct** because it replaces *do this* with *do so*, eliminating the problem of the missing noun/referent.

(E) is incorrect because *encouraged that it do so* should be *encouraged to do so*. The phrase *it should be encouraged that it do so* is wordy, awkward, and idiomatically unacceptable.

### 139. A: Verb form; Logical construction

When the Cooper Union for the Advancement of Science and Art opened its doors in 1859, the school represented for Peter Cooper <u>the realization of an idea that had occupied his imagination</u> for nearly three decades.

- **(A)** the realization of an idea that had occupied his imagination
- (B) the realization of an idea that was occupied by his imagination
- (C) the realizing of an idea that would occupy his imagination
- (D) that an idea which had occupied his imagination was realized
- (E) an idea whose occupation of his memory was realized

If you look through the answer choices, you can notice that they contain the same verb (*occupy*) in various forms, a pattern that indicates that the question is testing tense.

**(A) is correct** because the sentence describes two actions in the past, one of which preceded the other: 1) the idea of opening a school occupied Cooper's imagination for more than three decades; 2) Cooper Union opened. The past perfect (*had occupied*) is appropriately used to refer to the action that came first.

(B) is incorrect because it creates an illogical meaning. The idea of opening a school occupied Cooper's imagination; the idea was not occupied *by* Cooper's imagination.

(C) is incorrect because *realizing* should be *realization*, and because *would* + verb is used to refer to an action that, from the perspective of the past, has not yet taken place. That is not the case here: the sentence clearly indicates that Cooper's school did in fact open.

(D) is incorrect because *which* should be *that*, and because this version creates an illogical meaning when it is plugged back into the sentence, implying that Cooper's idea was realized for three decades—not that the idea had occupied his imagination for that length of time.

(E) is incorrect for the same reason as (D); the placement of the word *realized* at the end of the underlined portion implies that Cooper's idea was realized for three decades, not that it occupied his imagination for that length of time.

## 140. D: Faulty comparison; Grammatical construction

Although it is estimated that more than 15% of adults are afraid of flying, a condition known as aviophobia, modern air travel is <u>widely acknowledged to be safer than almost any form of transportation</u>—far safer, for example, than automotive travel.

(A)  widely acknowledged to be safer than almost any form of transportation
(B)  acknowledged widely as safer than almost any transportation form
(C)  widely acknowledged as being safer than almost any form of transportation
**(D)  widely acknowledged to be safer than almost any other form of transportation**
(E)  widely acknowledged that it is safer than almost any other form of transportation

The easiest way to answer this question is to spot the logic error in the original version. Because air travel itself is a form of transportation, it cannot be "safer than *any* form of transportation." Rather, it must be "safer than *any other* form of transportation." On that basis, (A), (B), and (C) can be eliminated.

**(D) is correct** because it creates a logical comparison: air travel is compared to *any other form of transportation*.

(E) is incorrect because it creates an extremely awkward and grammatically unacceptable construction when it is plugged back into the sentence: *Modern air travel is widely acknowledged that it is safer than almost any form of transportation...*

## 141. E: Idiom; Logical construction

Azurite, a carbonate mineral also known as Chessylite, has an exceptionally deep blue <u>hue that has been described to be reminiscent of the color of winter skies since antiquity</u>.

(A)  hue that has been described to be reminiscent of the color of winter skies since antiquity
(B)  hue that since antiquity described as reminiscent reminiscent of the color that winter skies have
(C)  hue, whose descriptions since antiquity are reminiscent of the color of winter skies
(D)  hue, of which the descriptions have reminisced since antiquity about winter skies' color
**(E)  hue, which since antiquity has been described as reminiscent of the color of winter skies**

**Shortcut:** If you know that the phrase *described to be* in (A) is incorrect and that the correct idiom is *described as*, you can simply look for that phrase among the answer choices. The only options that include it are (B) and (E), and (B) contains a tense error. That leaves (E), which is correct. Otherwise, you can work through the answers one-by-one.

(A) is incorrect because *described to be* should be *described as*. In addition the placement of the phrase *since antiquity* at the end of the underlined portion implies that the <u>color</u> of winter skies has only resembled that of azurite for a few millennia when, more logically, the <u>comparison</u> between the color of azurite and that of winter skies has been made for that length of time.

(B) is incorrect because *described* should be *has been described*; a deep blue hue cannot describe anything. A passive construction is required here for the sentence to make sense. The phrase *reminiscent of the color that winter skies have* should also be *the color of winter skies*. The existing phrase is awkward and not parallel, comparing a noun (color) to a relative clause (*that winter skies have*).

(C) is incorrect because this version illogically implies that the *descriptions* of azurite's color, not azurite's color itself, have resembled the color of winter skies. In addition, *are* should be *have been*. The word *since* is a tip-off that the present perfect is required.

(D) is incorrect because *have reminisced* should be *are reminiscent of*. This version is extremely illogical because descriptions cannot reminisce about anything.

**(E) is correct** because *which* is correctly set off with a comma and refers to the noun that immediately precedes it (*deep blue hue*). The idiom *described as* is presented correctly.

## 142. A: Verb form

<u>Should the Albert Bridge be demolished,</u> as some city planners regularly urge, Tower Bridge will become the only bridge in London to exist in its original form.

**(A) Should the Albert Bridge be demolished,**
(B) If the Albert Bridge were demolished,
(C) Had the Albert Bridge been demolished,
(D) Were the Albert Bridge to be demolished,
(E) The Albert Bridge, having been demolished,

Although the underlined portion of this sentence does not contain the non-essential clause, it is important that you cross out the non-essential clause because it is strategically placed to obscure what is being tested: "if" clauses and "result" clauses.

Crossed out: *Should the Albert Bridge be demolished...Tower Bridge will become the only bridge in London to exist in its original form.*

Now that there are only two clauses, the "if-then" structure is much more apparent.

The use of the future tense (*will become*) in the second clause limits the tense for the first clause to one possibility: the present tense (recall that when a main clause includes a verb in the future tense, the "if" clause must include a verb in the present tense.) If you're not sure about (A), leave it.

(B) is incorrect because *were* is in the past tense.

(C) is incorrect because *had* is in the past tense.

(D) is incorrect because *were* is in the past tense.

(E) is incorrect because *having* is a gerund; this version is a fragment because it lacks a main verb.

So that leaves **(A), which is correct** because *Should the Albert Bridge be demolished* is an acceptable way of indicating a hypothetical situation in the present. Grammatically, it is identical to the phrase *If the Albert Bridge is demolished*.

**143. C: Parallel structure**

Cumulus clouds, <u>clouds that produce little or no precipitation, cool the earth and reflecting the incoming solar radiation to come</u> in many distinct sub-forms.

(A) clouds that produce little or no precipitation, cool the earth and reflecting the incoming solar radiation to come
(B) clouds producing little or no precipitation, cooling the earth and reflecting the incoming solar radiation, which comes
**(C) clouds that produce little or no precipitation and that cool the earth by reflecting the incoming solar radiation, come**
(D) clouds that produce little or no precipitation to cool the earth, and the incoming solar radiation is reflected, come
(E) clouds that produce little or no precipitation, cooling the earth and reflecting the incoming solar radiation, comes

(A) is incorrect because *cool* and *reflecting* are not parallel, and because the phrase *incoming solar radiation to come* implies that the solar radiation comes in many distinct forms, not the cumulus clouds.

(B) is incorrect because the gerund *cooling* creates a fragment; this version of the sentence lacks a main verb.

**(C) is correct** because this version maintains parallel structure: *that produce = that cool*. In addition, the plural verb *come*, which appears after the non-essential clause, agrees with the plural subject *cumulus clouds*.

(D) is incorrect because the switch from active (*clouds that produce little or no precipitation...*) to passive (*and the incoming solar radiation is reflected*) disrupts parallel structure and is awkward as well as illogical.

(E) is incorrect because the singular verb *comes*, which appears after the non-essential clause, disagrees with the plural subject *cumulus clouds*.

**144. D: Pronoun: missing/ambiguous referent; Participle**

In the Southern Hemisphere, mild and rainy winters produce ideal breeding conditions for locusts, <u>which creates a surge in population outpacing authorities' ability to control their spread</u>.

(A) which creates a surge in population outpacing authorities' ability to control their spread
(B) which creates a population surge that outpaces authorities' ability to control their spread
(C) whose surge in population creates an outpacing of the ability to control their spread by authorities
**(D) creating a surge in population that outpaces the ability of authorities to control the insects' spread**
(E) and creates a surge in population which outpaces the ability to authorities to control their spread

Whenever *which* is underlined, check to see whether it logically refers to the noun that immediately precedes it.

In this case, that noun is *locusts*. Logically, it was the creation of ideal breeding conditions, not the locusts themselves, that led to the population. In addition, *which* is followed by the singular verb *creates* in both (A) and (B), and there is no singular noun that *which* could plausibly refer to. (A) is also incorrect because *a surge in population outpacing* should be *a surge in population that outpaces*.

(C) is incorrect because it consists of an awkward and ungrammatical construction. In addition, the phrase *control their spread by authorities* implies that the authorities themselves are facilitating the locusts' spread.

**(D) is correct** because it uses a participle (*creating*) to join the two clauses and makes it clear that the authorities are responsible for controlling the locusts' spread.

(E) is incorrect because *creates* is not parallel to *produce* and disagrees with the subject *winters* and because *which* should be *that*. In addition, the pronoun *their* is ambiguous because it is unclear whether it refers to the locusts or the authorities.

**145. A: Word pair: so...that; Grammatical construction**

The Must Farm archaeological site in Cambridgeshire, England, is considered so rich in Bronze age ruins that it has been compared to Pompeii, the Roman town buried by the eruption of Mount Vesuvius in the first century B.C.E.

**(A)** **is considered so rich in Bronze age ruins**
(B) is considered of such richness in Bronze age ruins
(C) is considered to have a great richness in Bronze age ruins
(D) considered to be so rich in Bronze age ruins
(E) which is considered to be so rich in Bronze age ruins

The key to answering this question quickly is to recognize that it is testing the word pair *so...that*. In order to do that, however, it is necessary to recognize the significance of the word *that* immediately after the underlined portion of the sentence. Because *that* cannot be changed, the correct version of the underlined portion must contain either *so* or *such*. That eliminates (C).

(A) is correct because it provides the first half of the word pair and includes the idiomatically correct phrase *so rich in Bronze Age ruins*.

(B) is incorrect because the phrase *of such richness in Bronze Age ruins* is awkward and ungrammatical.

**(D) is correct** on its own but incorrect in context. The verb *is* must be placed before *considered*; without the passive construction, this version does not make sense.

(E) is incorrect because it creates a nonsense fragment when plugged back into the sentence.

**146. B: Idiom: gerund vs. infinitive, like vs. as; Grammatical construction**

Even though individuals with Highly Superior
Autobiographical Memory (HSAM) can remember
details from their own lives' events in extraordinary
detail, <u>they appear to be no better than average to
recall impersonal information like random lists of
words</u>.

(A)  they appear to be no better than average to
     recall impersonal information like random lists of
     words
**(B)  they appear to be no better than average at
     recalling impersonal information such as random
     lists of words**
(C)  they appear as no better than average in
     recalling impersonal information such as random
     lists of words
(D)  they appear to be no better than average when
     recalling impersonal information like random
     word lists
(E)  but they appear to be no better than average
     when they recall impersonal information such as
     random lists of words

(A) is incorrect because the phrase *no better than average* should not be followed by an infinitive, and because *such as* or *including*, not *like*, should be used to set up an example.

**(B) is correct** because *appear* is followed by an infinitive and *average* is followed by a gerund. In addition, *such as* is correctly used to introduce the example that follows.

(C) is incorrect because *appear as* should be *appear to be*; *appear as* means "appear in the form of."

(D) is incorrect because *when* should be followed by subject + verb rather than a gerund, and because *such as* or *including*, not *like*, should be used to set up an example.

(E) is incorrect because two consecutive clauses should not begin with conjunctions.

**147. E: Word pair: between…and; Pronoun agreement**

Parrots are not only capable of mimicking human
speech but on some occasions also <u>demonstrate their
being able to form associations between words with
their meanings</u>.

(A)  demonstrate their being able to form associations
     between words with their meanings
(B)  demonstrate being able to form associations
     between words to their meanings
(C)  demonstrate the ability of forming associations
     between words to their meanings
(D)  demonstrate its ability to form associations
     between words and their meanings
**(E)  demonstrate the ability to form associations
     between words and their meanings**

The simplest way to answer this question is to recognize that *between* must be paired with *and*. On that basis, (A), (B), and (C) can all be eliminated.

(D) is incorrect because the singular pronoun *its* disagrees with the plural referent *parrots*.

**(E) is correct** because it correctly pairs *between* with *and*, and eliminates the pronoun disagreement found in (D) by eliminating the pronoun entirely.

### 148. C: Dangling modifier

Alvin Ailey Dance Theater became a resident company of New York City's Clark Center for the Performing Arts in 1960, and having established a permanent home for his troupe, <u>*Revelations*, Ailey's famous character dance accompanied by traditional spirituals and gospel songs, was choreographed</u>.

(A) *Revelations*, Ailey's famous character dance accompanied by traditional spirituals and gospel songs, was choreographed

(B) Ailey's famous character dance *Revelations*, accompanied by traditional spirituals and gospel songs, was choreographed

**(C) Ailey choreographed his famous work *Revelations*, a character dance accompanied by traditional spirituals and gospel songs**

(D) *Revelations*, was choreographed, which was Ailey's famous character dance accompanied by traditional spirituals and gospel songs,

(E) the choreography of *Revelations*, Ailey's famous character dance, was accompanied by traditional spirituals and gospel songs

Although this question might initially seem very complicated, it can actually be answered very quickly if you know what information to focus on. That said, it takes a commonly tested structure and gives it a twist: unlike most dangling modifiers, this one appears in the middle of the sentence rather than at the beginning.

The key is to recognize that the subject described in the participial phrase (*having established a permanent base for his troupe*) that immediately precedes the underlined portion must appear after the comma—that is, at the beginning of the underlined portion. That means it is possible to identify the correct answer using only the first few words of each answer.

So who had established a permanent home for his troupe? Ailey. So *Ailey*, the subject, must appear at the beginning of the correct answer.

**The only option that fulfills that criterion is (C), making it correct.**

Be careful with (B). Even though Ailey's name appears as the first word, it is possessive. The actual subject is not Ailey but rather *Ailey's famous character dance Revelations*.

All of the other options create dangling modifiers.

## 149. B: Parallel structure

Professional liability insurance, also known as
professional indemnity insurance, focuses on the
alleged <u>error in the performance or financial loss from</u>
a product sold by the policyholder.

(A)  error in the performance or financial loss from
**(B)  error in the performance of or financial loss from**
(C)  error in the performance of or financial loss
(D)  error in the performance and financial loss of
(E)  error of the performance and financial loss from

Because *performance* and *financial* are followed by different prepositions (*performance of* vs. *financial loss from*), the preposition *from* after *financial loss* cannot "apply" back to *performance*. Rather, a separate preposition must be included after each item.

(A), (D), and (E) are incorrect because they omit the preposition *of*.

(C) is incorrect because it omits the preposition *from*.

**(B) is correct** because it is the only option that includes both *of* and *from* after the appropriate nouns.

## 150. D: Logical construction

Although female authors were permitted to publish
under their own names in England during the
Victorian  era, Mary Ann Evans (George Eliot)
nevertheless elected to use a pseudonym <u>so as to
escape</u> the stereotype of the female romance novelist.

(A)  so as to escape
(B)  for the escape from
(C)  in order that she could escape
**(D)  so that she could escape**
(E)  in escaping

**(D) is correct** because it is the option that most clearly and idiomatically indicates this cause-and-effect relationship: Evans wrote under the pseudonym George Eliot in order to escape the stereotype of the female romance novelist.

All of the other options are idiomatically unacceptable. Although the phrase *in order to escape* would be an acceptable option, it does not actually appear. (C) is incorrect because *in order* should not be followed by *that*.

# ABOUT THE AUTHOR

Erica Meltzer earned her B.A., *magna cum laude*, from Wellesley College and spent more than a decade tutoring privately in Boston and New York City, as well as nationally and internationally via Skype. Her experience working with students from a wide range of educational backgrounds and virtually every score level gave her unique insight into the types of stumbling blocks students often encounter when preparing for standardized reading and writing tests.

She was inspired to begin writing her own test-prep materials in 2007, after visiting a local bookstore in search of additional practice questions for a student. Unable to find material that replicated the contents of the exam with sufficient accuracy, she decided to write her own. What started as a handful of exercises jotted down on a piece of paper became the basis for her first book, *The Ultimate Guide to SAT® Grammar*, published in 2011. Since that time, she has authored guides for SAT reading and vocabulary, as well as verbal guides for the ACT®, GRE®, and GMAT®. Her books have sold more than 200,000 copies and are used around the world. She lives in New York City, and you can visit her online at www.thecriticalreader.com.

Made in United States
Orlando, FL
25 May 2022

18174142R00165